The Great Disruption

FRANCIS FUKUYAMA

THE
GREAT
DISRUPTION

HUMAN NATURE AND THE
RECONSTITUTION OF SOCIAL ORDER

P

PROFILE BOOKS

First published in Great Britain in 1999 by
Profile Books Ltd
58A Hatton Garden
London EC1N 8LX
www.profilebooks.co.uk

This paperback edition first published in 2000

First published in the United States in 1999 by
The Free Press

Printed and bound in Great Britain by
St Edmundsbury Press, Bury St Edmunds

The moral right of the author has been asserted.

A CIP catalogue record for this book is available from the British Library.

ISBN 1 86197 217 2

TO MY MOTHER, TOSHIKO,

AND IN MEMORY OF MY FATHER, YOSHIO FUKUYAMA

Naturam expelles furca,
tamen usque recurret,
et mala perrumpet furtim fastidia victrix.

You can throw out Nature with a pitchfork,
But it always comes running back
And will burst through your foolish contempt in triumph.

—Horace, *Epistles* I. x. 24–25.

CONTENTS

ACKNOWLEDGMENTS

arts of this book were delivered as the 1997 Tanner Lectures at Brasenose College, Oxford. A version of Chapter 12, "Technology, Networks, and Social Capital," was delivered as the Krasnoff Lecture at New York University's Stern School of Business in February 1997. The Tanner Lectures were published in the United Kingdom as a pamphlet entitled *The End of Order* by the Social Market Foundation. I am grateful to the Tanner Foundation, the fellows of Brasenose College, the Stern School, and the Social Market Foundation for their support in these endeavors.

I profited greatly from two seminar series I cochaired—the first on new issues in science and the second on the dual revolutions in information technology and biology. These took place first at the Johns Hopkins School of Advanced International Studies' Foreign Policy Institute and then at the RAND Corporation and George Mason University.

There is a very long list of people I need to thank for their advice and comments on this project, both when this book was in lecture form and as it took its present shape. They include, but are not limited to, Karlyn Bowman, Dominic Brewer, Leon Clark, Mark Cordover, Tyler Cowen, Partha Dasgupta, John DiIulio, Esther Dyson, Nick Eberstadt, Jean Bethke Elshtain, Robin Fox, Bill Galston, Charles Griswold, Lawrence Harrison, George Holmgren, Ann Hulbert, Don Kash, Michael

Kennedy, Tjoborn Knutsen, Andrew Kohut, Jessica Korn, Timur Kuran, Everett Ladd, S. M. Lipset, John L. Locke, Andrew Marshall, Pete Molloy, David Myers, David Popenoe, Bruce Porter, Wendy Rahn, Marcella Rey, Steve Rhoads, Richard Rose, Abe Shulsky, Marcelo Siles and the Michigan State Social Capital Interest Group, Lord Robert Skidelsky, Tom Smith, Max Stackhouse, Neal Stephenson, Richard Swedberg, Lionel Tiger, Eric Uslaner, Richard Velkley, Caroline Wagner, James Q. Wilson, Clare Wolfowitz, Michael Woolcock, and Robert Wright.

The data on crime and family used in this book were collected by writing to a variety of national statistical agencies. I thank the countless individuals in these offices who kindly and helpfully responded to my requests, often with mountains of extremely useful data.

I thank the research assistants who helped me on this book: David Marcus, Carlos Arieira, Michelle Bragg, Sanjay Marwah, Benjamin Allen, and Nikhilesh Prasad. David Marcus generously volunteered to help; the work of the last five was supported by a grant from the Lynde and Harry Bradley Foundation. I am also grateful to my assistants, Lucy Kennedy and Kelly Lawler, for all of their work during the preparation of this manuscript and to Cynthia Paddock, Richard Schum, and Danilo Pellctiere for help with the science study groups.

I am grateful to Adam Bellow, formerly of The Free Press, who signed the book originally, and to Paul Golob, currently of The Free Press, who inherited the project and saw it through to completion with wise editorial comment. Andrew Franklin of Profile Books in the United Kingdom has been a long-time friend and helpful editor, for this as for my previous two books. Esther Newberg and Heather Schroder of International Creative Management have handled the business end in their usual excellent way for a similar length of time.

My wife, Laura, had the patience to read every version of the manuscript, and her judgment, according to my editor, was much surer than my own.

The manuscript was prepared for the most part on a self-assembled, dual-processor NT machine with 232 megs of RAM and a fast, open-GL graphics accelerator. This setup was a bit of overkill for word processing, but it was great for running AutoCAD and 3D Studio MAX in background.

PART ONE

THE
GREAT
DISRUPTION

I

Playing by the Rules

After the Industrial Era

Over the past half-century, the United States and other economically advanced countries have gradually made the shift into what has been called an "information society," the "information age," or the "postindustrial era."[1] Futurist Alvin Toffler has labeled this transition the "Third Wave," suggesting that it will ultimately be as consequential as the two previous waves in human history: from hunter-gatherer to agricultural societies and then from agricultural to industrial ones.[2]

This shift consists of a number of related elements. In the economy, services increasingly displace manufacturing as a source of wealth. Instead of working in a steel mill or automobile factory, the typical worker in an information society has a job in a bank, software firm, restaurant, university, or social service agency. The role of information and intelligence, embodied in both people and increasingly smart machines, becomes pervasive, and mental labor tends to replace physical labor. Production is globalized as inexpensive information technology makes it increasingly easy to move information across national borders, and rapid communications by television, radio, fax, and e-mail erodes the boundaries of long-established cultural communities.

A society built around information tends to produce more of the two things people value most in a modern democracy: freedom and equality. Freedom of choice has exploded, whether of cable channels, low-cost shopping outlets, or friends met on the Internet. Hierarchies of all sorts, whether political or corporate, come under pressure and begin to crumble. Large, rigid bureaucracies, which sought to control everything in their domain through rules, regulations, and coercion, have been undermined by the shift toward a knowledge-based economy, which serves to "empower" individuals by giving them access to information. Just as rigid corporate bureaucracies like the old IBM and AT&T gave way to smaller, flatter, more participatory competitors, so too did the Soviet Union and East Germany fall apart from their inability to control and harness the knowledge of their own citizens.

The shift into an information society has been celebrated by virtually everyone who has written or talked about it. Commentators as politically diverse as George Gilder, Newt Gingrich, Al Gore, Alvin and Heidi Toffler, and Nicholas Negroponte have seen these changes as good for prosperity, good for democracy and freedom, and good for society in general. Certainly many of the benefits of an information society are clear, but have all of its consequences necessarily been so positive?

People associate the information age with the advent of the Internet in the 1990s, but the shift away from the Industrial era started more than a generation earlier with the deindustrialization of the Rust Belt in the United States and comparable moves away from manufacturing in other industrialized countries. This period, from roughly the mid-1960s to the early 1990s, was also marked by seriously deteriorating social conditions in most of the industrialized world. Crime and social disorder began to rise, making inner-city areas of the wealthiest societies on earth almost uninhabitable. The decline of kinship as a social institution, which has been going on for more than two hundred years, accelerated sharply in the last half of the twentieth century. Fertility in most European countries and Japan fell to such low levels that these societies will depopulate themselves in the next century, absent substantial immigration; marriages and births became fewer; divorce soared; and out-of-wedlock childbearing came to affect one out of every three children born in the United States and over half of all children in Scandinavia. Finally, trust and confidence in institutions went into a deep, forty-year decline. A majority of people in the United States and Europe expressed confidence in their governments and fellow citizens during the late 1950s; only a small minority did so by the early 1990s. The nature of people's involvement with one another changed as well. Although there is no evidence that people associated with each other less, their mutual ties tended to be less permanent, less engaged, and with smaller groups of people.

These changes were dramatic, they occurred over a wide range of similar countries, and they all appeared at roughly the same period in history. As such, they constituted a Great Disruption in the social values that prevailed in the industrial age society of the mid-twentieth century, and are the subject of Part One of this book. It is highly unusual for social indicators to move together so rapidly; even without knowing why they did so, we have reason to suspect that they might be related to one another. Although conservatives like William J. Bennett are often attacked for harping on the theme of moral decline, they are essentially correct: the breakdown of social order is not a matter of nostalgia, poor memory, or ignorance about the hypocrisies of earlier ages. The decline is readily measurable in statistics on crime, fatherless children, reduced educational outcomes and opportunities, broken trust, and the like.

Was it just an accident that these negative social trends, which together reflected weakening social bonds and common values holding people together in Western societies, occurred just as economies in those societies were making the transition from the industrial to the information era? The hypothesis of this book is that the two were in fact intimately connected, and that with all of the blessings that flow from a more complex, information-based economy, certain bad things also happened to our social and moral life. The connections were technological, economic, and cultural. The changing nature of work tended to substitute mental for physical labor, thereby propelling millions of women into the workplace and undermining the traditional understandings on which the family had been based. Innovations in medical technology like the birth control pill and increasing longevity diminished the role of reproduction and family in people's lives. And the culture of intensive individualism, which in the marketplace and laboratory leads to innovation and growth, spilled over into the realm of social norms, where it corroded virtually all

5

forms of authority and weakened the bonds holding families, neighborhoods, and nations together. The complete story is, of course, much more complex than this, and differs from one country to another. But broadly speaking, the technological change that brings about what economist Joseph Schumpeter called "creative destruction" in the marketplace caused similar disruption in the world of social relationships. It would be surprising were this not true.

But there is a bright side too: social order, once disrupted, tends to get remade once again, and there are many indications that this is happening today. We can expect this to happen for a simple reason: human beings are *by nature* social creatures, whose most basic drives and instincts lead them to create moral rules that bind themselves together into communities. They are also by nature rational, and their rationality allows them to create ways of cooperating with one another spontaneously. Religion, often helpful to this process, is not the sine qua non of social order, as many conservatives believe. Neither is a strong and expansive state, as many on the Left argue. Man's natural state is not the war of "every one against every one" that Thomas Hobbes envisioned, but rather a civil society made orderly by the presence of a host of moral rules. These statements, moreover, are empirically supported by a tremendous amount of recent research coming out of the life sciences, in fields as diverse as neurophysiology, behavioral genetics, evolutionary biology, and ethology, as well as biologically informed approaches to psychology and anthropology. The study of how order arises, not as the result of a top-down mandate by hierarchical authority, whether political or religious, but as the result of self-organization on the part of decentralized individuals, is one of the most interesting and important intellectual developments of our time. Thus Part Two of this book steps back from the immediate social issues raised by the Great Disruption and asks the more general questions, Where does social order come from in the first place, and how does it evolve under changing circumstances?

The idea that social order has to come from a centralized, rational, bureaucratic hierarchy was one very much associated with the industrial age. The sociologist Max Weber, observing nineteenth-century industrial society, argued that rational bureaucracy was in fact the very essence of modern life. We know now, however, that in an information society, nei-

ther governments nor corporations will rely exclusively on formal, bureaucratic rules to organize the people over whom they have authority.
Instead, they will have to decentralize and devolve power, and rely on the
people over whom they have nominal authority to be self-organizing.
The precondition for such self-organization is internalized rules and
norms of behavior, which suggests that the world of the twenty-first century will depend heavily on such informal norms. Thus, while the transition into an information society has disrupted social norms, a modern,
high-tech society cannot get along without them and will face considerable incentives to produce them.

Part Three of the book looks both backward and forward for the
sources of this order. The view that society's moral order has been in
long-term decline is one long held by certain conservatives. The British
statesman Edmund Burke argued that the Enlightenment itself, with its
project of replacing tradition and religion with reason, is the ultimate
source of the problem, and Burke's contemporary heirs continue to argue
that secular humanism is at the root of today's social problems. But while
conservatives may be right that there were important ways in which
moral behavior deteriorated in the past two generations, they tend to ig-
nore the fact that social order not only declines, but also increases in long
cycles. This happened in Britain and America during the nineteenth century. It is reasonably clear that the period from the end of the eighteenth
century until approximately the middle of the nineteenth century was
one of sharply increasing moral decay in both countries. Crime rates in
virtually all major cities increased; families broke down and illegitimacy
rates rose; people were socially isolated; alcohol consumption, particularly in the United States, exploded, with per capita consumption in 1830
at levels perhaps three times as great as they are today. But then, with each
passing decade from the middle of the century until its end, virtually each
one of these social indicators turned positive: crime fell; families began
staying together in greater numbers; drunkards went on the wagon; and
new voluntary associations sprouted up to give people a greater sense of
communal belonging.

There are similar signs today that the Great Disruption that took
place from the 1960s to the 1990s is beginning to recede. Crime is down
sharply in the United States and other countries where it had become

epidemic. Divorce rates have declined since the 1980s, and there are now signs that the rate of illegitimacy (in the United States, at any rate) has begun to level off, if not fall. Levels of trust in major institutions have improved during the 1990s, and civil society appears to be flourishing. There is, moreover, plenty of anecdotal evidence that more conservative social norms have made a comeback, and that the more extreme forms of individualism that appeared during the 1970s have fallen out of favor. It is far too early to assert that these problems are now behind us. But it is also wrong to conclude that we are incapable of adapting socially to the technological and economic conditions of an age of information.

Gemeinschaft and *Gesellschaft*, One More Time

The disruption of social order by the progress of technology is not a new phenomenon. Particularly since the beginning of the Industrial Revolution, human societies have been subject to a relentless process of modernization as one new production process replaced another.[3] The social disorder of the late eighteenth and early nineteenth centuries in America and Britain can be traced directly to the disruptive effects of the so-called first Industrial Revolution, when steam power and mechanization created new industries in textiles, railroads, and the like. Agricultural societies were transformed into urban industrial societies within the space of perhaps a hundred years, and all of the accumulated social norms, habits, and customs that had characterized rural or village life were replaced by the rhythms of the factory and city.

This shift in norms engendered what is perhaps the most famous concept in modern sociology, the distinction drawn by Ferdinand Tönnies between what he called *gemeinschaft* ("community") and *gesellschaft* ("society").[4] According to Tönnies, the gemeinschaft that characterized a typical premodern European peasant society consisted of a dense network of personal relationships based heavily on kinship and on the direct, face-to-face contact that occurs in a small, closed village. Norms were largely unwritten, and individuals were bound to one another in a web of mutual interdependence that touched all aspects of life, from family to work to the few leisure activities that such societies enjoyed. Gesellschaft, on the other hand, was the framework of laws and other formal regulations that characterized large, urban, industrial societies. Social relationships were more formalized and impersonal; individuals did not depend on one another for mutual support to nearly the same extent and were therefore much less morally obligated.

The idea that informal norms and values will be replaced over time by rational, formal laws and rules has been a mainstay of modern sociological theory ever since. The English legal theorist Sir Henry Maine argued that in premodern societies, people were tied to one another by what he called a "status" relationship. A father was bound to his family or a lord to his slaves and servants in a lifetime personal relationship that consisted of a host of informal, unarticulated, and often ambiguous mutual obligations. No one could simply walk away from the relationship if he or she didn't like it. In a modern capitalist society, by contrast, Maine argued that such relationships are based on "contract," for example, a formal agreement that an employee will provide a certain quantity of labor in return for a certain quantity of wages from the employer. Everything is spelled out in the wage contract and is therefore enforceable by the state; there are no age-old obligations or duties that accompany the exchange of money for services. Unlike a status relationship, in other words, the contract relationship is not a moral one: either party can break it at any time, provided the terms of the contract are fulfilled.[5]

The consequences of the shift from agricultural to industrial societies on social norms were so large that they gave birth to an entirely new academic discipline, sociology, which sought to describe and understand these changes. Virtually all of the great social thinkers at the end of the nineteenth century—including Tönnies, Maine, Weber, Emile Durkheim, and Georg Simmel—devoted their careers to explicating the nature of this transition. Indeed, the American sociologist Robert Nisbet once characterized the entire subsequent thrust of his discipline as one long commentary on gemeinschaft and gesellschaft.

Many of the standard sociological texts written in the middle of the twentieth century treated the shift from gemeinschaft to gesellschaft as if it were a one-shot affair: societies were either "traditional" or "modern," and the modern ones somehow constituted the end of the road for social development. But social evolution did not culminate in middle-class American society of the 1950s, as industrial societies soon began transforming themselves into what Daniel Bell characterized as postindustrial societies or what we know as information societies. If this transformation is as momentous as the previous one, then it should hardly surprise us that the impact on social values should be equally great.

Why Social Order Is Important to the Future of Liberal Democracy

One of the greatest challenges modern information age democracies face today is whether they can maintain social order in the face of technological and economic change. From the early 1970s to the early 1990s there has been a sudden surge of new democracies in Latin America, Europe, Asia, and the former communist world that constitutes what Samuel Huntington has labeled another "Third Wave," this one of democracy.[6] As I argued in *The End of History and the Last Man,* there is a strong logic behind the evolution of political institutions in the direction of modern liberal democracy, one that is based on the correlation between economic development and stable democracy.[7] For the world's most economically advanced countries, there has been a convergence of political and economic institutions over time and no obvious alternatives to the liberal political and economic institutions we see before us.

This same progressive tendency is not necessarily evident in moral and social development, however. The tendency of contemporary liberal democracies to fall prey to excessive individualism is perhaps their greatest long-term vulnerability, and is particularly visible in the most individualistic of all democracies, the United States. The modern liberal state was premised on the notion that in the interests of political peace, government would not take sides among the differing moral claims made by religion and traditional culture. Church and state were to be kept separate; there would be pluralism in opinions about the most important moral and ethical questions concerning ultimate ends or the nature of the good. Tolerance would become the cardinal virtue. In place of moral consensus would be a transparent framework of law and institutions that would produce political order. Such a political system did not require that people be particularly virtuous, only that they be rational and follow the law in their own self-interest. In a similar fashion, the market-based capitalist economic system that went hand-in-glove with political liberalism required only that people consult their long-term self-interest to achieve a socially optimal production and distribution of goods.

The societies created on these individualistic premises have worked extraordinarily well, and as the twentieth century comes to a close there is little real alternative to liberal democracy and market capitalism as fundamental organizing principles for modern societies. Individual self-interest is a lower but more stable ground than virtue on which to base society. The creation of a rule of law is one of the proudest accomplishments of Western civilization, one whose benefits become all too obvious when one deals with countries like Russia or China that lack one.

But although formal law and strong political and economic institutions are critical, they are not in themselves sufficient to guarantee a successful modern society. Liberal democracy has always been dependent on certain shared cultural values to work properly. This can be seen most clearly in the contrast between the United States and the countries of Latin America. When Mexico, Argentina, Brazil, Chile, and other Latin countries gained their independence in the nineteenth century, many of them established formal democratic constitutions and legal systems patterned on the presidential system of the United States. Since then, not one Latin American country has experienced the political stability, economic growth, or efficiency of democratic institutions enjoyed by the United States, though fortunately most had returned to democratic government by the late 1980s.

There are many complex historical reasons for this, but the most important is a cultural one: the United States was settled primarily by Britain and inherited not just British law but British culture as well, while Latin America inherited various cultural traditions from the Iberian peninsula. Although the U.S. Constitution enforces a separation between church and state, American culture was nonetheless decisively shaped by sectarian Protestantism in its formative years. Sectarian Protestantism reinforced both American individualism and what Alexis de Tocqueville called the American "art of association"—that is, the tendency of the society to be self-organizing in a myriad of voluntary associations and communities. The vitality of American civil society was crucial for both the stability of its democratic institutions and its vibrant economy. The imperial and Latin Catholic traditions of Spain and Portugal, by contrast, re-inforced dependence on large, centralized institutions like the state and church, consequently weakening an independent civil society. There are similar contrasts between northern and southern Europe, whose differing abilities to make modern institutions work was also influenced by religious heritage and cultural tradition.

The problem with most modern liberal democracies is that they cannot take their cultural preconditions for granted. The most successful among them, including the United States, were lucky to have married strong formal institutions to a flexible and supportive informal culture. But there is nothing in the formal institutions themselves that guarantees that the underlying society will continue to enjoy the right sort of cultural values and norms under the pressures of technological, economic, and social change. Just the opposite is the case: the individualism, pluralism, and tolerance built into the formal institutions tend to encourage cultural diversity and therefore have the potential to undermine moral values inherited from the past. And a dynamic, technologically innovative economy will by its very nature disrupt existing social relations.

It may be, then, that while large political and economic institutions have been evolving along a long-term secular path, social life is more cyclical. Social norms that work for one historical period are disrupted by the advance of technology and the economy, and society has to play catch-up in order to renorm itself under changed conditions.

The Value of Rules

The cultural connections between the shift to an age of information and social disruption were symbolized by a series of television commercials that blitzed the airwaves during the 1996 Summer Olympic Games in Atlanta, Georgia. Sponsored by a major American telecommunications company, they showed a series of muscular, well-conditioned athletes doing some rather extraordinary things, like running up the sides of buildings, jumping off cliffs into thousand-foot canyons, and bounding from the roof of one skyscraper to another. The commercials were built around the theme that flashed on the screen at the end: "No limits." Consciously or not, the athlete's superb physique evoked the philosopher

Nietzsche's Superman, the godlike being unconstrained by ordinary moral rules, as he might have been lovingly portrayed by the Nazi filmmaker Leni Riefenstahl.

The telecommunications company that sponsored the commercials and the ad agency that produced them clearly wanted to create a powerful, positive, and future-oriented image: in the new age of information technology, old rules were breaking down, and the sponsoring company was at the forefront of the destruction. The implicit message said that the old rules—presumably the ones governing pre-Internet communications and regulated telephone monopolies—were unnecessary and harmful constraints, not just on telephone service but on the human spirit more generally. There was no telling what heights of human achievement could be reached if only these rules were lifted, and the sponsoring company would be perfectly happy to help its customers reach this promised land. Like the athletes, we might then become Godlike.

Whether consciously or not, the producers of these commercials were building on a very powerful cultural theme: that of the liberation of the individual from unnecessary and stifling social constraints. Since the 1960s, the West has experienced a series of liberation movements that have sought to free individuals from the constraints of many traditional social norms and moral rules. The sexual revolution, the women's liberation and feminist movements, and the movements in favor of gay and lesbian rights have exploded throughout the Western world. The liberation each one of these movements seeks concerns social rules, norms, and laws that unduly restrict the options and opportunities of individuals—whether of young people choosing sexual partners, women seeking career opportunities, or gays seeking recognition of their rights. Pop psychology, from the human potential movement of the 1960s to the self-esteem trend of the 1980s, sought to free individuals from stifling social expectations. Each one of these movements might well have adopted the slogan "No limits" as its own.

Both the Left and Right participated in this effort to free the individual from restrictive rules, but their points of emphasis tended to be different. To put it simply, the Left worried about lifestyles, and the Right worried about money. The former did not want traditional values to constrain unduly the choices of women, minorities, gays, the homeless,

13

people accused of crimes, or any number of other groups marginalized by society. The Right, on the other hand, did not want communities putting constraints on what they could do with their property—or in the particular case of the United States, what they could do with their guns. It was not an accident that the commercial promulgating the message of "no limits" was produced by a private, high-tech corporation trying to maximize its profits, for modern capitalism thrives on the breaking of rules wherein old social relationships, communities, and technologies are discarded in favor of new and more efficient ones. Both Left and Right denounced excessive individualism on the part of the other. Those who supported reproductive choice tended to oppose choice in buying guns or gas-guzzling cars; those who wanted unconstrained economic competition were appalled when they were mugged by unconstrained criminals on the way to the low-priced Wal-Mart. But neither side was willing to give up its preferred sphere of free choice for the sake of constraining the other.

As people soon discovered, there were serious problems with a culture of unbridled individualism, where the breaking of rules becomes, in a sense, the only remaining rule. The first had to do with the fact that moral values and social rules are not simply arbitrary constraints on individual choice; rather, they are the precondition for any type of cooperative enterprise. Indeed, social scientists have recently begun to refer to a society's stock of shared values as *social capital.* Like physical capital (land, buildings, machines) and human capital (the skills and knowledge we carry around in our heads), social capital produces wealth and is therefore of economic value to a national economy. It is also the prerequisite for all forms of group endeavor that take place in a modern society, from running a corner grocery store, to lobbying Congress, to raising children. Individuals amplify their own power and abilities by following cooperative rules that constrain their freedom of choice, allow them to communicate with others, and coordinate their actions. Social virtues like honesty, reciprocity, and keeping commitments are not choiceworthy just as ethical values; they also have a tangible dollar value and help the groups who practice them achieve shared ends.

The second problem with a culture of intense individualism is that it ends up being bereft of community. A community is not formed every time a group of people happens to interact with one another; true communities are bound together by the values, norms, and experiences shared among their members. The deeper and more strongly held those common values are, the stronger the sense of community is. The trade-off between personal freedom and community, however, does not seem obvious or necessary to many. As people were liberated from their traditional ties to spouses, families, neighborhoods, workplaces, or churches, they thought they could have social connectedness at the same time, this time the connections being those they choose for themselves. But they began to realize that such elective affinities, which they could slide into and out of at will, left them feeling lonely and disoriented, longing for deeper and more permanent relationships with other people.

The "no-limits" message is, then, a problematic one. We want to break rules that are unjust, unfair, irrelevant or outdated, and we seek to maximize personal freedom. But we also constantly need new rules to permit new forms of cooperative endeavor and to enable us to feel connected with one another in communities. These new rules always entail the limitation of individual freedom. A society dedicated to the constant upending of norms and rules in the name of increasing individual freedom of choice will find itself increasingly disorganized, atomized, isolated, and incapable of carrying out common goals and tasks. The same society that wants "no limits" to its technological innovation also sees "no limits" to many forms of personal behavior, and the consequent growth of crime, broken families, parents failing to fulfill obligations to children, neighbors not looking out for each other, and citizens opting out of public life.

Social Capital

Even if we agree in a general way that human society requires limits and rules, the question immediately arises, "Whose rules should prevail?"

In the rich, free, and diverse society constituted by the United States at the end of the twentieth century, the word *culture* has come to be associated with the concept of choice. That is, culture is something that artists, writers, or other imaginative people choose to create on the basis of an inner voice; for those less creatively inclined, it is something they choose to consume as art, cuisine, or entertainment. Culture is superficially but also commonly associated with food, particularly of an ethnic variety: what it means to have cultural diversity is to have a great choice among Chinese, Italian, Greek, Thai, or Mexican restaurants. More important cultural choices are up for grabs as well, as in the case of the Woody Allen character who, upon learning that he has terminal cancer, frantically tries to decide whether he will seek solace as a Buddhist, Hare Krishna, Catholic, or Jew.

We are taught, moreover, that in negotiating among these competing cultural claims, none can be judged to be better than any other. In the hierarchy of moral virtues, tolerance ranks high and moralism—the attempt to judge people by one's own moral or cultural rules—ranks as the vice among vices. *De gustibus non est disputandem*—there is no accounting for tastes—and like the taste for ethnic food, there is no way of judging whether one set of moral rules is better or worse than any other. This is a lesson taught not just by proponents of multiculturalism on the Left, but by libertarian economists on the Right, who boil down all human behavior to the pursuit of irreducible individual "preferences."[8]

It is to get around the problem of cultural relativism that this book concentrates not on cultural norms writ large, but on a certain subset of norms that constitute social capital. *Social capital* can be defined simply as a set of informal values or norms shared among members of a group that permits cooperation among them. If members of the group come to expect that others will behave reliably and honestly, then they will come to *trust* one another. Trust is like a lubricant that makes the running of any group or organization more efficient.

The sharing of values and norms does not in itself produce social capital, because the values may be the wrong ones. Look, for example, at southern Italy, a region of the world that is almost universally characterized as lacking in social capital and generalized trust, even though strong social norms exist. The sociologist Diego Gambetta tells the following story:

> A retired [mafia] boss recounted that when he was a young boy, his mafioso father made him climb a wall and then invited him to jump,

promising to catch him. He at first refused, but his father insisted until finally he jumped—and promptly landed flat on his face. The wisdom his father sought to convey was summed up by these words: "You must learn to distrust even your parents."[9]

The mafia is characterized by an extremely strong internal code of behavior, *l'omerta,* and individual mafiosi are spoken of as "men of honor." Nonetheless, these norms do not apply outside a small circle of mafiosi; for the rest of Sicilian society, the prevailing norms can be described more as "take advantage of people outside your immediate family at every occasion because otherwise they will take advantage of you first"—and as Gambetta's example suggests, even families may not be that reliable. Obviously such norms do not promote social cooperation, and the negative consequences for both good government and economic development have been documented extensively.[10] Southern Italy has been the source of the extensive corruption plaguing the country's political system, as well as one of the poorest parts of Western Europe.

The norms that produce social capital, by contrast, must substantively include virtues like truth telling, the meeting of obligations, and reciprocity. Not surprisingly, these norms overlap to a significant degree with those Puritan values that Max Weber found critical to the development of Western capitalism in his book *The Protestant Ethic and the Spirit of Capitalism*.

All societies have some stock of social capital; the real differences among them concern what might be called the "radius of trust."[11] That is, cooperative norms like honesty and reciprocity can be shared among limited groups of people and not with others in the same society. Families are obviously important sources of social capital everywhere. Whatever low opinions American parents may have of their teenage children, it is far more likely that members of the same family will trust and work with one another more than with strangers. This is the reason that virtually all businesses start out as family businesses.

But the strength of family bonds differs from society to society, and also varies relative to other types of social obligation. In some cases, there appears to be something of an inverse relationship between the bonds of trust and reciprocity inside and outside the family; when one is very strong, the other tends to be weak. In China and Latin America, families are strong and cohesive, but it is hard to trust strangers, and levels of honesty and cooperation in public life are much lower. A consequence is nepotism and pervasive public corruption. What made the Protestant Reformation important for Weber was not so much that it encouraged honesty, reciprocity, and thrift among individual entrepreneurs, but that these virtues were for the first time widely practiced outside the family.[12]

It is perfectly possible to form successful groups in the absence of social capital, using a variety of formal coordination mechanisms like contracts, hierarchies, constitutions, legal systems, and the like. But informal norms greatly reduce what economists label transaction costs—the costs of monitoring, contracting, adjudicating, and enforcing formal agreements. Under certain circumstances, social capital may also facilitate a higher degree of innovation and group adaptation.

Social capital has benefits that go well beyond the economic sphere. It is critical for the creation of a healthy civil society, that is, the realm of groups and associations that fall between the family and the state. Civil society, which has been the focus of considerable interest in former communist countries since the fall of the Berlin Wall, is said to be critical to the success of democracy. Social capital allows the different groups within a complex society to band together to defend their interests, which might otherwise be disregarded by a powerful state.[13] Indeed, so close is the association between civil society and liberal democracy that the late Ernest Gellner has argued that the latter is a virtual proxy for the former.[14]

Although social capital and civil society have been widely praised as good things to have, they are not always beneficial. Coordination is necessary for all social activity, whether good or bad. Plato's *Republic* is a discussion between Socrates and a group of friends over the meaning of justice. In Book I, Socrates points out to Thrasymachos that even a band of robbers must have a sense of justice among themselves, or they could not succeed in pulling off their robberies. The mafia and the Ku Klux Klan are constituent parts of American civil society; both possess social capital, and both are detrimental to the health of the broader society. In economic life, group coordination is necessary for one form of production, but when technology or markets change, a different type of coordination with perhaps a different set of group members becomes necessary.

The bonds of social reciprocity that facilitated production in the earlier time period become obstacles to production in the later one, as is the case for many Japanese corporations in the 1990s. To continue the economic metaphor, social capital at that point can be said to be obsolete and needs to be depreciated in the country's capital accounts.

The fact that social capital can on occasion be used for destructive purposes or can become obsolete does not negate the widely shared presumption that it is generally a good thing for a society to have. Physical capital, after all, is not always a good thing either. Not only can it become obsolete, but it can be used to produce assault rifles, thalidomide, tasteless entertainment, and a whole range of other social "bads." But societies have laws to forbid the production of the worst social bads, whether by physical or social capital, so we can presume that most of the uses to which social capital will be put will be no less good from a social standpoint than the products of physical capital.

And so it has been regarded by most people who have employed the concept. The first known use of the term *social capital* was by Lyda Judson Hanifan in 1916 to describe rural school community centers.[15] Jane Jacobs used the term in her classic work *The Death and Life of Great American Cities,* in which she explained that the dense social networks that existed in older, mixed-use urban neighborhoods constituted a form of social capital that encouraged public safety.[16] The economist Glenn Loury, as well as the sociologist Ivan Light, used the term *social capital* in the 1970s to analyze the problem of inner-city economic development: African Americans lacked the bonds of trust and social connectedness within their own communities that existed for Asian American and other ethnic groups, which went a long way toward explaining the relative lack of black small business development.[17] In the 1980s, the term *social capital* was brought into wider use by the sociologist James Coleman[18] and the political scientist Robert Putnam, the latter of whom has stimulated an intense debate over the role of social capital and civil society in Italy and in the United States.[19]

Perhaps the most important theorist of social capital was someone who never used the term but who understood its importance with great clarity: the French aristocrat and traveler Alexis de Tocqueville. Tocqueville observed in *Democracy in America* that in sharp contrast to his native

France, America possessed a rich "art of association," that is, a populace habituated to come together in voluntary associations for purposes both trivial and serious. American democracy and its system of limited government worked only because Americans were so adept at forming associations for both civil and political purposes. This ability to, in effect, self-organize not only meant that the government did not have to impose order in a hierarchical, top-down manner; civil association was also a "school of self-government" that taught people cooperative habits they would carry over with them to public life. Tocqueville would, one suspects, agree with the proposition that without social capital, there could be no civil society, and that without civil society, there could be no successful democracy.

How Do We Measure Social Capital?

Neither sociologists nor economists have been happy with the spreading use of the term *social capital,* the former because they see it as part of the broader conquest of the social sciences by economics, and the latter because they regard it as a nebulous concept that is difficult, if not impossible, to measure. And indeed, measurement of the total stock of cooperative social relationships based on norms of honesty and reciprocity is not a trivial task. If we argue that the Great Disruption has had an effect on social capital, we need to find an empirical basis for testing whether this is in fact true.

Robert Putnam has argued that the quality of governance in the different regions of Italy is correlated with social capital and that social capital has been in decline in the United States since the 1960s. The empirical validity of his claim with regard to the United States will be addressed in the next chapter. His work, however, illustrates some of the difficulties posed in measuring social capital. He uses two types of statistical measures of social capital. The first is information on groups and group memberships, from sports clubs and choral societies to interest groups and political parties, as well as indexes of political participation such as voter turnout and newspaper readership. In addition, there are more detailed time-budget surveys and other indicators of how people spend their waking hours. The second type is survey research, such as the

General Social Survey (for the United States) and the World Values Survey (for over forty countries around the world), that asks a series of questions concerning values and behavior.

The assertion that American social capital has been declining over the past two generations has been hotly contested. Numerous scholars have either pointed to contradictory data showing that groups and group memberships have actually been increasing over the past generation, or else argued that the available data simply do not capture the reality of group life in a complex society like that of the United States.[20] This evidence will be reviewed in Chapter 2.

Aside from the question of whether it is possible to count groups and group memberships comprehensively, there are at least three further measurement problems with this approach. First, social capital has an important qualitative dimension. A bowling league or a garden club might be, as Tocqueville suggests, schools for cooperation and public spiritedness, but they are obviously very different institutions from the U.S. Marine Corps or the Mormon church, in terms of the kinds of collective action they foster. A bowling league is not, to say the least, capable of storming a beach. An adequate measure of social capital needs to take account of the nature of the collective action of which a group is capable—its inherent difficulty, the value of the group's output, whether it can be undertaken under adverse circumstances, and so forth.

The second problem has to do with what an economist would call the positive externalities of group membership, or what we might label the "positive radius of trust." An externality is a benefit or cost falling on a party outside a given activity. Mowing your lawn and keeping your house looking nice are examples of positive externalities that benefit your neighbors. Pollution is the classic case of a cost that has to be borne by people who weren't responsible for creating it. Although all groups require social capital to operate, some build bonds of trust (and hence social capital) outside their own memberships. As Weber indicated, Puritanism mandated honesty not simply toward other members of one's religious community, but toward all human beings. On the other hand, norms of reciprocity can be shared among only a small subset of a group's members. In a so-called membership group like the American Association of Retired Persons (AARP), which has a membership of over 30 million, there is no reason to think that any two given members will trust one another or achieve coordinated action just because they have paid their yearly dues to the same organization.

The final problem concerns negative externalities. Some groups actively promote intolerance, hatred, and even violence toward nonmembers. The Ku Klux Klan, Nation of Islam, and Michigan Militia possess social capital, but a society made up of such groups would not be particularly appealing, and might even cease to be a democracy. Such groups have problems cooperating with each other, and the exclusive bonds of community uniting them are likely to make them less adaptive by sealing them off from influences in the surrounding environment.

It should be clear that coming up with a believable number expressing the stock of social capital for a large and complex society like the United States based on a census of groups is next to impossible. We have empirical data, of varying reliability, on only a certain subset of the groups that actually exist and no consensus means of judging their qualitative differences.

How, then, can we get a handle on whether a given society's stock of social capital is increasing or decreasing? One solution is to rely more heavily on the second of the two data sources: survey data on trust and values. Many of the long-running social surveys query respondents directly on questions relevant to social cooperation, such as whether they trust their fellow citizens, are willing to take bribes, or are likely to lie in their own interest. There are manifold problems with survey data, of course, beginning with the fact that responses will vary according to the way the question is phrased and who is asking it, to the absence of consistent data for many countries and many time periods. A general question such as, "Generally speaking, would you say that most people can be trusted or that you can't be too careful in dealing with people?" (asked in both the General Social Survey and World Values Survey) won't give very much precise information about the radius of trust among the respondents, or their relative propensities to cooperate with family, co-ethnics, co-religionists, complete strangers, and the like. Nonetheless, such data exist and will be used here to the extent that they shed light on general trends.

There is another alternative approach as well. Instead of measuring social capital as a positive value, it might be easier to measure the *absence* of social capital through traditional measures of social dysfunction, such as rates of crime, family breakdown, drug use, litigation, suicide, and tax evasion. The presumption is that since social capital reflects the existence of cooperative norms, social deviance ipso facto reflects a lack of social capital. Indicators of social dysfunction, while hardly unproblematic, are far more abundant than data on group memberships and are available on a comparative basis. This strategy has been used by the National Commission on Civic Renewal to measure civic disengagement.[21]

It should be noted at the outset that there is one very serious problem with using social dysfunction data as a negative measure of social capital: it ignores distribution. Just as conventional capital is unevenly distributed within a society (i.e., as measured by wealth and income distribution studies), so social capital is also likely to be unevenly distributed: strata of highly socialized, self-organizing people may coexist with pockets of extreme atomization and social pathology. Using social deviance as a proxy for social capital is a bit like using poverty data as a measure of a society's overall wealth, under which circumstances the United States would show up as one of the poorer countries in the developed world.

Taking these different considerations into account, this book will look at three major types of data to measure trends in social capital in the developed world since the 1950s: (1) data on crime, based mostly on the self-reporting of national criminal justice agencies; (2) data on families, including fertility, marriage, divorce, and illegitimacy, again from national statistical agencies; and (3) survey data on trust, values, and civil society. After the data are presented in Chapter 2, Chapter 3 considers the conventional explanations for the Great Disruption, most of which leave something to be desired. Chapters 4 and 5 discuss specific causes for each of the phenomena in question.

Inclusion of data on families in a list of indicators of social dysfunction will be controversial to many. There are those who argue that there is no "normal" type of family and that the massive changes that have taken place in family structure since the 1950s merely reflect the shift from one form of household to another. Families can constitute social capital, but as the Chinese and Latin Catholic cases cited above indicate, they can also be barriers to cooperation outside the family. It is my view that family norms both constitute social capital and are critical for propagating social capital to succeeding generations, and that phenomena like the rapid growth of households headed by single women is a very negative social development. These assertions are defended in Chapter 6.

There are other types of social capital indicators that could have been considered but are not included here. One is the level of litigation in a society. Americans are famously litigious and have a much higher number of lawyers per capita than any other developed society. To many Americans, it appears that issues that used to be settled with a handshake are now fought out in court. The apparent rise of litigation over what seem to be trivial or absurd issues, such as the woman who was awarded damages from McDonald's for having spilled coffee on herself that was too hot, or children suing parents for "wrongful life" (the failure to have an abortion), is evidence of the declining level of trust, not to say common sense, in the society.

Unfortunately, data on comparative levels of civil litigation are difficult to come by and even more difficult to interpret given the major differences between common law and civil code countries. Moreover, it is not clear that rising levels of litigation in the United States are necessarily indicators of lower levels of social capital. The United States tends to use tort law as a substitute for state regulation: instead of having a government agency monitor and inspect public swimming pools and rollercoasters, for example, it relies on the ability of private citizens to sue pool or amusement park operators for large sums of money to deter them from doing things dangerous to public safety. Rising rates of litigation in the United States may therefore actually be a positive indicator of social capital: rather than appeal to a hierarchical source of authority to resolve disputes, private parties seek to work out equitable arrangements among themselves, albeit with the help of a legion of highly paid lawyers.

A Note on Comparative Methodology

In the chapters that follow, I present social data for the United States, the United Kingdom, Sweden, and Japan, as well as draw on more extensive data for approximately ten other developed countries, including Canada, Australia, New Zealand, France, Germany, the Netherlands, Italy, Spain, Norway, Finland, and Korea. The choice of the first four countries in the book's charts is simply illustrative; readers who want to look at more detailed data for other countries should consult the Appendix. All of these countries are members of the Organization for Economic Cooperation and Development (OECD). (Data on additional countries is available at http://www.mason.gmu/~ffukuyam/.)

In studying phenomena like sudden shifts in social norms, it is extremely important to compare data from different countries. Unlike natural scientists, social scientists cannot carry out laboratory experiments in which a procedure is run under controlled circumstances to understand precisely what cause is responsible for what effect. The closest we can come is to compare two societies that are similar in many respects, but vary in one particular area. Thus, if we want to understand the impact of lower marginal tax rates on economic growth, we might compare New Zealand to Australia during the 1980s. Comparing New Zealand to Papua New Guinea on the effects of tax policy would make no sense. Not only are the two countries culturally very diverse, they are at such completely disparate levels of socioeconomic development that any differences in economic growth would be, as the phrase goes, "massively overdetermined."

Comparative methodology has a long history in the social sciences, beginning with classic studies like Emile Durkheim's *Suicide,* which developed the concept of anomie by looking at suicide rates in a series of different European countries at the end of the nineteenth century. Only by comparing the experience of one country to that of others that are similar can we hope to unpack explanations for complex phenomena and avoid excessive parochialism. Americans, for example, often attribute developments like the declining respect for authority to national experiences like the Vietnam War or the Watergate scandal. Although this may be true to some extent, the explanation seems less plausible once we learn that respect for authority has been declining in virtually all other developed countries.

Since many social outcomes are strongly correlated with a society's level of development (as measured by per capita gross domestic product), it makes sense to compare developed countries only with other developed countries. As we will see in the next few chapters, Asian countries when they reached the same level of development as Britain or France have experienced very different levels of social dysfunction, which would indicate that it is culture rather than level of development that is responsible for the contrast. This also explains why I have not included data on any developing countries in this book. It is not that their experiences are not important; rather, they tend to be different from the United States and other developed countries in so many ways that their experience is not particularly helpful in interpreting our own.

2

Crime, Family, Trust: What Happened

eginning in about 1965, a large number of indicators that can serve as negative measures of social capital all started moving upward rapidly at the same time. These fell into three broad categories: crime, family, and trust. These changes occurred in virtually all developed countries, with the exception of Japan and Korea. As we will see, there are a number of regularities in these changes: the Scandinavian countries, English-speaking nations (the United States, United Kingdom, Canada, Australia, and New Zealand), and Latin Catholic countries like Spain and Italy tended to behave in similar ways. Changes came later in some and reached different levels in other countries, and the United States was usually exceptional within this group for its high levels of social deviance. But all Western societies were affected sooner or later by the Great Disruption.

Crime

There is an intimate relationship between social capital and crime. If we define social capital as a cooperative norm that has become embedded in the relationships among a group of people, then crime ipso facto represents the absence of social capital because it represents the violation of a community norm. That is, formal criminal law defines a minimal set of social rules by which people in a society agree to abide. Breaking such a law represents an offense not just against the individual victim of the crime, but against the larger community and its system of norms as well. That is why, in criminal law, the state rather than an individual steps in to apprehend and punish violators.

We have, of course, defined social capital not as formal laws but rather as informal norms promoting cooperative behavior. On this level as well, there is a clear if somewhat more complex relationship between social capital and crime. Communities have both formal and informal means of establishing norms and controlling or punishing deviance. Ideally, the best form of crime control is not a large and repressive police force, but a society that socializes its young people to obey the law in the first place and to steer violators back into the mainstream of society through informal community pressures.

In *The Death and Life of Great American Cities,* Jane Jacobs described the ability of social networks in older urban neighborhoods to produce public safety.[1] A neighborhood like Boston's North End in the first half of the twentieth century was populated largely by Italian immigrants and their children. To outsiders, it looked squalid and disorganized. Yet although the community was indeed poor relative to others in the Boston area, it had a plentiful stock of social capital embedded in the relationships among families that existed on each block. Jacobs pointed out that crime control was largely a matter of adult supervision—literally, the number of adults out on the sidewalks keeping track of young people who were likely to get into trouble and outsiders who might lead them astray. In such a dense urban neighborhood, people were out on the street constantly, working, shopping, eating, and doing errands. Shopkeepers in particular had an interest in what was going on outside their stores because crime was bad for business. The mixed-use character of the neighborhood—the fact that it was partly residential, partly commercial, with some light industry—was critical for increasing the number of "eyes on the street" at any given moment of the day or night.

Jacobs illustrates the power of this kind of social network by describing an incident that happened outside her apartment in Manhattan, when a man tried to pull a little girl away on a sidewalk and the child resisted:

> As I watched from our second-floor window, making up my mind how to intervene if it seemed advisable, I saw it was not going to be necessary. From the butcher shop beneath the tenement had emerged the woman who, with her husband, runs the shop; she was standing within earshot of the man, her arms folded and a look of determination on her face. Joe Cornacchia, who with his sons-in-law keeps the delicatessen, emerged about the same moment and stood solidly to the other side. Several heads poked out of the tenement windows above, one was withdrawn quickly and its owner reappeared a moment later in the doorway behind the man. Two men from the bar next to the butcher shop came to the doorway and waited. On my side of the street, I saw that the locksmith, the fruit man and the laundry proprietor had all come out of their shops and that the scene was also being surveyed from a number of windows besides ours. That man did not know it, but he was surrounded. Nobody was going to allow a little girl to be dragged off, even if nobody knew who she was.[2]

Jacobs notes that, as it turned out, the girl was being dragged away by her father.

Neighborhoods like Jacobs's in Manhattan and the North End rely not on formal police controls or on the kinds of strong social ties that exist within families or in a rural village. Neighbors and passersby on the street are not necessarily friends or even acquaintances. Nonetheless, even in such crowded, dense urban environments, shared concern for order and community norms was sufficient to keep crime rates low. In later years, many such neighborhoods were bulldozed to make way for planned housing projects, often in the name of a high-modernist urbanism that saw tidy, geometrical cities as aesthetic ends in themselves.[3] Mixed-use neighborhoods were replaced with single-use tracts that kept working people out of residential areas during the day; in place of crowded streets were large, empty parks and playgrounds that gangs and drug dealers soon took over. The adults retreated from sidewalks to their high-rise apartments, and as a result, crime rates began to soar. Some of

America's most crime-infested neighborhoods, like the Cabrini-Green housing project and the Robert Taylor Homes on Chicago's South Side, are the results of urban renewal projects in the 1950s and 1960s that took no account of the social capital embedded in the older neighborhoods they replaced. It is not surprising that urban renewal strategies in the 1990s centered around dynamiting many of these projects from the 1950s.

The inverse relationship between social capital and crime has long been recognized in the criminological literature, though not necessarily using that term. Robert Park and the Chicago school of sociology argued that juvenile delinquency was associated with the social dislocations created by urbanization and that its prevention required the embedding of individual children in social structures like churches and schools.[4] Others, like the contemporary criminologists Robert Sampson and John Laub, have pointed to social norms maintained informally by communities beyond the family as a source of social order. In one study, Sampson, Stephen Raudenbush, and Felton Earls use survey data to measure what they call the "collective efficacy" of neighborhoods. The survey asks questions such as how likely it was for someone in the neighborhood to intervene if children were skipping school or hanging out on a street corner, whether children behaved respectfully toward adults, or whether neighbors trusted each other. Analyzing several hundred neighborhoods in Chicago, they showed that these social capital variables were strongly correlated with the absence of neighborhood violence.[5]

In police states, the importance of informal social norms in controlling crime is made evident when formal controls are relaxed. People in authoritarian or totalitarian societies often obey the law more strictly than their counterparts in democratic societies do, but we would not be inclined to say that their law-abidingness necessarily represents an abundance of social capital.[6] It may instead reflect fear of draconian punishments meted out by an omnipresent and repressive state. Under such conditions, crime frequently increases when the state collapses and people no longer fear the police. This happened throughout the former communist world, where crime rates rose dramatically after the fall of the Berlin Wall in 1989. What we were witnessing was not a precipitous drop in social capital in Russia, Hungary, Poland, and other countries, but rather the revelation that levels of social capital were low or depleted under communism to begin with. This should not surprise us, since the objective of Marxist-Leninism was to stamp out an independent civil society and the horizontal ties between citizens on which civil society was based.

Crime: The Big Picture

Americans are aware that crime rates began to escalate beginning some time in the 1960s, a dramatic change from the early post–World War II period when murder and robbery rates in the United States actually declined.[7] The beginning of the great postwar crime surge can be dated from approximately 1963 and accelerated rapidly thereafter. It is not surprising that the late 1960s became a period when "law and order" was exploited as a political issue among conservatives; Richard Nixon rode to victory over Hubert Humphrey in 1968 in part because he appealed to Americans' fears of rising crime.

After declining slightly in the mid-1980s, U.S. crime rates spurted upward again in the late 1980s and peaked around 1991–1992. Rates for both violent and property crimes have dropped substantially since then. Indeed, they have fallen most dramatically in areas where they had risen most rapidly in the 1960s, 1970s, and 1980s—in New York, Chicago, Detroit, Los Angeles, and other big cities. New York's murder rate is now back to where it was in the 1960s, when the Great Disruption began. Note that this great upsurge in crime coincided with the coming into adulthood of the postwar baby boom generation, as well as the period of decreasing trust and civic disengagement.

Americans may be less aware that this same increase in crime rates occurred in virtually all other non-Asian developed countries in approximately the same time period. Figure 2.1 shows that violent crime rose rapidly in England and Wales and in Sweden, while declining in Japan. Rates also rose rapidly in Canada, New Zealand, Scotland, Finland, Ireland, and the Netherlands (see the Appendix). The composition of violent crime was different in these countries; murders comprise a much higher proportion of violent crimes in the United States than in other countries, so on the whole the American record is probably worse than

Figure 2.1 indicates. High-income countries in Asia, like Japan and Singapore, show decreasing levels of violent crime in this period.

FIGURE 2.1

Total Violent Crime Rates, 1950–1996

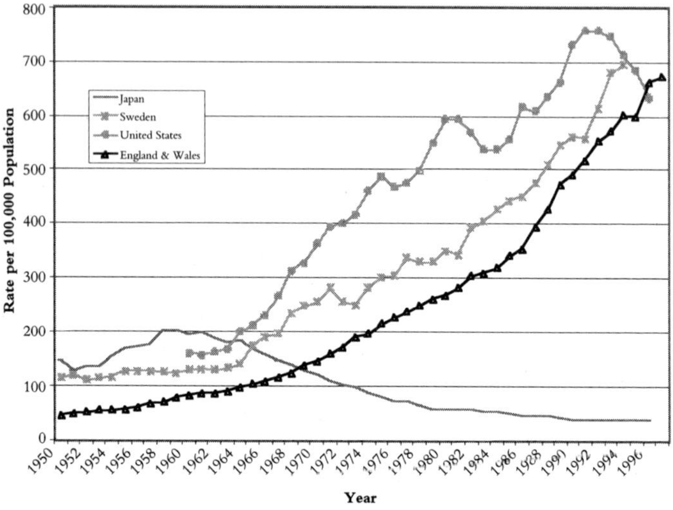

Source: See the Appendix for data.

Property crime rates are probably a better negative measure of social capital than violent crimes. The latter, and particularly murders, are relatively infrequent, individualistic acts that touch a comparatively small portion of a given population. Property crimes, by contrast, are far more widespread and reflect the behavior of a broader part of the population. In the United States in 1996, for example, there were 632 property crimes committed for every murder. Weighed against this is the fact that violent crimes tend to be more prone to media sensationalism, and hence contribute disproportionately to public perceptions of public safety and thus to social trust. As Figure 2.2 indicates, property crime rates have increased dramatically in England and Wales, and Sweden, as well as the United States. Many other countries saw sharp increases in theft rates, including Scotland, France, New Zealand, Denmark, Norway, Finland, and the Netherlands. Here, the United States is not exceptional: New Zealand, Denmark, the Netherlands, Sweden, and Canada ended up with higher theft rates than the United States over the past generation. Again, Singapore, Korea, and Japan are outliers, with relatively low rates and no discernable increases in property crime rates over the same period.

As Figure 2.2 illustrates, property crime rates fell during the 1990s in the United States, England and Wales, and Sweden. Rates also fell in New Zealand, Canada, Finland, France, and Denmark (see Appendix).

FIGURE 2.2

Total Theft Crime Rates, 1950–1996

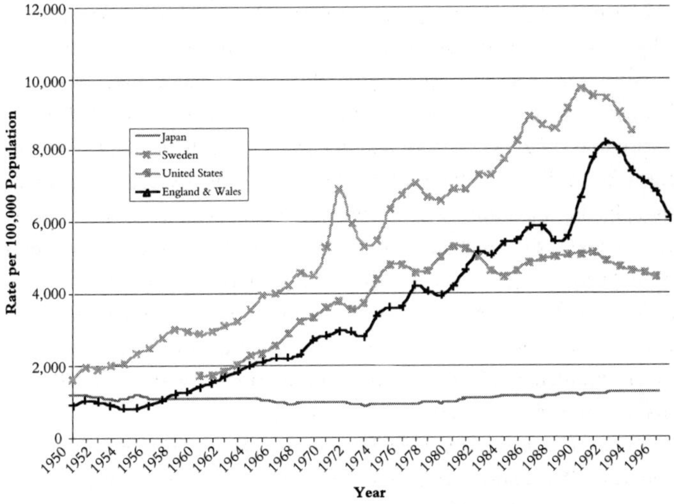

Source: See the Appendix for data.

White-collar crime might seem to be a useful measure of social capital since it is often committed not just by the poor and marginalized but also by the better-off members of society. Unfortunately, data on white-collar crime are far less usable than those on violent and property crime. Definitions vary widely between countries, and data collection and reporting is abysmal. Accordingly, it will not be used here.

In addition to the categories of violent, property, and white-collar crime, there is a fourth category of deviance for which very few statistics are kept, but which is in fact quite critical to the stock of social capital in a particular society. This is what certain criminologists have come to label *social disorder,* that is, acts like vagrancy, graffiti writing, public drunkenness, and panhandling.[8] Forty years ago, prior to the onset of the Great Disruption, most of these activities were considered crimes in the United States and other developed countries; indeed, much of what municipal police departments once spent their time doing was arresting drunks and chasing away panhandlers. In a series of court rulings over the past generation, almost all of these activities were decriminalized in the United States on the grounds that criminal sanctions violated the rights of individuals to free speech, due process, and the like. In San Francisco, for example, arrests for drunkenness declined from 60 or 70 percent of all arrests in the 1950s to 17 percent in 1992; public drunkenness, as well as homelessness, panhandling, and other forms of vagrancy, exploded.[9] In addition, during the 1970s large numbers of mentally ill people were released from the institutions where they had previously been housed; although the intention was to provide them with a more humane environment, the result was that city streets filled up with large numbers of mentally ill homeless people. Something similar happened in Britain as seriously disturbed people were discharged under "community care" policies. The consequence of these changes was to produce a sense of urban disorder in many cities that was, as criminologist Wesley Skogan has shown, often a precursor to increases in crime.[10]

The pattern in Asia is very different from that of Western developed countries. The four wealthiest societies in the Far East—Japan, Korea, Singapore, and Hong Kong—which (at least up to the Asian economic crisis of 1997–1998) had per capita GDPs comparable to those of Europe and North America, showed crime rates that were lower than for virtually all European countries. Japan's crime trends are of particular interest: not only are rates significantly lower overall than any other country in the OECD, but overall rates actually declined through the first half of the period in question, while violent crime rates declined over the entire period.

The data in Figures 2.1 and 2.2 and in the Appendix are based on the self-reporting of national justice or interior ministries.[11] Any criminologist will immediately note that there are many problems in using these data to represent actual levels of crime, much less more amorphous concepts like social capital.[12] The most serious concerns police underreporting (or, in much rarer circumstances, overreporting). That is, only a portion of crimes actually committed are ever reported to the police (by one estimate, reported robberies constituted only 44 to 63 percent of all actual ones), and the number of reported crimes that the police in turn report to national statistical agencies is only a portion of those reported to them.[13] Many reported crimes are dealt with by local police agencies on an informal basis without paperwork or audit trails. Criminologists agree that for most countries, the level of police reporting of crimes has increased as record-keeping systems improved and organizational rules for crime reporting were systematized. Many criminologists have turned to victimization surveys rather than police reports to get at the real level of crime in a society.[14] Such surveys ask a random sample of respondents whether they have ever been victims of crime, and hence are not dependent on police agencies. Unfortunately, many countries do not carry out systematic victimization surveys, and those that do (like the United States) have done so only since the 1970s.[15] These surveys indicate that police underreporting of crime in decades past may have been substantial. On the other hand, one recent comparative British study shows victimization rates more or less tracking police reporting rates, rising through the late 1980s in a number of countries and falling thereafter.[16]

The methodological problems with existing crime data have led many criminologists to shy away from comparative analysis of crime, or crime trends over long periods of time.[17] But they are missing the forest for the trees. Even if we posit that there have been gradual increases in police reporting rates for most developed countries, the overall rates of increase in reported crime have been extraordinarily dramatic in most cases. It is hard to imagine that the broad upturns in so many different countries over prolonged periods of time are simply a statistical artifact, corresponding as they do to popular perceptions that crime has been on the increase. The crime historian Ted Robert Gurr is skeptical that changes in police reporting practices could have been responsible for increasing numbers after World War II; he notes, for example, that crime rates declined between 1840 and the early twentieth century in most economically advanced countries even as reporting practices were improving. He argues that the real explanation for rising reported crime rates may be the simplest one: that "threatening social behavior . . . began an increase far more rapid than the earlier decline."[18] Indeed, many victimization studies have shown that police reporting corresponds fairly accurately with public perceptions of crime when those crimes are serious.[19] Moreover, it is difficult to explain why the four wealthiest Asian societies appear to be exempt from this trend. Are they the only developed countries that have not improved their crime reporting methods over the past two generations?

The Family

The most dramatic shifts in social norms that constitute the Great Disruption concern those related to reproduction, the family, and relations between the sexes. The sexual revolution and the rise of feminism in the 1960s and 1970s touched virtually everyone in the Western part of the developed world and introduced massive changes not just in households but in offices, factories, neighborhoods, voluntary associations, education, even the military. Changes in gender roles have had an important impact on the nature of civil society.

There is a strong relationship between families and social capital. Families in the first instance constitute the most basic cooperative social unit, one in which mothers and fathers need to work together to create, socialize, and educate children. James Coleman, the sociologist who was most responsible for bringing the term *social capital* into broader use, defined it as "the set of resources that inhere in family relations and in community social organizations and that are useful for the cognitive or social development of a child."[20] Cooperation within families is facilitated by the fact that it is underpinned by biology: all animals favor kin and are willing to undertake large one-way transfers of resources to genetic relatives, in ways that vastly increase the chances of reciprocity and long-term cooperation within kin groups. The propensity of family members to cooperate facilitates not just the raising of children, but other sorts of social activities like running businesses. Even in today's world of large, impersonal, bureaucratic corporations, small businesses, most of them run by families, account for as much as 20 percent of private sector employment in the American economy and are critical as incubators of new technologies and business practices.[21]

On the other hand, excessive dependence on kinship ties can produce negative consequences for the broader society outside the family. Many cultures, from China to Southern Europe to Latin America, promote what is called "familism," that is, the elevation of family and kinship ties above other sorts of social obligations. This produces a two-level morality, wherein the level of moral obligation to public authority of all sorts is weaker than that reserved for kin. In the case of a culture like that of China, familism is promoted by the prevailing ethical system, Confucianism. In this type of culture, there is a high degree of social capital inside families but a relative paucity of social capital outside kinship.

Much of the classical social theory written at the turn of the nineteenth century assumed that as societies modernized, the family would diminish in importance and be replaced by more impersonal kinds of social ties. This was one of the most basic differences between gemeinschaft and gesellshaft: in a modern society, instead of relying on your cousin or uncle when you need a loan or want to hire an accountant, you go to a bank, advertise, or look in the Yellow Pages. Familism led to nepotism. Hence, the demands of economic efficiency meant that business partners, clients, and bankers should be selected unsentimentally on the basis of qualifications and ability, and not blood. Modern bureaucracies (in theory, at least) are staffed not by family members and cronies, but by those who have met objective job criteria or have passed formal exams.

And so, indeed, the family has diminished in importance in virtually all modernizing societies. In colonial America, when the vast majority of Americans lived on family farms, the family was the basic productive unit, producing not just food but many household items as well. The family educated its children, took care of the elderly, and, in view of the physical isolation and lack of transportation of most farms, was also its own main source of entertainment. In subsequent years, nearly all of these functions were stripped away. First men and then women began seeking employment outside the household in factories and offices; children were sent off to public schools for education; grandma and grandpa were shipped off to retirement or nursing homes; and entertainment came to be provided by commercial companies like Walt Disney and MGM. By the middle of the twentieth century, the family had been reduced to its two-generation nuclear core, and all that was left as its unique province was the reproductive function.

The modernization theory that was popular in the social sciences in the middle of the twentieth century did not see family life as particularly problematic: extended families would simply evolve into nuclear ones that were more appropriate to the conditions of life in industrial societies. But the family did not stop evolving in the year 1950. The Great Disruption has put even the nuclear family into a long-term decline and consequently has jeopardized the family's core reproductive function. Unlike economic production, education, leisure time activities, and the other functions that were moved outside the family, it is not clear that there is a good substitute for reproduction outside nuclear families, and this in turn explains why changes in family structure have been so consequential for social capital.

The changes that have taken place in Western families are familiar to most people, and are captured in statistics on fertility, marriage, divorce, and out-of-wedlock childbearing.

Fertility

Although it sounds silly to state a point so obvious, social capital cannot exist without people, and Western societies are failing to produce enough of them to sustain themselves. The generation that came of age in America and Europe in the 1960s and 1970s grew up hearing about the population explosion and global environmental crisis, and many remain firmly convinced that "overpopulation" is one of the chief threats to future human existence. And so it may be for many parts of the Third World. But for any developed country, the problem is exactly the opposite: they are in the process of depopulating themselves.

By the 1980s, virtually all developed countries had undergone the so-called demographic transition in which total fertility rates (TFR, the average number of children per woman per lifetime) fell below the rate (a little over two) required to maintain the population at a steady level.[22] Figure 2.3 shows total fertility rates for the United States, the United Kingdom, Sweden, and Japan. Some countries, like Spain, Italy, and Japan, have fallen so far below replacement fertility that their total population in each successive generation will be more than 30 percent smaller than in the previous one.[23] Absent large-scale immigration from less developed countries, Japan and much of Europe will be losing population at a rate of well over 1 percent per year, year after year, until they dwindle to a fraction of their current sizes toward the end of the twenty-first century. Japan was the first developed country to see a rapid decline in fertility, which began plummeting as early as the 1950s. One consequence is that while demographic momentum will keep its total population growing into the next century, the Japanese labor force had already started to shrink in absolute numbers by the late 1990s, and by 2015 will fall by 10 million workers in the absence of massive immigration.[24]

FIGURE 2.3

Total Fertility Rates, 1950–1996

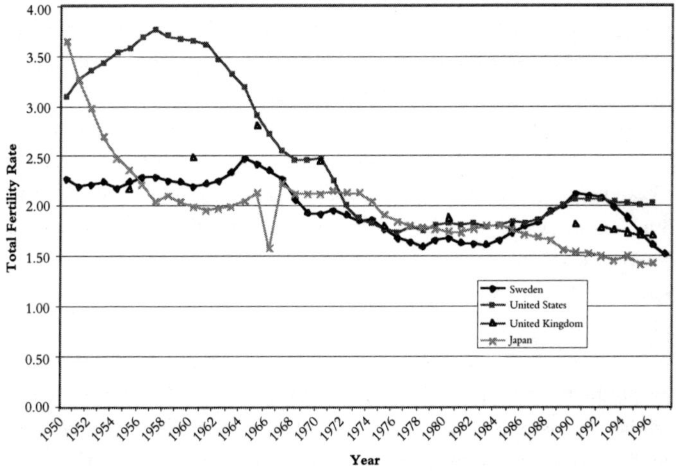

Year

Source: See the Appendix for data.

The shift to low TFR in the last two decades of the century has and will continue to have particularly disruptive social consequences because it followed a period of relatively high fertility during the post–World War II baby boom. For reasons that few demographers can fathom, the baby boom was particularly pronounced in certain English-speaking countries like the United States, New Zealand, and Australia. But it was not limited to these countries: the Netherlands, Denmark, Sweden, Norway, France, and Germany all experienced increases in fertility after the war. The baby booms in the English-speaking world began in the late 1940s and crested in the late 1950s or early 1960s; Italy, Sweden, and France reached their peak postwar fertility rates only in the mid-1960s or even later.

Low fertility rates are not new, though rates so far below replacement are without precedent. Fertility rates in France had already begun falling in the nineteenth century and were a preoccupation of French policy-makers, who worried about falling behind a rising Germany prior to World War I. Rates were also low across Europe during the 1930s, when some intellectuals began discussing the meaning and consequences of de-population.[25] Many European countries like France and Sweden have tried to implement pronatalist policies such as giving a per child subsidy to families along with social services like day care and generous maternal leave (and increasingly paternal leave) provisions. Most pronatalist policies are extremely expensive, though, and have had very little effect on fertility rates. Despite generous family allowances, French fertility rates have remained low. Sweden spent ten times as much as Italy or Spain to encourage its citizens to have children, and between 1983 and the early 1990s it managed to raise fertility back up to almost replacement levels. But the rate began to collapse again in the mid-1990s and is now back down to 1.5.

Marriage and Divorce

In addition to getting smaller and failing to reproduce themselves, Western families were also starting to split apart, with increasing numbers of children being born outside wedlock, or else experiencing the disruption of their parents' marriage at some point during childhood. In light of the massive evidence that the nuclear family has been in long-term decline and that this was having serious consequences for children, it is remarkable how social scientists tried for so long to assert that no significant change had occurred. The sociologist David Popenoe notes that in the very years that the Great Disruption was taking place, it was common for introductory sociology textbooks to heap scorn on the "myth of family decline."[26] In the 1950s and early 1960s, this may have reflected the fact that family cohesion in the United States and Western Europe actually improved, as did fertility rates during the baby boom. The Depression and World War II had caused a significant disruption in family patterns, but by the late 1950s stability had returned and actually improved over prewar levels.

By the 1970s and 1980s, however, the indicators began to turn dramatically downward. People began marrying later, stayed married less long, and remarried at a lower rate. Like fertility rates, marriage rates experienced a rise in the 1960s in the United States, the Netherlands, New Zealand, Canada, and other countries; since the 1970s, however, rates have been falling rapidly. The American divorce rate has increased in every decade since the Civil War, but the rate of change began to accelerate sharply beginning in the mid-1960s. Although the increase in the divorce rate has leveled off in the 1980s, this does not reflect so much an increase in marital stability as the passing of the baby boom cohort through the age when they are most likely to divorce. Approximately half of all marriages contracted in the 1980s in the United States could be expected to end in divorce. The ratio of divorced to married persons has increased at an even more rapid rate, due also to a parallel decline in marriage rates. For the United States as a whole, this rate has increased over fourfold in the space of just thirty years.[27]

As in the case of violent crime, the United States is exceptional in its propensity for divorce. The United States began the period of the Great Disruption with a significantly higher divorce rate than other developed countries, and it ended the period with a higher rate as well. But most European countries also experienced sharp increases in divorce rates. Figure 2.4 shows changes in divorce rates for our four countries. After settling down from relatively high wartime rates in the 1950s, families in the Netherlands, Canada, Britain, and virtually all of the Nordic countries began breaking apart in the second half of the 1960s. There are some individual variants—Germany and France have relatively lower rates, and the Nordic countries as well as Britain have higher ones. European Catholic countries like Italy, Spain, and Portugal did not legalize divorce until rather late in this period (1970, 1981, and 1974, respectively), and continue to have relatively low though rising rates.[28] Japan also stands out in this comparison for having a low rate, just a bit higher than the Catholic countries of Southern Europe.

FIGURE 2.4

Divorce Rates, 1950–1996 (per 1,000 total population)

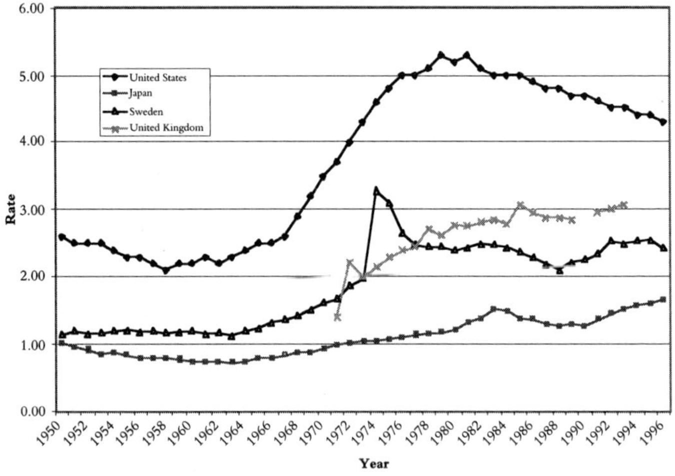

Source: See the Appendix for data.

Illegitimacy

Steadily increasing proportions of children have been born out of wedlock. Births to unmarried women as a proportion of live births for the United States climbed from under 5 percent to 31 percent from 1940 to 1993.[29] Illegitimacy ratios vary significantly by race and ethnicity. In 1993, the ratio for whites was 23.6 percent and for African Americans

68.7 percent.[30] Fatherlessness is the condition of a significant majority of black American children, and in certain areas of concentrated poverty, having a father married to one's mother can be extremely rare.

It should be noted that from 1994 to 1997, the ratio of births to single mothers in the United States ceased its upward trend and appears to have leveled off.[31] The drop in the rate of births to teenagers, the vast majority of whom are unmarried, has been more dramatic, falling from 62.1 per 1,000 women aged 15–19 years in 1991 to 54.7. The rate of decline for black teenagers has been especially steep, falling 21 percent between 1991 and 1996.[32] Although these changes are not as dramatic as the fall in crime rates during the 1990s, they suggest that the explosion of illegitimacy may not be a one-way street.

A number of observers have pointed out that the reason that the ratio of out-of-wedlock births to legitimate births has increased so dramatically is less because of an increase in the number of births to unmarried women than as a result of a steep drop in the fertility of married women.[33] This fact is sometimes adduced to argue that the relatively high U.S. illegitimacy ratio today should not be of concern. It is not really clear why the fact that those women best able to care properly for and raise children have decided to have fewer, while those less able to do so are having more, should be considered reassuring. The increase in fertility of unmarried women after the mid-1970s was not trivial, moreover, having more than doubled between then and 1990, while leveling off and then decreasing thereafter.[34]

If we turn from the United States to the rest of the OECD, we find that America is no longer such an outlier; virtually all industrialized countries, again with the exception of Japan and Catholic countries like Italy and Spain, have experienced extremely rapid rises in illegitimacy rates (see Figure 2.5 and the Appendix). While some countries like France and the United Kingdom saw increases in their rates somewhat later than the United States did, the increases, when they came, were even more dramatic. In Scandinavia, illegitimacy ratios are the highest in the world and significantly greater than those of the United States. Again, within Europe, Germany and the Netherlands, with their relatively large Catholic populations, have relatively low ratios, while Italy's ratios are

FIGURE 2.5

Births to Single Mothers, 1950–1996

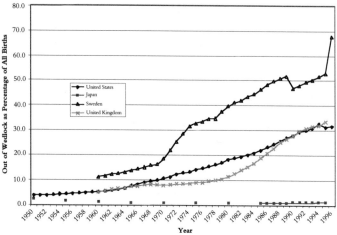

Source: See the Appendix for data.

lower still. With respect to illegitimacy, the real outlier is Japan, whose ratios are both significantly lower than that of any European country, and also show an insignificant rate of increase.

The meaning of illegitimacy is different in Europe than it is in the United States because of the high rate of cohabitation in most European countries. Between the ages of twenty and twenty-four years, 45 percent of Danish women, 44 percent of Swedish women, and 19 percent of Dutch women are already cohabiting, compared to only 14 percent of Americans.[35] In the United States, approximately 25 percent of all out-of-wedlock births are to cohabiting couples; in France, Denmark, and the Netherlands, the proportion is much higher, and in Sweden it reaches perhaps 90 percent.[36] It is very difficult to get accurate statistics on the number of cohabiting couples in various countries and how that number has changed as a percentage of all couples over time, but all observers agree that the shift from marriage to cohabitation has been substantial.[37] In Sweden, the marriage rate today is so low (3.6 per 1,000 inhabitants) and the cohabitation rate so high (30 percent of all couples) that one

44

could argue that the institution of marriage there has fallen into long-term decline.[38] The United States stands out both for the number of children born to mothers living alone and for the number born to teenagers.[39]

The number of children living in single-parent families in any given year is the product of several factors: the rate of out-of-wedlock births, the rate of cohabitation, the rate of divorce, the rate of dissolution of co-habitation arrangements, and the remarriage and re-cohabitation rates. The United States has a high rate of single-parent families because it has a high illegitimacy rate, a high divorce rate, and a low cohabitation rate, relatively speaking.

The fact that many European couples with children cohabit rather than marry does not mean that family life has continued without any of the disruptions American families have experienced. Cohabitation is more unstable than marriage. Demographers Larry Bumpass and James Sweet have found that not only are unions begun by cohabitation twice as likely to dissolve after ten years than first marriages, but that marriages entered into after a period of cohabitation are also less stable than marriages without prior cohabitation.[40] This contradicts the popular assumption that premarital cohabitation is good for marriage because partners are better able to size each other up before making a commitment. Other studies have shown that cohabitation is also more closely correlated with domestic aggression and social isolation than marriage.[41]

Sweden has both a high illegitimacy rate and a high rate of cohabitation. It is therefore much more likely that young Swedish children will live in a household with both biological parents present than young American children will. On the other hand, Sweden has a divorce rate that has grown rapidly recently and is at the high end of the spectrum for European countries. Since so few people in Sweden bother to get married, the rate of dissolution of cohabiting couples is a more meaningful measure of family stability than the divorce rate. This statistic is extremely hard to determine, however. One study of a sample of 4,300 Swedish women born between 1936 and 1960 indicated that cohabiting couples with one child were three times as likely as married couples to see their relationship dissolve. It stands to reason that cohabitation arrangements will be less stable than marriages. Presumably the reason that couples choose cohabitation is that there is less of a commitment to lifelong partnership. In any event, cohabitation poses significantly fewer legal obstacles to the breakup of households. This leads David Popenoe, among others, to speculate that Sweden may now have the highest rate of family dissolution in the industrialized world.[42]

Neither the divorce rate nor the illegitimacy rate nor the single-parent family rate alone captures the extent to which children will experience family breakdown and life in a single- or no-parent household. Of the 67 percent of children born to married parents in the United States in the 1990s, a full 45 percent of these will see their parents divorce by the time they are age eighteen.[43] In subcommunities like those of African Americans, the percentage is much higher, making the experience of continuously living with two biological parents throughout childhood relatively rare.

These kinds of rates are not entirely without historical precedent. In colonial America, fewer than half of all children reached the age of eighteen with both of their biological parents still living.[44] The difference, of course, was that in the eighteenth century, loss of parents was overwhelmingly due to disease and early mortality, while in the late twentieth century it has come about largely as a matter of parental choice. Some observers have used this precedent to argue that current rates of single-parent families are not as bad for children as commonly thought—a strange argument indeed. Presumably the death of a parent during childhood was a traumatic event in earlier ages, one fraught with great risks for the life chances of the child; the fact that life expectancies have increased dramatically since then is one of the proudest accomplishments of modern health care. The fact that we have managed to reproduce the conditions of colonial America in the late twentieth century is not something that we should regard with equanimity. There is, moreover, considerable evidence that the psychological damage done by a voluntary breakup of the family is greater than when it is involuntary.[45]

It is hard not to conclude that the nuclear family has weakened across the board and that the functions remaining to it like reproduction are being performed less well.[46] This presumably should have an important impact on social capital insofar as the family is both a source for and a transmitter of social capital.

The next set of data concerns measures of social capital outside the family.

Trust, Moral Values, and Civil Society

Anyone who has lived through the decades between the 1950s and the 1990s in the United States or other Western countries can scarcely fail to recognize the massive value changes that have taken place over this period. These changes in norms and values are complex, but can be put under the general heading of *increasing individualism*. To use Ralf Dahrendorf's terminology, traditional societies have few options and many ligatures (i.e., social bonds to others): people have little individual choice concerning marriage partner, job, where to live, or what to believe, and are tied down by the often oppressive bonds of family, tribe, caste, religion, feudal obligation, and the like.[47] In modern societies, options for individuals vastly increase, while the ligatures binding them in webs of social obligation are greatly loosened.

Under the most optimistic scenario, modern life does not abolish ligatures altogether. Instead, involuntary ties and obligations based on inherited social class, religion, gender, race, ethnicity, and the like are replaced by ties undertaken voluntarily. People do not become less connected to one another, but rather connect only with those with whom they choose to associate. The labor union or professional association replaces the occupational caste; one joins a Pentecostal church or becomes a Methodist rather than worshipping in a state church; children and not parents select marriage partners. In a way, the Internet represents a technology with the potential to take voluntary social bonds to new and undreamed-of heights: one can associate with people around the globe based on virtually any shared interest, from Zen Buddhism to Ethiopian cuisine, no longer limited by physical location.

The problem with this optimistic scenario, as countless authors like Peter Berger, Alasdair McIntyre, and Dahrendorf himself have noted, is that the dissolving of ligatures does not stop with the oppressive ones characterizing traditional or authoritarian societies, but goes on to corrode the social ties underlying those very voluntary institutions that populate modern societies. Thus people question the authority not just of tyrants and high priests, but of democratically elected officials, scientists, and teachers. They chafe under the constraints of marriage and family obligations, even though these were voluntarily undertaken. And they do not want to be excessively bound by the moral teachings imposed by religion, even though they are perfectly free to enter and exit the denomination of their choice whenever they wish. Individualism, the bedrock virtue of modern societies, begins to shade over from the proud self-sufficiency of free people into a kind of closed selfishness, where maximizing personal freedom without regard for responsibilities to others becomes an end in itself.

In societies where individuals enjoy more freedom of choice than at any other time in history, people resent all the more the few remaining ligatures that bind them. The danger for such societies is that people suddenly find themselves socially isolated, free to associate with everyone but unable to make the moral commitments that will connect them to other people in true communities. The arguments that have surfaced in the 1990s about social capital are in fact ones about the possibilities for creating and sustaining even the voluntary ties that permit collective action among groups of people, for purposes from the utilitarian to the sublime.

It is easy to sketch the broad outlines of the kinds of changes in social norms that have taken place during the Great Disruption, but much harder to document this change empirically. There are at least two ways of doing this: first, through survey data that ask people directly about their values and behavior, and second, through the direct measurement of the quantity and quality of social institutions, associations, and organizations that constitute a modern civil society.

Robert Putnam has argued that in the United States, both types of data move in the same direction: people have evinced less trust in institutions and in each other over time, and there has also been a decline in groups and group memberships. He argues, not unreasonably, that the two ought to be connected: that is, trust is necessary for people to work together and participate in groups in civil society, and both therefore are equally measures of social capital.[48]

The evidence, however, indicates that trust and group memberships are not necessarily related to one another. Although the decrease in levels of trust is fairly unambiguous, there are considerable data showing that many types of groups and group memberships are actually on the increase.

Beyond the United States, there is a similar kind of phenomenon. Trust in many traditional types of authority, like politicians, police, and the military, has declined in most Western developed countries, as has self-reported ethical behavior of the sort that ought to underlie trust relationships. At the same time, the evidence shows that while the mix of groups and group memberships has been shifting, overall there has been an *increase* in group participation.

How can it be that expressions of cynicism have increased dramatically, while civil society appears to be healthy? And how is the latter fact compatible with a shift toward greater individualism? The answer has to do with *moral miniaturization:* while people continue to participate in group life, the groups themselves are less authoritative and produce a smaller radius of trust. As a whole, then, there are fewer common values shared by societies and more competition among groups.

Trust: United States

Trust is a key by-product of the cooperative social norms that constitute social capital.[49] If people can be counted on to keep commitments, honor norms of reciprocity, and avoid opportunistic behavior, then groups will form more readily, and those that do form will be able to achieve common purposes more efficiently.

If trust is a significant measure of social capital, then there are clear signs that the latter has been in decline. Many Americans are aware that trust in institutions of all sorts, beginning with the U.S. government,[50] has been steadily declining over time and reached historic lows during the 1990s. In 1958, 73 percent of Americans surveyed said they trusted the federal government to do what is right either "most of the time" or "just about always." By 1994, this figure had fallen as low as 15 percent (depending on the poll), though by 1996–1997 confidence had increased again so that it averaged somewhere in the mid- to upper 20s. Correspondingly, those trusting the government either "none of the time" or only "some of the time" rose from 23 percent in 1958 to a range of 71 to 85 percent in 1995 (again, declining slightly in subsequent years).[51]

Most American institutions have fared only slightly better. Corporations, organized labor, banks, the medical profession, organized religion, the military, education, television, and the press all saw declines in the percentages of those expressing trust in them between the early 1970s and the early 1990s.[52] Within the government, only the Supreme Court has more Americans feeling a "great deal" of confidence rather than "hardly any," a situation that is reversed for the executive branch and is even worse for Congress. Only the scientific community has enjoyed a relatively constant level of confidence.[53]

While public trust has eroded, it would appear that private trust—a by-product of the cooperative relations citizens have with one another—has also declined. Surveys asking the question, "Generally speaking, would you say that most people can be trusted or that you can't be too careful in dealing with people?" show that while 10 percent more Americans evinced more trust than distrust in the early 1960s, this began to change in the following decade, and by the 1990s the distrusters had a 20 percentage point margin over those expressing trust. While some have suggested that distrust is a phenomenon specific to the baby boom generation, Figure 2.6 indicates comparable increases in distrust among high school students born in the period 1958–1972. This is confirmed by research by Wendy Rahn, which shows that Generation-Xers have lower levels of trust than baby boomers, who in turn had lower levels of trust than their parents' generation.[54]

Within the United States, different racial and ethnic groups express different levels of trust. African Americans are far more distrustful than other groups: 80.9 percent of blacks consider people untrustworthy compared with 51.2 percent of whites, while 60.6 percent of blacks consider other people unfair compared to 31.5 percent of whites.[55] Hispanics are less distrustful than blacks, and Asian Americans are more trusting still. Older people tend to be more trusting than younger ones, and religious people are more trusting than nonreligious ones, though fundamentalists show higher levels of distrust than members of mainline denominations. Trust is correlated with income and even more highly correlated with education: people with college educations and higher tend to have a relatively benign view of the world.[56] Finally, suburbanites tend to be much more trusting than residents of big cities.

FIGURE 2.6

Trust Among High School Seniors, 1975–1992

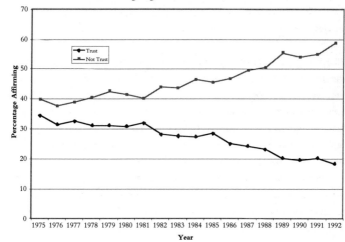

Source: Tom W. Smith, "Factors Relating to Misanthropy in Contemporary American Society," *Social Science Research* 26 (1997): 170–196.

Trust, it should be recalled, is not in itself a moral virtue, but rather the by-product of virtue; it arises when people share norms of honesty and reciprocity and hence are able to cooperate with one another. Trust is damaged by excessive selfishness or opportunism. It is difficult to measure levels of selfishness directly, but the belief that people have become more selfish recently has certainly grown among Americans. For example, in sociologist Alan Wolfe's Middle Class Morality Project, which conducted in-depth interviews with a wide variety of Americans, a strong majority agreed with the assertion that, compared with twenty years ago, "Americans have become more selfish."[57] In addition to the question concerning trust, the General Social Survey (GSS) asks whether people are fair and helpful. Answers to the former question show a slight trend from 1972 to 1994 of perceptions of decreasing fairness; the answers to the helpfulness question show no trend at all. On the other hand, the Monitoring the Future survey of American high school seniors showed fairly steady declines in trust, belief in fairness, and belief in helpfulness between 1976 and 1995.[58]

Civil Society: The United States

The wealth of data that Robert Putnam has assembled to demonstrate the decline of associational memberships in the United States is very impressive and includes, in addition to the survey data cited above, data on memberships from individual organizations from the Boy Scouts to parent-teacher organizations, panel data from various longitudinal studies, and detailed time-budget studies of how selected Americans spend their hours in the week. Putnam points to declines in memberships of many traditional societies like the Moose, Elks, Kiwanis, Shriners, and other "animal" organizations, as well as evidence from the GSS that shows a drop in group memberships among respondents of about one-quarter between 1974 and the mid-1990s.

In general, the Putnam thesis can be sustained only if one makes an important qualitative distinction between the kinds of ties binding different kinds of groups—what I referred to earlier as the "positive radius of trust." That is, tobacco interests may form a group to lobby Congress for lower excise taxes on cigarettes, but most Americans would consider this a very different kind of activity from a faith-based group like Habitat for Humanity that organizes the building of homes in poor, inner-city neighborhoods. The former group has a fund of social capital and achieves cooperative goals, but most of the individuals involved are motivated, one presumes, largely by the salary being offered them and would have little incentive to cooperate outside the boundaries of their interest group. The Habitat group, on the other hand, shares more in the way of common values, extends those values beyond their immediate group, and thereby produces a higher degree of social capital overall. The growth of large lobbying groups representing banking, health care, insurance, and other interests is undeniable, but one may question whether they build other kinds of cooperative ties among their memberships.

Commonsense moral reasoning would tell us that there is another important difference between the tobacco lobbying firm and Habitat for Humanity. The former makes no bones about the fact that it is trying to advance the interests of tobacco producers in Washington. One can argue that given a democratic political system, it is the right of all major interests in a society to have political representation. On the other hand, there are clear downsides to interest group politics: the buying of political influence through campaign contributions increases voter cynicism about the democratic political process. And as the economist Mancur Olson pointed out, the accumulation of entrenched interest groups can lead to rent seeking and other parasitic forms of behavior that are detrimental to economic growth.[59] Habitat for Humanity, on the other hand, is not trying to aggrandize itself or seek subsidies from the federal government; its explicit aim is to build affordable housing for poor people who need it. In fact, both types of groups are important to the success of a modern society, but our view of the health of civil society would be very different if it were populated exclusively by commercial interest groups rather than by charitable voluntary associations. Any argument that American civil society has been in decline must be based on a distinction between the two groups.

Everett Ladd of the University of Connecticut, who has directed Roper surveys for many years, has contested Putnam's data on U.S. civil society on virtually every point in his book *The Ladd Report*.[60] He begins with the charge that Putnam failed to count many new groups in American society, a formidable task given the size and diversity of the country. Some of the examples he cites are particularly telling. Putnam, for example, showed that memberships in parent-teacher associations (PTAs) declined sharply from a high of 12.1 million in 1962 to a low of 5.3 million in 1982, while rising somewhat thereafter; the decline in memberships over a thirty-year period persists when these memberships are converted to rates per pupil in U.S. public schools.[61] Ladd shows, however, that much of the decline in PTA memberships was due not to parents' disengaging, but rather to a shift in affiliations toward so-called parent-teacher organizations (PTOs). PTOs do not send their dues to a national organization, are less closely tied to the teachers' unions, and are less formally organized in general. A survey conducted by Ladd and the Roper Center suggested that PTAs had declined to perhaps one-fourth of the total number of parent-teacher organizations in most school districts. Thus parental involvement in their children's education appears to have actually increased monotonically throughout the previous three decades, a fact confirmed by survey data based on parents' self-reporting of their school-related activities.

What goes for PTAs is true for many other types of organizations. Groups like the all-male "animal" organizations have declined; on the other hand, the past decade has seen an explosion in informal AIDS support groups, whose numbers cannot be reliably estimated. American children now play soccer rather than join baseball Little Leagues, but there is no evidence that there has been an overall decline in the amount of time spent socializing around a sports event.

A number of attempts have been made to produce censuses of groups and associations in the United States. One was done by the U.S. Department of Commerce in 1949, which estimated that there were 201,000 nonprofit voluntary trade and business organizations, women's groups, labor unions, civic service groups, luncheon clubs, and professional groups at all levels of American society.[62] Lester Salamon, director of the Comparative Nonprofit Sector Project, estimates that by 1989 there were 1.14 million nonprofit organizations in the United States, indicating an overall rate of growth much higher than that of the population as a whole.[63] The near-impossibility of producing a complete census that catalogues the whole range of informal networks and cliques in a modern society is suggested by the Yankee City study, which counted some 22,000 different groups in a community of 17,000 people.[64] Changing technology changes forms of association. How do we account, for example, for the proliferation of on-line discussion groups, chat rooms, and e-mail conversations that have exploded with the spread of personal computers in the 1990s?[65]

The GSS data do not point unambiguously to a decline in group memberships. The GSS asks a series of specific questions about memberships in specific types of organizations, such as labor unions, professional associations, hobby groups, sports clubs, fraternal organizations, and church groups. It is difficult to detect a strong trend; some kinds of organizations like labor unions have seen declines, and others like professional associations have seen increases.[66] Other sources of data too show increasing levels of civic engagement. For example, a 1998 ABC/Washington Post poll shows the percentage of respondents saying they had done volunteer work in the past year up from 44 to 55 percent between 1984 and 1997. Another survey asking whether respondents had been involved in any charity or social service activities went from 26 percent in 1977 to 54 percent in 1995. Based on interviews with middle-class Americans, Alan Wolfe speculates that survey respondents tend to understate their group memberships because they don't include hobby clubs, social groups, and others regarded as less serious. His own interviewees express the view that people have less and less time for voluntary activities, but then contradict the generalization in their accounts of their own lives, which are filled with social activities of all sorts. The types of organizations to which people belong tend, moreover, to be civic or religious rather than merely social or fraternal.[67] The curious disjunction between social trust and group memberships is confirmed in both the Monitoring the Future survey of American high school seniors, where participation in community affairs and volunteer work increased while trust decreased,[68] and in a study done by the Pew Research Center for the People and the Press, which focuses on Philadelphia.[69]

Trust: Other Developed Countries

It is very difficult to find comparable data for countries outside the United States regarding the decline in trust over the past forty years. The only survey that asks a consistent set of value-related questions across a broad range of countries is the World Values Survey (WVS) directed by Ronald Inglehart of the University of Michigan. Unfortunately, it is very difficult to gauge trends over time using these data, since the survey has been administered only three times—in 1981, 1990, and 1995 (the 1995 data were not available at the time this book was being written). We cannot make too much of trends over time when we have only two data points for each country; many of the important changes not only in values but also in crime and family occurred between 1965 and 1981.

Despite small data sets, if we look at the WVS survey questions bearing on the question of trust, we do find some patterns that are not so different from those seen in the United States.[70] There are two categories of relevant questions: those having to do with confidence in major social institutions, and those having to do with ethical values. Trust, to repeat, is a by-product of shared norms of ethical behavior. If people profess to behave in less trustworthy ways—if they are more willing to take bribes, cheat on taxi fares, falsify their tax returns—then there should be less of an objective basis for trusting others, regardless of how people answer the direct question concerning trust.

The WVS data for fourteen Western developed countries, including the United States, show that between 1981 and 1990, confidence in most institutions decreased for a large number of countries; surprisingly, only the press and major companies showed increases in confidence in most countries.[71] In particular, the more traditional sources of authority—the church, the armed forces, the legal system, and the police—showed declines in a large majority of countries.[72] There are also WVS survey data for ethical values that could be related to trust, such as whether the respondent would ever consider doing things like keeping benefits to which he or she is not entitled, avoiding a fare on public transportation, or cheating on taxes.[73] The self-reported constraints against doing dishonest things appear to have declined for most developed countries.

Given America's antistatist political traditions, it should not be surprising that Americans express deeper levels of distrust in government than Europeans do.[74] A study by the Pew Research Center shows that in 1997, 56 percent of Americans said they distrusted the government, compared to an average of 45 percent of Europeans in five countries surveyed. More Americans than Europeans also agreed that government is inefficient and wasteful, by a margin of 64 to 54 percent. There is evidence, however, that European attitudes toward government are beginning to converge in some respects with those of Americans. Between 1991 and 1997, the number of Europeans agreeing with the assertion that "the government controls too much of our daily lives" increased from 53 to 61 percent (compared to 64 percent of Americans in 1997).[75]

These changes correspond in part to what Ronald Inglehart calls the shift to "postmaterialist" values that he finds occurring throughout the developed world.[76] According to Inglehart, materialists value economic and physical security, while postmaterialists value freedom, self-expression, and improving the quality of their lives. Based not just on WVS data but on data from the European Commission's Eurobarometer surveys, Inglehart has argued that this shift has been occurring since the 1970s for all of the major European countries and that it generally should help improve the quality of democracy where it has occurred by increasing political participation and concern for public policy issues.

It is possible to read Inglehart's data somewhat differently than he does, however. The labels he uses, *materialism* and *postmaterialism,* can be misleading because they suggest that people in the former category are selfishly concerned with their own economic and personal needs, while people in the latter category are interested in broader issues like social justice and the environment. Another way to interpret the former group, however, is that they are people willing to defer to the authority of a variety of large communal institutions like the police, the corporation, and the church, while the latter are much more individualistic in demanding recognition of their rights at the expense of community. Individualism is, of course, the cornerstone of modern democracy, but excessive individualism can have negative effects on democracy by making social cohesion less achievable. The shift to postmaterialist values thus is likely to signify the decline of certain types of social capital.

Civil Society: Other Developed Countries

If we turn from values to group memberships, we find much the same pattern in the rest of the world as in the United States: that is, while there is good evidence of decreasing levels of confidence in major institutions and in self-reported ethical behavior, there appears to be an increasing level of participation in a variety of groups in civil society.

The chief advocate of the view that civil society has been taking off around the globe is Lester Salamon, whose Comparative Nonprofit Sector Project has tried to document trends in civil society worldwide.[77] According to him, a veritable "'associational revolution' now seems underway at the global level that may constitute as significant a social and political development of the latter twentieth century as the rise of the nation-state was of the latter nineteenth."[78] Salamon provides extensive documentation showing an increase in numbers of nongovernmental organizations (NGOs) in the United States, and argues that this is also happening in Europe: "The number of private associations has similarly skyrocketed in France. More than 54,000 such associations were formed in 1987 alone, compared to 10,000 to 12,000 per year in the 1960s. Between

1980 and 1986, the income of British charities increased an estimated 221 percent. Recent estimates record some 275,000 charities in the United Kingdom, with income in excess of 4 percent of the gross national product."[79] Not only are the number of NGOs skyrocketing in Europe, they are said to be exploding around the Third World.[80]

There are a number of reasons for being skeptical of some of Salamon's claims about global civil society and what they tell us about social capital. In the first place, the new organizations that Salamon counts are formal nonprofit institutions, usually ones that have gone to the trouble of legally incorporating themselves. It may well be that there has been a global shift from informal networks and groups to formal ones, but civil society is the sum of both types, and it is not clear that there has been a net increase. Furthermore, many of the organizations that he considers parts of civil society are in fact very large, bureaucratic operations—universities, hospitals, research labs, educational foundations, and the like—which, while fitting the Internal Revenue Service's category of a nonprofit organization, are often virtually indistinguishable from either government bureaucracies or profit-making corporations. Indeed, one of Salamon's points is that the United States and other governments have increasingly offloaded a great deal of work that was formerly done directly by government agencies onto "third-sector" organizations, which accounts for a good deal of their growth. These groups did not come together spontaneously, but were created by government fiat and should be regarded as extensions of modern government.[81]

The second reason for skepticism about the global associational upsurge has to do with the quality of the data. As we have seen from a detailed examination of the empirical evidence on both sides of the Putnam debate, it is very hard to know whether civil society has been increasing, decreasing, or going in both directions at once for a country that has by far the richest sources of data about itself, the United States. The same data problems we find in the American case reappear in spades in other societies. We need to know not just how many new organizations have formed, but how many have died, what trends there have been in their memberships, and what the quality of community life has been.[82]

There are nonetheless grounds for thinking that in other developed societies, there has at least been no net decline in numbers of voluntary organizations, and in many cases an overall increase. The WVS asks respondents whether they are members of various categories of organizations, like churches, political parties, unions, or social welfare organizations, as well as whether they have performed unpaid work for each category of organization in the past year. The trends move in both directions. Some categories of organizations like trade unions and community action groups have declined in a majority of countries, while others, like educational, artistic, human rights, and environmental groups, have seen increases in a large majority of developed countries. The same trends are true for the amount of time spent doing unpaid work. Except for youth work, a strong majority of countries show increases in volunteerism in each category.

The Great Disruption is manifest in the shift in values that has taken place across the developed world in the past generation, a shift that is only imperfectly captured by the available empirical data on values. While the story of trust, values, and civil society is different in every Western developed country, certain overall patterns emerge. There is, first of all, a trend toward lower levels of trust in institutions, and particularly older ones associated with authority and coercion like the police, military, and church, in virtually all countries surveyed. There is, further, a trend toward lower levels of self-reported ethical behavior that would constitute the basis of trust: in most countries, more people said they would be willing to behave dishonestly in one way or another in 1990 than in 1981. Both of these patterns were also present in the United States.

On the other hand, trends in groups and group memberships appear to be on the upswing in most countries. Again, the story varies by individual country, and the mix of group types has shifted over time, but nonetheless the loss of confidence in institutions and the decay of ethical behavior do not seem to have particularly injured the ability of people to associate with one another on *some* level.[83]

On both counts, the United States remains exceptional: it has the highest levels of institutional distrust *and* the highest rates of group memberships and voluntary community activity.

In terms of the comparative values data we have available, Asian developed countries do not appear all that different from their Western counterparts. Japan and Korea (the only two high-income Asian countries included in the WVS) both show declines in confidence in institutions like their European and North American counterparts. Japan's self-reported belief in ethical values shows across-the-board increases (as was the case for Ireland and Spain), while data for Korea are incomplete. In terms of group memberships, there is no particular trend: Japanese group memberships (particularly trade unions) tended to go down, and Korean group memberships (particularly religious organizations) tended to increase.

Summing Up

The Great Disruption was characterized by increasing levels of crime and social disorder, the decline of families and kinship as a source of social cohesion, and decreasing levels of trust. These changes all began to happen in a wide range of developed countries in the 1960s, and occurred very rapidly when compared to earlier periods of shifting norms. There were several consistent patterns of behavior: Japan and Korea showed consistently lower rates of increase in crime and family breakdown, while suffering from distrust; Latin Catholic countries like Italy and Spain had relatively lower rates of family breakdown, while moving to extremely low rates of fertility. There are undoubtedly other measures of diminishing social capital we could have used, but the ones portrayed here suggest a striking pattern of growing disorder. We now need to explore possible reasons that these changes occurred.

3

Causes:
The Conventional Wisdom

hanges as massive as those described in the preceding chapter obviously have multiple causes and defy attempts to provide simple explanations. However, the fact that many different social indicators moved across a wide group of industrialized countries at roughly the same time simplifies the analytical task somewhat by pointing us to a more general level of explanation. If the same phenomena occur in a broad range of countries, then we can rule out explanations specific to one single country.

In the pages that follow, I present what amounts to the conventional wisdom concerning the causes of different aspects of the Great Disruption as they have been put forward by various social theorists. I begin with broad explanations that purport to explain all aspects of the Great Disruption simultaneously, and then move on to ones that are tailored to one or another specific aspect of it. Some of these explanations I regard as plausible, and others I think are wrong or insufficient.

American Exceptionalism

One of the first questions we need to raise is whether the Great Disruption happened at all. Many Europeans would be inclined to argue that deteriorating social order is a uniquely American phenomenon and that they have escaped most of the extreme social pathologies that plague the United States. As the data presented in the preceding chapter indicate, the United States has always had significantly higher rates of divorce, crime, inequality, and other ills, together with superior economic growth, innovation, technology, and a denser civil society.[1] American exceptionalism is particularly evident in rates of violent crime, where the United States has the distinction of having the highest murder, rape, and aggravated assault rates in the developed world. Murder rates are an order of magnitude greater in the United States than they are in many European countries and Japan; the number of murders taking place in New York City alone was at one point larger than the number of murders for the whole of Britain or Japan.[2]

If the Great Disruption happened only in the United States, we would be tempted to say that it was rooted in both the specific circumstances of American history and culture, and events taking place in the United States starting in the 1960s, such as Vietnam, Watergate, or Reaganism. Observers like Robert K. Merton and Seymour Martin Lipset have written at great length on the specific aspects of American culture—antistatism, hostility to authority, expectations of economic mobility, and the like—that make it particularly conducive to family disruption, crime, and social anomie.[3] America's minority population, larger than those of other developed countries, also skews the figures. The rate of illegitimacy for American non-Hispanic whites, for example, is in the middle of the European distribution.

Whatever the validity of these cross-cultural explanations for American exceptionalism, they cannot explain the rising rates of divorce, illegitimacy, crime, and distrust beginning in the 1960s that took place across a wide variety of developed countries at the same time. Indeed, the rate of increase in family breakdown and crime indicators for many European countries has been higher than those of the United States (though starting from a lower base).[4] This suggests, in turn, that these changes were triggered not by factors unique to the United States, but rather by factors common to the Western developed countries as a group.

Moreover, according to a broader set of indicators, the United States is not nearly as exceptional as many people think. We have seen that most Scandinavian countries have higher rates of illegitimacy than the United States, and other English-speaking nations like Britain, Canada, and New Zealand have rates that are quite comparable. The same is true for crime. The criminologist James Lynch points out that in terms of serious property crime, Australia had a burglary rate 40 percent higher than that of the United States, Canada 12 percent higher, and England and Wales 30 percent higher in 1988 and 1992. With the fall in rates in the United States during the 1990s, the number of European countries with property crime rates higher than that of the United States has increased. The popular perception that the United States has the most punitive criminal justice system is also incorrect: while the per capita incarceration rate of the United States is high, it also has the most violent crime. The propensity to incarcerate for a given crime and the length of time served for homicide are not dramatically higher for the United States and in some cases are actually lower.

What the United States has that Europe does not have is a large *underclass,* that is, a stratum of concentrated and chronic poverty, distinct from the working class, characterized by violent crime, drug use, unemployment, poor education, and broken families. The beginnings of an underclass are visible not in the center but on the outskirts of many European cities, particularly in areas with high concentrations of Third World immigrants. But European poverty tends to be more orderly than American poverty, and more structural rather than cultural in nature.[5]

General Causes

Broadly speaking, at least four arguments have been put forward to explain why the phenomena we associate with the Great Disruption occurred: first, they were brought on by increasing poverty and/or income inequality; second, and to the contrary, they were caused by growing wealth; third, they were the product of the modern welfare state; and fourth, they were the result of a broad cultural shift that included the decline of religion and the promotion of individualistic self-gratification over community obligation.

In my view, all of these perspectives are flawed as single explanations for why such rapid changes in social norms have occurred since 1965. These changes are indeed rooted in values and are therefore deeply embedded in broader shifts in culture that were described in the first chapter. But this still begs the question of why cultural values changed when they did, rather than a generation earlier or later. In the realm of sexual and family norms, these shifts can be explained, in my view, by two factors. The first is the broad shift in the nature of labor as societies made the transition from industrial to information age economies; the second is a single technological innovation, the birth control pill. These specific causes will be discussed in the two chapters following this one.

Explanation 1: The Great Disruption Was Caused by Poverty and Inequality

Everyone agrees that there is a strong correlation among broken families, poverty, crime, distrust, social atomization, drug use, poor educational achievement, and low social capital. The arguments made by the Left and the Right in what is a highly ideologized debate concern the direction of causality between economic and cultural factors. The Left argues that crime, family breakdown, and distrust are caused by lack of jobs, opportunity, education, and economic inequality more generally. Many observers would add racism and prejudice against minorities as factors. This causal link has led to calls for the United States to enact European-style welfare state protections to guarantee jobs or incomes to poor people, and to charges that the growing problem of family breakdown is due to the failure of the American welfare state to "modernize" adequately.[6]

The idea that such large changes in social norms could be brought on by economic deprivation in countries that were wealthier than any others in human history might give one pause. Poor people in the United States have higher absolute standards of living than Americans of past generations and more per capita wealth than many people in contemporary Third World countries with more intact family structures. The United States has not gotten poorer in the last third of the twentieth century; per capita income increased in constant dollars between 1965 and 1995 from $14,792 to $25,615 while personal consumption expenditures rose from $9,257 to $17,403.[7] Poverty rates, after coming down dramatically through the 1960s and rebounding slightly thereafter, have not increased in a way that would explain a massive increase in social disorder (see Figure 3.1).

Those favoring the economic hypothesis argue that absolute levels of poverty are not the source of the problem. Modern societies, despite being richer overall, have become more unequal, or else have experienced economic turbulence and job loss that have led to social dysfunction. In the case of family breakdown, a casual glance at the comparative data on divorce and illegitimacy rates shows that this cannot possibly be true. A look across the OECD reveals no positive correlation between level of welfare benefits seeking to increase economic equality, and family stability. Indeed, there is a weak correlation between high levels of welfare benefits and illegitimacy, tending to support the argument advanced by American conservatives that the welfare state is the cause and not the cure for family breakdown. The highest rates of illegitimacy are found in egalitarian Scandinavian countries like Sweden and Denmark, which cycle upwards of 50 percent of their GDP through the state.[8] This compares to the United States, which cycles less than 30 percent of GDP through the government and has higher levels of inequality yet lower rates of illegitimacy. Japan and Korea, which have minimal welfare state protections for poor people, also have what are among the lowest rates of divorce and illegitimacy in the OECD.[9]

It is true that the linkage between family breakdown and poverty is much weaker for countries that have extensive welfare state protections. Poverty rates for single-parent families tend to be higher in the United States than in other OECD countries with larger welfare states, which indicates that various family support and income maintenance programs appear to have been effective.[10] Many Europeans, seeing data like these, believe that their welfare states have spared them the costs of American-style social problems.

A closer look at the data, however, indicates that the welfare state has not solved the *underlying* social problem. That is, the state in these cases has simply taken over the role of the father, providing mother and children

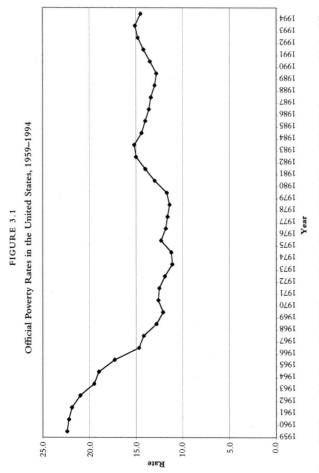

FIGURE 3.1

Official Poverty Rates in the United States, 1959–1994

Source: U.S. Bureau of the Census, *Statistical Abstract of the United States, 1997* (Washington, D.C.: U.S. Government Printing Office, 1997), p. 472.

with resources for their protection and upbringing in a process the anthropologist Lionel Tiger labels "bureaugamy."[11] The welfare state does not eliminate the social cost of family breakdown, but rather shifts it from individuals to taxpayers, consumers, and the unemployed. It is questionable whether states are adequate substitutes for fathers, who not only provide resources but play a role in socialization and education as well. Moreover, the European welfare state has run into serious economic problems in the 1990s, producing steadily rising rates of unemployment in virtually all continental countries. The contrast with Japan, which does not suffer from the underlying problem of family breakdown, is instructive and will be explored in later chapters.

The same is true for crime. The notion that poverty and inequality beget crime is commonplace among politicians and voters in democratic societies who seek reasons for justifying welfare and poverty programs. But although there is plenty of evidence of a broad correlation between income inequality and crime,[12] this hardly constitutes a plausible explanation for rapidly rising crime rates in the West. There was no depression in the period from the 1960s to the 1990s to explain the sudden rise in crime; in fact, the great American postwar crime wave began in a period of full employment and general prosperity. (Indeed, the Great Depression of the 1930s saw *decreasing* levels of violent crime in the United States.) Income inequality rose in the United States in the years following, but crime has also risen in other Western developed countries that have remained more egalitarian than the United States. While America's greater economic inequality may explain to some degree why its crime rates are higher than, say, Sweden's in any given year, it does not explain why Swedish rates began to rise during the same period as America's. Income inequality, moreover, has continued to increase in the United States during the 1990s when crime rates were falling; hence the correlation between inequality and crime becomes negative for this period.[13]

Poverty is also correlated with distrust. But if there was no broad increase in poverty in the United States corresponding to the Great Disruption, then poverty is unlikely to explain increasing levels of distrust over this period. In any case, the relatively small minority of Americans falling below the poverty line would not explain why large majorities of Americans began expressing distrust toward institutions and other Americans. On the other hand, it is possible that economic turbulence and increasing income inequality in themselves led to greater levels of cynicism. During the Great Disruption, Americans experienced rising economic insecurity. The 1970s saw a series of economic crises over oil and inflation; the early 1980s saw a major recession in the Rust Belt and a loss of jobs to overseas competition. In the early 1990s, U.S. companies downsized dramatically, and the idea of lifetime employment in large American corporations became a thing of the past.

Alan Wolfe's interviews may serve to illustrate some of the ways that economic change has fed distrust. In contrast to many Europeans, Americans are not prone to thinking that economic inequality per se is unjust or signifies a fundamentally unfair social system. Many interviewees expressed understanding for corporations that downsized, noting that they had to do so in order to stay competitive; many were also skeptical of unions that sought to preserve jobs and benefits without raising productivity in return. They were, however, critical of the disappearance of loyalty in the workplace due to a new, ruthless competitiveness, and CEOs who rewarded themselves with huge options as they cut payrolls in half.[14] The leaner, meaner corporate world of the 1990s meant that people had to divide and qualify their workplace loyalties to a much greater extent than in the previous generation. In the new world of part-time or temporary work, consultants, and job hopping, one had more ties but weaker ones.

Explanation 2: The Great Disruption Was Caused by Greater Wealth and Security

Paradoxically, a second general explanation for the shift in values that took place during the Great Disruption is the polar opposite of the first: far from being caused by poverty and inequality, the disruption took place *because* of increasing wealth. This argument has been made by the pollster Daniel Yankelovich, whose public opinion surveys have tracked the shift from community-oriented to individualistic values since the 1950s.[15] This view is also implicit in the work of Ronald Inglehart, whose concept of "postmaterialist values" suggests that satisfaction of basic economic needs engenders a different set of priorities as people move up a hierarchy of needs.

Yankelovich sees a three-stage "affluence effect." In the first stage, when people have recently become wealthy but still have memories of economic insecurity, they are too worried about day-to-day survival to think much about self-expression, personal growth, or self-gratification. In the second stage, as they are able to take prosperity for granted, they become more self-indulgent, an attitude that manifests itself in a lesser willingness of people to sacrifice themselves for their children and a greater willingness to take risks. Both family breakdown and increasing deviance might be results of this second stage. Finally, as people grow older, they find that they can't necessarily take affluence for granted and realize they need to think about the long term. Yankelovich argues that many Americans reached this third stage during the 1991–1992 recession and that this may explain the decline in measures of social dysfunction that has occurred during the 1990s.

The argument that growing individualism and the social problems resulting from it are the result of greater prosperity is on its face much more plausible than the opposite argument—that they are the result of growing poverty. We have seen, after all, that levels of family breakdown, crime, and distrust increased over an extended period of time during which the countries involved were growing steadily wealthier. Moreover, there is a broad correlation between value change and income levels within the OECD; wealthier nations like the United States, Canada, and the Scandinavian countries tend to have higher levels of disruption than poorer ones like Portugal, Ireland, and Spain. It makes intuitive sense to think that as income levels rise, the bonds of interdependence that tie people tightly together in families and communities will weaken, because they are now better able to get along without one another. In times of economic distress, abandoning family or neighbors might condemn loved ones to poverty or extreme hardship; one is cautious about guarding small advantages and unwilling to risk them for the sake of short-term gratification.

But although there is a great deal of truth to this line of argument, it is not wholly satisfactory. In the first place, those whose actual behavior changed the most dramatically during the Great Disruption in terms of family breakdown, crime, and distrust tended to be the least wealthy members of a given society. It was lower-income African Americans, for example, who had the least reason to take the economic gains they made during the 1960s for granted, and yet this community suffered the most dramatic breakdown in social norms in subsequent decades. The economic insecurity brought about by the 1991–1992 recession, moreover, was too brief to explain the shift to more conservative values in the 1990s. If prosperity and value change are related, they are clearly not related (as Inglehart's work also shows) in any terribly close way. That is, individualism does not shift up and down with short-term economic cycles; whatever connection exists between wealth and value change takes place over a period spanning a generation or more.

Explanation 3: The Great Disruption Was Caused by Mistaken Government Policies

The third general explanation for the increase in social disorder is one made by conservatives, and has been primarily associated with Charles Murray in his book *Losing Ground,* and before him by the economist Gary Becker. The argument is the mirror image of that of the Left: it maintains that it is the perverse incentives created by the welfare state itself that explain the rise in family breakdown and crime.[16] The primary American welfare program targeted at poor women, the Depression-era Aid to Families with Dependent Children (AFDC), provided welfare payments only to single mothers and thereby penalized women who married the fathers of their children.[17] The United States abolished AFDC in the welfare reform act of 1996, in part because of arguments concerning its perverse incentive effects.[18]

Similarly, many conservatives see rising crime as a result of the weakening of criminal sanctions that also occurred in this period. Gary Becker has argued that crime can be seen as another form of rational choice: when payoffs to crime go up or costs (in terms of punishment) go down, more crimes will be committed, and vice versa.[19] Many conservatives argued that crime began to rise in the 1960s because the society had grown permissive and that the legal system was "coddling criminals." By this reasoning, the tougher enforcement measures undertaken by communities across the United States in the 1980s—stiffer penalties, more jails, and in some cases more police on the streets—were one important reason for falling crime rates in the 1990s. The U.S. incarceration rate in 1997 was double that of 1985 and triple that of 1975.[20] Ignoring deterrent effects and simply calculating the number of crimes the recidivists in this population would have committed had they not been in prison accounts for a substantial proportion of the downturn in crime rates during the 1990s.[21] James Q. Wilson argues that the more rapid fall in U.S. crime rates when compared to Britain in the 1990s is related to the more punitive policies undertaken in America.[22] In addition to being more punitive, police methods also shifted in the direction of community policing, an innovation that may have had a positive effect in helping to bring down crime rates.

There is little doubt that welfare benefits create what economists call "moral hazard" and discourage work.[23] What is less clear is their impact on family structure. The comparative data at first glance give greater support to the Murray hypothesis on welfare benefits as a cause of family breakdown than to its left-wing counterpart: high-benefit welfare states like Sweden and Denmark have higher rates of illegitimacy than low-benefit ones like Japan. There are numerous anomalies, however, beginning with the fact that the United States, which has a substantially lower level of welfare benefits than, say, Germany, has much higher illegitimacy rates. Detailed econometric studies of welfare benefits in the United States have found similar discrepancies when correlating levels of welfare benefits with illegitimacy either across states (which are allowed to set their own levels of benefits) or across time.[24] In the latter case, welfare benefits in real terms stabilized and then began to decline in the 1980s, while the rate of family breakdown continued unabated through the mid-1990s.[25] One analyst suggests that no more than perhaps 15 percent of family breakdown in the United States can be attributed to AFDC and other welfare programs.[26]

The more fundamental weakness of the conservative argument is that illegitimacy is only part of a much larger story of weakening family ties, a story that includes declining fertility, divorce, cohabitation in place of marriage and the separation of cohabiting couples. Illegitimacy is primarily, though not exclusively, associated with poverty in the United States and most other countries. Phenomena like divorce and cohabitation, however, are much more prevalent among middle- and upper-class individuals throughout the West. It is very difficult to lay soaring divorce rates and declining marriage rates at the government's doorstep, except to the extent that the state made divorce legally easier to obtain.

While improved police methods and penalties may well have had a lot to do with declining crime rates in the 1990s, it is much harder to argue that the great upsurge in crime in the 1960s was simply the product of police permissiveness. It is true that U.S. courts constrained police and prosecutors in the interests of the rights of criminal defendants through a series of Supreme Court decisions in the 1960s, most notably *Miranda v. Arizona*. But police departments quickly learned how to accommodate what were perfectly legitimate concerns over police procedure. As will be seen in later chapters, a great deal of recent criminological theory ascribes crime to poor socialization and impulse control relatively early in the life course. It is not that potential criminals do not respond rationally to punishment; rather, the propensity to commit crimes and respond to a given level of punishment is heavily influenced by upbringing. What is more relevant to understanding a sudden upsurge in crime may be less the level of punishments than changes in mediating social institutions like families, neighborhoods, and schools that were simultaneously taking place in this period, and in the signals that the broader culture was sending to young people.

Explanation 4: The Great Disruption Was Caused by a Broad Cultural Shift

This brings us to cultural explanations, the most plausible of the four presented here. Increasing individualism and the loosening of communal controls clearly had a huge impact on family life, sexual behavior, and the willingness of people to obey the law. The problem with this line of explanation is not that culture was not a factor, but rather that it gives no adequate account of timing: Why did culture, which usually tends to evolve extremely slowly, suddenly mutate with extraordinary rapidity after the mid-1960s?

In Britain and the United States, the high point of communal social control was the Victorian period in the last third of the nineteenth century, when the ideal of the patriarchal conjugal family was broadly accepted and adolescent sexuality was kept under tight control. The cultural shift that undermined Victorian morality may be thought of as layered. At the top is a realm of abstract ideas promulgated by philosophers, scientists, artists, and academics, with the occasional huckster and fraud, who lay the intellectual groundwork for more broadly based changes. The second level is one of popular culture, as simpler versions of complex abstract ideas are promulgated to broader audiences through books, newspapers, and other forms of mass media. Finally, there is the layer of actual behavior, as the new norms implicit in the abstract or popularized ideas become embedded in the actions of large populations.

The decline in Victorian morality can be traced to a number of intellectual developments taking place at the end of the nineteenth century and the beginning of the twentieth, and in a second wave that began in the 1940s. At the highest level of thought, Western rationalism began to undermine itself by concluding that there were no rational grounds supporting universal norms of behavior. This was nowhere more evident than in the thought of Friedrich Nietzsche, the father of modern relativism. Nietzsche in effect argued that man, the "beast with red cheeks," was a value-creating animal and that the manifold "languages of good and evil" spoken by different human cultures were products of the will, rooted nowhere in truth or reason. The Enlightenment did not lead to self-evident truths about right or morality; rather, it exposed the infinite variability of moral arrangements. Attempts to ground values in nature or in God were doomed to be exposed as willful acts on the part of the creators of those values. Nietzsche's aphorism, "There are no facts, only interpretations," became the watchword for later generations of relativists under the banner of deconstruction and postmodernism.

In the social sciences, the undermining of Victorian values was in the first instance the work of psychologists. John Dewey, William James, and John Watson, founder of the behavioralist school of psychology, for differing reasons all contested the Victorian and Christian notion that human nature is innately sinful and argued therefore that tight social controls over behavior were not necessary for social order. The behavioralists argued that the human mind is a Lockean tabula rasa waiting to be filled with cultural content; the implication was that human beings are far more malleable through social pressure and policy than people had heretofore believed. Sigmund Freud and the school of psychoanalysis that he founded were enormously influential in promulgating the idea that neurosis lay in the excessive social repression of sexual drives. Indeed, the spread of psychoanalysis got an entire generation accustomed to talking about sex and seeing everyday psychological problems in terms of the libido and its repression.

It is easy to oversimplify what were extremely complex intellectual trends. Jameseans, behavioralists, and Freudians all had distinct views on the role of instinct, culture, and human nature more generally. Perhaps more important than the influence of any given school of psychology was the rise of psychology itself, both as a discipline and as a way of looking at the self. It is safe to say that nineteenth-century Americans (and nineteenth-century Europeans, for that matter) did not spend a lot of time introspectively plumbing the depths of their innermost feelings for therapeutic purposes. To the extent that people were encouraged to be introspective, it was for the purpose of aligning their inner thoughts and behavior with externally sanctioned norms and rules, ones that connected them with larger communities and institutions. The twentieth-century emphasis on psychology, by contrast, has done a great deal to legitimate the pursuit of individual pleasures and gratifications. The result of this "psychologization" of contemporary life is the rise of what the sociologist James Nolan describes as the "therapeutic state,"[27] that is, a government that seeks to minister to the inner psychological needs of its citizens and stands or falls on its ability to make them feel better about themselves. The California "self-esteem" movement, by which public schools were to seek to raise the self-esteem of young people by freeing them from anxiety about being unable to meet unwarranted standards of behavior, is just another dim echo of intellectual trends begun nearly three generations earlier.

As the twentieth century progressed, a second source of high-level ideas about sexuality came out of anthropology. The Columbia anthropologist Franz Boas attacked earlier social Darwinist theories of racial and ethnic hierarchy and criticized the ethnocentrism of Western attempts to judge primitive cultures. Boas's student Margaret Mead wrote *Coming of Age in Samoa* in 1928, applying the concept of cultural relativism directly to the issue of American sexual practices. Samoan girls, she argued, unlike their Puritan- and Victorian-influenced American counterparts, could express their sexuality as adolescents; because of the absence of repressive norms, Samoan society as a whole was much freer of guilt, jealousy, and competitiveness.[28] It is hard to overestimate Mead's influence, not just through her books but through her regular columns in *Life* magazine and the new media of radio and television.

On the level of popular culture, the cultural historian James Lincoln Collier points to the years on either side of 1912 as critical to the breakdown of Victorian sexual norms in the United States. It was in this period that a series of new dances spread across the nation, as well as the opinion that decent women could be seen in dance clubs; the rate of alcohol consumption increased; the word *jazz* was first mentioned in print, along with the growing popularity of black popular music genres like ragtime and later Dixieland among whites; the feminist movement began in earnest; movies and the technology of modern mass entertainment appeared; literary modernism, whose core was the perpetual delegitimization of established cultural values, moved into high gear; and sexual mores (from what little empirical knowledge we have of this period) began to change.[29] Collier argues that the intellectual and cultural grounds for the sexual revolution of the 1960s had already been laid among American elites by the 1920s. Their spread through the rest of the population was delayed, however, by the Depression and war, whose insecurities led people to concentrate more on economic survival and domesticity than on self-expression and self-gratification, which most, in any event, could not afford.

The crucial question about the changes that occurred in social norms during the Great Disruption is therefore not whether they had cultural roots, which they obviously did, but how we can explain the timing and speed of the subsequent transformation. Everything we know about culture is that it tends to change very slowly when compared to other kinds of factors, such as shifts in economic conditions, public policies, or ideology. Where cultural norms have changed quickly, such as in rapidly modernizing Third World societies, cultural change is clearly being driven by economic change and is therefore not an autonomous factor.

So with the Great Disruption: the shift away from Victorian values had been occurring gradually for two or three generations by the time the Disruption began; then, all of a sudden, the pace of change sped up enormously. It is hard to believe that people throughout the developed world simply decided to alter their attitudes toward such elemental issues as marriage, divorce, child rearing, authority, and community so completely in the space of two or three decades, without that shift in values being driven by other powerful forces. Those explanations that link changes in cultural variables to specific events in American history like Vietnam, Watergate, or the counterculture of the 1960s betray an even greater provincialism: Why were social norms disrupted in other societies from Sweden and Norway to New Zealand and Spain?

If these broad explanations for the Great Disruption are unsatisfactory, we need to look at the different elements of the Disruption more specifically and ask whether they were in some way related to one another.

4

Causes:
Demographic, Economic,
and Cultural

Why Rising Crime?

Assuming that the increases in crime rates are not simply a statistical arti-fact of improved police reporting, we need to ask several questions. Why did crime rates increase so dramatically over a relatively short period of time and in such a wide range of countries? Why are rates beginning to come down or level off in the United States and several other Western countries? And why do Asian developed countries appear to be excep-tions to this pattern?

As in the case of rising divorce rates, the first and perhaps most straightforward explanation for increasing crime rates from the late 1960s to the 1980s, and decreasing rates thereafter, is a simple demographic one. Crime tends to be committed overwhelmingly by young males between the ages of fourteen and twenty-five. There is doubtless a genetic reason for this, having to do with male propensities for violence and aggression, and it means that whenever birthrates go up, crime rates will also rise fifteen to twenty-five years later.[1] In the United States, the number of young people between the ages of fourteen and twenty-four increased by 2 million between 1950 and 1960, while the next decade added 12 million to this age group—an onslaught that has been compared to a barbarian invasion.[2] Greater numbers of young people not only increased the pool of potential criminals; their concentration in a youth culture may have led to more-than-proportional increases in efforts to defy authority. It is possible to control for age by comparing numbers of crimes not to the total population, but to the population of young males in a given society. Were this done, most of the curves in Figures 2.1 and 2.2 would flatten out both on ascending and descending slopes. Indeed, the fact that fertility increased more rapidly in the United States than in other developed countries during the baby boom years is part of the explanation for higher U.S. crime rates from the 1960s to the 1990s.[3] New Zealand, which experienced a sharper increase in fertility after World War II than the United States did, also saw its property crime rates go up faster in the 1970s and 1980s.

But the baby boom is only part of the explanation for rising crime rates in the 1960s and 1970s. One criminologist has estimated that the increase in the United States murder rate was ten times as high as would be expected from shifts in the demographic structure of the country alone.[4] Other studies have shown that changes in age structure do not correlate well with increases in crime cross-nationally.[5]

A second explanation links crime rates to modernization and related phenomena like urbanization, population density, and opportunities for crime. It is a commonsense proposition that there will be more auto theft and burglary in large cities than in rural farm areas because it is easier for criminals to find automobiles and empty homes in the former than the latter. "Ecological" theories like those of Henry Shaw and Clifford McKay in the 1940s[6] or Rodney Stark more recently connect crime to specific kinds of environments—for example, densely populated urban areas, mixed-use neighborhoods, or neighborhoods that encourage transience.[7] These types of environments tend to be created as societies modernize economically, so there is reason to expect higher crime rates as people move off farms and from villages to urban areas.

Urbanization and changing physical environment are poor explanations for rising crime rates in developed countries after the 1960s. By 1960, the countries under consideration were already industrialized, urbanized societies; there was no sudden shift from countryside to city that began in 1965. In the United States, murder rates are much higher in the

South than in the North, despite the fact that the latter tends to be more urban and densely populated. Indeed, violence in the South tends to be a rural phenomenon, and most observers who have looked closely into the matter believe that explanations for high crime rates there are cultural rather than ecological.[8] Japan, Korea, Hong Kong, and Singapore are among the most densely populated, overcrowded urban environments in the world, and yet they did not experience rising crime rates as that urbanization was occurring. Indeed, if we are to believe Jane Jacobs's account of crime as inversely proportional to the number of "eyes on the street," precisely the sorts of urban conditions said to breed crime, including crowded sidewalks and mixed-use neighborhoods, are for her exactly the reasons that crime is low in neighborhoods with plentiful social capital. This suggests that the human social environment is much more important in determining levels of crime than the physical one: the same few city blocks can deteriorate or go through a renewal when new groups of people move in. We are back, in other words, to the social capital argument: crime increases because the social capital of a neighborhood or a society decreases, and vice versa.

A third category of explanation is sometimes euphemistically labeled "social heterogeneity."[9] That is, in many societies crime tends to be concentrated among racial or ethnic minorities; to the extent that societies become more ethnically diverse, as virtually all Western developed countries have over the past two generations, we can expect crime rates to rise. The reason that crime rates are frequently higher among minorities is very likely related, as criminologists Richard Cloward and Lloyd Ohlin argued,[10] to the fact that legitimate avenues of social mobility are blocked for them in ways that are not true for members of the majority community. In other cases, the simple fact of heterogeneity in itself may be to blame: neighborhoods that are too diverse culturally, linguistically, religiously, or ethnically never come together as communities able to enforce informal norms on their members. And finally, not all minorities whose advancement is blocked by the larger society engage in crime at similar rates. Higher rates of crime in certain minority communities may simply be the product of that community's own culture.

As an overall explanation for rising crime rates, social heterogeneity is probably a stronger explanatory factor in Europe than in the United

States. In the United States, ethnic diversity has been increasing as a result of new immigration, particularly from Latin America and Asia. It is not clear, however, that overall crime rates for Hispanic immigrants are significantly higher than for the native-born, and in any case crime rose for native as well as foreign-born groups after the 1960s. In Europe, a great deal of anti-immigrant sentiment exploited by right-wing groups like Jean-Marie Le Pen's Front National in France and the Republikaner party in Germany is fueled by the perception that immigrants are disproportionately responsible for crime. But here as well crime rates have been increasing for native-born groups.[11]

A further explanation has to do with drugs. Based on the maturing of the baby boom cohort alone, we should have expected the decline in crime to occur in the late 1980s (just as divorce rates began to level off) rather than in the late 1990s. One explanation for the continuation of high levels of violent crime, and for the sudden rapid drop in rates in the late 1990s, has to do with the introduction of crack cocaine in American cities in the mid-1980s and the subsequent stabilization of crack markets.[12] This factor does not, however, explain the reasons for the initial growth of crime, only the crime wave's prolongation.

Given the limitations of these explanations, we are led to ask whether increases in crime rates might not be related to other aspects of the Great Disruption, particularly to more or less contemporaneous changes in the family. The currently dominant school of contemporary American criminology holds that early childhood socialization is one of the most important factors determining the level of subsequent criminality. That is, most people do not make day-to-day choices about whether to commit crimes based on the balance of rewards and risks, as the rational choice school sometimes suggests. The vast majority of people obey the law, particularly with regard to serious offenses, out of habit that they learned relatively early in life. By contrast, most crimes are committed by repeat offenders who have failed to learn this basic level of self-control. In many cases, they are not acting rationally, but out of impulse. Failing to anticipate consequences, they are frequently undeterred by expectations of punishments.

One of the most famous criminological studies that demonstrated the importance of early childhood socialization was that of Sheldon and Eleanor Glueck, whose results were published in their book *Unraveling Ju-*

venile Delinquency.[13] The Gluecks conducted a longitudinal study following the same group of boys from a poor Boston neighborhood well into their adult lives, trying to discern what caused some of them to commit crimes and others to live productive lives. One of the study's findings was that boys who committed crimes continued to have problems as adults— further criminal behavior, failed marriages, addiction to alcohol or drugs, inability to keep jobs, and the like. This suggested that the propensity for low self-control is established relatively early in life, and that this is one of the most important forms of what is in effect social capital provided by families.

This is also the conclusion of criminologists Travis Hirshi and Michael Gottfredson, who argue that it is more useful to speak of "criminal careers" rather than individual acts of crime, since life courses were established by the way parents socialized their children at relatively early ages.[14] In a comprehensive survey of studies linking family to crime, Rolf Loeber and Magda Stouhamer-Loeber confirmed what most people know by common sense: that parents influence their children's subsequent criminal behavior through neglect, conflict with the child, deviant behavior on the part of the parents themselves, and marital conflict and parental absence.[15]

The Gluecks' data were reanalyzed in the 1990s by Robert Sampson and John Laub, who found that they confirmed the importance of what they call "age-graded informal social control," and the continuity in life-course criminal behavior on the part of children who were not socialized properly.[16] Sampson and Laub differ slightly from the Gluecks and other "control" theorists in their conclusions that subsequent social relationships, like school, jobs, and peers, could also have an effect on an individual's propensity toward a criminal career. For them, it is not just families that are important sources of social capital; the social capital embedded in neighborhoods can also influence the amount of crime committed by delinquents. But they would not dispute the basic linkage between family and crime or the importance of families to the maintenance of social capital in neighborhoods.

Can family breakdown account for the broad rise in developed country crime rates after 1965? It would make sense that the deterioration of family life that began in this period also accounted for the large rise in crime rates, and there is indeed a good deal of empirical evidence linking the two.[17] Family breakdown often proves to be an important mediating variable that explains how poverty is related to crime:[18] poor families are not simply ones whose job opportunities are blocked by lack of education or transportation; they are often ones without fathers present in the home who can encourage, discipline, serve as role models, and otherwise socialize sons.

On the other hand, the statistical relationship between family breakdown and crime is not as open and shut as it may first appear, since the former is often correlated with a host of other factors like poverty, bad schools, and dangerous neighborhoods, which also have an impact on how children are socialized.[19] Disentangling these different factors is often difficult and varies by country. In Sweden, for example, the community outside the family—neighbors, other adults, day care professionals, teachers, and the like—probably plays a significantly greater role in socializing children than it does in the United States. The negative consequences of a child growing up in a single-parent family are thus mitigated.

Even in the United States, there is a problem in using family breakdown to explain rising crime rates in the 1960s. If family breakdown were the major factor responsible for crime, one would expect crime rates to rise with a lag of fifteen to twenty years after the rise in rates of divorce and illegitimacy, since presumably it would be the children of such broken families who would lead the crime wave. And yet crime, divorce, and illegitimacy all began to rise during the same period. Those young people committing crimes in the late 1960s and early 1970s would have been born in the period 1945–1960, during the postwar baby boom when the stability of the American family was increasing. There was evidently something beneath the surface of family domesticity in the 1950s that wasn't entirely right, since the generation growing up in it proved more than ordinarily vulnerable to a variety of temptations when they came into adulthood. Family disruption clearly had something to do with continued high rates of crime through the early 1990s, but it would appear that the onset of the Great Disruption needs to be traced to a factor common to both crime and family breakdown.

And yet the link between family and crime clearly exists—more so, I suspect, in the United States than in Europe or Japan. Broadly speaking, the central problem that any society faces is controlling the aggression, ambition, and potential violence on the part of its young men, directing it into safe and productive channels. In most human societies, this job almost always falls to the older men in the community, who seek to ritualize aggression, control access to women, and generally establish a web of norms and rules to constrain young men's behavior.[20] The older man who plays this role can be the biological father of the younger one, but he can also be an older brother, uncle, or a male from the mother's side of the family. In contemporary American society, those older males can take the form of Marine Corps drill instructors, who, as Thomas Ricks has shown in *Making the Corps,* have proved superb in taking undirected boys from broken homes and turning them into self-disciplined, purposeful men.[21]

The link between family breakdown and social disorder is weaker in Europe than in America, I suspect, not just because there is a larger welfare state to provide resources to single-parent families, but also because there are more males around to socialize and educate boys. In some cases, this is the biological father who continues to cohabit with the mother even though the two are not married to one another. In other cases norms of behavior are enforced by neighbors, more distant relatives, or simply others in the community. The much lower degree of physical, not to mention socioeconomic, mobility of Europeans as compared to Americans means that neighborhoods and local communities are more stable and homogeneous. In Jane Jacobs's terms, there are more "eyes on the street" in a typical European neighborhood than in a typical American one. Single mothers thus get greater help raising their sons than do their American counterparts.

If we move from general crime rates to child abuse more specifically, the relationship between changes in family structure and increasing levels of abuse becomes much more clear-cut. The Children's Defense Fund asserts that based on interviews with child care professionals, the number of children seriously injured by abuse nearly quadrupled between 1986 and 1993—a truly astonishing increase to take place over a seven-year period.[22] A study by the U.S. Department of Health and Human Services shows less dramatic but still large increases in physical, sexual, and emotional abuse between 1980 and 1993.[23] Although press sensationalism has tended to exaggerate popular perceptions of this problem,[24] there is reason to think that rates of child abuse did in fact increase during the Great Disruption.

From a biological point of view, it should not be surprising if increasing rates of divorce and illegitimacy led to abuse on the parts of substitute parents, particularly by men whose primary interest is in having sex with the mother and for whom the children are at best an inconvenience. According to Martin Daly and Margo Wilson, two evolutionary psychologists who have studied the issue closely, "Perhaps the most obvious prediction from a Darwinian view of parental motives is this: Substitute parents will generally tend to care less profoundly for children than natural parents."[25] They point to the near universality of Cinderella-type stories of evil stepparents in the folklore of virtually every culture around the world. In cities with good police records that distinguish between violence perpetrated by substitute rather than natural parents, a child is anywhere from ten to one hundred times as likely to experience abuse at the hands of a substitute parent as a biological one. A study by the Family Education Trust in Britain came up with similar findings: a child living with both natural parents is approximately half as likely to experience child abuse as the average child, those living with a single mother are anywhere from 1.7 to 2.3 times as likely, and those living with their mother and a father substitute 2.8 to 5.0 times as likely to suffer abuse.[26] A U.S. Health and Human Services study of child abuse and neglect showed that children living with a single parent suffered abuse at a rate that was "more than one and three-fourths times the rate of overall maltreatment under the Harm Standard for children living with both parents." Rates of neglect for single-parent families were 2.2 times the rate for two-parent families.[27] Indeed, in some cases, the violence against children spills over and becomes a risk factor for the mother as well.[28]

It is true that child abuse is also highly correlated with family income and other measures of socioeconomic status, and that none of the studies cited has performed a more complex multivariate analysis to disentangle the relative impacts of class and family structure. Poverty, then, plays a role in promoting child abuse. It should be noted, however, that poverty rates (in the United States, at least) tend to move with economic cycles, and that there was no general increase in poverty that corresponded to the large increase in child abuse cases.[29] As in other aspects of the Great Disruption, it is difficult to explain these dramatic changes in social indicators in terms of broad economic variables alone.

Of course, there are very many devoted stepparents around the world who care for their stepchildren with no less love and attention than they would for their own biological offspring.[30] People may prefer kin, but they also have an ability to bond with other creatures, from children to pets, when they are so inclined. Indeed, it is likely that many substitute parents overcompensate and spend extra effort with their stepchildren precisely to show that they are not playing favorites. The delicacy of the situation in remade households involving substitute parents can lead to an entirely different kind of problem, where the new father is unwilling to step in to intervene and discipline a child because he feels he has no right to do so as a nonbiological relative.[31]

Why Rising Distrust?

In the realm of trust, values, and civil society, we need to explain two separate phenomena: first, why there has been a broad-based decline in trust in both institutions and other people, and how we can reconcile the shift toward fewer shared norms with an apparent growth in groups and in the density of civil society.

The reasons for the decline of trust in an American context have been debated extensively. Robert Putnam argued early on that it might be associated with the rise of television, since the cohort that first grew up watching television was the one that experienced the most precipitous decline in trust levels.[32] Not only does the content of television breed cynicism in its attention to sex and violence, but the fact that individuals are sitting on their living room couches watching television limits their opportunities for face-to-face social activities in a country whose average resident watches over four hours per day.

One suspects, however, that a broad phenomenon like the decline of trust is a complex one that has a number of different causes, of which television is only one. Tom Smith of the National Opinion Research Center has performed a multivariate analysis of the survey data on trust and found, as noted above (see p. 50), that distrust is correlated with low socioeconomic status, minority status, traumatic life events, fundamentalism, failure to attend a mainline church, and age cohort (e.g., whether one is a baby boomer or a member of generation X). The traumatic life events affecting trust are, not surprisingly, whether one has been a victim of crime or whether one is in poor health.

Which of these factors has changed since the 1960s in a dramatic way that could explain the decrease in trust? Income inequality has increased somewhat, and Eric Uslaner of the University of Maryland has suggested that this may account for some of the increase in distrust.[33] Poverty rates have fluctuated but have not increased overall in this period, and the so-called middle-class squeeze did not represent a drop in real income for the vast majority of Americans so much as a stagnation of earnings. We have seen how the economic instability of this period, from oil crisis to downsizings, may have fostered an increase in cynicism.

Crime saw a dramatic increase between 1965 and 1995, and it makes a great deal of sense to think that someone who has been victimized by crime or watches the daily cavalcade of grisly crime stories on the local television news is likely to feel distrust not for immediate friends and family, but for the larger world. Hence crime would seem to be an important explanation for the increase in distrust after 1965, a conclusion well supported in more detailed analyses.[34]

The other major social change that has led to traumatic life experiences has been the rise of divorce and family breakdown. Commonsensically, one would think that children who have experienced the divorce of their parents, or who deal with a series of the mother's boyfriends in a single-parent household, would tend to become cynical about adults in general, and that this might go far to explain the increase in levels of distrust that show up in survey data. However, in Smith's analysis, divorce or single parenthood does not emerge as an important explanatory variable.[35] On the other hand, plenty of indirect connections exist: family breakdown is related to both crime and poverty, and both of these are clearly incubators of cynicism. A study by Wendy Rahn and John Transue shows that father absence in the household increases the likelihood that children will hold materialistic values, which in turn is correlated with distrust.[36]

Religion apparently has contradictory effects on trust; fundamentalists as well as those who do not attend church tend to be more distrustful than others. While many Americans believe that their own society has grown more secular in the past generation, this is true primarily of the public sphere, where strict separation of church and state has been progressively enforced; it is not clear that in their private beliefs, Americans have shown a dramatic decline in religious conviction.[37] However, it is possible that some of the decrease in trust can be explained by shifts to a more secular society, a trend that would, paradoxically, be amplified by a simultaneous increase in members of fundamentalist churches.

The fact that younger cohorts tend to be more mistrusting than older ones does not explain the rise of distrust; rather, it begs the question of why the young are more cynical. On the other hand, it shows that the rise of distrust is not simply a life cycle effect—that is, something that characterizes people at a certain stage in their lives. Nor is it characteristic of only one birth cohort—say, the baby boom generation—since it appears to be even more characteristic of so-called Generation-Xers.

We can statistically verify that rising crime and economic insecurity have had negative effects on trust and suspect that family breakdown also played a role. One gets the feeling, however, that empirical measures of cultural change like the ones used above are rather crude instruments and that we need to take a more qualitative look at what has been happening.

The Miniaturization of Community

The fact that groups and group memberships could be increasing even as trust and shared values appear to be in retreat can be explained in a number of ways, all of them consistent with the broad assertion at the beginning of this book that the most important change in contemporary societies is an increase in individualism. There has in fact been an important transformation in the nature of American civil society, which probably also applies to other Western developed countries. But the important change that has occurred cannot be captured in any of the quantitative measures of the number and size of organizations that have been bandied about in the so-called Putnam debate. The important changes are *qualitative,* in the nature of the groups that tend to predominate today and in the character of the moral relationships that exist between individuals in the broader society.

The most obvious way to reconcile lower levels of trust and greater levels of group membership has to do with a reduction in what has been called the radius of trust. Consider the case of a family joining a neighborhood watch organization that patrols local streets because there has been a sudden rash of burglaries. The neighborhood watch serves as one of Tocqueville's schools of citizenship and constitutes a new group that would be counted as part of the broader civil society. Its members learn to cooperate with one another and thereby build social capital. On the other hand, the reason that the organization exists in the first place is as a result of crime and the *distrust* that people in the neighborhood have for those in the broader society who are making them feel insecure. If the growth of civil society is based on the proliferation of such small-radius, defensive groups, then one might well expect that levels of generalized social trust would decline.

Even worse would be a situation in which people retreated into bigoted or actively aggressive groups that diminished the larger society's stock of trust. The science-fiction writer Neal Stephenson presents a dark and humorous picture of a United States of the future in his novel *Snow Crash,* where the country has been divided into hundreds of thousands of individual "burbclaves"—in effect, subdivisions and homeowners' associations that have turned into sovereign entities requiring passports and visas to enter. In this world, the authority of the federal government has been reduced to those few dilapidated buildings that it still occupies. Blacks, bikers, Chinese, even racists in a gated community called New South Africa all enjoy community life in mutual ignorance of and hostility toward one another.

Contemporary America has not quite reached this point, but it has moved in that direction. It is hard to interpret the data on either values or civil society in any way other than to suggest that the radius of trust is diminishing, not just in the United States but across the developed world. People continue to share norms and values in ways that constitute social capital, and they join groups and organizations in ever larger numbers, but the type of group has shifted dramatically. The authority of most large organizations has declined, and the importance of a host of smaller associations in people's lives has grown. Rather than taking pride in being a member of a large and powerful labor federation, or working for a large corporation, or for having served in the country's military, people seek sociability in a local aerobics class, a new age sect, a codependent support group, or an Internet chat room. Rather than seeking authoritative values in the national church that once shaped the society's culture, people are picking and choosing their values on an individual basis, in ways that link them with smaller communities of like-minded folk.

The shift to smaller-radius groups is mirrored politically in the almost universal rise of interest groups at the expense of broad-based political parties. A political party like the German Christian Democrats or the British Labour party takes a coherent ideological stand on the whole range of issues facing a society, from national defense to social welfare. Although usually based on a particular social class, it unites within itself a broad coalition of interests and personalities. The interest group, on the other hand, focuses on a single issue like saving rain forests or the promotion of poultry farming in the upper Midwest; it may be transnational in scope, but it is much less authoritative in the range of issues it deals with or the numbers of people it brings together.

Alan Wolfe's interviews with middle-class Americans provide plenty of confirmation concerning the miniaturization of community and morality in contemporary American society. Wolfe argues that there are no real "culture wars" going on in the United States today, with different groups pitted irreconcilably against one another. The reason that no one is at war is that, with the exception of certain issues like abortion and homosexuality, most middle-class Americans don't believe in anything strongly enough to want to impose their values on one another, and therefore have no motive for serious cultural warfare. Many of Wolfe's interviewees are religious and concerned with the ethical shortcomings of contemporary American society. They also prize community and can be quite hostile to those who make community more difficult, from entrepreneurs in racial politics to downsizing corporations. But they are even more committed to being nonjudgmental about the values of other people. They have no interest in imposing their religious or ethical beliefs on anyone else, and are even more hostile to the idea that any form of external authority should tell them how to live.

Wolfe argues that this easygoing moral relativism is in the end a good thing: it enshrines the central liberal virtue of tolerance, it is nuanced on a range of issues from affirmative action to feminism to patriotism, and it means that there is a great deal of shared pragmatism at the center of the American moral universe. He criticizes conservative intellectuals like Irving Kristol and Robert Bork for arguing that most Americans want a return to religious and moral orthodoxy. His first reason is empirical: from everything we know of the opinions of most Americans, they want the benefits of orthodoxy in terms of community and social order, but they do not want to give up any significant amount of personal freedom to achieve these ends. They deplore the loss of family values, but oppose the move away from no-fault divorce; they want friendly mom-and-pop stores but are enamored of low prices and consumer choice. It is as if Emile Durkheim's prediction that in a modern society, the only values uniting people would be the value of individualism itself had come true: people reserve their greatest moral indignation for moralism on the part of other people.[38]

We will defer, for the time being, the question of what "morality writ small" portends for the future of democratic societies. It is clear, however, that moral relativism is a key link between the apparently contradictory findings of decreasing trust and a growing civil society. Community is based on shared values: the more authoritative and widely held those values, the stronger the community and higher the level of generalized social trust. But growing individualism and the desire to maximize personal autonomy lead to a questioning of authority across the board, particularly the authority of large institutions that are endowed with substantial power.

Contemporary Americans, and contemporary Europeans as well, seek contradictory goals. They are increasingly distrustful of any authority, political or moral, that would constrain their freedom of choice, but they also want a sense of community and the good things that flow from community, like mutual recognition, participation, belonging, and identity. Community has to be found elsewhere, in smaller and more flexible groups and organizations where loyalties and memberships can be overlapping, and where entry and exit entail relatively low costs. People might thus be able to reconcile their contradictory desires for community and autonomy. But in this bargain, the community they get is smaller and weaker than most that have existed in the past. Each community shares less with neighboring ones, and the ones to which they belong have relatively little hold. The circle of people they can trust is necessarily narrower. The essence of the shift in values that is at the center of the Great Disruption is, then, the rise of moral individualism and the consequent miniaturization of community.

5

The Special Role of Women

We have seen that crime and, to a lesser extent, distrust can be linked to changes that have taken place in family structure. That the family has undergone such dramatic change in the past thirty years is obviously related to the two major upheavals of the 1960s and 1970s: the sexual and feminist revolutions. Many people regard these developments as purely voluntary cultural choices. The Right decries a decline in family values, while the Left sees traditional norms as a matter of men who "just don't get it." These value changes were stimulated, however, by important technological and economic developments related to the end of the industrial era that alone can explain their timing. It is not that people don't have free will or make moral choices. But moral choices take place within a technological and economic framework that makes certain outcomes more likely in some periods than in others.

Fertility

The widespread availability of birth control and the legalization of abortion in many developed countries from the 1960s on is a background condition explaining the extraordinarily low levels of fertility since then. But birth control and abortion are only part of the story. Many countries, like France and Japan, saw their fertility drop well before the 1960s. Nor does the simple existence of birth control explain why fertility moves to a particular level. Why didn't the total fertility rate of Italy drop to 0.2 rather than 1.2 in the 1990s, since birth control made the lower figure just as possible as the one that actually emerged?

The models that demographers use to explain fertility tend to be economic ones. Parents, the argument goes, want children the way they want other economic goods.[1] Of course, they love them and treasure them, but they do not love them to the exclusion of all other good things in life. The cost of a child consists of a number of components: the direct costs of feeding, clothing, housing, and educating children, and the opportunity costs to the parents—and especially to the mother—of having to forgo time and income while bringing up the child. The child repays this through the love and affection the parents feel for him or her, and perhaps may repay some of these costs directly by supporting the parents when the child is able to earn an income. But having children represents a net one-way transfer of resources from parents to children, a cost that the former balance against other types of expenditures.

In a modern, information-based society, both the direct costs and opportunity costs of having children have gone up substantially. As wealth, measured by per capita income, rises and the technological sophistication of an economy increases, skills and education (or what economists call human capital) become increasingly important to the life chances of a young person. In a poor country like India, children can become economic assets by going to work when they are seven or eight years old. In the United States, by contrast, there is little remunerative work an eight year old can do, and increasingly little work even for someone with only a high school diploma. In the 1990s, it can cost well over $100,000 to give a single child a four-year college education. At the same time, the child's parents—and particularly mothers—are more likely to be in the labor force and earning larger salaries. For women, the cost of taking off several months or years to raise children can amount to tens or hundreds of thousands of dollars. Parents for biological reasons want to maximize their reproductive success, but they are also rational and understand that their children are likely to do well only if equipped with the proper skills, education, and other appurtenances of life in a modern society.

Although this may seem like a broadly satisfactory account of fertility, there are many specific facts and anomalies for which it does not provide a good explanation. Why, for example, did France's total fertility rate (TFR) begin to fall in the nineteenth century, well before the TFRs of other countries at a comparable level of development began to do so? Why did Japan, which in the 1950s had a much lower per capita GDP and much lower female labor force participation than the United States, Britain, or Canada, experience a sudden and drastic fall in fertility, while the latter three countries were experiencing a baby boom?[2] Why did the baby boom itself take place? And why did the Swedish pronatalist policy, which was supposed to shift the economic incentives toward having more children, appear to work in the 1980s and then collapse during the 1990s?

It would seem that in addition to the economic model, a host of other factors determine fertility, including some cultural ones that are difficult to quantify. Culture can often trump economic considerations. In the United States, there are communities, like Hasidic Jews or Mormons, whose fertility is considerably higher than the national average because their religious beliefs dictate large families. The postwar baby boom has been explained in terms of the deferred expectations of the cohort that would have started families during the Depression and war years and by their need to retreat into the security and domesticity of family life after years of upheaval.

Similarly, it is hard to believe that the drop in fertility over the past generation in Europe is not also related to changing cultural preferences regarding the importance of family life per se relative to other good things, and not just a child-by-child calculation of costs and forgone earnings.[3] For many educated Europeans and Americans, having children and raising families has simply become less fashionable. One young Swedish woman, quoted in the *New York Times,* explained, "There are times when I think that perhaps I will be missing something important if I don't have a child. . . . But today women finally have so many chances to have the life they want. They travel and work and learn. It's exciting and demanding. I just find it hard to see where the children would fit in."[4]

Trends in fertility in turn explain, to some extent, increases in divorce rates that characterized the Great Disruption. Couples tend to divorce at higher rates during the first few years of marriage; hence countries experiencing baby booms can expect higher divorce rates when the children born during them reach their twenties and thirties. In addition, greater longevity means that marriages must last longer; by the law of averages, they will tend to be disrupted more by divorce than by the death of a spouse. Hence the fertility and mortality patterns described earlier would lead us to expect an increasing degree of marital disruption during the 1970s and 1980s.

The disruption in family life that actually occurred, however, was much more dramatic than these demographic factors by themselves would imply, so we need to look for other causes. But before we can identify these social factors, we need to understand the biological context within which these changes operated.

Biological Origins of the Family

One of the staples of post-Boas anthropology is the idea that there is no such thing as a natural or normal human family. Much of the discipline of anthropology is given over to the study of the enormous variety that exists in human kinship systems, and it is indeed hard to discern clear universals in family patterns. Certainly what anthropologists call the conjugal or nuclear two-generation family of the United States in the 1950s was not characteristic of much of the rest of the world in that period and was not typical of many Western societies at earlier stages in their development. Therefore the breakdown of the nuclear family after the 1960s in the West did not ipso facto represent deviation from some kind of age-old norm.

On the other hand, if we put human kinship in the broader context of kinship among other animal species, we see that it serves certain evolutionary purposes, despite the surface variety of kinship systems. Few people would contest the notion that the relationship between a mother and her children is biologically grounded, as it is in the case of other animal species. A new mother will let down milk at the sound of a baby's cry; she instinctively cradles the baby in her left arm, where the infant will be calmed by the sound of the mother's heartbeat.[5] A host of studies show that mothers and infants communicate spontaneously and interact in a variety of ways that appear to be under genetic rather than cultural control.[6] Mothers are essential to the well-being of their children; many sociopathic behaviors that appear later in life can be traced back to a disruption of the mother-child bond at a relatively early age.[7]

The male role in rearing offspring is more problematic, and in other species shows considerable variability. Much as humans like to look on monogamous pair-bonding in birds as a natural model for human families,[8] in the great majority of sexually reproducing species, males do not contribute much more than a single sperm cell to the creation and upbringing of their children. This is true of man's closest primate relatives, the great apes. Chimpanzees, for example, are promiscuous and do not form pair-bonds for any appreciable length of time; although males contribute to the defense and feeding of dependents in their troop, young chimpanzees are raised in what are in effect single-parent families. What determines the degree of male parental involvement in any given species has to do with the kinds of resources that are necessary, given the animal's environment, for the successful upbringing of the young and the male's ability to contribute to them.[9]

In the case of human beings, males are pulled in contradictory directions. On the one hand, human children require much more parental investment than offspring of other species, leaving an important role for males. Human beings have such large brains that despite a rather long pregnancy period, they are in effect born premature, with much of the maturation that in other animals occurs during pregnancy done outside the womb. Human infants are therefore far more helpless at birth than those of most other animal species, including any of the great apes. Human children take an extraordinarily long time to become viable on their own, during which time they are weak, vulnerable, and dependent on their parents. Mothers are, of course, the sine qua non of their children's survival, but the human child's needs are so great that males come to play important roles. In hunter-gatherer times, during which the present human genetic makeup was established, males were important in providing protein in the form of animal meat and in protecting these communities from both other human groups and the natural environment. Hence it is understandable that some form of monogamous pair-bonding is much more common among human societies than among other animals.

On the other hand, the nature of this bond remains fragile because of biological factors that make the male's incentives for staying with his children much weaker than the female's. Any animal's most basic biological drive is to get its genes into the next and succeeding generations. For a human mother, as for most other mothers in the animal kingdom, that means providing her children with the best possible genes at the start of life and providing those children with the resources thereafter to make them viable and able to reproduce themselves. Females generally have to provide a higher level of what biologists call "parental investment" than males. Particularly among mammals, females must gestate, nurse the young, find food to feed their children, and often fight to protect them from predators and the environment. While human males invest more in their children than the males of many other species, the contribution (and cost) to having children remains smaller than for females. There is, for example, a rather low natural limit to the number of offspring a female can bear during a lifetime compared to the number a male can beget. For humans, a woman can produce perhaps a dozen children in a lifetime, while a man can sire thousands. A female, then, will increase the chances of passing on her genes if she is highly selective in her choice of mate—in the first place to make sure that her children have the best available genes and, second, to ensure that the male's resources are available to her children after birth. Males, on the other hand, tend to maximize their chances for passing on their genes by mating less discriminately with as many females as possible.

The fact that females tend to be more selective than males in their choice of sexual partners is a generalization that, as it turns out, can be made not just of virtually all known human cultures, but of virtually all animal species that reproduce sexually. According to the biologist Robert Trivers,

> In most species females are highly discriminating in their choice of sex partners, while males are much less discriminating. A female is typically courted by many males and refuses access to all but one or a few. This

choice is by no means random. Wherever female preference has been studied in nature, females have been shown to choose in very particular ways. Most females in a species choose in a similar way, so that the result of female choice is to give some males many copulations and many other males none. . . . By contrast, males court many females and will copulate with most or all if accepted. In addition, males will court inappropriate objects. For example, males have been observed courting other males, females of the wrong species, stuffed females, portions of stuffed females, and inanimate objects. Sometimes they are seen courting a combination of the above.[10]

According to Trivers, there are only a few known species where these sexual preferences are reversed, including the phalarope, the Mormon cricket, and certain kinds of seahorses.[11]

Men, in other words, have a biological disposition to be in effect more promiscuous and less discriminating than women in their search for sexual gratification.* This finding accords with our everyday observation of male and female sexuality and explains why men rather than women are the primary consumers of prostitutes and pornography. It also explains why gay men have a much larger, and lesbian women a much smaller, average number of partners than heterosexuals: it is not gayness

---

*One may ask how it can be that heterosexual men can be more promiscuous than heterosexual women, since for every sex act, there has to be a partner of the opposite sex. This is, strictly speaking, true; but what tends to happen in most societies is that wealthy or high-status men have much greater sexual access to women (and therefore many more partners and children from those partners) than low-status ones. The low-status men by and large would like the same degree of access but simply can't get it. In some strongly polygamous societies (the Aztec emperor Montezuma was said to have four thousand concubines; the Indian emperor Udayama sixteen thousand, and the Chinese emperor ten thousand), this literally means that a significant proportion of low-status men passed their entire lives without the prospect of either sex or families of their own. In modern societies, polygamy has been outlawed, but high-status men continue to enjoy greater sexual opportunities, the only difference being that American corporate executives have their wives and children serially rather than simultaneously, as in the case of Ottoman pashas or Chinese mandarins. And the same sex act tends to be interpreted differently by men and by women. For men, it is a notch on their belt; for women, it is a chance to draw a man into a relationship of greater intimacy. Even if both end up having sex, their intentions are different, and one or the other usually ends up having been deceived.

but maleness unconstrained by female selectivity that produces the high numbers in the former case.[12]

Biology, then, tells us that there will be some male role in the family centered around the provision of resources to the woman and her children, but it also suggests that that role will be fragile and subject to disruption. The extent to which males will stay in monogamous pair-bonds and play an active role in the nurture of children will depend less on instinct than on the kinds of social norms, sanctions, and pressures that are brought upon them by the larger community. As the anthropologists Lionel Tiger and Robin Fox explain, although the forms of human kinship vary enormously across cultures, the underlying structure remains constant: "Whatever else a social system does, it has to have some means of ensuring the security of the relationship between mother and infant until at least that point when the infant is independently mobile and able to survive with a reasonable chance of reaching adulthood."[13] This can be done by the father, the mother's brothers, or other members of the community, but it has to be done by somebody. The problem is ensuring that this function be performed: "Most societies create elaborate and formidable rules to keep the pairs together, once they have mated. Far from representing the intrinsic normality of the mating bond, these rules suggest how precarious it really is. The great variety and depth of customs surrounding kinship and marriage are not expressions of an innate and ready tendency to form families: they are devices to protect the mother-child unit from the potential fragility of the mating bond."[14]

The contradictory biological incentives operating on human males, to invest in families *and* to escape the bonds of family, may explain the variability of family forms and the complex provenance of the nuclear family. The latter is neither as historically recent nor as transitory as its critics believe, nor as universal and natural as its defenders would like to think. On the one hand, it was commonly argued in the nineteenth century, and still believed by many people today, that the nuclear family is a modern invention that arose only after industrialization.[15] Prior to that, the belief went, everybody lived in much larger kinship groups like tribes and lineages, in which nuclear families constituted only small subordinate parts. Such lineages can still be seen in southern China, the Middle East, and other parts of the Third World. Over time, these lineages broke down into joint or extended families, with three or more generations living in an extended household; and then, with the Industrial Revolution, extended families turned into nuclear ones. The nuclear family, by this account, is only an evolutionary waystation and may well give way to single-parent families or more free-form types of household association in the future.

In fact, nuclear families, although not universal, have actually been much more prevalent throughout human history than this account suggests and were the dominant form of kinship in hunter-gatherer times.[16] According to anthropologist Adam Kuper, "Contemporary social anthropologists are skeptical about the models, current until recently, which represented African, American, and Pacific societies as associations of large corporations of kin that swallow up the family and the individual in a great collective of bloodkin. On the contrary, nuclear families crop up everywhere, and they are usually the most important domestic institutions, their heads making pragmatic choices of political alignment."[17] Australian aborigines, the Trobriand Islanders of the South Pacific, pygmies, Kalahari bushmen, and the indigenous peoples of the Amazon all organize themselves into nuclear families.[18] The large, diverse kinship systems studied by anthropologists appear to have originated with the discovery of agriculture. In some sense, the rediscovery of the nuclear family, which historian Peter Laslett has shown occurred in northern Europe well prior to the Industrial Revolution, marks a return to a very ancient pattern.[19]

Monogamous pair-bonding and the nuclear family, then, are not necessarily recent historical inventions. But while fathers have a clear role to play in human kinship, a role that is much more important and closely linked to his children than for any of the great apes, the precise nature of that role has shown tremendous variability over historical time and among different human societies. In other words, while the role of mother can be safely said to be grounded in biology, the role of father is to a much greater degree socially constructed.[20] In the words of Margaret Mead, "Somewhere at the dawn of human history, some social invention was made under which males started nurturing females and their young." The male role was founded on the provision of resources, "who among human beings everywhere helps provide food for women and children."

But being a learned behavior, the male role in nurturing the family is subject to disruption: "The evidence suggests that we should phrase the matter differently for men and women—that men have to learn to want to provide for others, and this behaviour, being learned, is fragile and can disappear rather easily under social conditions that no longer teach it effectively."[21] The role of fathers, in other words, varies by culture and tradition from intensive involvement in the nurturing and education of children, to a more distant presence as protector and disciplinarian, to the largely absent provider of a paycheck. It takes a great deal of effort to separate a mother from her newborn infant; by contrast, it usually takes a fair amount of effort to get a father to be involved with his.

Birth Control and Working Women

Once we put kinship and family in a biological context, it is easier to understand why nuclear families have started to break apart at such a rapid rate in the past two generations. The family bond is relatively fragile, based on an exchange of the woman's fertility for the man's resources. Prior to the Great Disruption, all Western societies had in place a complex series of formal and informal laws, rules, norms, and obligations to protect the mother-child bond by limiting the freedom of fathers to ditch one family and start another. Today many people have come to think of marriage as a kind of public celebration of a sexual and emotional union between two adults, which is why gay marriage has now become a possibility in the United States and other developed countries. But it is clear that historically, the institution of marriage existed to give legal protection to the mother-child unit and to ensure that adequate economic resources are passed from the father to allow the children to grow up to be viable adults. These legal protections were supplemented by a host of informal norms as well.

What accounts for the breakdown of these norms constraining male behavior and the bargain on which the family rested? Two very important changes occurred sometime during the early postwar period. The first involved advances in medical technology—primarily the birth control pill, which permitted women to better control their own reproductive cycles. The second was the movement of women into the paid labor force in most industrialized countries and the steady rise in their incomes—hourly, median, and lifetime—relative to men over the next thirty years.

The significance of birth control was not simply that it lowered fertility, since fertility had already been on the decline in some societies in the nineteenth century, prior to the widespread availability of birth control or abortion.[22] Indeed, if the effect of birth control is to reduce the number of unwanted pregnancies, it is hard to explain why its advent should have been accompanied by an explosion of illegitimacy and a rise in the rate of abortions[23] or why use of birth control is positively correlated with illegitimacy across the OECD.[24]

The main impact of the Pill and the sexual revolution that followed was, as the economists Janet Yellen, George Akerlof, and Michael Katz have shown, to alter dramatically calculations about the risks of sex and thereby to change *male* behavior.[25] The reason that the rates of birth control use, abortions, and illegitimacy all went up in tandem is that a fourth rate—the number of shotgun marriages—declined substantially at the same time. By these economists' calculations, in the period 1965–1969 some 59 percent of white brides and 25 percent of black brides were pregnant at the altar. Young people were evidently having quite a lot of premarital sex in those years, but social consequences like out-of-wedlock childbearing were mitigated by the norm of male responsibility for the children they produced. By the 1980–1984 period these proportions had dropped to 42 and 11 percent, respectively. Since the Pill and abortion permitted women for the first time to have sex without worrying about the consequences, men felt liberated from norms requiring them to look after the women whom they had gotten pregnant.

The second factor altering male behavior is the entry of women into the paid labor force. That female incomes should be related to family breakdown is an argument accepted by many economists and elaborated most fully by Gary Becker in *A Treatise on the Family*.[26] The assumption behind this relationship is that many marriage contracts are entered into with imperfect information: husbands and wives discover, once married, that life is not a perpetual honeymoon, that their spouse's behavior has changed from what it was before marriage, or that their own expectations for partners have changed. Trading in a husband for one you like better, or getting rid of an abusive mate, was restricted by the fact that many women were unable to support themselves for lack of job skills or experience. As female earnings rise, women become better able to support themselves and to raise children without husbands. Rising female income also increases the opportunity costs of having children and therefore lowers fertility. Fewer children means less of what Becker characterizes as the joint capital in the marriage, and hence makes divorce more likely.

Substantial empirical evidence links higher female earnings to both divorce and extramarital childbearing.[27] Figure 5.1 plots female labor force participation rates against divorce rates in 1994 for a series of OECD countries. The points lie along a southwest-northeast axis, with Japan and Italy having both low female labor force participation and low divorce rates and Scandinavian countries like Sweden having high rates of both. Similar results can be obtained if we plot female labor force participation against illegitimacy.

FIGURE 5.1

Divorce versus Female Labor Force Participation, 1994

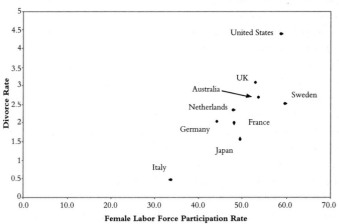

Source: International Labor Organization, Bureau of Statistics, *The Economically Active Population, 1950–2010* (Geneva, 1996); divorce statistics: see Appendix.

A more subtle consequence of women entering the labor force was to weaken further the norm of male responsibility and reinforce the trend created by ready access to birth control. In divorcing a dependent wife, the husband would have to face the prospect of either paying alimony or seeing his children slip into poverty. With wives now making incomes rivaling that of those husbands, this obviously became less of an issue. The weakening norm of male responsibility reinforced, in turn, the need for women to arm themselves with job skills so as not to be dependent on increasingly unreliable husbands. With the substantial probability of marriages' ending in divorce, contemporary women would be foolish not to prepare themselves to work.

There are, of course, many ways to characterize the transition from an industrial to an information age economy, but certainly one of the most important concerns the nature of work itself. An information economy, at the margin, substitutes information for material product: instead of building more freeways, a smart transportation system routes drivers through existing highways more efficiently; instead of maintaining large inventories of raw materials, a just-in-time factory coordinates the delivery of just the right amount of inputs at just the right moment. In this kind of world, services constitute an ever larger proportion of the national economy, and traditional manufacturing shrinks. Human capital comes to be rewarded at higher and higher rates. It is not the low-skill clerk at the Wal-Mart scanning items over the bar code reader who draws the big salary, but the programmer who helps design the bar code reader.

In an era when automation has penetrated every aspect of the work environment, it is easy to forget how physically demanding most work was throughout much of the Industrial Revolution. According to Shoshana Zuboff, who has written perceptively about the transition from an industrial to an information economy, workers were necessarily far more aware of their bodies during the Industrial Revolution. As she explains,

> Coal was excavated by pick and shovel—"tools of the most primitive description, requiring the utmost amount of bodily exertion." Clay-getting required working with a heavy pick. Masses of slime had to be stirred and trampled into the right consistency. Bakeries produced bread almost entirely by manual labor, the hardest operation being that of preparing the

dough, "usually carried on in one dark corner of a cellar, by a man, stripped naked down to the waist, and painfully engaged in extricating his fingers from a gluey mass into which he furiously plunges alternately his clenched fists."[28]

In addition to being heavily physical, low-skill industrial jobs were relatively abundant. In 1914 Henry Ford doubled the prevailing hourly wage rate at his automobile factories by offering five dollars per day because he needed to attract more low-skilled labor; Detroit was flooded with new workers and grew several-fold in size in the first decades of the century. Studies showed that, earlier in the century, going to college did not pay big rewards; not only were the salaries of college graduates not that much higher than those of people holding a high school diploma, but the college graduate lost four years of pay and benefits in the process.[29] Unionization guaranteed steadily rising real wages, making the 1940s and 1950s the heyday of low-skill, blue-collar jobs in the auto, steel, meatpacking, and similar industries.

This world of abundant low-skill, blue-collar work disappeared during the 1970s and 1980s. As a result of international competition, deregulation, and (most important) technological change, many new high-skill jobs were created and many low-skill jobs began to disappear. The returns to education, and consequently the gap between those receiving four or more years of higher education and those with a high school diploma or less, began to widen steadily. Table 5.1 shows the large drops in manufacturing employment that occurred in the countries of the Group of Seven (G-7) between 1970 and 1990, most dramatically in the United States and the United Kingdom.

TABLE 5.1

Manufacturing Employment as a Percentage of Total Employment for the G-7

	United States	United Kingdom	Italy	Germany	Japan	Canada	France
1970	25.9	38.7	27.3	38.6	26	19.7	27.7
1990	17.5	22.5	21.8	32.2	23.6	14.9	21.3

Source: Manuel Castells, *The Rise of the Network Society* (Malden, Mass.: Blackwell, 1996).

Put in its starkest form, an information age economy substitutes mental for physical labor, and in this sort of world women inevitably have a much larger role to play. Between 1960 and 1995, total female labor force participation in the United States rose from 35 to 55 percent; the labor force participation of women in the prime child-bearing years of twenty to thirty-nine increased from 37 to 76 percent. Male labor force participation, on the other hand, declined slightly, from 79 to 71 percent. These changes also took place throughout the industrialized world (see Figure 5.2), particularly in Scandinavia. Japan's female labor force participation rate began the period at higher levels than for most Western countries (presumably due to the shortage of men as a result of the Pacific war), but increased at a much lower rate thereafter.

FIGURE 5.2

Female Labor Force Participation, Ages 20–39, 1950–2000

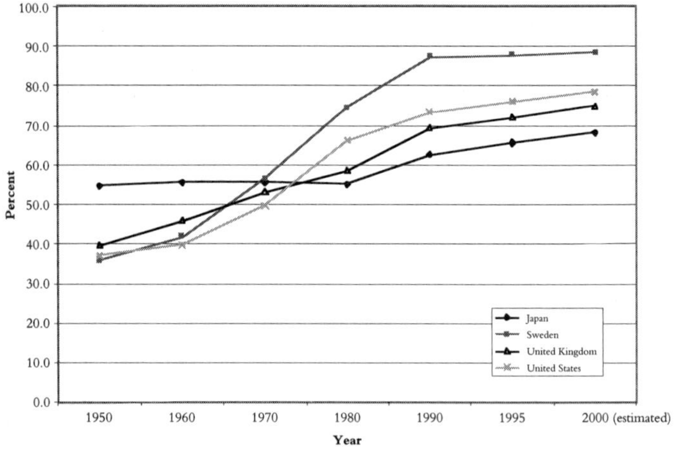

Source: International Labor Organization, Bureau of Statistics, *The Economically Active Population, 1950–2010* (Geneva, 1996).

In addition to more women joining the labor force, female incomes were increasing as well. Figure 5.3 shows male and female median incomes, as well as the ratio of the two, between 1947 and 1995. Women made steady absolute gains throughout this period, although the rate of

FIGURE 5.3

Male-Female Median Incomes, United States, 1947–1995

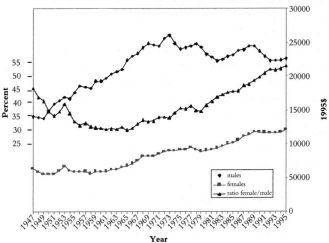

Source: U.S. Bureau of the Census web site [http://www.census.gov:80/hhes/income/histinc/p02.htm].

increase tapered off slightly in the 1990s. The economists who study this phenomenon attribute rising female incomes to a number of factors, including increasing accumulated work experience, better remuneration for that experience, higher levels of education, and the different types of careers being chosen by women (choosing to be, say, lawyers rather than schoolteachers).[30] The most important of these is probably the first. Instead of taking off several years to raise children, thereby losing seniority, experience, and access to the most demanding jobs, women were having fewer children and working at the same time they were raising the ones they had. Instead of being shunted into traditionally female occupations of typist or clerk, they could compete directly with men on an upward career track.

The period from the end of World War II to the early 1970s had been a good one for American men generally, with real incomes peaking in 1973. Indeed, relative gains were such that in the early baby boom years in the late 1940s and 1950s, the ratio of female-to-male incomes shifted in favor of men. After 1973, however, the position of men began to slip, such that by the mid-1990s, their real median incomes had fallen by over 13 percent.[31]

The reasons for this decline, as well as for the fall in male labor force participation, are complex. Lower labor force participation rates were in part due to the fact that more men were living long enough to retire, and therefore voluntarily leaving the labor force at the end of their careers. But labor economists note another important component to the decline as well: young men, and especially those with poor skills and education, were increasingly detaching themselves from the labor force, even in the presence of jobs.[32] Indeed, for males in this group, the crisis was much more severe than the aggregate figures indicate. Growing income inequality hit men more sharply than it did women; although men at the top of the income distribution made off like bandits, those at the bottom saw their real incomes fall at what was often an astonishing rate.[33] Deindustrialization was a largely male phenomenon, given that 41 percent of men remained in blue-collar jobs compared to only 9 percent of women at the end of the 1980s.[34] The setbacks for men have indeed been directly related to the gains for women. Particularly at the low end of the job market, the new women entrants were smarter, tougher, and more ambitious, and they outcompeted men for employment.[35] Although few human resource managers will say this out loud, in situations where a man and a woman with identical formal qualifications are competing for the same low-skill but nonphysical job, they will probably prefer the woman because they know she will present fewer behavioral problems than the man.

The effect of this shift on working-class marriages was clear. Contrary to popular perceptions, the women making strong employment and income gains in the 1970s and 1980s were not highly paid newscasters or lawyers, but relatively low-skill women in the bottom half of the income distribution.[36] The relative value of a blue-collar husband suddenly fell through the floor. In sharp contrast to the situation a generation earlier, many working-class women suddenly found themselves bringing home larger paychecks than their husbands or boyfriends were. The situation was probably also made worse for low-skill men by the fact that women are more likely to marry upward in the social hierarchy than are men, leaving the latter fewer suitable partners. The relative importance of manufacturing may explain some of the variance in relative rates of family disruption; the United States and Britain were hit with deindustrialization much harder than Germany and Japan were, and suffered steeper increases in divorce and illegitimacy.

The crisis was particularly severe for young black men. Traditionally youth unemployment has tended to go up and down with economic cycles; after the economic turmoil of the 1970s, however, black male youth unemployment rates went up and failed to come down as rapidly as one would expect when jobs became more plentiful in the 1980s. Figure 5.4 shows unemployment rates for black and white teenagers. For most of the 1970s, black male unemployment was lower than black female unemployment; by the 1990s, it was substantially higher.

FIGURE 5.4

U.S. Unemployment Rates by Race and Sex,
Ages Sixteen Through Nineteen, 1972–1996

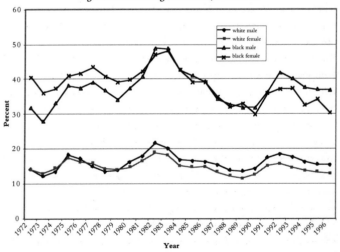

Source: U.S. Department of Labor, Bureau of Labor Statistics web site. [http://www.bls.gov/webapps/legacy/cpsatab2.htm].

The reverse side of the coin of black male joblessness and stagnating incomes has been the remarkable gains made by black women. By the late 1990s, black women had largely caught up with their white counterparts in terms of incomes, level of education, life expectancies, and the like even as the gap between black and white men widened. Why this should be the case—whether it was the result of racism, structural flaws in the economy, or cultural problems unique to African American males—is one of the great mysteries of this period.[37] (This problem exists for white male teenagers as well, though in a less severe form.) There is evidence that black women's high rate of attachment to the labor force cannot be explained except by cultural factors.[38]

As the work of Herbert Gutman has shown, while blacks have had higher rates of family instability than whites, family breakdown at these levels is historically unprecedented.[39] Analysts like sociologist William Julius Wilson have stressed the high rates of black male youth unemployment as an explanation for the breakdown of inner-city families, and as the earlier data on unemployment rates suggest, there is a great deal to this.[40] However, although family instability is particularly concentrated among poor African Americans, it has also affected middle-class black families. For middle-class blacks, the ratio of female-to-male incomes may be more important than relative rates of unemployment. Figure 5.5 compares changes in the female-male median income ratio for United States blacks compared to all U.S. workers from 1951 to 1995. The black ratio shifts much more rapidly in favor of black women than does the ratio for all races. In the immediate postwar period, the ratios are roughly the same for blacks as for all Americans; by the end of the period, black women gained on black men by 15 percentage points more than the population as a whole. When this shift in relative earnings for people with jobs is combined with the rise in black male unemployment relative to that of females, it is clear that black men as a group have lost a tremendous amount of ground in the past generation.

In accordance with an economic theory of the family, the ratio of female-to-male earnings portrayed in Figure 5.3 largely tracks the fortunes of the American family. In the late 1940s and 1950s—the period of the baby boom, rising fertility, and the return to domesticity after

FIGURE 5.5

Female-Male Median Income ratios, 1951–1995 (percent)

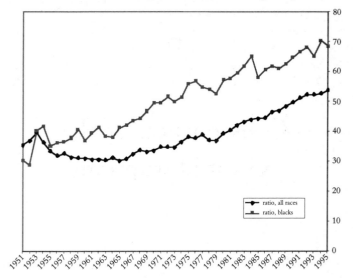

Source: U.S. Bureau of the Census web site [http://www.census.gov:80/hhes/income/histinc/p02.htm].

wartime disruption—the ratio shifted in favor of men. Beginning in the mid-1960s, however, the ratio started moving in favor of women and has continued in that more or less continuous rise until the mid-1990s, when it began to come down slightly, for reasons that puzzle most observers.[41] The mid-1960s, as we have seen, is a good starting date for the beginning of the Great Disruption.

6

Consequences of the
Great Disruption

I began this book with the assumption that crime, family breakdown, and diminished trust were negative measures of social capital. It remains to elucidate more precisely how the shift in norms detailed in previous chapters has affected the ability of people to associate for cooperative ends, and their levels of trust.

Consequences of Falling Fertility for Social Relatedness

Falling fertility rates have been discussed primarily in the context of the social security liability that will be incurred as members of earlier birth cohorts retire and have to be supported by ever-dwindling numbers of younger workers.[1] Important as that issue is, what is more central to this book's concerns is the impact of falling fertility on family life and on social capital. These consequences are both difficult to predict and potentially contradictory. In one obvious way, falling birthrates should increase the overall level of social order, since social disorder is typically the product of hotheaded young men, who will constitute increasingly small proportions of the population. Within a couple of generations, half the population of Europe and Japan will be older than age fifty. The over-fifty age group has never been known for revolutionary passion or its propensity to commit crime. Economically as well, there is no obvious cost to depopulation: while absolute GDP may start shrinking, per capita income could well rise substantially. With smaller populations and shrinking national incomes, these countries will project less power and influence on the international scene, but it is not clear that their elderly populations will have great international ambitions for empire and conquest in any case.

The increasing longevity that is one source of the demographic situation in which advanced countries find themselves should increase social capital in other ways as well. A number of years ago, the French sociologist Jean Fourastié argued that increases in life expectancies vastly increased the number of people living to ages when they could acquire educations and lead peak creative lives, which he said occurred in one's forties and fifties.[2] With modern societies no longer being forced to ration high-quality education, a far larger portion of the population that survived into older years would see its "tertiary life"—that is, life as a fully educated adult—flourishing. Social capital is formed through education in a variety of ways, as students are trained not just to acquire skills and knowledge, but are socialized to the standards of trades and professions. Hence, aging populations are better socialized not only because they lack juvenile hormones, but because they have been better shaped by their societies.

On the other hand, falling fertility poses some difficult problems for social cohesion by further weakening kinship as a source of social capital. One additional reason for rising divorce rates during the Great Disruption is greater longevity. Marriage contracts today must last much longer than previously. Today it is not uncommon for unhappy couples to wait to divorce until after their children are grown and have left the house. In the nineteenth century, most couples would not live so long, being more likely to be separated by the death of one or the other spouse by the time their children had reached adulthood.

Families have become smaller, and will continue to do so into the foreseeable future. In a couple of generations, most Europeans and Japanese may be related only to their ancestors. For the first time in human history, it may become common for families to have three generations of adults alive simultaneously. According to the calculations of demographer Nicholas Eberstadt, by projecting current fertility patterns forward two generations, three-fifths of Italy's children will have no siblings, cousins, aunts, or uncles; only 5 percent of all children will have both siblings and cousins.[3] For a culture like that of Italy, which has prized family relationships so deeply, life will be very different. The number of people living alone has vastly increased, abetted by the fact that women tend to live significantly longer than men at later ages (see Table 6.1). Scandinavia, which has seen the nuclear family deteriorate the furthest, appears loneliest, with almost half of all households composed of single individuals. (In Oslo, the number of people living alone rises to some 75 percent of all households.[4]) Some countries may be tempted to make up for the shortfall in native-born population by encouraging higher levels of immigration. While the United States and Canada have grown adept at handling an influx of culturally different foreigners, their presence is much more likely to provoke social instability and backlash in Europe and Japan. There may be new forms of conflict among the native born as well—for example, intergenerational fights if and when cohorts of older people refuse to give way to younger ones.

TABLE 6.1

Persons Living Alone as a Percentage of All Households

Country	Households	Year
Austria	29.2	1993
Denmark	50.3	1997
Ireland	21.5	1996
Netherlands	31.8	1996
Norway	45.6	1997
Switzerland	32.4	1990
United Kingdom	12.0	1995
United States	25.1	1997

Source: Various national statistical agencies; see Appendix.

What other consequences will emerge for societies that in effect refuse to reproduce themselves, we can scarcely imagine.

Consequences of Family Disruption

The decline of nuclear families in the West had strongly negative effects on social capital and was related to an increase in poverty for people at the bottom of the social hierarchy, to increasing levels of crime, and finally to declining trust.

One of the most important consequences of the decline in social capital in families is a decrease in the human capital of subsequent generations. The 1966 Coleman Report, commissioned by the U.S. Department of Health, Education and Welfare, was a massive study that sought to identify the sources of educational performance. It found that family and peers have a much greater impact on educational outcomes than the inputs over which public policy has control, like teacher salaries, classroom sizes, and spending on facilities.[5] Since that time, the Coleman Report's findings have been supported by a great deal of subsequent research. Much of the disastrous decline in test scores that occurred in the United States over the period of the Great Disruption can be laid at the door of families that were disrupted, distracted, impoverished, or in other ways less able to pass on skills and knowledge. Conversely, the strong performance of many Asian American children reflects the relatively more intact family structure and family-based cultural traditions of this community.

The effects of divorce, out-of-wedlock birth, and single-parent families on the welfare of children growing up in such households—on the human and social capital passed on from one generation to another—have been researched and argued to death since the publication of the Moynihan report in 1965.[6] This report, written while Daniel Patrick Moynihan was a Labor Department official in the Johnson administration, argued that family structure was a critical intermediate variable explaining poverty among American blacks. The report engendered tremendous controversy as opponents argued that Moynihan was either "blaming the victim" or imposing white, middle-class family values on a

115

minority whose family structure was different but not necessarily inferior.[7]

There is probably little that can be added to this debate at this point, except to say that nearly thirty-five years later, Moynihan has been vindicated. I believe that any fair reading of this literature leads to the conclusion that, all other things being equal, it is much better to grow up in a traditional two-parent family than in a single- or no-parent one. The reason that some people persist in arguing that family structure does not make much difference to the welfare of children is that disrupted or single-parent families are highly correlated with a host of other social ills, beginning with poverty and including bad schools, dangerous neighborhoods, and drugs. It is very difficult for even the most sophisticated statistical analysis to disentangle the chains of causality linking these phenomena, and it is possible to show that if one controls for socioeconomic status—the social scientist's term for the parent's income and education—the impact of divorce and single-parent families on child welfare is not all that great.[8]

Money, in other words, can mitigate much of the human and social capital deficit caused by family disruption. I suspect that many readers of this book personally know children who are the product of divorce or other unhappy domestic situations, but who after some personal turmoil have ended up "just fine" and matured into healthy adults. Many great individuals in history have been raised by nannies or mistresses or have otherwise been the products of bizarre and seemingly unhealthy households. But with enough tutors, good schools, and the right sorts of friends, these domestic situations often prove a shallow encumbrance and may even help to shape character in positive ways later on.

There are three problems with this point of view. First, not everyone has money. Family breakdown for the poor can be mitigated only through intervention by a welfare state that in effect takes the place of the father. This unfairly shifts the burden from the missing father to taxpayers. Although the state can alleviate the problem of poor single-parent families to some extent, doing so is expensive and also creates moral hazard by encouraging the very behavior it was intended to ameliorate. Charles Murray may exaggerate the effects of welfare on family breakdown, but it has certainly contributed to the problem.

The second problem is that family breakdown is in itself a cause of poverty. Any number of studies have demonstrated what we would assume from common sense: households with only one parent lose economies of scale, drawing on only half as much of the income, labor, and social capital of those with two, and cease to benefit from the division of labor between two parents. Empirical studies have confirmed that following divorce, households with children experience substantial drops in income, regardless of the parents' predivorce socioeconomic status.[9] This almost always works to the detriment of women: for nonpoor families, the mother and children are left with less than 50 percent of total predivorce household income, on average, while the father's income actually rises.[10] Socioeconomic status is thus what social scientists call a dependent, rather than an independent, variable.

The third problem is that statistical studies usually fail to capture important qualitative elements of childhood education and socialization, particularly the role of fathers in raising children. As we have seen, the role of father is socially constructed to a much greater degree than that of mother, and varies across societies and individuals from minimalist provider of sperm and income to nurturing parent who takes the lead in educating and socializing children. At a minimum, fathers present in the household allow mothers to spend more time with their children.[11] But it defies common sense to think that for most children, the only positive role that a father plays is providing a paycheck. Fathers are important role models for their sons: male aggression becomes manly virtue when older men show younger ones the proper ways in which to compete and to dominate. Fathers also shape their daughters' expectations about men in important ways. If the mother's husband, much less her boyfriends, shows her little respect, the daughter is unlikely to have high expectations for her own choice in mates. The belief that fathers have not been living up to their responsibilities has been growing in the United States during the 1990s,[12] and properly so, given the fragility of this role.[13]

Although the breakdown of a family in itself constitutes a loss of social capital, this breakdown may actually lead some family members to greater levels of association with people and groups outside the family, whether friends, support groups, or women's or men's rights organizations. Just as the strong bonds of kinship in familistic societies in China or

Latin America may produce a deficit of trust among strangers, it is possible that the weakening of bonds within contemporary Western families leads to an increase in social ties outside the family.

There are other respects in which changes in the family may have affected civil society. Most survey data tend to show that women who work outside the home participate in a larger number of organizations than women who do not.[14] This should not be surprising: one of the chief complaints of stay-at-home women in suburban America in the 1950s was that they were socially isolated—more isolated than women of earlier generations who were filling traditional roles in rural or village communities where men and neighbors were closer at hand. Presumably the nature of the organizations that working women join is rather different. Instead of volunteering in a church or school, women are now joining unions, professional associations, and other kinds of work-related groups. But while work outside the home improves social connectedness, single-parent status injures it for the simple reason that raising children alone consumes a much larger share of time. Again, this is a problem that can be solved to some extent, though not entirely, by money. Even children of wealthy parents need time with their mother and father.

The social capital impact of the changes that have occurred in Western families is complex. It clearly reduces the social capital represented by families themselves, but it has a neutral to possibly positive effect on trust and social connectedness outside the family.

The decline of kinship may lead, however, to an important change in the *quality* of relationships. The saying, "You can choose your friends but not your relatives," indicates that people may not like their relatives all that much, but nonetheless feel specially obligated to them. Consider the nursing home test. Suppose someone you know goes into a nursing home or other institution because he or she has become physically and mentally impaired. The person is no longer sexy, lively, or particularly fun to be with and is not in a position to do anything for you. The person has in effect returned to childlike dependency, but without a child's cuteness. What circle of people would you be willing to visit in that nursing home every weekend, year in and year out, into the indefinite future? Only relatives—a parent, sibling, possibly a spouse—are likely to pass this test. From the hundreds or even thousands of our other friends and acquaintances, we are prone to demand some reciprocal attention in turn, before we lose interest or decide that our time is simply too valuable.

Consider the difference in the situation of an elderly person falling into decrepitude and senescence in Europe or North America sometime in the early twenty-first century, compared with that of an old person three hundred years earlier, at the beginning of the eighteenth century. In the latter case, simply to have survived into one's seventies or eighties was a major accomplishment; half of all children died by the age of fifteen, and only a small minority could expect to last until the ripe old age of fifty-two. Jean Fourastié explained that such a person could legitimately be looked up to as remarkable, since reaching an advanced age represented an uncommon accomplishment. By contrast, people over the age of fifty-two in the early twenty-first century may think of themselves as "survivors," but in fact they will constitute an absolute majority of the society. The older person in the earlier era would likely die at home, surrounded by two, three, or even more generations of descendants, relatives with whom he or she would have passed the greater part of life. That person's life would be structured by rituals large and small, from daily prayers and ceremonies at the family table to the familiar funeral cortege at the end of life.

By contrast, the older person of the early twenty-first century—let us say, an aging baby boomer—twice or thrice divorced, will pass his or her waning years living alone in a house or apartment, visited occasionally by a son or daughter who are themselves past retirement age and seeking ways to deal with their own deteriorating health. The connection with these relatives will be tenuous, because the long and tumultuous personal lives they led when younger—the different marriage and sexual partners, the separated homes and conflicts over division of household goods and child custody—have left their descendants with a sentimental but slightly detached relationship—one that will have to compete with the demands of physical distance and activities more pleasant than family duties. It may be that a grandchild or a former spouse takes a sudden interest in the older person's whereabouts or well-being, but that is a matter of pure accident. Having grown up in the age of computer networks, the older person has a huge circle of friends and contacts both locally and in distant countries, and stays in touch daily with people whose interests intersect in ways important and trivial, from politics and religion to gardening and cooking. But the very thing that made modern communications appealing—its apparent abolition of distance and erosion of cultural and political borders—becomes a progressive disadvantage. Moving into a nursing home, the older person is suddenly surrounded by strangers; those friends and acquaintances reached over the network express sympathy and concern but find it too inconvenient to visit. Life has become completely deritualized. The different transitions from one phase of life to another are not marked by familiar and comforting ceremonies that connect the individual to generations past and those yet to come, but are rather a matter of improvisation. The ability to innovate and remake oneself, which had seemed like such a valuable characteristic in early phases of life, now leads only to incredible loneliness. The end, when it comes, is faced alone.

Cui Bono?

Pointing to the negative consequences for social capital of changes in the family is in no way to blame women for these problems. The entry of women into the workplace, the steady closing of the earnings gap with men, and the greater ability of women to control fertility are by and large good things. The most important shift in norms was the one that dictated male responsibility for wives and children. Even if the shift in the norm was triggered by birth control and rising female incomes, it was men who were to blame for the consequences that followed. And it is not as if men always behaved well prior to that. The stability of traditional families was often bought at a high price in terms of emotional and physical distress, as well as lost opportunities, costs that fell disproportionately on the shoulders of women.

On the other hand, these massive changes in gender roles have not been the unambiguously good thing that some feminists pretend. There have been losses accompanying the gains, and those losses have fallen disproportionately on the shoulders of children. This should not surprise anyone. Given the fact that female roles have traditionally centered around reproduction and children, we should hardly expect that the movement of women out of households and into workplaces would have no consequences for families.

Moreover, women themselves were often the losers in this bargain. The bulk of labor market gains for women in the 1970s and 1980s were not in glamorous *Murphy Brown* types of occupations, but in low-end service sector jobs. In return for the meager financial independence this brought, many women found themselves abandoned by husbands who moved on to younger wives or girlfriends. For reasons that are directly biological (men remain more sexually attractive at later ages than do women), they had much lower chances of ever remarrying than the husbands who left them. The widening of the gap between rich and poor among men had its counterpart among women as well. Educated, ambitious, and talented women broke down barriers, proved they could succeed at male occupations, and saw their incomes rise; but many of their less educated, less ambitious, and less talented sisters saw the floor collapse under them as they tried to raise children by themselves in low-paying, dead-end jobs or, for the poor, on welfare. Our consciousness of this process has been distorted by the fact that the feminists who talk, write, and shape the public debate about gender issues come almost exclusively out of the former category.

By contrast, men have, on balance, come out about even. Although many have lost substantial status and income, others (and sometimes the same individuals) have been quite happily freed of burdensome responsibilities for wives and children. Hugh Hefner did not invent the Playboy lifestyle in the 1950s; casual access to multiple women has been enjoyed by powerful, wealthy, high-status men throughout history and has been one of the chief motives for seeking power, wealth, and high status in the first place. What changed after the 1950s was that many rather ordinary men were allowed to live out fantasy lives of hedonism and serial polygamy formerly reserved only for a tiny group of men at the very top of society. One of the greatest frauds perpetrated during the Great Disruption was the notion that the sexual revolution was gender neutral, benefiting women and men equally, and that it somehow had a kinship with the feminist revolution. In fact, the sexual revolution served the interests of men, and in the end it put a sharp limit on the kinds of gains

121

that women might otherwise have expected from their liberation from traditional roles.

The Consequences of Crime for Social Capital

While high crime rates can reflect an absence of social capital, it is clear that the causality can work the other way around as well. That is, high crime rates can cause otherwise law-abiding and norm-obeying members of a community to become distrustful of others, and therefore less likely to cooperate with them on many different levels. In the words of James Q. Wilson,

> Predatory crime does not merely victimize individuals; it impedes and, in the extreme form, prevents the formation and maintenance of community. By disrupting the delicate nexus of ties, formal and informal, by which we are linked with our neighbors, crime atomizes society and makes of its members mere individual calculators estimating their own advantage, especially their chances for survival amidst their fellows. Common undertakings become difficult or impossible, except for those motivated by a shared desire for protection.[15]

People who are too afraid of crime to venture out of their houses at night are not likely to participate in voluntary organizations like PTAs or the Boy Scouts (the exception being, as Wilson notes, organizations like neighborhood watches). As noted earlier, there is a strong correlation between crime victimization and trust: the increase in crime rates beginning in the 1960s is one of the most important explanations for declining trust. Even when neighborhoods are not physically dangerous (as is the case in the vast majority of American neighborhoods), the perception of rising crime rates, fueled by local television coverage, adds considerably to levels of individual cynicism. In this respect, the media often play a large and unhelpful role.

The way in which perceptions of crime have affected people's abilities to bond together is illustrated by the issue of child abuse. As indicated in Chapter 4, there is evidence that rates of child abuse have increased in the United States, Britain, and perhaps other industrialized countries over the past generation. But public perceptions of the magnitude of this problem in the United States were vastly overblown by a series of sensational cases in the 1980s, including the trial (and eventual acquittal) of the operators of a day care center in Manhattan Beach, California, the Amirault case in Massachusetts, and the Snowden case in Miami. As Dorothy Rabinowitz has carefully reported over the years in the *Wall Street Journal,* many of these cases, including those leading to successful convictions, were driven by overzealous prosecutors and were probably responsible for the jailing of many innocent people.[16] Nonetheless, media coverage of these cases created a popular belief that an epidemic of child abuse was taking place across the land. This belief had wide-ranging effects on how parents taught their children to behave. By the end of the 1980s, the essential message drilled into every preschooler was that he or she should actively distrust all strangers.

The net effect of this perception of an increase in the rate of crimes against children was to make socialization of children a more individualistic matter. In tightly knit traditional communities, the socialization of children is usually a community responsibility. Even in liberal-individualist America, adults other than a child's parents would typically monitor, supervise, reward, and even punish deviant behavior. The authority of adults outside the family has been slipping steadily as America urbanized and neighborhoods became more anonymous. After the child abuse sensationalism of the 1980s, however, a parent seeing a stranger sanctioning his or her child is more likely to call the police against the stranger than to see this as a legitimate exercise of community authority. It has also deterred positive displays of affection. Schoolteachers reportedly avoid hugging children because a number of them have been charged with sexual abuse.[17]

Understanding the relationship between social capital and crime has led to some highly productive innovations in American police practices during the 1980s and 1990s. Beginning in the 1960s and culminating in the late 1980s, there was, in addition to rising levels of serious crime, a huge increase in "social disorder"—small crimes like graffiti writing, vagrancy, and petty vandalism in virtually every American city. This increase was driven by the decriminalization of petty deviance and the deinstitutionalization of the mentally ill. There was a period during the 1980s when virtually every square inch of the surfaces of New York

City's subway trains was covered with graffiti. The apparent inability of public authorities to prevent this from happening gave people a strong sense that their society was out of control.

In an influential 1982 article, George Kelling and James Q. Wilson argued that the police ought to pay attention to social disorder as well as to the usual rapes, murders, and armed robberies that were grabbing headlines.[18] They argued that failure to fix a building with broken windows tended to invite crime, because it broadcast the message that the people who lived in the neighborhood didn't care about its physical appearance, and therefore wouldn't be interested in enforcing other types of norms as well. Kelling and Wilson argued that even if this approach didn't have an impact on levels of serious crime, it made people feel much better about their neighborhoods and hence encouraged community building and higher levels of social capital.

Community policing grew out of such ideas, and by the late 1990s had been introduced into a majority of U.S. communities.[19] Community policing began with efforts to get the police out of their patrol cars and onto sidewalk beats, where they could interact with communities. In its more ambitious forms, the police help organize community volunteers into neighborhood watches and sports leagues and pay attention to a wide variety of minor problems, such as noisy parties or barking dogs. In the 1980s, New York City began to invest serious resources in cleaning the graffiti off its subway cars, shooing vagrants out of the parks in which they had taken up residence, and taking other measures to let people know that rules would be enforced across the board. The earlier trend in policing, exemplified by the Los Angeles Police Department under Chief Daryl Gates, sped police into neighborhoods only after trouble had occurred, and only for the most serious offenses. While this economized on manpower and other police resources, it disconnected the patrol officer from the neighborhood, denying the authorities the kinds of intelligence information that arise out of trust relationships with the local citizens.[20] More traditional police departments were skeptical and even contemptuous of a form of policing that allegedly turned cops into social workers, but by the 1990s the payoffs to community policing were becoming more and more obvious.[21]

It could be, in fact, that changes in criminal law and police practices had a much greater impact on social capital in the United States than we have been suggesting up to now. There were, of course, many legitimate reasons for decriminalizing social disorder, reasons rooted in the American system's respect for the rights and dignity of the individual. The American Civil Liberties Union (ACLU) and other advocates for the disadvantaged argued that laws that criminalized a status like vagrancy were in effect criminalizing poverty. The fact that middle-class people were offended by dirty and ill-smelling vagrants, or that children were frightened by homeless people talking to themselves, was not, according to this view, a sufficiently compelling community interest to warrant their being arrested or moved out of public streets and parks. Subway graffiti, it was argued, was a victimless crime; those who disliked it were simply displaying their own cultural prejudices. Activities falling under the heading of social disorder were felt to be, in effect, small potatoes, not just by advocacy groups and liberal reformers but by hard-bitten police officers trying to stem a rising tide of murder, rape, and drugs.

The long-term impact of social disorder proved much more consequential, however, precisely in terms of urban social capital. George Kelling and Catherine Coles have pointed to numerous surveys showing that one of the most important factors driving middle-class people out of inner cities was not serious crime but disorder—the inability to cross a public park without being accosted by a panhandler, not wanting one's children to have to walk past sex shops and prostitutes, and the like.[22] There were, of course, many other reasons motivating flight to the suburbs, including race and schools. But one of the most significant unintended consequences of relaxing controls over petty deviance was to encourage the departure from many urban neighborhoods of precisely those respectable, middle-class residents with a strong stake in maintaining community standards of behavior. This process went on in African American neighborhoods as well as white ones, particularly after the abolition of formal racial housing segregation in the 1960s. Many American urban centers like Harlem, Boston's Roxbury, and the South Side of Chicago were literally depopulated as the more successful residents moved to the suburbs or to safer neighborhoods.[23] The people who remained were the poorer, less-educated, and more crime-prone members of the community; representing a rising proportion of the population, the community values underlying social capital began rapidly to deteriorate. By a circuitous route, petty social disorder led to more dangerous forms of criminal behavior and the disintegration of communities.

Gated communities of the sort that sprung up like mushrooms in the suburbs during the 1970s and 1980s have been seen by many as vivid symbols of a distrustful, atomized, and isolated America, the America of "Bowling Alone." And so they are. In place of Jane Jacobs's crowded urban sidewalks or the front porches open to the street of small town America, the residents of the gated community pass through a security checkpoint and move directly from their cars to the couch in front of their television sets when they come home at night, not having even to acknowledge their immediate neighbors. But the reason that this kind of community sprang up in the first place was not just a matter of automobiles, cheap gas, and mean-spiritedness on the part of its members. The gated community was trying to recreate within its walls the kind of physical security that once existed within the urban neighborhoods or small towns in which many suburbanites grew up. If public authorities were no longer going to keep panhandlers and graffiti at bay, then residents would do it themselves, walling themselves off in the process from the broader society. Once public safety and social order could be assured, people began in the late 1980s and 1990s to flock back to cities, since cities are, after all, much more interesting places to live. In this respect, community policing and other public policy innovations taking account of social capital may have had a far more important impact in revitalizing New York and other American cities than crime statistics alone would indicate.

7

Was the Great Disruption
Inevitable?

The fact that the American legal system's unwillingness to control
low-level social disorder in the 1970s and 1980s contributed to
the depletion of social capital, and the possibility that the advent
of community policing helped restore it, suggests that public policy can
have a role in either undermining communal values or helping to reinforce them. To what extent was the Great Disruption under society's
control, and to what extent was it the inevitable by-product of larger
economic and technological progress?

When we speak of something being under society's control, we can
mean this in two senses. First, societies seek to shape developments directly through public policies, that is, formal interventions by state authority designed to produce certain desirable social outcomes. Second,
societies can affect social outcomes culturally, through informal rules
and habits that are under no one's formal control. Often the two go together: public policies are designed to support cultural preferences, as
when Catholic legislators seek to ban divorce or abortion. But equally
often they don't; culture constrains public policy or is shaped by the
latter.

Understanding which social outcomes are the result of deeply rooted technological and economic change and which are under greater societal control helps us to avoid two common mistakes. The first is one typically made by the Left: the belief that all social problems can be remedied by public policy. When crime began to rise in the 1960s, the Johnson and Nixon administrations called on social scientists to come up with solutions. Many pointed to root causes like the ones laid out in earlier chapters: the breakdown of the family, poverty, poor education, and the like. This was all well and good. But they then went on to recommend that the federal government seek to address these root causes, an initiative that ultimately resulted in the Johnson administration's War on Poverty.[1] This fantastically ambitious effort did not even begin to scratch the surface of the poverty problem, much less reduce crime rates; it was very expensive, frequently counterproductive, and led to voter backlash. As James Q. Wilson has pointed out, there is a big difference between social science and public policy; the former seeks to understand deep and fundamental causes of social behavior, which almost by definition are not susceptible to manipulation by public policy. It is safe to say that today, thirty years later, public policy has become much less ambitious and more realistic. Initiatives like community policing can do a great deal of good in their own limited spheres, but no one should be fooled into believing that they even begin to touch root causes.

The second mistake is more commonly made by conservatives, which is to believe that undesirable social changes are the result of moral flaccidity, and that they can be corrected with enough hectoring and appeal to the right sorts of values. People are in fact capable of free moral choice, and there has indeed been a great deal of moral flaccidity in the past forty years. But in many cases, people make different moral choices in the context of different economic incentives, and no amount of preaching and cultural argument will be sufficient to shift the overall direction of change more than marginally unless those incentives are changed.

The fact that the Great Disruption occurred in such a wide variety of developed countries with great speed and at roughly the same time in world history points to causes that are broad and fundamental. At the beginning of this book, I suggested that the Great Disruption was an updated version of the transition from gemeinschaft to gesellschaft that occurred during the nineteenth century, only this time taking place as we move from an industrial to an information economy rather than from an agrarian to an industrial one. Chapter 5 argued that changes in technology—the substitution of mental for physical labor, information for material product, services for manufacturing, as well as medical advances that allowed people to live longer and to control reproduction—laid the basis for the enormous shift in sex roles that has taken place in the second half of the twentieth century.

Some years ago, the demographer Kingsley Davis argued that the feminist revolution was made virtually inevitable by the simple fact of increasing human longevity.[2] In the year 1900, the average woman in Europe or America could expect to spend almost no time outside a family: she would move directly from her birth family to the family she set up with her husband at age twenty-two; given female life expectancies of about sixty-five, she would likely die shortly after her last child left home. By 1980, the average woman had 32.5 extra years to live—more than half her adult life—outside her birth family or free from the demands of raising her own children. Even if a woman wanted to devote herself to family and even if the information age had not opened up so many new career possibilities, what was she to do with all of that extra time? Until such time as biotechnology frees women from the necessity of having to give birth, women will necessarily be more heavily involved with families and children than men, which means that female labor force participation may never quite equal that of men, nor will the gender gap in incomes be fully overcome. But the gap will close, and women will be all the more firmly attached to the labor force.

Nonetheless, the fact that certain industrialized countries did not experience many aspects of the Great Disruption, or experienced them to a much lesser degree, suggests that the latter was not the inevitable product of economic and technological change, and that culture and public policy play an important role in shaping norms. The high-income societies in Asia—Japan, Korea, Taiwan, Singapore, and Hong Kong—constitute an interesting contrast to the rest of the developed world because they appear to have avoided many of the effects of the Great Disruption. This fact alone suggests that the Great Disruption was not an inevitable product of a certain stage of socioeconomic modernization, but rather is influenced heavily by culture. But culture may in the end only delay and not avoid the Disruption's onset in Asian societies.

Asian Values and Asian Exceptionalism

The distinctiveness of Asian values was raised in the early 1990s by Singapore's former prime minister, Lee Kuan Yew, to explain Asia's then-striking economic success, as well as to justify his own brand of paternalistic authoritarianism. Lee argued that Asian culture, stressing obedience to group authority, hard work, family, savings, and education, was critical to the rapid and unprecedented postwar economic growth in Asia. These values were said to have a political component in the soft authoritarian regimes that predominated in Southeast Asia and justified the absence of Western-style democracy in Singapore, Malaysia, and Indonesia. But they were also reflected, according to Lee, in lower rates of crime, drug use, poverty, and family breakdown than those characterizing the United States and, increasingly, other Western developed countries.[3] Malaysia's prime minister, Mahathir bin Muhammed, also promoted the idea of the superiority of Asian values.

In the wake of the Asian economic crisis that began in 1997, the Asian values argument has not been repeated with great enthusiasm on either side of the Pacific. Asian values evidently did not prevent countries all over the region from making a series of long- and short-term mistakes in economic policy. The serious economic recession that followed succeeded in cutting as much as 50 percent (in dollar terms) off the national wealth of many Asian countries. Since much of the legitimacy of Asian values was grounded in economic performance, the end of growth was sufficient to undermine the argument as a whole.[4]

It is evident, however, that some Asian values are quite distinctive from Western ones, even if they do not have the clear-cut relationship to economic success that Lee and Mahathir asserted. Granted that Asian societies differ substantially from one another, they still collectively demonstrate a very different pattern of social adjustment to economic modernization. The discussion that follows will focus on the two Asian members of the OECD, Japan and Korea, because data are most complete for them and because their values and social patterns are in many ways similar to one another and dissimilar from their Western counterparts.

Japan and Korea are distinct from the West in a number of areas.[5] In both countries, crime rates are very low relative to Europe and particularly the United States. In Japan, most types of crime have actually decreased over the past forty years (see Chapter 2 and the Appendix). Postwar Korea has always been prone to greater political violence than Japan, and Koreans have sometimes been characterized as the "Irish of the East" for their propensity to fight. Crime rates picked up somewhat in 1982, apparently in connection with the Kwangju uprising and the political repression associated with Chun Du Hwan's rule. But overall, levels of crime in Korea have been remarkably flat. Low crime rates in these two countries ipso facto invalidate any general theory that urbanization and industrialization inevitably encourage higher levels of criminal behavior.

The same is true with regard to the stability of the nuclear family. Divorce rates have increased in both Japan and Korea somewhat over the past forty years, but neither society has experienced the explosion in family breakdown that occurred in most Western countries after 1965. The stability of nuclear families is evident also in both countries' extremely low rates of illegitimacy.

It is not clear what is responsible for the low crime rates in these two countries. Possibly the answers are different in each case. While Japanese society tends to smother deviance in a web of informal communal norms and obligations, the Koreans have been more inclined to use the naked power of the state to keep people in line. Even after Korea's post-1987 democratization, police authority has been strong when necessary to maintain public order.

The reasons for the much greater stability of the nuclear family in both countries are clearer and would seem to be related to the position of women in these societies. Although female labor force participation has been rising steadily in both Japan and Korea, it remains at the low end of the spectrum for OECD countries. More important is the fact that these countries (as well as the less developed ones in Southeast Asia) continue to have M-shaped female labor force participation curves: young women tend to enter the labor force in light manufacturing or service jobs, but

131

by their mid-twenties leave to marry and raise children, reentering only when their children have grown up.

The weaker attachment of women to the labor force in Japan and Korea is paralleled by the relatively low ratio of female-to-male incomes in both societies. The ratio of female-to-male incomes has increased over time for most developed countries; Japan's ratio is notable both for being substantially lower than for any other OECD country and also for increasing only marginally between 1970 and 1995.[6] A great deal of Japanese female employment is temporary, or actually represents a form of underemployment, such as the legions of young women who greet people coming into department stores or elevators.

Labor law in both Japan and Korea continues to treat men and women differently. In the West, this would be called gender discrimination; in Asia, it is more often seen as an effort to protect women. In Japan, the Labor Standards Law of 1947 prohibited women over the age of eighteen from working more than six hours of overtime a week, on holidays, or late at night. Given the notoriously workaholic nature of Japanese employees, this effectively barred women from full participation in most workplaces and from the lifetime employment system. The Equal Employment Opportunity Law of 1986 lifted these restrictions for managers and certain white-collar occupations, a change that had a relatively small effect given the low numbers of Japanese female managers.[7] The legislation to lift these restrictions for blue-collar workers was not finally passed until 1997, to be implemented over the following three years.[8]

Although these kinds of laws may appear discriminatory to Japanese and Western feminists, it is not clear that they were regarded this way by most Japanese women. In poll after poll, majorities of Japanese women have expressed a preference for quitting work when they marry and have children, and returning only after the children have grown up.[9] The fact that their earnings are thereby unlikely to keep up with those of men appears to bother them less than it does Western women. The division of labor by gender thus appears to reflect deeper cultural values and will not be ended simply by changes in labor legislation.

The situation in Korea was similar, if on a later time schedule due to Korea's later industrialization. Korean women increased their labor force participation from 34.4 percent in 1963 to 40.4 percent in 1990, again low by OECD standards. Like Japanese women, Korean women tend to drop out of the labor force while raising children. Korean workers were less well protected in general than Japanese workers under the country's postwar military rulers, and workplace discrimination against women was widespread. It was only a year after the end of military rule, in 1988, that the Equal Employment Act, codifying the principle of equal pay for equal work and the end to other discriminatory labor practices, was put into place.[10] Korean feminists complain that this law is inadequately enforced by the Ministry of Labor. As in Japan, there continues to be a preference on the part of many women not to work while raising children.

Another difference between Japan and Korea, on the one hand, and the United States and other Western developed countries on the other, is that manufacturing remains a larger share of GDP for the two Asian countries. Manufacturing in all developed societies has been primarily a male occupation in the latter half of the twentieth century in Asia as well as in the West,[11] and only in the 1990s has faced the same kind of "hollowing out" that hit the American Rust Belt in the 1970s and 1980s. As Table 5.1 indicated, manufacturing employment dropped in Japan a relatively small amount, from 26.0 to 23.6 percent of the total employment, compared to a much larger drop, from 25.9 to 17.5 percent, for the United States in the period 1970–1990. This may provide further explanation of why the relative earnings of women have not caught up more quickly to those of men. During the 1990s, the Japanese economy has been subject to the same pressures for exporting manufacturing jobs and replacing workers with technology as Western societies. A more rapid shift into services as a result of the recession of the late 1990s combined with falling population will likely lead to greater numbers of women working in the future.

In the account of the reasons for the breakdown of nuclear families in the West, birth control as well as female incomes was cited as a factor that played a large role in changing male norms of responsibility. It is interesting to note that in Japan, the Pill was still not fully approved as of 1999. The primary means of controlling fertility continue to be abortion (something that has been freely available to Japanese women since the early 1950s), condoms, and the rhythm method. Although abortion was much easier to obtain in Japan than in the West, it retains a stigma. (Abortion is disapproved of by both Buddhism and Shinto; Japanese temples do considerable business erecting shrines to the souls of aborted fetuses.)[12] The dissociation of sex from reproduction that took place in the West thus never occurred in Japan to the same extent.

The much greater likelihood that Japanese and Korean women will drop out of the labor force to raise children, their more limited possibilities for earning incomes on their own, and the stronger link between sex and marriage in both societies does a great deal to explain the greater integrity of the Japanese and Korean nuclear families. Women in both societies by and large do not regard themselves, in the derisive phrase of some Western feminists, as "reproductive machines." Part of the reason that children in both societies do so well on international tests has to do with the investments their mothers make in their education. On the other hand, their career opportunities are clearly much more limited than in the West. While Japanese and Korean marriages are much more stable than American ones, it would seem that they are also emotionally more distant.[13]

When we get to Asia outside Japan and Korea, entirely different patterns emerge that would seem to invalidate most universal theories of how economic modernization affects family life. In peninsular Malaya and in much of Indonesia, for example, divorce among Muslim Malays was extremely high in the first half of the twentieth century and actually declined dramatically with modernization, falling below Western rates only in the 1970s.[14] The high preindustrial divorce rate was an artifact of the way Islam was practiced there, with polygamy and relatively easy terms for divorce. Such an increase in marriage stability accompanying economic growth does not have an obvious parallel in twentieth-century Europe.

Whether women in Japan and Korea will continue to work less and earn less than their Western counterparts is questionable. Due to its sharply declining fertility rate, Japan faces a shrinking labor pool; in the late 1990s, for the first time, the Japanese workforce declined in absolute numbers. As we have seen, absent an unanticipated increase in fertility, Japan's total population will begin to decline early in the next century at a rate of well over 1 percent per year. The aging of Japan's population and the declining ratio of working-age to retired persons create a huge future social security liability, which has already constrained Japan's ability to spend its way out of the 1998–1999 recession. One method of mitigating this situation would be to allow more foreign workers into the country, something that Japan has resisted strongly. The other possibility would be to encourage more women to enter the workforce, not just prior to marriage but throughout their working lives. Of these two possibilities, it would appear that Japanese policymakers are much more likely to choose the latter than the former. And if this happens, it seems likely that the stability of the Japanese family will decrease and that the country will experience social problems not unlike those faced by the West.[15]

Kultur Über Alles?

The fact that Japan and Korea have so far resisted the Great Disruption is testimony to the power of culture to shape economic choices. Both countries have shown strong cultural preferences for more traditional female roles, and both have retained discriminatory formal laws that make it less likely for women to enter the workforce. Particularly in Korea, Confucianism gives broad support to the patriarchal family. Culture plays an important role in Europe as well. Italy, Spain, and Portugal are outliers in the rate at which they have experienced change in family structure. (It is interesting to note, however, that Spain and Italy have the lowest fertility rates in Europe, despite having relatively low divorce and illegitimacy rates. One wonders whether these two facts may be related. Although I know of no evidence to support this speculation, it may be the case that Spanish and Italian women, being much less able to assert control through divorce, have sought to do so by having fewer children.) Catholicism has succeeded in keeping the family more intact—at least formally—than in northern Europe.[16] Germany and the Netherlands, with their substantial Catholic populations, generally end up in international comparisons somewhere between Italy and Japan, on the one hand, and the English-speaking countries and Scandinavia, on the other.

Indeed, one could argue that culture and public policy are much more important than may appear on the surface and have rivaled technology in shaping norms of work and family. Women did not automatically move into occupations that are today thought of as traditionally women's work, like clerk or typist, when such positions were created in large numbers in the late nineteenth century. Women and their families first had to convince themselves that it was appropriate to do so. While it is true that men on average have significantly more upper-body strength than women, this does not necessarily bar women from work in many physically demanding occupations. In America during World War II and in the Soviet Union, women were moved by state necessity into heavy manufacturing and agricultural jobs that had traditionally been the province of men, and by all accounts they acquitted themselves well. The questions to be answered are thus: Are deindustrialization and the shift from manufacturing to service sector employment necessarily to the advantage of women, or are they the accidental historical by-products of the fact that men found themselves more heavily represented in blue-collar jobs? Cannot societies protect themselves from the consequences of technological change by, for example, seeking to protect the jobs of male heads of households, as both Japan and many European countries have sought to do?

The untangling of technological and cultural causation is thus very difficult, and the interplay between the two highly complex. Culture seems to play an important role in determining at least the pace of norm change; societies can exercise control over the degree to which changes in technology and labor markets alter social relationships. The countless stratagems by which Japanese health bureaucrats slowed legalization of the birth control pill over thirty years is just one example. While the passing of no-fault divorce laws, first in Scandinavia and then in the English-speaking countries, was not the *cause* of these countries' high divorce rates, the absence of legal divorce slowed family disruption in Catholic countries like Italy and Ireland. Certain states in the United States have passed laws in the 1990s permitting so-called covenant marriages, in which couples can opt for marriage contracts that are harder to break. This innovation will not bring down the divorce rate to 1950s levels, but it may permit couples to place extra constraints on themselves that will help stabilize some marriages.

Reconstituting Social Order

The question remains as to how we can rebuild social capital in the future. The fact that culture and public policy give societies some degree of control over the pace and degree of disruption is not in the long run an answer to how social order will be established at the beginning of the twenty-first century. Japan and some Catholic countries have been able to hold on to more traditional family values longer than Scandinavia or the English-speaking world, which may have saved them some of the social costs the latter experienced. But it is hard to imagine that they will be able to hold out over the coming generations, much less reestablish anything like the nuclear family of the industrial era, where the father worked and the mother stayed at home to raise children. Such an outcome would not be desirable, even if it were possible.

We appear to be caught in an unpleasant circumstance: going forward seems to promise ever-increasing levels of disorder and social atomization, at the same time that our line of retreat has been cut off. Does this mean, then, that contemporary liberal societies are fated to descend into increasing levels of moral decline and social anarchy, until they somehow implode? Were critics of the Enlightenment like Edmund Burke right that this kind of anarchy was the inevitable product of the effort to replace tradition with reason?

The answer, in my view, is no, for the simple reason that we human beings are by nature designed to create moral rules and social order for ourselves. The situation of normlessness—what Durkheim labeled anomie—is intensely uncomfortable for us, and we will seek to create new rules to replace the ones that have been undercut. If technology makes certain old forms of community difficult to sustain, then we will seek out new ones, and we will use our reason to negotiate different arrangements that will suit our underlying interests, needs, and passions.

To understand why our current situation isn't as hopeless as it may seem, we need to study the origins of social order per se, on a more abstract level. Many discussions of culture treat social order as if it were a static set of rules handed down from earlier generations. If you were stuck in a low-social capital or low-trust country, there was nothing you could do about it. It is true, of course, that public policy is relatively limited in its ability to manipulate culture and that the best public policies are ones shaped by an awareness of cultural constraints. But culture is a dynamic force that is constantly being remade, if not by governments, then by the interactions of the thousands of decentralized individuals who make up a society. Although culture tends to evolve less quickly than formal social and political institutions, it nonetheless adapts to changing circumstances.

What we find is that order and social capital have two broad bases of support. The first is biological, and emerges from human nature itself. There have been important recent advances in the life sciences, which have the cumulative effect of reestablishing the classical view that human nature exists and that their nature makes humans social and political creatures with great capabilities for establishing social rules. While this research in a certain sense does not tell us anything that Aristotle didn't know, it allows us to be much more precise about the nature of human sociability, and what is and is not rooted in the human genome.

The second basis of support for social order is human reason, and reason's ability to spontaneously generate solutions to problems of social cooperation. Mankind's natural capabilities for creating social capital do not explain how social capital arises in specific circumstances. The creation of particular rules of behavior is the province of culture rather than nature, and in the cultural realm we find that order is frequently the result of a horizontal process of negotiation, argument, and dialogue among individuals. Order does not need to proceed from the top down, from either a lawgiver (or in contemporary terms, a state) establishing laws or a priest promulgating the word of God.

Neither natural nor spontaneous order is sufficient in itself to produce the totality of rules that constitute social order per se. They need to be supplemented at crucial junctures by hierarchical authority. But if we look back in human history, we will see that decentralized individuals have been creating social capital for themselves continuously and have managed to adapt to technological and economic changes greater than those faced by Western societies in the past two generations. And, as we will see, human beings are creating social capital today in the heart of the most high-tech workplaces and factories.

We need, then, to look at the two broad sources of social order: human nature and the spontaneous process of self-organization.

PART TWO

ON THE GENEALOGY OF MORALS

8

Where Do Norms Come From?

Slugs

Several miles south of my home in suburban Washington, D.C., a curious ritual takes place every weekday morning.[1] Outside the Bob's restaurant at the corner of Bland Street and Old Keene Mill Road in Springfield, Virginia, a line of people forms during the morning rush hour. A car pulls up, and two or three commuters—none of whom is known to the driver—get in to ride north into downtown Washington. In the evening the same ritual unfolds in reverse, with cars full of strangers returning from downtown and dropping their passengers off so that they can pick up their own vehicles and head home.

The people who share rides in this fashion call themselves slugs, and the practice of slugging began in 1973 when the government, reacting to the oil crisis, declared the inside lanes of Interstate 95 leading from the southern suburbs into the District of Columbia HOV-3. HOV stands for "high-occupancy vehicle," and means that during rush hours, each car using the lane must have a minimum of three passengers. I-95 is notorious as the most congested artery in the Washington area. By taking advantage of the HOV restrictions, both drivers and passengers can shave forty minutes off their round-trip commute.

The slugs have established an elaborate set of rules over the years. Neither cars nor passengers may jump the line; passengers have the right to refuse to get into a particular car; smoking and the exchange of money are forbidden; slug etiquette demands that conversations stay away from controversial issues like sex, religion, and politics. The process is remarkably orderly. In the past thirteen years, there have been only two criminal incidents, both occurring on dark winter mornings when few people were waiting. As a result, no one will leave a woman alone on a slug line.

The slugs have, in effect, created social capital. They have agreed on cooperative rules that allow them to get to work a little bit faster. What is interesting about the slug culture is that it wasn't deliberately established by anybody. No government bureaucracy, historical tradition, or charismatic leader initially laid down the rules of where to meet and how to behave; it simply emerged out of the desire of commuters to get to work faster. The government, of course, is responsible in a way for the existence of the slugs. Had it not mandated the HOV-3 lanes, the practice would never have evolved, and it could shut the slugs down in an instant by converting, as some have suggested, the HOV-3 restriction to HOV-2. But the practice of slugging emerged spontaneously in the ecological niche created by the government mandate, a bit of social order created from the bottom up by people pursuing their own private interests in getting to work.

There are further points to be made about the practice of slugging. Although it was not deliberately created by anybody, it could not emerge just anywhere. There are many neighborhoods in the Washington area where this kind of order would be very unlikely. Some neighborhoods are too dangerous for people to wait on the street; in others the residents are too transient or culturally heterogeneous to agree on rules. Slugs are willing to get into the cars of complete strangers—to *trust* them—because, in the words of one participant, "They're government workers. . . . They're harmless."[2]

The Universe of Norms

The slugs may seem very distant from the issues of crime, family break-down, and trust that were discussed in Part One of this book, but they are relevant because through them we can see social capital in the making. Social capital is not, as sometimes portrayed, a rare cultural treasure passed down across the generations—something that, if lost, can never again be regained. Rather, it is created all the time by people going about their daily lives. It was created in traditional societies, and it is generated on a daily basis by individuals and organizations in a modern capitalist society. Indeed, social capital becomes even more important as technology advances, organizations flatten their managerial structures, and networks replace hierarchies as ways of structuring business relations.

Slugging is revealing because it is a small example of how a degree of social order—limited, but effective—can evolve from the ground up. This runs counter to the way that most people think about social order. If asked, they are most likely to say that order comes about because someone imposes it on society. Thomas Hobbes, who stands at the fountainhead of modern political thought, argued that man's natural condition was a war of all against all, and that to avoid this kind of anarchy, the mighty Leviathan of the state was necessary to impose order. It is for this reason that many people don't like the connotations of the phrase *social order*. Particularly to American ears, it sounds vaguely authoritarian and menacing. On the other hand, people tend to become Hobbesians when faced with the prospect of disorder. If they are progressives who are suspicious of the working of "untrammeled markets," they want order imposed by the state in the guise of a regulatory agency; if they are traditionalist conservatives, they frequently want people to obey the dictates of religious authority.

The systematic study of how order, and thus social capital, can emerge in a spontaneous and decentralized fashion is one of the most important intellectual developments of the late twentieth century. Leading the charge have been the economists—not a surprising development, given that the discipline of economics centers around markets, which are themselves prime examples of spontaneous order. It was Friedrich von Hayek who laid out the program of studying what he called "the extended order of human cooperation," that is, the sum total of all of the rules, norms, values, and shared behaviors that allow individuals to work together in a capitalist society.[3] Although Hayek is famous for his antistatist and free market views, he believed strongly in the need for order, and much of the research agenda that he set out involved understanding how order could come about in the absence of centralized, hierarchical institutions like states.

But the notion of spontaneous order is not unique to economics. Scientists since Darwin have concluded that the high degree of order represented by the biological world was not created by God or some other Creator, but rather emerged out of the interaction of simpler units. As Kevin Kelley, executive editor of *Wired* magazine, points out, a swarm of bees exhibits complex behavior, but is not controlled by the queen or any other bee; it is generated instead by individual bees' following relatively simple behavioral rules (e.g., fly toward nectar, avoid running into obstacles, stay close to other bees).[4] The elaborate mounds of various species of African termites, taller than a human being and equipped with their own heating and air-conditioning systems, were not designed by anyone, much less by the neurologically simple creatures that built them. And so on, throughout the natural world, order is created by the blind, irrational process of evolution and natural selection.[5] Computers can simulate complex behavior not by executing detailed, top-down programs that define all aspects of that behavior, but by modeling simple agents that follow simple rules, and watching what emerges as a result. The Santa Fe Institute was created in the 1980s to study just this type of phenomenon—so-called complex adaptive systems.[6]

No one would deny that social order is often created hierarchically. But it is useful to see that order can emerge from a spectrum of sources that extends from hierarchical and centralized types of authority, to the completely decentralized and spontaneous interactions of individuals. Figure 8.1 illustrates this continuum. Hierarchy can take many forms, from the transcendental (e.g., Moses coming down from Mount Sinai with the Ten Commandments) to the mundane (as when a CEO announces a new corporate ethos that will govern customer relations). Spontaneous order has similarly diverse origins, ranging from the blind interaction of natural forces (as in the case of the incest taboo, described

FIGURE 8.1

A Continuum of Norms

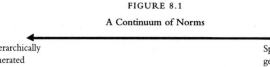

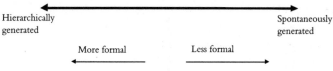

below) to highly structured negotiations among lawyers over underground water rights. By and large, the norms created spontaneously tend to be informal; that is, they are not written down and published, whereas norms and rules created by hierarchical sources of authority tend to take the form of written laws, constitutions, regulations, holy texts, or bureaucratic organization charts. In some cases, the boundary between spontaneous and hierarchical order is blurry. In English-speaking countries like Britain and the United States, for example, common law evolves spontaneously through the interaction of a myriad of judges and advocates, but is also recognized as binding by the formal judicial system.

Besides arraying social norms along a continuum from hierarchically generated to spontaneously generated, we can overlay another continuum of norms that are the product of rational choice, and those that are socially inherited and arational in origin. Combining our two axes produces a four-quadrant matrix of possible types of norms, as illustrated in Figure 8.2. *Rational* as used here refers only to the fact that alternative norms are consciously debated and compared ahead of time. Clearly, rational discussion can lead to bad choices that don't serve the true interests of the people making them, while arational norms can be quite functional, as when religious belief supports social order or economic growth.

In many respects, this distinction between rational and arational corresponds to the disciplinary boundary between sociology and economics. Sociology is, in the end, a discipline devoted to the study of social norms. Sociologists assume that as human beings grow and mature, they are socialized into a whole series of roles and identities—Catholic, worker, deviant, mother, bureaucrat—defined by a series of complex norms and rules. These norms bind communities together and are tightly enforced by them, sharply limiting the kinds of choices people can make about

FIGURE 8.2

The Universe of Norms

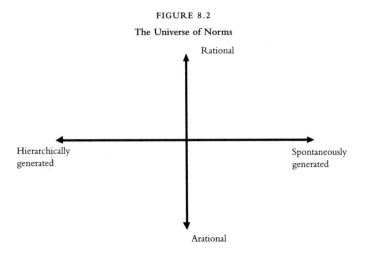

Rational

Hierarchically generated

Spontaneously generated

Arational

their lives. Mothers are expected to love their children; if they drown them in a car, as Susan Smith did in South Carolina in 1994, the community extracts a fearsome punishment through formal law and in terms of moral opprobrium.

Emile Durkheim argued that sociology trumped economics in getting to the most fundamental layer of human motivation. Economists assume that when human beings meet, they will exchange goods in markets. Durkheim argued that market exchange presupposes noneconomic social norms that dictate, for instance, that buyers and sellers will negotiate peacefully rather than, for example, pulling out guns and trying to rob and murder each other.[7] The economist's assumption that raising the piece rate will increase worker output was wrong, according to Max Weber, because utility maximization was itself a historically conditioned social norm. In some traditional societies, a higher piece rate would mean that peasants quit working earlier because they sought to earn only a minimum that allowed them enough to live from day to day.[8]

The sociologist's emphasis on social norms may lead one to think that what distinguishes sociology from economics is that sociology is about constraints, while economics is about freedom of choice. In an often-cited article, Dennis Wrong complained about his fellow sociologists' "oversocialized" view of man: if human beings were all norms and constraints, how is it possible to understand the ways in which individuals strike out on their own and become entrepreneurs, innovators, or deviants?[9] Modern neoclassical economics is, by contrast, based on a model of rational utility-maximizing human behavior in which human choice is placed front and center. Human beings choose to do things, in other words, because they have a rational self-interest in doing so. In some versions of neoclassical thought, economists talk as if human action consisted of a series of sequential rational choices in response to changing environmental conditions, in which internalized social rules of behavior play very little role.

Over the past generation, however, economists have paid increasing attention to the importance of norms and rules in economic life.[10] Ronald Heiner pointed out that rational human beings simply cannot make rational decisions at every point in their day-to-day lives. Were we to do so, our behavior would be both unpredictable and subject to paralysis as we perpetually calculated whether we should tip the waiter, stiff the cab driver of his fare, or put away a different amount of our paycheck every month in our retirement account.[11] In fact, it is rational for people to impose simplifying rules on their own behavior even if these rules do not always yield correct decisions in every circumstance, because decision making is in itself costly and often requires information that is unavailable or faulty. Self-imposed rules like, "Don't buy anything on impulse" or "Don't let him touch you *there* on the first date," may lead to the wrong decision when you run into the prize-of-a-lifetime sweater or boyfriend, but on average and in the long run, people feel their interests are better served by constraining their choices by clear-cut rules. As we will see, there also appears to be a strong biological basis for human rule following: people want to obey rules and want other people to obey rules. They feel guilt when they fail to do so and anger when others do not.

The entire subdiscipline within economics of the "new institutionalism" is built around the observation that rules and norms are critical to rational economic behavior.[12] What the economic historian Douglass North labels an "institution" is a norm or rule, formal or informal, governing human social interaction.[13] He points out that norms are critical for reducing transaction costs. If we did not have norms—for example, requiring mutual respect for property rights—we would have to negotiate ownership rules on a case-by-case basis, a situation that would be conducive to neither market exchange, nor investment, nor economic growth.

Thus economists do not differ from sociologists in stressing the importance of norms. Where they do differ is in their self-perceived ability to give an account of the origins of norms and rules. Sociologists (as well as anthropologists) are, by and large, much better at describing social norms than in explaining why they came to be that way. Many sociological descriptions paint a highly static picture of human society, observing, for example, that lower-class boys in Italian neighborhoods in New York are socialized by "peer group pressure" to join gangs.[14] But this kind of assertion simply begs the question of where those peer group norms came from in the first place. We can trace them back a generation or two into the historical past, but ultimately face an absence of evidence for their more distant origins. There was for a period a school of "functionalist" sociology and anthropology that tried to find rational utilitarian reasons for the most bizarre social rules. The Hindu ban on eating cows was ascribed, for example, to the fact that cows were resources that had to be protected for other uses, like plowing and dairy farming. What could not be explained is why the Muslims in India, who faced the same ecological and economic conditions, ate cows with gusto, or why the ban persists when a McDonald's in New Delhi can import all the beef it wants from Australia or Argentina.[15]

Into the breach have stepped the economists, who are not shy about applying their methodology to ever-wider aspects of social behavior. The large and well-developed branch of economics known as game theory seeks to explain how social norms and rules come about.[16] Economists do not deny that human action is bounded by rules and norms. How human beings get to these norms, however, is for them a rational and therefore explicable process.

To oversimplify a bit, economic game theory starts from the premise that we are all born into the world not as Dennis Wrong's oversocialized communitarians with lots of social ties and obligations to one another, but rather as isolated individuals with bundles of selfish desires or preferences. In many cases, however, we can satisfy those preferences more effectively if we cooperate with other people, and therefore end up negotiating cooperative norms to govern social interactions. People can act altruistically, by this account, but only because they have calculated at some level that altruism is of benefit to themselves (presumably because other people will then behave altruistically as well). The mathematics behind game theory seeks to understand in a formal way the strategies by which people can move from selfish interests to cooperative outcomes.

The economist's game-theoretic understanding of the origins of social norms is essentially a vast elaboration of the views of classical liberals like Hobbes, Locke, and Rousseau on the origins of society. Each of these thinkers characterized the state of nature as one populated by isolated, self-regarding individuals.[17] Civil society for Hobbes came about when these individuals negotiated a social contract among themselves establishing the Leviathan—a state that would promote order and guarantee the rights they possessed but were unable to realize fully in the state of nature. Although Locke's vision of the state of nature is gentler than Hobbes' war of all against all, he, like Hobbes, does not posit any natural social instincts on the part of human beings, outside the family. For Rousseau, the isolation of primitive human beings is even more extreme: while sex is natural, the family is not. Society is created later, by humans interacting in historical time. This "methodological individualism" continues to dominate the thinking of the contemporary heirs of the tradition,[18] including game theorists and economists like Gary Becker and James Buchanan who have tried to push their discipline into the study of noneconomic aspects of social life like politics, race relations, and the family.

If we try to locate various types of norms within our previous four-quadrant matrix, we come up with something like Figure 8.3. The rules concerning slugging, with which this chapter began, belong in the rational, spontaneously generated quadrant. The rules evolved in a decentralized fashion, but presumably after some discussion and trial and error among the participants. Formal law, whether promulgated by dictatorships or democracies,[19] belongs in the rational hierarchical quadrant, as do constitution writing, social engineering, and all other efforts to guide communities from the top. Common law, on the other hand, is generated

FIGURE 8.3

Sources of Order

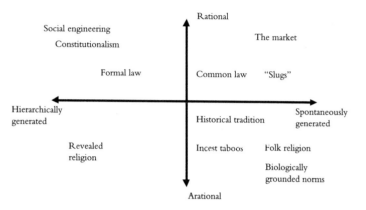

just like the slugs' rules, spontaneously and rationally. Organized revealed religion usually comes from a hierarchical source—indeed, the ultimate hierarchical authority, God—and the rules it dictates are not adopted with rational debate. Some folk religions (for example, Taoism or Shinto in East Asia) and quasi-religious cultural practices may have evolved in a decentralized, arational way. In modern times, folk religion has been replaced by a voluntary, congregational sectarianism that depends less on hierarchical authority than on the collective beliefs of small communities. These forms of religious norms belong, therefore, in the lower left and lower right quadrants, respectively. Finally, certain norms are grounded in biology and belong firmly within the arational, spontaneously generated quadrant. The incest taboo is in this category. The most recent research indicates that human incest taboos, while conventional, draw on natural aversions of human beings to having sex with close relatives. Some version of the incest taboo would likely exist even if there was no overt cultural support for it.

Finally, it is possible to locate the different social sciences in this same matrix (see Figure 8.4). Economics, the study of markets, is primarily concerned with the rules of rational, spontaneous exchange. Political science, the study of the state, focuses on law and formal governmental institutions. Sociology is heavily concerned with religion and other hierarchical, arational norms, while anthropology and increasingly biology deal with norms that are arational and arise in a nonhierarchical manner. Clearly, each of these disciplines has tended to spill out of its home quadrant. There is a sociology of law and of economics, political scientists pay attention to political culture and other arational, nonhierarchical political norms, and economics recently has sought to apply its formidable methodological apparatus of rational choice to virtually all aspects of human behavior.

FIGURE 8.4

The Disciplinary Division of Labor

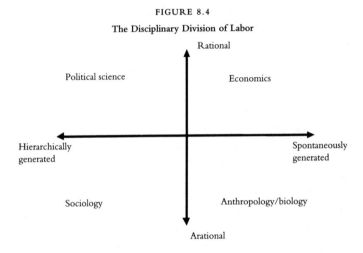

Now that we have identified four broad categories of norms, we can address the question of how they are generated.

9

Human Nature and
Social Order

uriously, the economists, who tend to be on the Right politically, share with the sociologists (who are by and large on the
Left) the belief that norms are socially constructed. The way
they interpret this construction is different, however. For the economists,
it tends to be a matter of rational bargaining among more or less equal individuals, while for the sociologists it is frequently the stronger (whether
defined by social class, gender, race, or some other status category) making up rules by which they can dominate the weaker. But for much of
this century, the social sciences have been dominated by the assumption
that social norms are socially constructed, and that if one wants to explain
some particular social fact one must refer, in Durkheim's words, to "prior
social facts" rather than to biology or genetic inheritance.[1] Social scientists do not deny that human beings have physical bodies shaped by nature rather than nurture. But the so-called standard social science model
asserts that biology governs only the body; the mind, which is the source
of culture, values, and norms, is a completely different realm.[2]

That realm is defined by a set of assumptions about the nature of
human cognition. In a tradition that stretches from the seventeenth-

century English philosopher John Locke to the behavioralist school of John Watson and B. F. Skinner, the mind is a tabula rasa, or blank slate, consisting of the capability to calculate, associate, and remember, but little else. Whatever knowledge, habits, associations, and the like that exist in an adult mind have entered that mind only after birth and are based wholly on experience. The rules by which we constrain our choices have been put there either as a matter of rational choice (the economists) or early childhood socialization (the sociologists and anthropologists).

There is, however, an increasing body of evidence coming out of the life sciences that the standard social science model is inadequate; instead, human beings apparently are born with preexisting cognitive structures and age-specific capabilities for learning that lead them naturally into society. There is, in other words, such a thing as human nature. For the sociologists and anthropologists, the existence of human nature means that cultural relativism needs to be rethought and that it is possible to discern cultural and moral universals that, if used judiciously, might be used to evaluate particular cultural practices. Moreover, human behavior is not nearly as plastic and therefore manipulable as their disciplines have assumed for much of this century. For the economists, human nature implies that the sociologists' view of humans as inherently social beings is more accurate than their own individualistic model. And for those who are neither anthropologists, sociologists, nor economists, an essential humanity confirms a number of commonsense understandings about the way people think and act that have been resolutely denied by earlier generations of social scientists—for example, that men and women are different by nature and that we are political and social creatures with moral instincts. This insight is extremely important to the discussion of social capital, because it means that the latter will tend to be generated by human beings as a matter of instinct.

The Historical Origins of Relativism

To understand the importance of the recovery of a concept of human nature, we need to go back into the history of social thought in the first half of the twentieth century.

Cultural relativism is the belief that cultural rules are arbitrary, socially constructed artifacts of different societies (or groups within societies) and that there are no universal standards of morality and no way by which we can judge the norms and rules of other cultures. Belief in the relativity of values is today imbibed by every schoolchild and has taken deep roots in American society. Cultural relativism can trace its roots ultimately to modern philosophers like Nietzsche and Heidegger and their critique of Western rationalism. As Allan Bloom explained in *The Closing of the American Mind,* the liberal virtue of tolerance was slowly but surely transmuted in this century into the belief that there are in principle no rational grounds on which to make moral or ethical judgments. Instead of being asked to tolerate diversity, we are today enjoined to celebrate it, and this change has wide-ranging implications for the possibility of community in a democratic society.

Relativism became a household word in the United States not just as a result of the influence of the highbrow thinkers cited by Bloom, but also because of the popularization of certain key anthropological concepts. In this, the Columbia University anthropologist Franz Boas and his students Margaret Mead and Ruth Benedict played key roles.

Boas argued that perceived differences between human groups—for example, their level of technology, their artistic and intellectual accomplishments, indeed, even their intelligence—were not genetically determined, but were the product of upbringing and culture. Boas argued, quite rightly, against an earlier social Darwinist tradition in the late nineteenth and early twentieth centuries in which thinkers like Herbert Spencer claimed that existing social stratifications reflected a natural hierarchy of abilities, or where writers like Madison Grant argued that white northern Europeans represented the top rung of a racial evolutionary ladder. Boas's most famous work was a study of the head sizes of immigrant children, which showed that those from the "wrong" parts of Europe and Asia were no less intelligent or capable than northern Europeans if fed an American diet, and that consequently efforts to preserve the purity of the white race through anti-immigration and eugenics measures were deeply misguided. Boas endorsed the standard social science model that there were no significant cognitive or psychological differences between human groups and argued forcefully that attempts by Americans or Europeans to judge the cultural practices of so-called primitive peoples were hopelessly ethnocentric. Ruth Benedict and Margaret Mead did much to popularize these ideas and to apply them directly to Western cultural practices regarding sex, family, and gender roles.

While these developments in academic and popular anthropology prepared the ground intellectually, it was the Nazi genocide that thoroughly discredited the idea that biology could tell us anything relevant about human behavior. The Nazis' belief in racial hierarchy and their cruel misuse of biological arguments to legitimate it created a backlash against any type of argument that saw behavior grounded in genetics rather than culture, a backlash that is still very much evident in Europe today. The discrediting of biological theories was directly linked to the rise of cultural relativism, for if there is no such thing as a stable human nature underlying social behavior, then there can be no universal standards by which any given cultural practice could be judged. Henceforth, all human behavior was understood to be "socially constructed," that is, driven by cultural norms that shaped behavior after birth. The absence of broad patterns of cultural behavior led anthropologists like Clifford Geertz to argue that the discipline of cultural anthropology necessarily had to center around what he called "thick description," the detailed ethnographic explication of an individual cultural system that sought to understand its complexity but without fitting it into a theoretical framework.[3]

The New Biology

The sources for the biological revolution that has been underway in the second half of the twentieth century are multiple. The most startling advances have been made on the level of molecular biology and biochemistry, where discovery of the structure of DNA has led to the emergence of an entire industry devoted to genetic manipulation. In neurophysiology, large advances have been made in understanding the chemical and physiological bases of psychological phenomena, including an emerging view that the brain is not a general-purpose calculating machine, but a highly modular organ with specially adapted capabilities. And finally, on the level of macrobehavior, there has been a tremendous amount of new work done in animal ethology, behavioral genetics, primatology, and evolutionary psychology and anthropology, suggesting that certain behavioral patterns are much more general than previously believed. A generalization like the one made in Chapter 5 that females tend to be more selective than males in their choice of mates proves to be true not only across all known human cultures, but across virtually all known species that reproduce sexually. It would seem to be only a matter of time before the micro- and macro-levels of research are connected. With the mapping of complete gene sequences for rats, fruit flies, nematodes, and eventually human beings, it will be possible to turn on and off individual gene sequences and directly observe their effects on behavior.

In contrast to the thoroughly relativistic assumptions of cultural anthropology, much of the new biology suggests that human cultural variability is not as great as it might seem on the surface. Just as human languages may be infinitely varied but reflect common deep linguistic structures stemming from the linguistic areas of the neocortex, so too may human cultures reflect common social requirements determined not by culture but by biology. No respectable biologist would deny that culture is important and often exercises an influence that can overwhelm natural instincts and drives. Culture itself—the ability to transmit behavioral rules across generations in a nongenetic way—is itself hard-wired into the human brain and constitutes a major source of evolutionary advantage for the human species. But that cultural content rests on top of a natural substructure that limits and channels cultural creativity for populations of individuals. What the new biology suggests to sensible observers is not biological determinism, but rather a more balanced view of the interplay of nature and nurture in the shaping of human behavior.

By and large, the genetically controlled behaviors that influence social phenomena like kinship or the propensity to form groups in civil society are mediated through culture, so that no direct causal connections can be made between, say, the nuclear family and some genetic disposition toward reproduction. In human beings, many of the behaviors that appear to be under biological control are not deterministic drives or instincts, but rather propensities to learn at certain stages in the development of an individual. Again, the example of language is a helpful means of understanding the interplay of genetic and cultural forces. The ability to learn a language appears to be under strict genetic control, appearing at the age of twelve months or so and leading to the astonishing ability of young children to acquire many new words per day. This ability lasts for only a few years; children who have grown up without learning to speak, or adults who try to learn new languages, never develop the same fluency that children have. The structure of language also appears to be present at birth; children expect certain regularities in rules about tenses, plurals, and the like without having to be laboriously taught. On the other hand, the words themselves and much of the syntactical structure of a given language are culturally determined, as well as all of the subtle implications of certain phrases in the context of a particular culture. *That* children will learn certain things at certain times according to a certain structure is set by biology; *what* they learn is the province of culture.

The Incest Taboo

Perhaps one of the best illustrations of how natural instincts can shape social norms in a rather direct way concerns the incest taboo. Incest taboos are virtually universal among human societies. Despite this universality, social scientists for many years believed that the taboo was socially constructed and acted to suppress a deep-seated natural desire. Freud argued in *Totem and Taboo* that the desire to commit incest was one of man's deepest and darkest urges, and therefore needed to be controlled by particularly powerful social norms. It was commonly believed that animals were indifferently promiscuous and routinely committed incest. Incest avoidance, by this interpretation, was the primordial cultural act that began to separate a species like *homo sapiens* that transmitted behavior culturally from animal species whose behavior was governed solely by instinct. The incest taboo, according to Freud, was a uniquely human and artificial contrivance.

As Robin Fox has pointed out in his authoritative account of the incest taboo, Freud's theory of incest was not the only one in play at the time.[4] A young Finnish scholar named Edward Westermarck published a theory that in many ways was diametrically opposed to Freud's. Westermarck argued that animals, including human beings, had a natural aversion to committing incest and that the cultural taboos against incest didn't so much suppress as support natural inclinations. There is no need to recount the Freud-Westermarck debate here, which has been done at length by a number of recent writers.[5] Fox shows that there is a huge amount of contemporary evidence that supports Westermarck over Freud, including several remarkable studies from Israel and Taiwan showing that young children raised as siblings from an early age develop a positive aversion to sexual relations with one another.[6] Theories that early humans as well as animals are promiscuous and incestuous have proved untrue; incest appears to be relatively rare among, for example, mankind's primate relatives. Fox argues that norms concerning incest are universal to all societies and have the ultimate purpose of controlling the access of younger men to females.[7]

Incest norms are formulated and enforced in a wide variety of ways. The Apache Indians regarded it as a heinous crime and imposed draconian punishments on those who violated the taboo. The Trobriand islanders studied by Bronislaw Malinowski, on the other hand, treated it much more leniently, and certain royal families actually encouraged the practice. All societies, however, have to have a mechanism for forcing exogamous relations so that people will leave the bosom of the families in which they grew up and set up a system of social exchange, as Claude Levi-Strauss postulated.[8]

The incest taboo is therefore a good illustration of a norm from the arational, spontaneous quadrant of Figure 8.2. The norm appears to have evolved spontaneously in virtually all human societies on the basis of the natural aversion people have toward incestuous acts and on the need of human groups to regulate sexual access and social exchange. It does not appear to have been created by any hierarchical source of authority; on the other hand, religion and culture have given it strong support and have shaped the particular forms that the ban takes in different societies.[9]

The Fate of *Homo Economicus*

A tremendous amount of cross-fertilization has taken place between biology and economics over the past three decades.[10] However, the fact that biology shares a great deal methodologically with economics has obscured the fact that that the new evolutionary biology's substantive conclusions are more supportive of *homo sociologus* than *homo economicus*. That is, it tends to show that humans are by nature political and social creatures, and not isolated and selfish individuals. But human sociability is not an undifferentiated kind of altruism toward others. Even as humans have special capabilities for cooperation and creating social capital, they do so in ways that protect their interests as individuals.

Both evolutionary biologists and economists accept what is called methodological individualism, that is, they seek to explain behavior of groups in terms of the interests of individuals rather than the other way around.[11] Many thinkers and social observers in the past have assumed that the primary human unit was the group and that nature prepared individuals to sacrifice their own interests for the sake of larger groups. Darwin himself occasionally spoke as if natural selection acted on races or species rather than individuals, and many early social Darwinists applied the idea of natural selection to the competition of nations or races.[12] The last major biological theory of group selection was put forward by British biologist V. C. Wynne-Edwards, who argued that animals sometimes reduce their own reproductive chances for the sake of the survival of the species.[13]

The revolution in evolutionary biology that began in the 1960s occurred when George Williams and William Hamilton attacked Wynne-Edwards's theory of group selection and argued that all instances of altruistic behavior in the animal world had to be explained in terms of the self-interest of the individuals practicing it. Williams argued that groups cannot pass on genes, only individuals can. If an altruistic gene geared toward species survival existed but endangered the reproductive chances of the individual carrying it, it would soon die out.[14] Group interest had to correspond to individual interest over a time period short enough that altruistic individuals had better chances of passing their genes on to their descendants.

The game theory that economists developed to explain the behavior of markets, and particularly evolutionary game theory, proved to be extremely useful to biologists as a means of mathematically modeling how certain altruistic behavioral characteristics could be selected and spread within populations of competing individuals.

Despite methodological borrowing between biology and economics, the substantive findings from biology in many ways undermine many of the behavioral premises of economics. Although individual self-interest may be the ultimate explanation for the development of any altruistic tendencies, certain forms of altruism and social cooperation provide substantial advantages for individuals. Indeed, the capacity to create social capital through elaborate forms of social cooperation is perhaps the chief advantage that the human species possesses and explains why the current global human population of over five billion individuals today so completely dominates the earthly natural environment. Moreover, this process plays itself out over evolutionary time, and its results become genetically coded in later generations of individuals. That is, the people who are the actual products of this evolution have the cooperative tendencies embedded, so to speak, in their brain tissue and therefore do not have to reinvent the wheel in every generation.[15]

Economists frequently express surprise that there is as much cooperation in the world as there is, since game theory suggests that cooperative solutions are often difficult to achieve. They have a hard time explaining why so many people turn out to vote, or donate to charities, or remain loyal to employers, since their models of self-interested behavior suggest that it is irrational to do so. Most non-economists would reply that cooperation occurs readily because people are naturally sociable, and do not need to strategize extensively in order to find ways of working with one another. Evolutionary biology supports the latter claim and provides a much more precise understanding of how this sociability arose and how it manifests itself. It shows how rule making, rule following, and the punishment of those who break community rules (including oneself) have a natural basis, and how the human mind has special cognitive abilities that allow it to distinguish between cooperators and cheaters.

From Great Ape to Human Being

Perhaps the easiest way to demonstrate that cooperative behavior in human beings has a genetic basis and is not simply culturally constructed is by observing not humans but their closest genetic relative, the chimpanzee. Chimpanzees demonstrate social behavior that is often uncannily human. The Dutch primatologist Frans de Waal observed chimp behavior over long periods of time in the world's largest captive chimp colony at the Burger's Zoo in Arnhem, Netherlands. In the 1970s, a struggle worthy of Machiavelli unfolded. The aging alpha male of the colony, Yeroen, was gradually unseated from his position of dominance by a younger male, Luit. Luit could not have done this on the basis of his own physical strength, so he entered into a coalition with Nikkie, a younger male. No sooner was Luit on top, however, than Nikkie turned on him and formed a coalition with the deposed leader to achieve dominance himself. Nikkie was not regarded as a good leader by the other chimps, however; alpha males are expected to, among other things, maintain order within the colony. Luit remained in the background as a threat to his rule, so one day, he was deliberately and brutally murdered by Nikkie and Yeroen.[16]

De Waal and other primatologists point out that chimps do not achieve alpha male status by physically dominating the others. In colonies of twenty to thirty individuals, no single chimp is strong enough to bend the others to his will; rather, he must assemble coalitions and engage in what amounts to politicking in order to beg, wheedle, cajole, bribe, and threaten others into going along with him. Establishing coalitions involves a standard repertoire of gestures and facial expressions. Chimps hold out their hands in an imploring fashion when seeking help, and hoot and point at others against whom the coalition partner's help is being sought. Chimps express goodwill or peaceable intentions by grooming one another; they show their rear ends to rivals in gestures of submission. The alpha male is even required to dispense what amounts to a rough form of justice within the colony, intervening as a third party to break up fights that threaten the stability of the group as a whole.

Like human beings, chimpanzees compete intensely in social hierarchies. Indeed, social order is achieved in a chimp colony primarily through the establishment of a dominance hierarchy. The biological anthropologist Richard Wrangham explains that

> we exaggerate only barely in saying that a male chimpanzee in his prime organizes his whole life around issues of rank. His attempts to achieve and then maintain alpha status are cunning, persistent, energetic, and time-consuming. They affect whom he travels with, whom he grooms, where

163

he glances, how often he scratches, where he goes, and what time he gets up in the morning. (Nervous alpha males get up early, and often wake others with their overeager charging displays.) And all these behaviors come not from a drive to be violent for its own sake, but from a set of emotions that, when people show them, are labeled "pride" or, more negatively, "arrogance."[17]

Chimps evidently feel anger when they are not accorded the respect they feel is due them by virtue of their rank in the hierarchy—in other words, when they are "dissed."

Chimps are very much like human beings in their capacity to organize for group competition and group violence, and in the phenomenon of male bonding. Wrangham describes the way in which the chimps at the Gombe National Park in Tanzania broke up into what could only be described as two rival gangs in the northern and southern parts of the range.[18] Parties of four or five males from the northern group would go out, not simply defending their range but often penetrating deeply into the rival group's territory, and systematically pick off individuals they caught alone or unprepared. The murders were often grisly, and the attackers celebrated with hooting and feverish excitement. Every one of the males and several of the females in the southern group were eventually killed, and the remaining females were forced to join the northern group. A generation earlier, the anthropologist Lionel Tiger had argued that human males have special psychological resources for bonding together, based on their need to hunt cooperatively.[19] Wrangham's research indicates that male bonding has much earlier biological roots and predates the human species.

These instances of social behavior in chimpanzees are significant because humans and chimpanzees are so closely related. Primatologists now think that chimps and human beings are descended from a common, chimp-like ancestor that lived less than five million years ago. Not only are behavioral patterns closer than for all of the thousands of other mammalian species that exist, but on a molecular level, the chimp and human genomes appear closely related. Moreover, although there is evidence that monkeys and apes can develop something like culture—that is, behavior learned and passed on from generation to generation—no one would argue that much in chimp social life is socially constructed. Chimps do not have language, the most important tool for creating and transmitting culture.[20]

It is, of course, both easy and dangerous to draw facile comparisons between animal and human behavior. Human beings are different from chimpanzees precisely because they do have culture and reason, and can modify their genetically controlled behavior in any number of complex ways. On the other hand, findings from primatology give us a certain insight into the debates over the nature of human nature that are at the root of modern political theory and contemporary notions of morality and justice. As noted earlier, philosophers like Hobbes, Locke, and Rousseau who were the sources of modern liberalism, all based their political theories on their view of man in the "state of nature," that is, prior to the changes that took place as a result of man's entry into civil society and the subsequent development of civilization. Although we have no direct empirical knowledge of what man in the state of nature was like, we cannot argue that behavior that existed among man's chimpanzee progenitors was an artifact of human civilization. Unless early humans were very different from the primates who preceded them and the civilized people who followed, we can presume that continuities between chimp and human behavior also existed in the state of nature. And thus it would appear that a number of the postulates put forward by these philosophers were not correct.

Hobbes's most famous assertion, for example, is that the state of nature is characterized by a war of "every one against every one," and that consequently life is "nasty, poor, brutish, and short." It would appear more accurate to say that the state of nature was characterized by a war of "some against some," that is, that from the beginning early humans had rudimentary social organization that permitted cooperative enterprise and domestic peace. This peace was, of course, punctuated by domestic conflict as people competed with one another for dominance within the small group or tribe in which they lived, and by foreign war as they fought other groups or tribes. Based on what we know of hunter-gatherer societies and from the archaeological records of prehistoric ones, it appears that the level of violence was at least as great as in contemporary societies, despite the vast differences in social organization and technology.[21] But there was no dramatic transition from a state of nature and violence to civil society and peace: civil society often served as a means of organizing human groups so that they could conduct external violence in a more organized fashion.

Similarly, Rousseau in the *Second Discourse* argued that man in the state of nature was so isolated and solitary that even the family was not natural. While *amour de soi* ("self-interest") existed naturally, what Rousseau termed *amour propre* ("selfishness") and vanity—the comparing of oneself to others—emerged only with the development of civilization and the invention of private property. Human beings had few other natural feelings for one another, apart from the emotion of pity.

Little of this, again, would seem to be true. Human beings are naturally gregarious; it is isolation rather than sociability that produces pathological symptoms of distress for most people. While a particular form of family may not be natural, kinship is, and has certain common structures across both human and nonhuman species. Not just humans but other primates compare themselves to one another. And from everything we can tell, chimps feel intense emotions of pride when their social status is recognized and feelings of rage and anger when it is not.

It is true, of course, that Hobbes, Locke, and Rousseau did not necessarily intend the "state of nature" to be taken literally as a description of a particular period of human evolution. It was rather a metaphor for human nature stripped of all of its cultural accretions. But even on this level, primatological research is revealing because it shows us that a great deal of social behavior is not learned but is part of the genetic inheritance of both man and his great ape forebears.

The problem common to all of these classical liberal accounts of the state of nature is their assumption of primordial individualism. They all begin, in other words, with the premise that human beings are what legal theorist Mary Ann Glendon calls "lone rights bearers," that is, individuals with no natural inclination for society, and who come together in cooperative enterprises only as a means of achieving their individual ends.[22] This is not the only possible philosophical view of human nature, however. Aristotle begins the *Politics* by asserting that man is a *political* animal by nature, somewhere between a beast and a god.[23] This is based on the commonsense observation that human beings organize themselves everywhere and at all times into political communities, whose character is different in kind from other types of social structure like the family or village, and whose existence is necessary for the complete satisfaction of what humans by nature desire.[24] They are not potential gods, as the Marxist wing of the Enlightenment assumed—that is, "species-beings" capable of unlimited altruism. But they are not beasts either. By nature, they organize themselves into not just families and tribes, but higher-level groups, and are capable of the moral virtues necessary to sustain such communities. To this, contemporary evolutionary biology would wholeheartedly agree.

10

The Origins of Cooperation

I f we grant that the human propensity to cooperate in groups is not simply socially constructed or the product of rational choice, and that cooperation has a natural or genetic basis, the question arises as to how it got there. As noted earlier, contemporary evolutionary biology starts from the same premise as modern economics: it is impossible to explain group behavior except in terms of the interests of the individuals who make it up. How then do we explain the emergence of altruism and social behavior?

In the Beginning, Kinship

The two primary routes by which individual interests lead to social cooperation are kin selection and reciprocity. Kin selection, also referred to as inclusive fitness, was a theory developed by William Hamilton in the 1960s[1] and popularized by Richard Dawkins in his book *The Selfish Gene*.[2] While any theory of social behavior must begin with the selfish interests of individuals, those self-interests lie in passing on their genes to offspring, and not necessarily in the creature's own survival. Hence,

Dawkins argues, it is genes and not individual organisms that are selfish. Hamilton showed that relatives would be altruistic toward one another in strict proportion to the number of genes they shared. Parents and children and full brothers and sisters share half of their genes (unless the siblings are identical twins, in which case they share 100 percent); one would therefore expect twice the altruism between them as between cousins or between aunts and nieces who share only a quarter of their genes.[3] Ground squirrels have been observed to discriminate between littermates and half-sisters in nesting behavior, and similar behavior has been observed in a wide variety of species.[4]

The story of kin selection is much more complicated than this, of course, for relatives sharing only a part of their genetic inheritance will compete as well as cooperate. Robert Trivers has shown that within families, there are varying incentives for parental altruism, not only between mothers and fathers but also for parents as the child ages and is more viable on his or her own.[5] Knowing who is and is not kin is also a nontrivial problem for many species, including human beings. The cuckoo's reproductive success depends on other birds not being able to distinguish the cuckoo's egg and fledgling from their own. Among humans, only the advent of DNA testing could assure men fully of their paternity.

Human sociability thus begins with kinship; altruism exists in proportion to the degree of relatedness. This is the sort of conclusion that you don't, as the saying goes, need a college education to understand. But it is useful nonetheless to remember that even in the strictest rule-of-law society, nepotism and favoritism toward kin continue to be powerful drives. This explains the huge one-way transfers of resources that take place between parents and children, and why the vast majority of new businesses that start up across the world's varied cultures tend to be family businesses, often drawing on the unremunerated labor of kin. It explains why not even the dearest nonrelative will pass the nursing home test, but your mother will. It also explains a number of social outcomes that are not immediately obvious—for example, that only a very small proportion of domestic homicides occur between blood relatives[6] and the fact noted above that child abuse has risen in the United States and other Western countries as a result of the prevalence of stepparents.[7]

Reciprocity

While sociability may begin with kinship, there is also clearly altruistic and cooperative behavior that takes place in the natural world between nonkin. The examples of cooperation among chimps cited at the beginning of the previous chapter, such as male-bonded raiding parties and coalitions to achieve dominance, were largely undertaken between unrelated animals. There are many other cases of this sort, like vampire bats that feed nonrelatives and baboons that protect children in the troop not their own.[8] Indeed, in the case of certain species of cleaner fish and the fish they clean, altruistic bonds exist between different species.[9] Anthropologists know full well that what passes for kinship in many human societies is actually fictive. Members of a Chinese lineage believe that they are related to one another when in fact they share no more than a single ancestor tens of generations in the past.[10] And yet they manage to cooperate with one another as if they shared a large proportion of their genes.

Beyond kin selection, the second commonly recognized natural source of social behavior is reciprocal altruism.[11] Biological theories of reciprocal altruism borrowed heavily from economics and game theory to show how reciprocity could develop on the part of individuals governed by selfish genes, in particular by making use of Robert Axelrod's iterated solution to the prisoner's dilemma.[12]

Game theory poses the problem of cooperation as follows: How do rational but selfish agents manage to arrive at cooperative norms that maximize group welfare, when they are tempted to defect from the cooperative solution and achieve more certain individual payoffs? The classic problem in game theory is called the prisoner's dilemma. Sam and I are prisoners in jail, and we agree on a plan to make a break for it. If we cooperate, we get out. But if I live up to my part of the bargain while Sam snitches on me to the guards, I will be severely punished. Conversely, if Sam lives up to his part of the bargain and I snitch on him, the guards will reward me. If we both snitch, neither of us gets anything. We will both do better if we stick to our original agreement, but the risk of Sam's betraying me is substantial, and I will get a reward if I betray him. Thus, both of us decide to snitch. Despite the mutual advantages of cooperation, the danger of being taken for a sucker prevents it from emerging.

Prisoner's dilemma games are problematic for their players because the solution in which both players cheat constitutes what game theorists call a Nash equilibrium. For you, it is the best available strategy: it minimizes the chances that you will be caught in a so-called sucker's payoff, where the other player walks off with a reward for snitching because you stuck to your agreement. At the same time, it gives you a shot at doing the same to him. But while cheating is a better strategy than cooperating for you as an individual, it leads to a worse result when the actions of both players are taken into account—what economists call a socially sub-optimal outcome. The question, then, is how the individual players can arrive at a cooperative result.

A one-shot prisoner's dilemma game, in which the players meet only once, does not have a cooperative solution short of elaborate strategies for committing themselves in advance to the cooperative outcome. (Pre-commitment doesn't solve a prisoner's dilemma; it only transforms the problem into one of how the players can signal their commitment ahead of time and have it be believed.) By hosting a tournament of strategies, Robert Axelrod showed how a cooperative solution could emerge in an *iterated* (that is, repeated) game in which the same players were forced to interact with one another repeatedly.[13] By playing a simple tit-for-tat strategy in which one player reciprocated cooperation for cooperation and defection for defection, a learning process ensued in which each player eventually recognized that over the long run, the cooperative strategy produced a higher individual return than the defection strategy, and hence was rationally optimal.

The reason that tit-for-tat works as a solution to the prisoner's dilemma can be understood in non-game-theoretic terms. If one faces a decision of trusting another person whom one doesn't know and will never see again, one is likely to be cautious because there are insufficient grounds for trust. Repeated interaction, on the other hand, allows people to build reputations, for either honesty or betrayal.[14] Those in the latter category will be shunned, while those in the former category will gravitate toward working with one another. Since the past is no inevitable predictor of the future, it is always possible that a person who cooperates today will betray me tomorrow. But even an imperfect ability to distinguish cooperators from betrayers confers a substantial advantage on an individual's ability to establish cooperative relationships.

Game theory has moved on considerably since the publication of the results of Axelrod's tournament, and many other strategies have emerged beyond tit-for-tat that prove to be as, if not more, stable over time. But his fundamental insight tells us an enormous amount about how trust and cooperation emerge in different situations, from the men learning to hunt together in hunter-gatherer societies, to modern-day corporations seeking to persuade consumers of the quality of their products. The key is *iteration:* if you know that you have to work with the same group of people over an extended period of time, and if you know that they will remember when you have been honest with them and when you have cheated, then it will be in your own self-interest to act honestly. In such a situation, a norm of reciprocity will emerge spontaneously because reputation becomes an asset. The cave man will not evade his responsibility for flushing the mastodon out of the forest, because he will have to face his angry companions tomorrow; the drug company will pull its defective product from the shelves immediately because it does not want to injure its reputation for product quality.

Axelrod's iterated tit-for-tat is a strategy that is normally played by rational human agents, and if they learn to cooperate on the basis of experience within a group, that norm becomes a cultural artifact. The game can be played out, however, by nonrational agents (i.e., animals) interacting blindly with one another, and the learning can take the form not of culture but of genetic dispositions toward rewarding collaborators and punishing defectors. That is, nonrelatives who exchanged benefits with one another over time would enhance their own reproductive success over those who defected, to the point where reciprocity could became coded into the genes governing social behavior.

Reciprocal altruism would be most likely to develop in species that experience repeated interactions, have relatively long lives, and have the cognitive capabilities to distinguish cooperators from betrayers based on a host of subtle signals. The biologist Robert Trivers argues that precisely such mechanisms for reciprocal altruism developed among human beings:

It seems likely that during our recent evolutionary history (at least the last 5 million years) there has been strong selection on our ancestors to develop a variety of reciprocal interactions. I base this conclusion in part on the strong emotional system that underlies our relationships with friends, colleagues, acquaintances, and so on. Humans routinely help each other in times of danger (for example, accidents, predation, and attacks from other human beings). . . . During the Pleistocene, and probably before, a homonid species would have met the preconditions for the evolution of reciprocal altruism: for example, long lifespan, low dispersal rate, life in small, mutually dependent and stable social groups, and a long period of parental care leading to extensive contacts with close relatives over many years.[15]

The above is, of course, one of those "just-so" stories that sociobiologists are frequently accused of inventing. But one needs to ask why it is that the human emotional system is equipped with feelings like anger, pride, shame, and guilt, all of which come into play in response to people who either are honest and cooperate, or who cheat and break the rules, in prisoner's dilemma–type situations.

The role of hunting as a source of both male and human sociability has been suggested by other evolutionary anthropologists. Big-game hunting in particular provided incentives for sociability. In hunter-gatherer societies, meat is shared beyond the nuclear family much more readily than plant food or insect grubs, for self-evident reasons. Large animals require the cooperative efforts of several men to kill, giving each an equity share in the proceeds. At the same time, the amount of protein thus acquired is more than can be eaten by a single family and cannot be stored, thus placing a premium on sharing.[16] It is notable that in virtually all known human cultures, the act of eating is almost always a public event. While we exercise most bodily functions only in private, we seem to have a natural desire to share food with other people, from power lunches to company picnics to family dinners. The anthropologist Adam Kuper points out that even in the United States, where individualism and competition rule supreme as cultural values, the two most important holidays are Thanksgiving and Christmas, festivals built around large banquets that celebrate not individual achievement but social solidarity.[17] All of this suggests that the environmental conditions of early man supported the development of a propensity for reciprocity that was not simply cultural.

There is a tendency to be sloppy in the use of the terms *reciprocity* or *reciprocal altruism* and to assume that they are the same as *market exchange*. They are not. In market exchange, goods are exchanged simultaneously, and buyers and sellers keep accurate tabs on the rate of exchange. In the case of reciprocal altruism, the exchange is time-shifted; one party can give a benefit without expecting any immediate return and does not expect to be exactly compensated. Reciprocal altruism is much closer to what we understand as moral exchange within a community, and as such is invested with a very different emotional content from market exchange. On the other hand, reciprocal altruism is not the same as altruism *tout court*. Apart from genetic relatives, it is difficult to find many examples of true one-way altruism in nature. As we will see later in a discussion of the difference between market exchange and moral exchange in Part Three, almost all behavior we understand to be moral involves two-way exchange of some sort and ultimately confers mutual benefits on the parties participating in it.

Cooperation for the Sake of Competition

In the polemical debates that occur over individualism versus collectivism or capitalism versus socialism, people tend to cite selectively examples from the natural world to prove that humans are by nature either aggressive, competitive, and hierarchical or, alternatively, cooperative, peaceful, and nurturing. A moment's thought, however, will indicate that these apparently dichotomous characteristics are in fact intimately linked to one another in evolutionary terms. Cooperation and reciprocal altruism emerged initially because they conferred benefits on the individuals who possessed them. The ability to work together in groups—social capital—constituted a competitive advantage for early humans and their ape progenitors, and so those qualities that sustained group cooperation spread. As groups form, competition between them begins, providing an incentive for higher levels of cooperation within the group. The social behavior of the chimps at Gombe is related at least in part to the fact that they need to compete against each other in groups. In the biologist Richard Alexander's words, human beings cooperate to compete.[18]

Students of political development have described a phenomenon labeled "defensive modernization": the appearance of a new military technology in one state forces competing societies not only to acquire the technology, but to acquire the political and economic institutions necessary to produce that technology, like tax and regulatory powers, standardized weights and measures, and educational systems. Something like this happened to Turkey in the early nineteenth century and to Japan forty years later as they faced Western military power.[19] Foreign military competition, in other words, drives domestic political cooperation.

The large size and rapid growth (in evolutionary time) of the human brain is related to a similar series of arms races between human beings, a development that then made possible language, society, the state, religion, and all of the subsequent cooperative social institutions that human beings have devised. Wrangham points to the pygmy chimp, or bonobo, as an evolutionary alternative that shows that human beings did not need to turn out as violent and aggressive as they are. Bonobos are a liberal's dream animal: the males are much less violent than chimpanzees; both males and females compete less in status hierarchies; females play a much more important political role in a bonobo troop; and all indulge constantly in sex, both hetero- and homosexual. The question, which we may never have the evidence to answer, is whether it is just an accident that humans descended from a chimp-like ancestor rather than a bonobo-like one, for it may well have been that the aggression and violence of the chimp-like progenitor of both humans and present-day chimps was what drove intelligence, sociability, and a host of other cooperative characteristics of human nature.

Between Angel and Devil

Evolutionary game theory is useful not just in providing an explanation for how social instincts may have developed in primates and man. It can also tell us something about why human cognitive and emotional traits developed as they did. And ironically, it helps us understand why most game-theoretic accounts of human behavior aren't terribly realistic in their depiction of how people actually behave.

When I say that human beings are social by nature, I do not mean that they are angels. That is, they do not have limitless reservoirs of altruism, they are not completely honest, and they do not have any special drives that incline them to put the good of their species, or even of more limited numbers of nonrelatives, ahead of their own. Evolutionary game theory explains why this is so. Even if we could imagine a society of angels where everyone is totally honest and inclined to cooperate with fellows in common endeavors for either genetic or cultural reasons, such a situation would not be stable. Knowing that everyone else will keep his commitments, an opportunist would potentially make much greater gains than among a group of noncooperators. And all it takes is one spectacularly successful opportunist to turn angels into ordinary, distrustful mortals. This is true on a genetic level and on a cultural level: a gene for opportunism will spread among a population of cooperators, just as opportunistic behavior will spread in a society of honest people. This explains why pyramid schemes have worked particularly well in Utah, where the honesty and trustfulness of the Mormon community has at times been shamefully exploited by crooks of various sorts (often by a fellow Mormon, who knows better than most others the community's vulnerabilities).

On the other hand, a society in which people are all devils seeking to cheat and double-cross their fellow humans at every opportunity would not be stable either. The introduction of a small number of honest cooperators in the society of devils will lead the cooperators to make large gains at the expense of the devils. The devils will not be able to work with one another and will steadily lose ground to the angels, who are cooperative. In the classic example from evolutionary game theory, a mixed population of hawks and doves will not be stable if all the doves are eaten by the hawks; the latter will turn on each other for lack of food.

What evolutionary game theory tells us, then, is that all societies will have mixed populations of angels and devils or, more accurately, they will consist of people who have different proportions of angelic and demonic qualities at the same time. The proportion of angels and devils will depend on the payoffs to each—that is, the rewards that accrue to angels who can cooperate with one another and to the devils who succeed in their opportunism. Given these payoffs, game theory can help predict what the proportion of angels and devils will be and what evolutionarily stable strategies will emerge in the mix.

Given that all human beings live in a mixed world of angels and devils, what psychological traits would be most useful for prospering? Clearly the answer is not that we should all evolve into angels, since this will create vulnerabilities when we confront devils. Rather, what we need are traits that would allow us to solve the multiple prisoner's dilemma problems that we have to face from day to day. We could use, first, special cognitive capabilities that allow us to distinguish angels from devils. And second, we would require special emotions or instincts that ensure that we play tit-for-tat consistently: we need to reward the angels and go out of our way to punish the devils. And this, it would seem, is exactly what happened during the evolution of the human psyche.

The psychologist Nicholas Humphrey and the biologist Richard Alexander separately suggested that one reason the human brain developed as quickly as it did was the need for humans to cooperate, deceive, and decipher each other's behavior.[20] In the five million or so years since the human line broke off from that leading to chimpanzees, the brain has more than tripled its size and expanded to the limits of the mother's birth canal. In evolutionary terms, this change occurred with extraordinary rapidity. People thought for many years that the advantages of the intelligence a large brain made possible were obvious in terms of the requirements of hunting, toolmaking, and the like. But other animals hunt, make and use tools, and indeed create and pass on a kind of elementary culture without nearly as developed cognitive capabilities. Humphrey and Alexander argued that the most important and dangerous part of a human being's environment quickly became other human beings, such that developing cognitive skills for social interaction quickly became the most critical requirement for evolutionary fitness. Once groups of human beings became the main source of competition, an arms race situation developed where there was no real limit to the degree of intelligence required to master social life, since the other social actors were gaining intelligence at an equal rate.[21]

Human beings can rely on a wide range of behavioral indicators to detect whether they are being deceived by another human being, and have specialized neurological mechanisms to help in the process of social cognition.[22] Lying correlates with many physiological characteristics such as changes in the tone of voice, averted eyes, sweaty palms, an increased heartbeat, and nervousness. Much of the highly sophisticated human visual cortex is designed to recognize faces—important if you are trying to keep track of who is a relative or who did you a favor—as well as to interpret facial expressions.[23] To this day, computers do not come close to the human ability to interpret subtle changes in facial expression or body language, which may explain why the Internet has not been able to replace face-to-face meetings in many social circumstances.

Beyond direct observation of other people's behavior, the most important source of information about the trustworthiness of another individual comes from the evaluations of other people who have dealt with him or her—a kind of collective social memory that substitutes for iterated interaction in many social dealings. In effect, it has been the need to gossip—to pass on information about other people in social settings, to evaluate their credibility and ability as mates, business associates, teachers, colleagues-in-arms, and the like—that has driven human intelligence per se. To gossip, you must have language, and this is something that chimps and other primates, for all their social sophistication, do not have. (Imagine how a chimp might communicate the following thought: "He's reliable enough in routine situations, but when the going gets tough, he's likely to bug out and then later claim the credit.")[24]

Language is the medium for lying, but also for the detection of lying. Linguistic ability is uniquely human and physically takes up a huge portion of the neocortex, that is, the part of the brain that developed most recently in evolutionary terms.[25] There are auditory cues that a person is lying, just as there are visual ones. Most important, and cognitively difficult, however, is the evaluative capability that permits one to assimilate knowledge about an interlocutor's past behavior with knowledge about his or her present actions into a judgment about future truthfulness and reliability—making judgments on, for example, the inherent plausibility of the story being told ("I'm offering you this special deal that's much too good to pass up . . ."). Much of this problem solving involves cultural information—for example, Should I avoid that strangely dressed fellow coming up to me on a dark street late at night? But the ability to gather and process such information is natural.

John L. Locke (a neurophysiologist and not the seventeenth-century philosopher) points out that what he labels "intimate talking" is in fact a critical and unique human activity.[26] He argues that people talk not necessarily to communicate specific facts or information, but rather to establish a bond of social relationship with their interlocutor. Small talk in this sense—about the weather, about mutual friends, about personal problems—universally constitutes the bulk of conversations from societies of hunter-gatherers to present-day postindustrial ones, and exists primarily for the purpose of enmeshing people in a web of social relationships and obligation.

Geoffrey Miller has argued that it was specifically the cognitive demands of courtship—being entertaining, witty, as well as deceitful and good at detecting deceit—that drove the development of the neocortex.[27] Males and females are constantly playing games with each other, males seeking to maximize the number of their sexual partners and females seeking the fittest male who can provide for them and their offspring.[28] The male has strong incentives to pretend that he will provide resources and loyalty when he has no intention of doing so, while the female has strong incentives to detect this deception. The female, on the other hand, has a strong incentive to make sure her children are fathered by a male with the best possible genes, regardless of whether he is the one actually providing for her economically, while the male has a strong incentive to avoid being cuckolded and wasting his resources raising someone else's offspring. Indeed, avoidance of this particular form of deception is what has driven a host of social practices—virgin marriages, chastity belts, the purdah, cloistering, clitorectomies, and the differential punishments under many human legal systems of male and female infidelity.[29] The cognitive abilities of a creature that can accurately answer the question in the song, "But will you love me tomorrow?" would have to be substantial.

Brain Modularity

The Lockean view that the mind is a general-purpose computer that is filled with data only after birth has been seriously challenged and replaced by the much different idea that the brain is a series of specialized modules. These modules have been shaped by the specific requirements of the environment faced by early humans in the years that the contemporary brain was being formed, and therefore contains innate knowledge for solving problems posed by that environment. Contrary to Locke and Skinner, infants appear to have some innate empirical knowledge of the world. When shown an image that implies that two objects are occupying the same physical space, for example, they become upset and disoriented because they somehow know that this cannot happen.[30]

The most famous brain modules are the left and right hemispheres of the cortex, which appear to perform partially specialized and partially overlapping functions, functions that can be tested separately by cutting the corpus callosum or nerve bundle that connects the two halves.[31] But there are also specialized modules for speech, vision, music, decision making, and even moral choice.

Some of the most intriguing work concerning brain modules that may be specialized to perform social cooperation tasks is that reported by the psychologists John Tooby and Leda Cosmides concerning the so-called Wason test. The Wason test was devised in the 1960s to see whether subjects could correctly falsify conditional if-then propositions by turning over a series of cards on which were printed several possible answers. In Wason's original test, this kind of logical reasoning proved very difficult for most people when it concerned abstract propositions; only 25 percent of the subjects tested were able to provide correct answers. On the other hand, when Tooby and Cosmides administered the same test using conditional rules that expressed social contracts, the performance of the test subjects improved dramatically. That is, falsifications of propositions of the type, "You can drink beer if you are twenty-one years old" or "You are entitled to receive a benefit if you contribute to the common fund," were much more readily identified by the test subjects than propositions involving familiar situations but with no implied social contract (e.g., "If a person goes to Boston, then he takes the subway").[32] Tooby and Cosmides argue that these results suggest the existence of a special, evolved brain function for solving prisoner's dilemma–type social cooperation problems.

Irrational Choice

While evolutionary game theory explains why a population of devils won't prosper, it doesn't predict that we will become true angels either. What it predicts, rather, is that we will become what Immanuel Kant called "rational devils," that is, devils who are led to moral or altruistic behavior because it is in their self-interest. A true angel, according to Kant, would follow a rule for its own sake, and especially in cases where moral behavior injured one's own self-interest. In Plato's *Republic,* Socrates describes the Ring of Gyges, whose wearer becomes invisible.[33] Is there any reason that we should act justly, he asks, if we could wear the Ring of Gyges and carry out crimes without being caught? Game theory would tell us no: what pays off is a reputation for honesty, not honesty itself. The economist Robert Frank extends the theory a bit further by suggesting that the best way to establish a reputation for honesty is actually to be honest, since people who are being honest only by calculation eventually slip up and undermine their credibility.[34] But in the end, only perceptions count.

Ultimately the most refined game theory will not provide an adequate account of human moral behavior. To be sure, we are good and act altruistically much of the time out of calculation. Certainly no one would argue that the drug company that pulls its defective product off the shelf is doing so out of ethical principle alone. But people have always believed that moral behavior is an end in itself, and they reserve their highest approbation not for rational devils but for true angels. Not just Plato and Kant, but virtually every other serious philosopher has wrestled with the question of whether our moral rules are just instrumental means to other ends, or ends in themselves. Even if we conclude that they are means to ends, the fact that we debate the issue constantly suggests that moral behavior has a special status in the human psyche.

I earlier suggested that evolutionary theory could explain the emergence of reciprocal altruism in human beings and that much of what we understood to be moral behavior involves a time-shifted, two-way exchange of benefits that in the long run improve the fitness of those practicing it. Yet people also insist on purer forms of altruism, even if they achieve it only rarely. Does this reflect, as Kant and Hegel would have argued, the fact that human beings are in fact free moral agents undetermined by biology? Or is there an evolutionary basis for strict rule following, even when it violates the individual's survival interests?

Recent advances in neurophysiology may provide some insight, as well as help to explain why human moral behavior—the making and following of norms—is far more complicated than the game-theoretic rational choice accounts favored by economists suggest. What economists call preferences, and what others refer to as desires, wishes, impulses, and the like, originate in the limbic system, an ancient part of the brain that includes the hippocampus and the amygdala. The limbic system is the seat of the emotions, and the hypothalamus interacts directly with the endocrine system, which in turn secretes hormones regulating body temperature, heartbeat, and the like.[35] Rational choice, on the other hand—the ordering and comparison of available alternatives and the selection of an optimal one—takes place in the neocortex, the most recently evolved part of the brain possessed by mammals, which is the seat of consciousness, language, and the like.

So far, so good. An economist would say that the limbic system offers up preferences, while the neocortex seeks strategies for satisfying them in a game-theoretic rational process. The problem with this view is that the emotions appear to play a much larger role in rational choice than this model suggests, as indicated by the work of Antonio Damasio, a neurophysiologist who has spent his career studying patients with damage to the ventromedial part of the prefrontal cortex.[36] The most famous of these brain-damaged patients was a railway worker named Phineas Gage, who in the 1840s suffered a horrendous accident in which an iron rod an inch and a half thick was blasted from his cheek through the top of his skull. Gage miraculously survived, but his personality changed dramatically after the accident. Where formerly he was a modest, industrious worker, he suddenly became profane and totally insensitive to the effects of his behavior on others. He was unable to hold a job and spent the rest of his life wandering in and out of freak shows, before eventually dying in penury.

Both Phineas Gage and the other patients Damasio studied with damage to the prefrontal cortex share common characteristics.[37] They remained capable of rational choice in the sense of being able to analyze a situation, break it down into alternative courses of action, and compare one to another. But they had no initiative and could not bring themselves to choose among the courses of action they had analyzed. Moreover, they had lost what can only be described as their moral sense: they were unable to empathize with other people and, like Gage, became insensitive to the impact of their actions on other people. Elliott, a patient of Damasio, showed no emotional reaction when shown pictures that were disturbing, disgusting, or erotic; he could talk rationally about what their effects on other people might be, but was himself totally disconnected from them.

Damasio argues that the process of rational choice is pervaded by the emotions, and not just as a source of preferences. Human beings are acutely aware of the impact that their behavior has on others. Driven by the emotions of sympathy and embarrassment, they are constantly adjusting their actions to take account of other people's feelings. This is not a matter of rational calculation: neither Phineas Gage nor Elliott could successfully negotiate the social world surrounding them because they had become, in effect, mere rational optimizers.

Damasio argues that the brain creates numerous somatic markers— feelings of emotional attraction or repulsion that help the brain do its calculating by short-circuiting many of the possible choices that lie before it. When a thought process reaches a somatic marker, it stops calculating and makes a decision. He gives the example of a business owner who is trying to decide whether to do business with the archenemy of his best friend. A purely rational-choice approach to the problem will necessitate an extremely complex calculation of what economists call "expected value" of the business he thinks he will do with the client but also the costs to his friendship. There are also a huge number of possible strategies he can follow, for example, trying to hide the new relationship from his friend or getting the friend's approval in advance. Somatic markers make the decision significantly easier by attaching emotional responses to certain outcomes and foreclosing further rational consideration of the alternative, for example, when the businessman imagines the look on his best friend's face when told about the new client.

In other words, the human mind attaches somatic markers to norms and rules themselves, which at first were nothing more than intermediate by-products of a rational calculation.[38] From that point on, we follow the norm not because it is useful for us to do so, but because following the norm has become an end in itself—one that is heavily invested with emotion. What may once have been a means to an end now takes on an importance greater than the end itself. We are all familiar with people who become obsessed by following simple behavioral rules, such as not ratting on a friend, even when following that rule is costly both to themselves and to the broader society they live in. Shakespeare's *Measure for Measure* revolves around the moral dilemma facing Isabel, who refuses to give up her chastity as a condition for sparing her brother's life. There is no question what the outcome of a purely utilitarian calculation would have been in this case.

The emotions most involved in norm following are the same as those associated with competition for status and recognition: anger, guilt, pride, and shame. People often act against their own material interests out of anger at someone else's injustice in violating a cherished norm or out of guilt at having violated such a norm oneself. We can illustrate the emotionally loaded nature of norms by asking why it is that people follow what Axelrod calls "metanorms." An ordinary norm directly regulates social cooperation ("divide the inheritance equally between brothers"), while a metanorm concerns the correct means of defining, promulgating, and enforcing ordinary norms ("a harmonious society can best be established through consultation of the Confucian classics"; "people should respect the authority of the police").[39] Everyone is interested in enforcing the ordinary norms they have negotiated, because it is in their immediate self-interest to do so. If I don't make sure my brother follows the norm on inheritance, I may get cut out of mine. However, rational people should in theory have little interest in enforcing metanorms. Metanorms are what economists call public goods: it is very difficult for an individual to capture the benefits of their enforcement, so private individuals should have little incentive to do so.

And yet people do go out of their way to see that metanorms are enforced—or, to put it in plainer language, to see that justice is done—all the time, and in situations where they have no direct stake. They display, in other words, what the biologist Robert Trivers calls "moralistic aggression."[40] Witness the crowds of people who demonstrated when O. J. Simpson was acquitted in Los Angeles to protest what they believed was an unjust verdict. Surely they were not there out of any directly self-interested concern that Simpson was going to come after them with a knife if he wasn't sent to jail. In the game-theoretic account of how one solves a prisoner's dilemma, the possibility of cheating is considered as one alternative strategy that may or may not be followed according to how one calculates a range of possible interactive outcomes. In the real world, cheating is never an emotionally or morally neutral choice. Almost every language is full of pejorative terms for defectors, like *traitor, scab, ingrate,* and *turncoat.* While the words are conventional, the emotions associated with them like anger and shame are natural.

People become angry not just at others who violate rules; they can also become angry or disappointed with themselves in an emotion we know as guilt. People frequently feel guilty for things that they are quite capable of rationalizing away: I didn't help that homeless man who asked me for money because he would have wasted it on alcohol or drugs; though I cheated the insurance company by filing a false claim, it's a big firm and won't notice, and in any event it expects people to pad their claims. In game-theoretic terms it makes no sense to worry oneself to death for having violated a norm, which is just the outcome of a rational calculation; and yet norms have such a powerful emotional hold that we call people who calculate their self-interest with absolutely cool rationality psychopaths, not normal human beings.

It would appear that human beings and their primate progenitors have been playing prisoner's dilemma games with one another for hundreds of thousands, if not millions, of years, seeking the cooperation of others and becoming increasingly attuned to the ever-increasing ability of their fellows to engage in deception. Since the enforcement of meta-norms is very useful in solving cooperative problems, we seem to have evolved specialized emotions to drive individuals to, in effect, supply this public good voluntarily.

Robert Frank suggests another reason that the emotions have become so closely associated with norm following in the course of the evolution of the human brain. The emotions serve the function of solving the credible commitment problem in one-shot prisoner's dilemma situations. It is commonly understood that a one-shot prisoner's dilemma game does not have a cooperative solution unless the parties can somehow precommit themselves, which simply transforms the game into one of how to signal credible commitment. Frank argues that the emotions serve to lock individuals into choices that appear to violate their short-term interests, but serve their long-term interests by demonstrating credible commitment.[41] In the "ultimatum bargaining game," the first player is given $100 to split between himself and player 2. If the two players do not agree on the split, neither gets any money at all. A rational strategy for player 1 would be to keep $99 and give player 2 $1, on the grounds that player 2 will still elect to keep the $1 rather than receive nothing at all. It turns out that when this game is played with real human beings, the first player almost always offers something closer to a fifty-fifty split of the money, because he assumes that a ninety-nine-to-one split will be (and indeed usually is) regarded as demeaning by the second player and will therefore be refused. In other words, the pride of the second player in refusing an inequitable split credibly precommits him to a narrower range of cooperative outcomes than would exist in the absence of the emotion of pride, and therefore serves player 2's long-run interests. Frank goes on to note that the emotions control many physiological phenomena like flaring nostrils and heavy breathing that serve as signals to other people about one's credibility.

Not only does the brain contain innate mechanisms to detect defectors and to reason about social contracts; it also has an emotional structure designed to punish defectors even at the expense of immediate interest. Thus, to say that human beings are by nature social animals is *not* to argue that they are inherently peaceful, cooperative, or trustworthy, since they manifestly are often violent, aggressive, and deceitful. Rather, it means that they have special facilities for detecting and dealing with deceivers and cheaters, as well as for gravitating toward cooperators and others who follow moral rules. As a result, they arrive at cooperative norms much more readily than more individualistic assumptions about human nature would predict.

11

Self-Organization

uman biology creates a predisposition to solve collective action problems, but the particular norms and metanorms chosen by a given group of individuals are cultural choice, not a product of nature. Just as human beings are born with the ability to learn and use language, the actual language they acquire depends on the culture in which they grow up. Hence it is necessary to move beyond cognitive and emotional structures that are universal to all human beings, to the actual norms that have been generated and evolved by human societies.

To do so, two separate problems must be addressed: how norms are created in the first place, and how they evolve once they have been created. The four quadrants of Figure 11.1, based on the taxonomy of norms developed in Chapter 8, outline four ways in which norms can be created. They may arise as a result of rational, hierarchical choice, as in the case of the American Constitution; they may come from arational hierarchical sources, as when Moses brought the Ten Commandments down from Mount Sinai; they may be the result of rational, spontaneous negotiation, as in the case of the slugs or common law in the Anglo-Saxon legal tradition; or they may arise spontaneously from arational sources, as

FIGURE 11.1

The Universe of Norms, 2

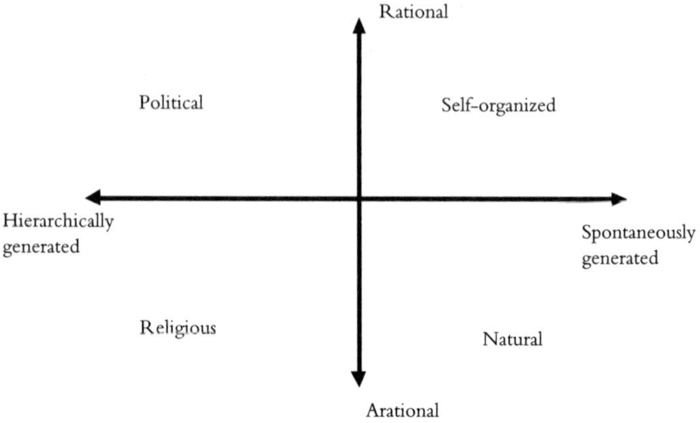

in the case of the incest taboo or folk religion. To oversimplify a bit, we might describe these quadrants as norms that are alternatively political, religious, self-organized, or natural. It would be foolhardy and empirically unsupportable to make generalizations concerning the relative importance of each of the four quadrants to the creation of new norms, other than to say that each of them constitutes a nontrivial category.

It is possible to hypothesize, as many have done, that as societies modernize, norms tend to be created less in the lower than in the upper quadrants, and particularly in the upper left one (by government authority). The terms that classically have been associated with modernization by theorists like Maine, Weber, Durkheim, and Tönnies—*rationalization, bureaucratization, the shift from status to contract,* and *gemeinschaft to gesellschaft*—all suggest that formal, rational legal authority, often vested in the state, becomes the chief source of order in modern societies. Yet as anyone who has tried to wade through the thicket of unwritten rules concerning gender relations in a modern American workplace or school knows, informal norms have not disappeared from modern life and are not likely to do so in the future.

Do formal laws merely codify existing social practices, or do they play a role in shaping morality? Each viewpoint has its advocates. Legal theorist Robert Ellickson labels "legal peripheralists" those who regard formal law as a reflection of informal norms, and those who regard law as critical to shaping norms "legal centralists."[1] The analysis of where norms come from is colored by the strong ideological preferences people have as to where they *ought* to come from. The fondest dream held in common by nineteenth-century anarchists, hippies from the 1960s, anti-government libertarians on the Right, and technolibertarians on the Left is that the state should wither away, to be replaced not by a Hobbesian war of all against all but by peaceful coexistence based on the voluntary adherence to informal social norms. The best type of order, in other words, is spontaneous order. By contrast, there are plenty of people on the Left who regard informal norms as vestiges of an elitist, bourgeois, racist, or sexist past and want to use the formal hierarchical power of the state to remold individuals in their favored image (e.g., "new Soviet man" or the feminized, caring, contemporary male). Their counterparts on the Right call on hierarchical religion to achieve similar ends.

Since people tend to be more aware of norms issuing from hierarchical authority than from Hayek's "extended order of human cooperation," it may be useful to look more closely at the two quadrants on the right side of Figure 11.1 to begin to understand the extent and limits of spontaneous order. *Self-organization* has become a buzzword not only among economists and biologists, but among information technology gurus, management consultants, and business school professors, many of whom have made a living advising organizations to abandon hierarchy and to organize themselves "biologically," that is, through highly decentralized forms of voluntary cooperation.[2] But while self-organization is an important source of social order, it can come into being only under certain distinct conditions and is not a universal formula for achieving co-ordination in human groups.

Natural selection proceeds blindly in the way it produces variance; although the results end up being adaptive, the process itself is often wasteful. Human norm creation can proceed equally blindly. As we have seen, incest taboos appear to have evolved out of an arational, natural aversion to incest. We assume that many folk customs were neither hierarchically mandated nor rationally negotiated, but began simply because some cultural entrepreneur decided, for example, to treat a local rock as a source of luck in the hunt, only to see rock worshipping spread throughout the community. Even in modern economies it is not necessary to assume that organizations innovate rationally; they often vary their technologies or internal organization on a random basis and hope for the best. Competition in the long run automatically weeds out the inferior alternatives.[3]

Human norm creation, however, is often a good deal more complex and purposive than random genetic mutation. Although norms can perhaps be created on a quasi-random basis, they are more often the products of explicit negotiation and bargaining. The greatest number of theoretical and empirical studies of spontaneous order have come, over the past generation, out of economics and related fields like Law and Economics and Public Choice. Many early studies in this genre had to do with the origin of norms regarding property rights.[4] So-called common pool resources that are shared within communities—resources like meadows, fisheries, forests, underground water, the air we breathe—constitute especially difficult problems of cooperation because they are subject to what Garrett Hardin referred to as the "tragedy of the commons."[5] Such common resources are public goods that can be enjoyed among a group of people regardless of the individual effort put in to create or maintain them, or else subject to positive and negative externalities (an individual who restocks a trout stream benefits not just himself but anyone else who fishes there; conversely, he can pollute the stream and impose a social cost on the rest of the community).

The tragedy of the commons is actually nothing other than an enlarged, multiple-player prisoner's dilemma game, where each participant has a choice between contributing to the upkeep of the common resource (cooperating) or free-riding on them (cheating). Unlike a two-sided prisoner's dilemma, the free-rider problem cannot be as readily solved through simple iteration, particularly when the size of the group of cooperating people grows large. In larger groups, free riding becomes much more difficult to detect. The free-rider problem has been the subject of an extraordinary amount of attention by economists and other social scientists over the past generation as a key to solving the broader problem of the origins of human cooperation.[6]

Hardin argued that the tragedy of the commons led to social disaster as seas were overfished and meadows overgrazed. The problem of sharing common resources could be solved, according to him, only through hierarchical authority, presumably by a coercive state or even a supranational regulatory body.[7] The example he gave was overpopulation, where parents' interest in having children is collectively depleting the planet's resources and needs to be restricted through strong population control measures. The economist Mancur Olson argues in his classic treatment of the subject that the problem of the provision of public goods can be solved either through Hardin's hierarchical methods (a coercive state that, for example, forces people to pay income taxes) or by a single user of the public good much larger than all the others who is willing to provide it unilaterally and tolerate free riding because the good is necessary.[8]

In contrast to this hierarchical approach to norm generation, a number of economists suggested more spontaneous approaches. One simple solution is to turn common-pool resources into private property. Economist Howard Demsetz argued that by "internalizing the externalities," that is, by converting public property to private property, individual owners would then have an incentive to protect it.[9] This, he argued, was the actual historical pattern among the Indians of the Labrador peninsula at the beginning of the eighteenth century. Douglass North and Robert Thomas extended this argument to explain the emergence of property rights in Europe over an extended period, from A.D. 1000 to 1800.[10] The problem with this approach is that many common-pool resources, public goods, or externalities cannot readily be converted into private property, because they move around (like air and fish) or are not readily divisible (like aircraft carriers and nuclear weapons).

The fountainhead of the entire Law and Economics field was University of Chicago economist Ronald Coase's often-cited article, "The Problem of Social Cost," in which he argues that when transaction costs are zero, a change in the formal rules of liability will have no effect on the allocation of resources.[11] Put differently, if negotiations between private parties were costless, it should not be necessary for governments to intervene to regulate polluters or other producers of negative externalities, because the parties negatively affected will have a rational incentive to organize and buy off the miscreant. The example Coase used to illustrate this point was the conflict between ranchers and farmers over range cattle that wandered onto farmers' fields and caused damage. The state could intervene to make the ranchers legally liable for the damage that their cattle caused, but Coase pointed out that the farmers would have an incentive simply to pay off the ranchers to have them prevent their cattle from doing damage. Social regulatory norms, in other words, will arise out of self-interested interactions of individual agents and do not have to be mandated through law or formal institutions.

The problem of applying the Coase theorem to real-world situations is that transaction costs are almost never zero. It is usually costly for private individuals to work out fair agreements with one another, particularly when one is substantially richer or more powerful than the other. On the other hand, transaction costs have been low enough in many cases that economists have been able to identify quite a number of intriguing cases of self-organization, whereby social norms have been created through a bottom-up process. Robert Sugden describes rules for the sharing of driftwood on English beaches, where first come is first served—but only if they take a moderate amount.[12] Robert Ellickson gives numerous examples of spontaneous economic rules. Nineteenth-century American whalers, for example, often faced potential conflicts when a whale harpooned by one ship would break free and be captured and sold by another ship that hadn't invested time and effort hunting it. Whalers developed an extensive set of informal rules to regulate such situations and divide the catch equitably.[13] Ellickson's own detailed field research shows that ranchers and farmers in Shasta County, California, have in fact established a series of informal norms to protect their respective interests, just as Coase predicted they would.[14]

Much of the spontaneous order literature tends to be anecdotal and does not give a good sense of how often new norms are actually created in a decentralized manner. One exception is the work of political scientist Elinor Ostrom, who has collected well over five thousand case studies of common-pool resources, a sufficient number to allow her to begin making empirically grounded generalizations about the phenomenon.[15] Her broad conclusion is that human communities in a variety of times and places have found solutions to the tragedy of the commons much more often than is commonly predicted. Many of these solutions involve neither the privatization of common resources (the solution favored by many economists) nor regulation by the state (the solution often favored by noneconomists). Rather, communities have been able to devise informal and sometimes formal rules rationally for sharing common resources in a way that is both equitable and does not lead to their premature depletion or exhaustion. These solutions are facilitated by the same condition that makes a two-sided prisoner's dilemma soluble: iteration. That is, if people know that they have to continue to live with one another in bounded communities where continued cooperation will be rewarded, they develop an interest in their own reputations, as well as in the monitoring and punishment of those who violate community rules.

Many of Ostrom's examples of rules regarding the sharing of common-pool resources involve traditional communities in preindustrial societies. Self-organization also occurs in developed communities as well. One of her examples concerns the sharing of underground water resources by various communities in southern California.[16] These resources could have been allocated by a higher-level hierarchical authority like the federal government, but Ostrom shows that local counties and cities negotiating with one another through the court system were able to devise fair rules that shared resources without depleting them. Not all southern California counties were able to reach this kind of agreement, however, indicating that self-organization cannot always be relied on.

In addition to scattered examples of ranchers, whalers, fishermen, and other communities sharing common-pool resources, we also find self-organizing behavior cropping up in the heart of the modern, high-tech workplace. The early twentieth-century corporation and the factories and offices it created were bastions of hierarchical authority, controlling thousands of workers through a system of rigid rules in a highly authoritarian manner. What we see in many contemporary workplaces, however, is something of the opposite: formal, rule-bound, hierarchical relationships are being replaced by flatter ones that give subordinates greater scope for authority, or else by informal networks. In these workplaces, coordination bubbles up from below rather than being imposed from the top, and is based on shared norms or values that allow individuals to work together for common ends without formal direction. It is based, in other words, on social capital, which becomes more rather than less important as the complexity and technological intensity of an economy increases.

12

Technology, Networks, and
Social Capital

The End of Hierarchy?

Max Weber argued that rational, hierarchical authority in the form of bureaucracy was the essence of modernity. What we find in the second half of the twentieth century, instead, is that bureaucratic hierarchy has gone into decline in both politics and the economy, to be replaced by more informal, self-organized forms of coordination.

The political version of hierarchy was the authoritarian or, in an even more extreme form, totalitarian state, in which a dictator or small elite at the top had power over the whole society. Authoritarian states of all stripes, from Franco's Spain and Salazar's Portugal to East Germany and the Soviet Union, have collapsed since the 1970s. They have been replaced with, if not well-functioning democracies, at least states that aspire to permit a greater degree of political participation.

Democracies themselves are also organized hierarchically. A modern president of the United States in some respects has much more power than an oriental despot ever dreamed of, including the power to vaporize much of the world with nuclear weapons. The difference is less a matter of hierarchy than the fact that authority in a democracy is legitimized through popular consent and is limited in its power over individuals. Democratic hierarchies have produced inefficiencies just like their authoritarian counterparts, and so within virtually all contemporary democracies, there has been substantial pressure to decentralize, federalize, privatize, and delegate authority.

Corporate hierarchies have also been under attack. There have been a number of setbacks to large, overly hierarchical and rigid companies— AT&T and IBM in the early 1980s were classic examples—which fell prey to smaller, quicker, and more nimble competitors. Business school professors, management consultants, and information technology gurus have all stressed the virtues of highly decentralized firms, and some have argued that in the coming century, the large, hierarchical corporation will be replaced entirely by a new form of organization, the network.

Centralized, authoritarian corporations have been failing for the same reason that centralized, authoritarian states have failed: they cannot deal with the informational requirements of the increasingly complex world they inhabit. It is no accident that hierarchies have gotten into trouble precisely at the time that societies around the world have been making the transition from industrial to high-tech, information-based forms of production.

The problems that centralized hierarchies have in dealing with information were laid out in a classic article by Friedrich von Hayek fifty years ago, which itself was based on a critique of socialism made earlier by Ludwig von Mises.[1] To control everything in his domain, an authoritarian ruler needs to have the information and knowledge necessary to make decisions. In an agricultural society where lords rule over peasants, knowledge of horseback riding, swordplay, and some politics, as well as the blessing of the local bishop, were probably sufficient to ensure a monopoly of power. But as economies developed and became more complex, the informational requirements for ruling increased exponentially. Modern governance requires technological expertise, which no ruler can hope to master on his own, so he must rely on technical experts for everything from weapons design to fiscal management. Moreover, the overwhelming proportion of information generated in an economy is *local* in nature. If a supplier is providing low-quality rivets, it is the riveter who is more likely to know this than an economic bureaucrat in a centralized planning ministry or a corporate vice president in the company headquarters.[2]

But the delegation of power downward, to either technical experts or those who generate and use local knowledge, begins to dilute the dictator's power. A process like this occurred in the Soviet Union and is one of the reasons that socialism collapsed on itself there. Stalin found himself relying on technical experts—the so-called Red directors—as well as a host of scientists, engineers, and other specialists.[3] Although he could control them through fear (the famed aircraft designer Tupolev created airplanes while in a jail cell), his successors found it increasingly difficult to do so. Technical experts could withhold knowledge and bargain with those holding political power. This bought them autonomy, and thereby the freedom to start thinking for themselves. Further, despite the fact that all decisions concerning pricing and transfers of materials were in theory controlled by a ministry in Moscow, the center had no way of keeping track of all the local knowledge being generated in the periphery. Consequently lower-level officials like provincial party secretaries and enterprise directors closer to local sources of knowledge began to accumulate substantial power. By the time Gorbachev came along in the 1980s, the totalitarian model of power had already failed.

The same process occurs within companies where CEOs enjoy similarly authoritarian powers over their employees. Certain CEOs, particularly first-generation entrepreneurs who have built companies from scratch, tend to want to control everything that goes on within their companies, and treat employees as if they were robots designed to carry out their orders. But as their companies grow larger and the problems they face become more complex, this type of decision making becomes too inflexible, and the boss becomes a bottleneck. Firms no less than governments need to devolve power to experts and to decision makers who are closer to local sources of information. Some present-day management experts talk as if the concepts of decentralization and employee empowerment are new, but as the business historian Alfred Chandler has shown, large firms have been devolving power to lower levels of their organizations steadily over at least the past hundred years.[4] Large multidivisional firms like General Motors and Du Pont Chemical were hierarchically organized, but still rather decentralized in terms of managerial authority when compared to, say, a small family business.

The problems afflicting large, hierarchical organizations are not trivial ones, and it is reasonable to think that the devolution of power and authority within them will continue. But then a new problem emerges: coordinating the activities of all of the players in a decentralized organization where low-level employees have newly acquired powers. One solution is the market, where decentralized buyers and sellers achieve efficient results without central control. The outsourcing craze in American business during the 1990s is an effort to replace hierarchical control with market relationships. But market exchange generates transaction costs, and in any event firms can't organize their core functions as markets with everyone competing against everyone else.

The other solution to the problem of coordinating highly decentralized organizations is the network, a form of spontaneous order that emerges as the result of the interactions of decentralized actors, without being created by any centralized authority. If networks are to be truly productive of order, they necessarily depend on informal norms taking the place of formal organization—in other words, on social capital.

The Rise of the Network

The classic theory of the firm laid out by Ronald Coase in 1937 argues that hierarchies exist because of transaction costs.[5] A complex activity like building cars could be done, in theory, by small, decentralized firms contracting with one another to produce all of the component parts, with separate companies providing design, systems integration, and marketing. The reason cars are not made this way but by giant, vertically integrated firms is that the costs of all of the negotiating, contracting, and litigating required to outsource everything are much greater than the costs of bringing these activities in-house, where the firm can control the quality of all of the inputs and outputs by managerial fiat.[6]

There is a substantial literature on the rise of the network as an intermediate form of organization between traditional markets and hierarchies, said to be better suited to the development of technology than large, hierarchical organizations.[7] Thomas Malone and Joanne Yates argued that the advent of cheap and ubiquitous information technology should reduce the transaction costs involved in market relationships, and thereby reduce the incentive to create managerial hierarchies.[8] Many apostles of the information revolution have seen the rise of the Internet not simply as a useful new communications technology, but as the harbinger of an entirely new, nonhierarchical form of organization uniquely adapted to the requirements of a complex, information-intensive economic world.

Much of the prevailing literature understands the shift that is going on in terms of formal organization. The classic hierarchical organization takes the shape of a pyramid, while Figure 12.1 shows the consequences of organizational flattening. The flat organization remains ultimately a centralized and hierarchical one; all that has been changed is the number of management layers intervening between the top and bottom. Flat organizations create enlarged spans of control; properly executed, they should not overburden senior managers with micromanagement responsibilities, but rather should push authority down to the lower levels of the organization.

FIGURE 12.1

A Flat Organization

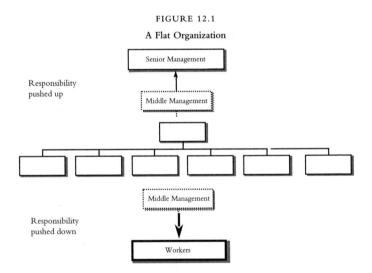

198

Sociologists have used the concept of networks for years, and at times express annoyance that business school professors are now reinventing the wheel. The definition of network commonly used by sociologists, however, is extremely broad and encompasses both markets and hierarchies as they are understood by economists.[9] There is a striking lack of precision in the use of the term *network* among the management specialists, however. Networks are commonly understood to be different from hierarchies, but it is often not clear how they differ from markets. Indeed, Malone did not use the term *network* when he originally talked about the decline of hierarchies; coordination would be performed by classical market mechanisms.[10] Some people treat the network as a category of formal organization in which there is no formal source of sovereign authority, while others understand it to be a set of informal relationships or alliances between organizations, each of which may be hierarchical but related to one another through vertical contractual relationships. Japanese *keiretsu* groups, alliances of small family firms in central Italy, and Boeing's relationships with its suppliers are equally understood to be networks.

If we understand a network not as a type of formal organization, but as *social capital,* we will have much better insight into what a network's economic function really is. By this view, a network is a moral relationship of trust:

A network is a group of individual agents who share *informal* norms or values beyond those necessary for ordinary market transactions.

The norms and values encompassed under this definition can extend from the simple norm of reciprocity shared between two friends to the complex value systems created by organized religions. Nongovernmental organizations like Amnesty International and the National Organization for Women achieve coordinated action on the basis of shared values. As in the case of friends or members of a religious denomination, the behavior of the organization's individual members cannot be explained on the grounds of economic self-interest alone. A society like the United States is characterized by a dense, complex, and overlapping set of networks (see Figure 12.2). The large ellipse may represent the United States

FIGURE 12.2

Multiple Networks of Trust

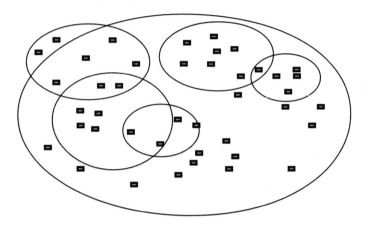

as a whole, whose inhabitants share certain political values related to free-dom and democracy. The overlapping ellipse may denote an immigrant group like Asian Americans, who partly share and partly stand outside mainstream American culture. The wholly enclosed ellipses could repre-sent anything from religious sects to firms with particularly strong corpo-rate cultures.

Note two features of this definition. A network is different from a market insofar as networks are defined by their shared norms and values. This means that economic exchange within a network will be conducted on a different basis from economic transactions in a market. A purist might argue that even market transactions require *some* shared norms (the willingness, for example, to engage in exchange rather than violence), but the norms required for economic exchange are relatively minimal. Exchange can occur between people who don't know or like one an-other, or who speak different languages; indeed, it can occur anony-mously between agents who never know each other's identities. Exchange among members of a network is different. The shared norms give them a superordinate purpose that distorts the market relationship. Hence mem-bers of the same family, or of the Sierra Club, or an ethnic rotating-credit association, sharing as they do certain common norms, do not deal with each other the way that anonymous individuals meeting in a marketplace do. They are much more willing to engage in reciprocal exchange in addition to market exchange—for example, conferring benefits without expecting immediate benefits in return. Although they may expect long-term individual returns, the exchange relationship is not simultaneous and is not dependent on a careful cost-benefit calculation as it is in a market transaction.

On the other hand, a network is different from a hierarchy because it is based on shared *informal* norms, not a formal authority relationship. A network understood in this sense can coexist with a formal hierarchy. Members of a formal hierarchy need not share norms or values with one another beyond the wage contracts that define their membership; formal organizations, however, can be overlaid with informal networks of various sorts, based on patronage, ethnicity, or a common corporate culture.

When networks are overlaid on top of formal organizations, the results are not necessarily beneficial, and indeed can be the source of a good deal of organizational dysfunction. Everyone is familiar with old-boy and patronage networks, based on kinship, social class, friendship, love, or some other factor. Members of such a network share important norms and values with one another (particularly reciprocity) that they do not share with other members of the organization. Within the patronage network, information passes readily, but its outer boundaries constitute a membrane through which information passes much less readily. Patronage networks are problematic in organizations because their structure is not obvious to those outside them, and they often subvert formal authority relationships. Common ethnicity may facilitate trust and exchange among members of the same ethnic group, but it inhibits exchange among members of different groups. When a boss is unwilling to criticize or fire an incompetent subordinate because the latter is a protégé, personal friend, or lover, the network's reciprocity becomes a clear liability.

The other problem with informal networks is the inverse relationship between the strength of the values or norms linking the community (and therefore the degree of coordination they can achieve) and their openness to people, ideas, and influences from outside the network. Being a member of the U.S. Marine Corps or the Mormon church involves much more than membership in a formal organization. Members are socialized into a strong and distinctive organizational culture that creates a high degree of internal solidarity and potential for coordinated activity. On the other hand, the cultural gap between Marine and civilian, or Mormon and non-Mormon, is much greater than for organizations with lesser degrees of moral relatedness. The impermeability of the communal walls around such groups can often make them intolerant, inbred, slow to adapt, and oblivious to new ideas. Building on the work of sociologist Mark Granovetter,[11] there has been a large literature on the importance of "weak ties" to the effectiveness of information networks. It is the deviant individuals straddling different communities who are often responsible for bringing in heterodox ideas that are ultimately necessary if the group is to adapt successfully to changes in its environment.

Networks, understood as informal ethical relationships, are therefore associated with phenomena like nepotism, favoritism, intolerance, inbreeding, and nontransparent, personalistic arrangements. Networks in this sense are as old as human communities themselves, and in many respects they were the dominant form of social relationship in many premodern societies. In some sense, many of the institutions we associate with modern life, such as contracts, the rule of law, constitutionalism, and the institutional separation of powers, were all designed to counteract the defects of informal network relationships. That is why Max Weber and other interpreters of modernity argued that its essence is the replacement of informal authority with law and transparent institutions.[12]

So why is it, then, that anyone should believe that human organizations in the future will rely less on formal hierarchies and more on informal networks? In fact, it is highly doubtful that formal hierarchies are about to go away anytime soon. To the extent that networks become important, they will exist in conjunction with formal hierarchies. But why should informal networks not wither away altogether? One answer has to do with the problems of coordination through hierarchies under conditions of increasing economic complexity.

Changing Methods of Coordination

The importance of social capital in a hierarchical organization can be understood in terms of the way information moves around in it. In a manufacturing firm, hierarchy exists in order to coordinate the flow of material resources in a production process. But although the flow of material product is determined by the formal structure of authority, the flow of information proceeds in a much different fashion. Information is a peculiar commodity. It can be extremely difficult and expensive to produce, but once in existence, further copies are essentially free.[13] This is all the more true in the digital age, when a mouse click can create endless copies of a computer file.

This means that any information generated within an organization in theory should optimally flow freely to all other parts of the organization where it can be of use. Since the organization in principle owns the rights to all information generated by its workers, there should be no cost to transferring information from one part of the organization to another.

Unfortunately, information never flows as freely within an organization as leaders at the top would like. The reason has to do with the fact that organizations have to delegate authority downward to lower levels of the hierarchy. This creates what economists call *principal-agent problems,* where the agent hired by the principal has his or her own agenda that is not always that of the boss or of the organization as a whole. Many managers think that the solution to the problem is to align individual incentives with organizational incentives so that the agents work in the principal's best interests. This is often easier said than done, however. Individual and organizational interests are at times in direct conflict. A middle manager who discovers a new application of information technology or a new plan for flattening the managerial structure that will eliminate his own job has no incentive to implement this discovery.[14] In other cases where it is difficult to measure the quality of a worker's output, such as a therapist counseling a patient or an artist painting a picture, monitoring individual performance for the sake of individualized incentives becomes prohibitively expensive.

Thus, although it is in the organization's overall interest to promote the free flow of information, it is often not in the individual interests of the various people within the hierarchy to allow it to do so. Information, as the saying goes, is power, and the granting or withholding of information becomes one important means by which various individuals within an organization seek to maximize their power relative to others. Everyone who has worked in a hierarchical organization knows that there is a constant struggle going on between superiors and subordinates, or between rival branches, to control information.

In addition to principal-agent problems, hierarchical organizations suffer from other inefficiencies related to their internal processing of information. We are all familiar with bureaucracies in which Department X doesn't know what Department Y on the next floor is doing. Some decisions require higher-level monitoring and therefore generate internal transaction costs in order to carry out that monitoring. In other cases, organizations assign monitoring responsibilities unnecessarily, incorrectly, or inefficiently.

The formality of hierarchies can also create problems in dealing with complex information. Management through a hierarchy usually entails the creation of a system of formal rules and standard operating procedures—the essence of Weberian bureaucracy. Formal rules become problematic when decisions have to be made on the basis of information that is complex or hard to measure and evaluate. In labor markets, advertising and listings of formal job requirements are used to match supply and demand for simple, low-skill jobs;[15] informal networks take over when universities or firms need to hire hotshot economists or software engineers, because their skills and performance are much harder to define in formal terms. Tenure decisions in American universities are made on the basis not of detailed formal criteria, but based on the fuzzier judgment of other tenured professors as to the quality of the candidate's work.

Finally, hierarchies can be less adaptive. Formalized systems of control are much less flexible than informal ones; when conditions in the outside world change, they are often more visible to lower levels of the organization than to higher-level ones. Hence overcentralization can be a particular liability in areas of rapid change in the external environment, such as the information technology industry.

The reason that networks, defined as groups sharing informal norms and values, are important is that they provide alternative conduits for the flow of information through and into an organization. Friends do not typically stand on their intellectual property rights when sharing information with each other and therefore do not incur transaction costs. Friendships thus facilitate the free flow of information within the organization. Nor do friends usually spend a lot of time strategizing over how to maximize their relative power positions in relation to each other. Someone in marketing knows someone in production and tells her over lunch about customer complaints concerning product quality, thereby bypassing the formal hierarchy and moving information to the place where it is most useful more quickly. A corporate culture ideally provides an individual worker with a group as well as an individual identity, encouraging effort toward group ends that again facilitate information flow within the organization.

Social capital is also critical to the management of highly skilled workers manipulating complex, diffuse, tacit, or hard-to-communicate knowledge and processes. Organizations from universities to engineering, accounting, and architectural firms generally do not try to manage their professional staffs through detailed bureaucratic work rules and standard operating procedures. Most software engineers know much more about their job than do the people who manage them; they alone can make informed judgments about their own productivity. Such workers are usually trusted to be self-managing on the basis of internalized professional standards. A doctor presumably will not do something unethical to a patient if someone pays him enough; he has taken an oath to serve the patient's interests rather than his own. Professional education is consequently a major source of social capital in any advanced information age society and provides the basis for decentralized, flat organization.

Indeed social capital is important to certain sectors and certain forms of complex production precisely because exchange based on informal norms can avoid the internal transaction costs of large hierarchical organizations, as well as the external transaction costs of arms-length market transactions. The need for informal, norm-based exchange becomes more important as goods and services become more complex, difficult to evaluate, and differentiated. The increasing importance of social capital can be seen in the shift from low-trust to high-trust manufacturing, among other places.

From Low-Trust to High-Trust Production

The early twentieth-century workplace, exemplified by Henry Ford's huge factories, was a hierarchical organization characterized by a high degree of formality. That is, there was an extensive division of labor mandated and controlled through a centralized, bureaucratic hierarchy, which laid down a large number of formal rules for how individual members of the organization were to behave. The principles of scientific management as elucidated by industrial engineer Frederick Winslow Taylor and implemented by Ford contained an implicit premise that there were economies of scale in managerial intelligence and that an organization could be more efficiently operated if its intelligence were segregated in a white-collar managerial hierarchy rather than being distributed throughout the organization.

In such a system there was no need for trust, social capital, or informal social norms: every worker was told where to stand, how to move his arms and legs, and when to take breaks and generally was not expected to display the slightest degree of creativity or judgment. Workers were motivated by purely individual incentives, whether rewards or punishments, and were readily interchangeable with one another. Reacting to this system through their unions, the blue-collar labor force demanded formal guarantees of their rights and the narrowest possible specification of duties—hence, the rise of job control unionism and labor contracts that were as thick as telephone books.[16]

Taylorism was an effective means—perhaps the only means—of coordinating the activities of a low-skill industrial labor force. In the first two decades of the century, half of Ford's blue-collar workers were first-generation immigrants who could not speak English, and as late as the 1950s 80 percent did not have a high school education.[17] But Taylorism ran into all of the problems of large, hierarchical organizations, with slow decision making, inflexible workplace rules, and an inability to adapt to new circumstances.

The move from a hierarchical Taylorite organization to a flat or networked one involves offloading the coordination function from formal bureaucratic rules to informal social norms. Authority does not disappear in a flat or networked organization; rather, it is internalized in a way that permits self-organization and self-management. A lean or just-in-time automobile factory is an example of a flat, post-Fordist organization. In terms of formal authority, many of the functions previously assigned to white-collar middle managers have now been undertaken by blue-collar assembly line workers who themselves are acting in teams. It is the factory floor workforce itself that manages day-to-day scheduling, machine setup, work discipline, and quality control.

The degree to which power has been moved down to the bottom layer of the organization is symbolized by the famous cord at each work-station in Toyota's Takaoka assembly plant, which allows individual workers to stop the entire assembly line if they see a problem in the production process. The cord constitutes what game theorists would call a unit veto, by which each actor can sabotage the entire group's effort. This kind of authority can be safely delegated only under certain conditions: the workforce has to be adequately trained to be able to undertake the management duties formerly performed by white-collar middle managers, and they have to have a sense of responsibility to use their power to further group ends rather than individual ones. Such authority cannot be implemented in a region with a history of poisonous labor-management relations. The post-Fordist factory requires, in other words, a higher degree of trust and social capital than the Taylorite workplace with its comprehensive workplace rules.

As any number of studies have indicated,[18] lean manufacturing has succeeded in improving productivity in the automobile industry by substantial margins, at the same time that it has improved product quality. The reason is that local information is processed much closer to its source: if a door panel from a subcontractor doesn't fit properly, the worker assigned to bolt it to the chassis has both the authority and the incentive to see that the problem is fixed rather than letting the information get lost while traveling up and down a long managerial hierarchy.

Regions and Social Networks

There is one further example of where social capital is critical to implementing a flat or networked form of organization: the American information technology industry. Silicon Valley might at first glance seem to be a low-trust, low–social capital part of the American economy, where competition rather than cooperation is the norm and efficiency arises out of the workings of rational utility maximizers meeting in impersonal markets as described by neoclassical economics. Firms are numerous, small, and constantly fissioning from one another; they bubble up and die as a result of cutthroat competition. Employment is insecure, lifetime employment and loyalty to a given company unheard of. The relatively unregulated nature of the information technology industry, combined with well-developed venture capital markets, permits a high degree of entrepreneurial individualism.

This picture of unbridled competitive individualism is belied, however, by any number of more detailed sociological studies of the actual nature of technological development in the Valley, such as Annalee Saxenian's *Regional Advantage*.[19] In a modern economy, social capital does not have to exist only within the boundaries of individual companies, or be embodied in practices like lifetime employment.[20] Saxenian contrasts the performance of Silicon Valley with Boston's Route 128, and notes that one important reason for Silicon Valley's success had to do with the different culture there. Saxenian makes clear that beneath the surface of apparently unbridled individualistic competition were a wide array of social networks linking individuals in different companies in the semiconductor and computer businesses. These social networks had a variety of sources, including common educational background (e.g., an electrical engineering degree from Berkeley or Stanford) and common employment histories (many key players in the semiconductor industry like Robert Noyce and Andy Grove worked closely with one another in the early days of the industry at Fairchild Semiconductor), or they arose out of the norms of the Bay Area counterculture of the late 1960s and 1970s.

Informal networks are critical to technology development for a number of reasons. A great deal of knowledge is tacit and cannot be easily reduced to a commodity that can be bought and sold in an intellectual property market.[21] The enormous complexity of the underlying technologies and of the systems integration process means that even the largest firms will not be able to generate adequate technical knowledge in-house. While technology is transferred between firms through mergers, acquisitions, cross-licensing, and formal partnerships, the literature on technology development in Silicon Valley stresses the informal nature of a great deal of the R&D work there. According to Saxenian,

> The informal socializing that grew out of these quasi-familial relationships supported the ubiquitous practices of collaboration and sharing of information among local producers. The Wagon Wheel bar in Mountain View, a popular watering hole where engineers met to exchange ideas and gossip, has been termed the fountainhead of the semiconductor industry. . . .
>
> By all accounts, these informal conversations were pervasive and served as an important source of up-to-date information about competitors, customers, markets, and technologies. . . . In an industry characterized by rapid technological change and intense competition, such informal communication was often of more value than more conventional but less timely forums such as industry journals.[22]

She argues that the proprietary attitudes of a Route 128 firm like Digital Equipment proved to be a liability. Unable ultimately to be a self-sufficient vertically integrated producer of technology, it lacked the informal links and trust necessary to share technology with rivals.

That these technology networks had an ethical and social dimension critical to their economic function is clear from the following comment: "Local engineers recognize that the quality of the feedback and information obtained through their networks depends upon the credibility and trustworthiness of the information provider. This sort of quality is only assured with individuals with whom you share common backgrounds and work experiences."[23] These shared professional and personal norms thus constituted an important form of social capital.

Other writers have analyzed the growth of so-called communities of practice in other areas of technology development.[24] That is, individual engineers working on the development of a specific technology tend to share information with one another on the basis of mutual respect and trust. The communities that emerge are sui generis; while they may be based on common educational or employment backgrounds, they frequently span the boundaries of individual organizations and areas of professional specialization.

These informal networks are probably more important in the information technology industry than in other sectors. In the chemical-pharmaceutical industry, where a large revenue stream can rest on knowledge of a single molecule, companies are understandably more cautious about sharing their intellectual property. Information technology, by contrast, is much more complex, involving the integration of a large number of highly advanced product and process technologies. The likelihood that a given bit of proprietary knowledge shared with a potential competitor will lead to direct losses is relatively small.

The social capital produced by such informal social networks permits Silicon Valley to achieve scale economies in R&D not possible in large, vertically integrated firms. Much has been written about the cooperative character of Japanese firms and the way in which technology is shared among members of a *keiretsu* network. In a certain sense, the whole of Silicon Valley can be seen as a single large network organization that can tap expertise and specialized skills unavailable to even the largest vertically integrated Japanese electronics firms and their *keiretsu* partners.[25]

The importance of social capital to technology development has some paradoxical results. One is that despite globalization, geographical proximity remains important—perhaps even more important—than previously. Michael Porter among other observers has noted that despite advances in communications and transportation technology, a number of industries, and particularly high-tech R&D, remain highly concentrated in particular geographical locations.[26] If information can now be readily shared over electronic networks, why is there not further geographical dispersal of industries? It would appear that the impersonal sharing of data over electronic networks is not enough to create the kind of mutual trust and respect evident in places like Silicon Valley; for that, face-to-face contact and the reciprocal engagement that comes about as a result of repeated social interaction is necessary. Thus, although the manufacture of commodity-like goods can be outsourced to parts of the world with low labor costs, it is much more difficult to do this with sophisticated technology development.

The fact that regions remain important does not imply that the world is returning to some kind of small-town clubbiness. In a global economy, even large and technologically sophisticated regions like the area around Provo, Utah, home to a booming software industry that includes the now-failing giants Novell and WordPerfect, can find themselves lacking the scale they need to stay on the cutting edge. "Weak" ties remain important; networks need to overlap one another if ideas and innovation are to flow freely. On the other hand, it is hard to turn ideas into wealth in the absence of social connectedness, which in the age of the Internet still requires something more than bandwidth and high-speed connectivity.

13

The Limits of Spontaneity and the Inevitability of Hierarchy

We can see, then, that there is a large and apparently robust set of cases where social norms have been spontaneously generated through rational bargaining and negotiation. We can also see that informal norms and self-organization will play a critical and perhaps increasing role in the high-tech workplaces typical of an information society. The question then arises as to the limits of such spontaneous order solutions to collective action problems. There are many people in the Law and Economics tradition with a libertarian agenda who have pushed the envelope in seeking to substitute spontaneous order solutions for hierarchical ones. The classic example, which works quite well, is the trading of pollution credits as an alternative to state regulation of air quality, a concept that American negotiators tried to introduce to their more statist-minded colleagues at the Kyoto summit on global warming in 1997. But some have suggested establishing markets for organs and babies as well. Where does spontaneous order stop, and hierarchy reassert itself?

Where Spontaneous Order Fails

It is clear from the work of Elinor Ostrom and others that spontaneous order occurs only under certain well-defined conditions, and that in many situations it either fails to materialize or leads to situations that are not good from the standpoint of society as a whole. Ostrom notes many instances of failed efforts to establish norms for the sharing of common pool resources.[1] Building on her conditions for self-organization, we can list several reasons that societies will not always be able to come up with spontaneous order solutions.

Size

Mancur Olson pointed out in *The Logic of Collective Action* that the free-rider problem becomes more severe as group size increases because it becomes increasingly difficult to monitor the behavior of any one individual. Members of a medical practice or partners in a law firm will likely know if one of them is not pulling their weight; the same is not true in a factory employing ten thousand workers. Free riding was a universal problem in the former Soviet Union and other socialist countries, because most people tended to work in giant factories or offices, and all pay and benefits were provided as a public good. The various biological mechanisms already described for detecting defectors are optimized for the group sizes that were typical in hunter-gatherer societies, groups no larger than fifty to one hundred people. Gossip is an ideal form of social control with this kind of social circle. Information about who is reliable, honest, lazy, or actively asocial is readily passed around in an informal network, and monitoring is done by the group itself without the use of specialized agents. When groups grow larger than this, the system begins to break down. It becomes difficult to associate faces with reputations; monitoring and enforcement become increasingly costly and subject to economies of scale that dictate designating certain members of the group to specialize in these activities. This is the historical point at which police, courts, and other instruments of formal hierarchical authority must come into play. Pervasive information technology can help us keep track of a wider circle of reputations, but here the desire for privacy will ultimately limit the information available to strangers.

Boundaries

For spontaneous order to occur, it is important to put clear boundaries on group membership. If people can enter and exit the group at will, or if it is not clear who is a member (and therefore who has a right to benefit from the common resources of the group), then individuals will have less incentive to worry about their reputations. This explains, among other things, why crime rates tend to be higher and levels of social capital lower in neighborhoods with a great deal of transience, such as those undergoing rapid economic change or around railroad or bus stations.[2] Because no one is sure who is really part of the neighborhood, it is impossible to establish community standards.

Repeated Interaction

Axelrod showed that iteration was the key to the solution of prisoner's dilemma problems and the key to spontaneous order. Many of the communities Elinor Ostrom studied that have successfully solved common-pool-resource problems are traditional ones with virtually no social mobility or contact with the outside world, like mountain villagers, rice farmers, and fishermen. People worry about their reputations only if they know they will have to continue to deal with one another for an extended period in the future. A newspaper article described the growing popularity of Cancun, Mexico, as a destination for partying college students on spring break. In Cancun's bars and discos, young men and women engage in feats of alcohol consumption and sexual promiscuity that they would not dare duplicate at home. In the words of one young woman, "You let loose because you know you won't ever see these people again."[3]

Prior Norms Establishing a Common Culture

The establishment of cooperative norms often presupposes the existence of a set of prior norms held in common by the individuals making up the group. In the example of the slugs in Chapter 8, slug culture owed its existence to the shared perception among the commuters that they were all harmless government workers who had reason to trust one another. Bargaining over rules for sharing a common resource requires at minimum that the participants speak the same language. A culture provides a common vocabulary not just of words, but of gestures, facial expressions, and personal habits that serve as signals of intent. Culture supplements biology in helping people distinguish cooperators from cheaters, as well as in transmitting behavioral rules that make action within a community more predictable. People are much more willing to demand the punishment of deviants who have broken the rules of their own culture than those of another. Conversely, new cooperative norms are much harder to generate across cultural boundaries. Communication is poor; people can mistake silence as a sign of contempt or unfriendliness when it wasn't intended that way. In extreme cases (Bosnia is an example), cultural groups define themselves in violent opposition to others.

The role of culture as a source of information for solving prisoner's dilemma problems explains the reasons why economic enterprise is so readily organized along ethnic lines in multiethnic societies like the United States. The substantive norms supported by different cultures around the world vary greatly with respect to what was earlier called the radius of trust.[4] There are certain cultures (like that of southern Italy) that do not promote cooperation because they are based on rules like "trust only members of your immediate nuclear family and take advantage of everyone else before they have the chance to do the same to you first."[5] On the other hand, other moral systems like Puritanism promoted honest behavior among a wide range of people unrelated to one another.[6] The existence of cultural rules promoting trust between strangers explains why a Puritan group settling in colonial New England should have had little difficulty establishing cooperative relations with one another. What is harder to understand is why low-trust groups like Sicilians also tend to organize themselves in ethnic communities and do business along ethnic lines when they move to the United States. It would make more sense for a southern Italian to patronize a high-trust Yankee merchant than a member of his own community.

The answer, of course, has a lot to do with the unwillingness of the Yankee merchant to deal with (in his eyes) an untrustworthy Sicilian, and there is indeed a long history of ethnic prejudice that explains the emergence of ethnic enclaves. But even apart from the Yankee merchant's behavior, the fact that the southern Italians and the Yankees each share common cultural norms within their own group gives them additional advantages in interpreting the behavior of their co-ethnics. That is, although the relative number of trustworthy people may be higher among the Yankees than among the Sicilians, the difference is only relative. No group is free of cheaters, liars, or opportunists. (Remember the earlier assertion that all human populations will be mixtures of angels and devils.) The Yankee as much as the Sicilian needs to be able to distinguish devils from honest and reliable people. What each group's culture gives its members is a leg up on the interpretation of other people's characters and a social network through which this information can be distributed and processed. Thus, even if a Sicilian may on average be less likely to act in a trustworthy way than a Yankee, he may still have a better chance at detecting opportunism among his fellow Sicilians than among taciturn Yankees.

Power and Justice

The next factor limiting the effectiveness of spontaneous order solutions to cooperative dilemmas concerns questions of power and justice. Informal social norms can frequently reflect the ability of one group to dominate another through its greater wealth, power, cultural capacity, or intellectual ability or through outright violence and coercion. The norms justifying slavery are an example. Many people would argue that such norms do not represent the results of a voluntary bargain, and hence cannot be described as spontaneous. But many such norms were more voluntary than people think. In ancient Greece and Rome, people did not want to be slaves, but nonetheless believed in the legitimacy of the institution of slavery and would accept their fate as slaves if they found themselves on the losing side of a war. Many women in traditional societies accept and even celebrate their subordinate position to men; while the norm legitimizing patriarchy may have been rooted in coercion, it was not always seen as coercive.

Certain social norms, in other words, may be seen as unjust even though they are voluntarily accepted by the communities that practice them. The judgment as to whether norms are inherently just or unjust is beyond the scope of any social science to make. The dilemma that twentieth-century philosophy has found itself facing is the conclusion that such judgments *cannot* be legitimately made: cultural relativism and the various strands of postmodernism argue on epistemological grounds that no set of cultural alternatives can be judged better or worse than another. The more libertarian forms of liberalism often end up making similar assertions: there is no accounting for preferences, and in any event there is no hierarchical source of authority that can legitimately tell an individual that his or her preference is wrong, provided its pursuit does not interfere with other individuals' pursuit of their preferences.[7] While limitations of space prohibit fuller discussion of this issue, there have been any number of serious grounds on which people have argued that there are universal norms of right and wrong, ones that should apply regardless of what the individuals or communities upholding contrary norms may believe.[8] If this is so, then we have grounds for saying that a community's spontaneously evolved norms are wrong or unjust.

The question of when hierarchical authority ought to intervene to correct a spontaneous outcome in the interests of justice or fairness constitutes the central issue that has historically divided Left and Right. The growth of rational hierarchical authority—"big government," in American parlance—has been driven first and foremost by the perceived need to correct a variety of societal abuses—slavery, Jim Crow laws, child labor, unregulated and unstable markets, unsafe working conditions, misleading advertising, and so on. State authority has been enormously abused from the French Revolution on, in the name of abstract concepts of social justice. Even discounting extreme cases like Stalin's Russia and Mao's China, the ability of public policy to achieve its goals without producing unintended or counterproductive consequences has been legitimately questioned on the basis of American experience in the twentieth century. Nonetheless, the need for hierarchical intervention under appropriate circumstances is not something that can ever be discounted on principled grounds. Apart from the most extreme libertarians, most people would agree that state intervention is often necessary to fix a range of problems that are both morally serious and not susceptible to spontaneous correction.

Lack of Transparency

An informal norm that has evolved through the repeated interactions of individuals within a community will necessarily lack transparency, particularly when viewed by outsiders. This can have any number of unhappy consequences. Within the community, individuals may be sanctioned unjustly because they didn't understand the norm, were falsely accused, or received disproportionate punishment. The fact that norms tend to arise in stable, closed communities means that outsiders will be viewed with suspicion and integrated into the community less easily than in a situation where order is the product of a strict, formal rule of law. Everyone knows that it is much easier to move into a big, anonymous city than a small town where everyone knows everyone else. The town may be friendlier, but it is also pervaded by a host of unwritten rules and norms that may take years for outsiders to understand.

The lack of transparency of informal norms often serves to disguise their origins in involuntary power relationships. Is the deference lower-class people show to upper-class ones a matter of voluntary agreement, or a lingering artifact of the former's violent domination by the latter? The movie *The Remains of the Day* (based on a novel of the same name by Kazuo Ishiguro) depicts an English butler, portrayed by Anthony Hopkins, who has devoted his life to service of a master who in the end is revealed to be both a fool and a Nazi sympathizer. The poignancy of the story revolves around the butler's final recognition that his life, which he had believed was given meaning by the code of service to which he adhered, was in fact wasted. Since the origins of most evolved, informal norms are buried in the mists of time, we often know very little about the interests that were and were not served by their creation and continued existence.

The Persistence of Bad Choices

Even if unjust, inefficient, or counterproductive norms came into being, one could argue that they would spontaneously disappear precisely because they did not serve the interests of the communities that practiced them. The Law and Economics literature often contains an explicit evolutionary assumption that whatever survives represents fitness in some sense and that there is therefore over time an "evolution toward efficiency." That is, firms compete with one another and the weaker ones go bankrupt; laws and institutions compete within a society, and the maladaptive ones are weeded out; societies compete among each other and are selected on the basis of superior performance.[9]

Evil, inefficient, or counterproductive norms can persist in a social system for generations, however, because of the influence of tradition, socialization, and ritual. *Path dependence* is a currently fashionable bit of jargon that signifies the dependence of current social relationships on history or tradition. The basic metaphor is that of a path through the woods whose twists and turns reflect the problems and limitations of those originally building it, like the presence of fords over rivers or dangerous wolves in the forest. Were the path to be built in later years, it would follow a straighter course due to better road-building technology or the clearing of forests, but past investments in the existing road mean that it is less costly to stay with the old road.[10] So too with human institutions. For example, the Electoral College that ultimately chooses U.S. presidents probably would not be included were the Constitution to be drafted from scratch today, but no one is going to take the effort to abolish it.

Traditions are critical to understanding norms because people frequently act on the basis of habit rather than anything resembling rational choice. Even if social norms are created initially through rational bargaining or deliberate choice, they are passed on to subsequent generations through a process of socialization, which is the habituation of people to certain patterns of behavior. Since many social norms place long-term interest over short-term interest or group interests over individual interests, they are often unwelcome and burdensome to those asked to obey them. As Aristotle points out in the *Ethics,* moral virtue, unlike intellectual virtue, is learned through habit and repetition, such that initially unpleasant activities eventually become either pleasant or, at any rate, less unpleasant. Moral education is not a cognitive exercise in which people are made to see that their own self-interest is in fact embodied in a norm. Rather, it is a type of habituation in which individual preferences are shaped to support virtuous behavior. This naturally means that a social habit, once learned, cannot be changed nearly as easily as an idea or belief that can be discredited on the basis of simple information.

Socialization is reinforced by ritualization. Rituals serve to connect individuals to communities by creating patterned modes of behavior that are transmitted over generations. Most rituals may seem arbitrary and pointless from a rational-choice point of view, but they are capable of being invested with enormous amounts of emotion; their interruption or modification challenges the integrity of the underlying community and therefore is met with tremendous resistance. The British monarchy makes absolutely no sense in terms of the democratic principles underlying the British polity today. To the contrary, it has the negative effect of reinforcing the social stratification of British society and elevates bloodlines over merit. One suspects that but for the rituals surrounding the monarchy and the emotion invested in them, it would be gone tomorrow.

The influence of bad initial choices is often greatly magnified by a phenomenon known to economists as increasing returns. That is, under the right circumstances, having something will lead to the production of even more of that thing, like feedback running through an amplifier. One such example is the peacock's tail. Evolutionary biologists beginning with Darwin have assumed that the peacock's tail is the result of sexual selection, that is, males and females competing with members of the same sex to choose the best partners in an endless interaction. Biologists theorize that the peacock's tail possibly developed out of an accident. For some unknown reason, some females began to prefer males with brightly colored tails. This created an increasing-returns situation: because some females want to mate with males with flashy tails, other females chose those males as well because their offspring would be able to find mates more easily. The more females preferred such males, the greater incentive later females had to do so as well, in a runaway interaction.

So too in human institutions: many exist not because they are efficient or well adapted to their environment, but simply because they crowded out other alternatives at an early stage of development. Very small, rather arbitrary differences can be magnified into very large ones as time goes on. The choice of Microsoft's DOS and Windows operating systems over competitors like CP/M or OS2 has been cited by economists as an example of increasing returns leading to the lock-in of an early choice. The Microsoft operating system was not technologically superior to its rivals, but its large, installed base gave everyone an incentive to use it because they would be able to use and share more applications.[11]

All of these factors constitute reasons that communities will not be able to generate cooperative norms in the first place, why such norms may be unjust even when they have been created, and why unjust or counterproductive norms may persist for a long time. This means that spontaneous order will never constitute order per se in any society. Rational hierarchical authority, in the form of government and formal law, will have to serve as supplements. The social norm legitimating slavery in the antebellum American South could not be corrected through spontaneous, evolutionary means—at least, not on a time scale that anyone thought was morally justifiable—but had to be ended decisively by the sword and imposed on an unwilling group of people in a highly authoritarian manner. State authority in the form of formal law will always be a necessary complement and corrective, as Hayek himself points out, to the extended order of human cooperation.[12]

Deficiencies of Networks

The network is the contemporary, corporate version of spontaneous organization. Some visionaries like Manuel Castells, author of *The Rise of the Network Society,* have declared that we are on the verge of a broad shift from authoritarian hierarchy to networks and other radically democratized power structures. For understandable reasons, the vision of a corporate world in which decisions are taken on a voluntary, egalitarian, peer-to-peer basis is an attractive one, and matches the libertarian utopia of those who would prefer to see the power of the government superseded entirely by voluntary community and internalized constraints. This egalitarian impulse explains the extraordinary popularity of biological metaphors in organizational discourse, where top-down, Newtonian, mechanical control is seen as bad, and bottom-up, organic self-organization is seen as good.

We can argue that networks will become more important in the technological world of the future and yet concede that there are at least three reasons why hierarchy will remain a necessary part of organization for the foreseeable future. First, we cannot take the existence of networks and their underlying social capital for granted, and where they don't exist, hierarchy may be the only possible form of organization. Second, hierarchy is often functionally necessary for organizations to achieve their goals. And third, people by nature *like* to organize themselves hierarchically.

Networks, as we have seen, are simply a form of social capital, in which individuals are related to one another by common norms and values in addition to their economic ties. To some extent, companies can create social capital by socializing their employees to certain shared values. But this is often a long and costly process, and individual firms in any event can't create the social ties that link their workers with those in different companies. For this, they must rely on social capital that exists in the larger society around them, which may or may not exist. Self-organizing networks are more likely to emerge when people in the broader society have other strong communal institutions and are not divided by class, ethnic, religious, racial, or other kinds of cleavages.

An example comes out of the auto industry. When Japanese auto manufacturers like Toyota and Nissan began to build factories in North America to get around political opposition to their imports, they generally stayed away from Michigan and other auto-building regions with histories of union militancy. Far more important to them than the high cost of union wages was the fact that American communities with a long tradition of unionism would be much less amenable to the kind of high-trust management that underlies lean manufacturing. Not only do lean plants require much greater flexibility in work rules; they also require two-way communications between workers and managers and a sense that they are part of a common enterprise. That is why the Japanese transplants ended up in places like rural Ohio, Kentucky, and Tennessee. These communities were less sympathetic to unions and had a small-town character similar to that which prevails in much of Japan. I do not know whether any lean manufacturer has ever considered setting up a factory in Sicily or other low-trust parts of southern Italy, but one would have good reason to think that this would not be a wise investment. Self-organization does not take place just anywhere.

American automakers that wanted to take advantage of social capital had to make substantial investments to create it, since they had much less flexibility in where to locate their North American plants than their Japanese rivals. Ford, after going through serious crisis and downsizing in the 1970s, moved rapidly to more efficient lean production methods in the 1980s. Ford understood that since it couldn't sidestep its unions, it would have to co-opt them by undertaking a long-term effort to build a relationship of trust with its workers. Ford assigned a senior vice president to work closely with the head of the United Auto Workers (UAW) and established a general policy of not dealing with union-bashing parts suppliers. In 1997, the company refused to buy parts from Johnson Controls, which was at the time involved in an acrimonious strike and lockout with the UAW.[13] This stance enraged Johnson Controls, but the strategy paid off later as Ford enjoyed substantial labor peace and was able to implement its own lean operations smoothly.

General Motors, by contrast, established a just-in-time supply operation without understanding that social capital was critical to its proper operation. It spent scant effort winning the trust of the UAW, assigning labor relations to a minor executive far down the corporate ladder. The tight delivery schedules of just-in-time production make it critically dependent on trust and cooperation; if a part is not delivered when promised, delays propagate throughout the system. In 1996 and 1998, GM faced two costly strikes that were started by UAW locals and quickly spread across GM's entire North American operations. The 1998 strike resulted in the loss of $1.6 billion in profits.

Thus the Japanese transplants made use of existing social capital in the communities where they located their plants; Ford invested heavily to create social capital where there was originally very little; and General Motors failed to understand the need for social capital in the first place, and paid a heavy price.

In the absence of social capital, hierarchical organization makes a great deal of sense, and in fact may be the *only* way in which a low-trust society can be organized. Classical Taylorism requires no trust whatsoever between workers and managers. It requires only that workers lower down in the hierarchy follow formal rules. Workers are motivated by simple carrots and sticks; Taylor was a big proponent of the piece-rate system for stimulating output. There is no reason that workers have to internalize the organization's goals or regard their bosses as part of an extended family. At low levels of skill and education, hierarchical centralization ensures that workers do not have to think for themselves. Taylorism was used very effectively by Soviet managers during the USSR's headlong industrialization in the 1930s and 1940s, as peasants were yanked off farms and rushed into giant industrial enterprises. There was at the time no other choice: the experience of Stalinism and the Terror atomized Soviet society, severing horizontal links between people and destroying all vestiges of social trust.

As educational requirements and skill levels rise throughout contemporary economies like that of the United States, the number of sectors demanding Taylorite organization will decrease. Part of the workforce will remain difficult to train, however, and the country's many social, ethnic, class, gender, and racial cleavages will prevent the spread of shared norms that are the basis of social capital among even well-educated workers. This guarantees that hierarchical organization will continue to be an important means of coordination.

A second reason that organizational hierarchy is not likely to disappear applies not just to low-skill labor forces in declining industries, but to even the most advanced high-technology companies. There are a variety of situations in which hierarchical control works much more effectively than decentralized management. Although a network may be more innovative by putting more brains to work taking risks and seeing what flies, there are times when the decisiveness of a centralized hierarchy is absolutely critical.

Consider an activity like the invasion of Normandy in June 1944. To preserve secrecy and surprise, the Allied command had to impose tight controls over the movement of troops and information; to make sure that forces ended up on the right beach at the right time, it needed dictatorial control over resource allocation. Centralized organizations can move much more quickly than networks, which are bogged down by the latter's consensus-style decision making. Suppose the Germans had gotten wind of the Allied invasion plans on June 4 and started moving troops to Normandy. If you were Eisenhower, would you prefer that the Allied armies be run at that point by a hierarchy or a network? In an experiment on network decision making, a theater of people was allowed to pilot a virtual plane by, in effect, voting whether to steer it up, down, or to one side.[14] The experiment showed that after a certain learning process, the crowd of people was able to maneuver the plane successfully, despite the fact that no one individual had control over it. This was an impressive instance of network coordination, but most people, I suspect, would much prefer to risk their own bodies in a 747 piloted by a single, competent pilot.

Network coordination can also be extremely risky. One of the great advantages of networks is that many individuals or subunits close to sources of local knowledge are constantly innovating, experimenting, and taking risks. But this advantage can become a huge liability when a company entrusts a single, low-ranking individual with the authority to "bet the firm." This is in effect what happened to the venerable British investment house of Barings, when it allowed a twenty-nine-year-old trader in Singapore named Nicholas Leeson to risk so much of the firm's capital that he was able to single-handedly undermine a 234-year-old institution. Firms luckier than Barings that are able to survive bad decisions on the part of low-ranking employees are usually quick to impose new layers of hierarchical controls on their workers to prevent similar disasters from happening again.

In fact, the craze for decentralization, organizational flattening, and networks that swept American management circles in the 1990s often takes on the quality of a naive reinvention of the wheel. Highly decentralized firms with "empowered" lower-level employees have existed in the past, and have failed. One example was the giant retailer Sears, which under the leadership of General Robert E. Wood in the 1930s and 1940s devolved substantial powers to territorial vice presidents and local store managers. The logic was the same as now: a store manager in Tallahassee would know much better than an executive in the Sears Tower in Chicago what items to put on sale for the local market. The problem that developed was that these various empowered lower-level executives began to pursue their own agendas, which often did not correspond to that of the company as a whole, as when certain auto repair managers in the 1970s traded on Sears's reputation for honest and reliable service and engaged in bait-and-switch marketing tactics.[15]

In decentralized organizations, dysfunction often takes the form of "tribalism," where one division's chief interest comes to lie in beating another division rather than defeating an outside competitor. Something like this happened at the Ford Motor Company in the 1950s, when two factions within the company clashed over the marketing of the Continental Mark II. One faction wanted to use it to draw high-income families into Ford showrooms to better market their entire line of cars; the other faction blocked development of a four-door model in the name of cost-cutting and undermined the strategy.[16]

In the absence of formal managerial controls, a firm can prevent unscrupulous individuals from behaving in damaging ways by having them internalize an acceptable code of behavior. Only social capital, in other words, can keep these kinds of problems under check in an organization with highly decentralized authority. This can and usually is done by training, or by screening prospective employees for good character, but such an investment in social capital is often expensive. Moreover, the tribalism that affects decentralized companies is more typically not the product of dishonesty or poor training but of the overzealous pursuit of the goals of a subunit at the expense of the organization as a whole. Informal norms controlling behavior in a decentralized organization may achieve an optimal balance between flexibility and risk, but it is no guarantee that either will be achieved. When the risks become great enough, formal control becomes necessary.

Paradoxically, hierarchical organization is frequently necessary to create the very social capital that is needed to make flat organizations or networks work properly, under the general heading of *leadership* and *charisma.* These are concepts familiar to sociologists and political scientists, but foreign to economists. The vast literature on organization and bureaucracy has always recognized that organizations have formal and informal structures and has pointed to the importance of the latter to the proper working of the former. More often than not, the informal ethos that guides a particular organization is taught by example. As in political life, great leaders are ones who can get people to behave in characteristic ways through the force of their personalities and example. The management expert Edgar Schein gives numerous small-scale examples of how leaders shape corporate cultures by, for example, getting out of their offices and walking around the shop floor, sharing personal risks with their workers, or bypassing the corporate hierarchy to reach workers directly.[17] The most effective government bureaucracies, like the U.S. Forest Service and the Federal Bureau of Investigation under J. Edgar Hoover, all had informal cultures that were shaped, often idiosyncratically, by the forceful personalities of their leaders.[18] Networks, by definition, are leaderless; examples and norms have to bubble up from below. If the norms that create social capital are not there in the first place, the organization will have much more trouble generating them internally than one that is organized hierarchically under a strong leader.

Homo Hierarchicus

There is a final reason why hierarchy is not about to disappear from modern organizations any time soon: human beings *by nature* like to organize themselves hierarchically—or to put it more precisely, those on the top of hierarchies find the satisfaction that recognition of their social status brings so enjoyable that it frequently outweighs money and material wealth as a source of happiness. Those on the bottom of hierarchies like it much less, but they usually have no choice. In any case, there are enough hierarchies scattered about in modern societies that most people can end up in the middle to upper range of at least one of them. Either way, what people dislike most is not hierarchy in principle, but hierarchies in which they end up on the bottom. Most radical egalitarians who have succeeded in coming to power, like the French, Bolshevik, and Chinese Communist revolutionaries, managed in short order to set up different but no less hierarchical social structures of their own, where the party secretary rather than the king or business tycoon ended up at the top of the heap. Today we tend not to award status on the basis of bloodlines; it would seem a bit ridiculous to choose one's neurosurgeon on the grounds that she was the granddaughter of a neurosurgeon. But the hierarchy of talent and ability is no less stratified. Most people would not think to rank the neurosurgeon together with the hospital janitor in the same category of "health care worker"— least of all the neurosurgeon herself.

Competition in status hierarchies is characteristic of much of the animal world, and particularly of our closest primate relatives. Most hierarchies in the animal world arise as a result of sexual selection, the process by which males compete with one another for access to females. Male chimpanzees are preoccupied with competition for alpha male status, a drive that is deeply embedded in their neurological systems. Chimpanzees feel a "serotonin high" when they achieve dominance in a hierarchy.[19] Indeed, researchers in one experiment were able to increase and decrease the dominance of different monkeys in a hierarchy by manipulating the levels of serotonin in their brains.[20] The antidepressant drug Prozac achieves its effect by artificially manipulating the brain's receptivity to serotonin.

Among human beings, the quest for status is similarly built into the emotional system. The desire for recognition—of one's own status and the status of one's gods, country, ethnicity, nationality, ideas, and so forth—is the central driving force behind political life.[21] The feeling of pride occurs when one is recognized as having the appropriate status, while anger results from inadequate recognition. These emotions are inherently social: when one feels anger at a lack of recognition, one does not want a material object outside the body; rather, one wants evidence of a mental state—recognition—on the part of another subjective consciousness. It is frequently the case that the passion of anger will lead human beings to do things that are manifestly not in their material self-interest, such as fighting wars over the recognition of national or religious identity, getting into duels, engaging in retaliatory spirals of violence, or sitting in court for months on end until the murderer of one's wife or son is brought to justice.

It should be clear that competition for status and the recognition of status are also important factors in economic life. Much of what passes for economic motivation—the satisfaction of "preferences" through the acquisition of material goods—is motivated not so much by the desire for consumption, but by the desire for what economist Robert Frank calls "positional goods"—one's standing relative to other people in a social hierarchy. This was a point that Adam Smith understood quite well when he explained in *Theory of Moral Sentiments* that the rich sought riches not from need, which is usually modest, but because "the rich man glories in his riches" and "feels that they naturally draw upon him the attention of the world."[22]

The importance of status in contemporary life is evident from a number of phenomena. Robert Frank points out that earnings schedules in American corporations are actually flatter than they should be were workers being compensated, as economic theory predicts, strictly according to their marginal productivity.[23] The reason is that the more highly paid employees are being partially compensated in terms of status—a corner office, a parking space near the door, or a vice president's nameplate—while the lower-ranking ones have to be compensated monetarily for their lack of status.

Perhaps the most convincing evidence that what economic life is all about concerns status rather than wealth is the fact that pollsters have found in repeated surveys that people judge themselves to be happier the richer they are in relation to other people. That is, people in the top 20 percent of the income distribution consider themselves to be happier than those in the next quintile, and so on down to the bottom fifth, who judge themselves the least happy. While this might appear to prove that money buys happiness, Frank points out that this has *always* been true, going back to the first surveys in the 1940s, when the richest fifth were no better off in terms of absolute wealth than, say, the middle fifth in the 1990s. Moreover, people at the top of the income distribution in very poor countries, who might barely qualify as middle class in the United States, also consider themselves the happiest.[24] All of this suggests that happiness is linked not to absolute but to relative income, and that the satisfaction that money brings is related, as Smith indicates, to the degree that the rich can "glory" in their riches.

Once human beings seek status rather than ordinary goods, they become engaged in a zero-sum rather than a positive-sum game. That is, high status is achievable only at the expense of someone else. In zero-sum competitions, many of the traditional remedies of neoclassical economics like unregulated market competition no longer work. Status competitions frequently lead to deadweight losses in social utility, as the competing parties seek to outbid each other. To keep up with the Joneses next door, you buy a fancy BMW; they retaliate by buying a Rolls Royce. Your relative position has not changed, but two luxury car companies have captured a significant part of your wealth and that of the Joneses. In such situations, it is often better either to agree not to compete (as in an arms control agreement, which seeks to resolve a similar zero-sum game) or to have a third-party arbiter limit the degree of competition.

Imagining a flat, networked, nonhierarchical world of the future is tantamount to imagining a world without politics. This particular libertarian dream—shared, incidentally, by many human rights activists in Eastern Europe before the fall of the Berlin Wall—is no more realistic than the socialist dream in which politics becomes everything, or the radical feminist dream in which men somehow cease being men.[25] Each generation may seek to redefine the line that separates politics from civil society and the market. In our generation, the line has been shifted away from government. Functions that were earlier defined as political have been given back to civil society or the market through privatization and deregulation. Similarly, on a corporate level, power and authority have been devolved, decentralized, outsourced, and divided. But the line itself separating the political from the social will never disappear: social order, whether on a society-wide or an organization-wide level, will always derive from a mixture of hierarchical and spontaneous sources.

14

Beyond Cave 76

Let them all go to hell, except for Cave 76.

—"The Anthem of Cave 76,"
from Mel Brooks's *2000-Year-Old Man*

Human beings by nature are social creatures with certain built-in, natural capabilities for solving problems of social coopera-tion and inventing moral rules to constrain individual choice. They will, without much prompting, create order spontaneously simply by pursuing their daily individual ends and interacting with other people. The Pied Piper, leading the children of Hamelin to another land, will probably not witness these children destroying themselves in a descent into Lord-of-the-Flies-type violence (unless there is a grave imbalance in the sex ratio, and assuming that the Pied Piper himself has no political ambitions). Rather, those children, remembering little of their parents' cultural traditions, will make up new ones not much different. Their new social world will have a kinship system, private property, a system of ex-change of goods, status hierarchies, and numerous other norms con-straining the behavior of individuals. Honesty, trustworthiness, the keeping of commitments, and reciprocity in various forms will be practiced by many people much of the time and valued, at least in principle, by nearly everyone. There will also be dishonesty, crime, and other forms of de-viance, as well as community mechanisms for controlling deviance. Little children without much coaching will divide up the world between good guys and bad guys. They will have powerful feelings of solidarity with those inside their community, and anything from wariness to outright hostility toward those on the outside. They, their children, and their children's children will gossip endlessly about who is naughty and who is nice, who kept promises and who snitched, who had easy virtue and who lost interest the morning after. All of this gossip will serve to sustain ordinary morality—the kind that is practiced within families and between friends and neighbors—and is the source of social capital.

The children of Hamelin, to repeat, *will spontaneously create all of these rules without the benefit of a prophet who will bring the word of God to them and without the benefit of a lawgiver to establish government.* They will do this because they are human beings who are by nature moral animals and have sufficient rationality to create cultural rules that will allow them to live with one another.

If ordinary morality is in some sense natural and the product of spontaneous human interaction, what, then, is missing from this picture? What do the prophet and the lawgiver bring to the table that is missing from what we might call New Hamelin? In what ways does spontaneous order need to be supplemented by these hierarchical forms of authority?

What is missing, in the first instance, is scale. The children of Hamelin and their descendants will live in a little colony of perhaps fifty to one hundred people, not too different in some respects from the chimp colony at Arnhem. Most members will be related to one another at various removes; indeed, it will be rare to encounter a nonrelative unless New Hamelin bumps into another colony. New Hamelin, though organized hierarchically, will be relatively egalitarian, with no large differences between leaders and led. But it will not be capable of building a city or of creating all the things that flow from life in a city. There will be no division of labor, no impersonal market, no economies of scale, no legal guarantees of property rights and therefore no long-term investment, and almost nothing by way of cultural diversity. There will be no high art—no Michelangelos or Bachs—for their output was critically dependent on the large surpluses produced by well-organized agricultural societies. There will be no pyramids, no Parthenon, certainly no Palace of Versailles. Novels, scientific research, libraries, universities, hospitals—

while the children of Hamelin may on some theoretical level be capable of producing these things, they won't, because their self-organized, egalitarian tribe will remain petty and too hopelessly mired in poverty to worry about much more than their day-to-day survival.

In other words, the various biological mechanisms detailed in Chapters 8 through 10, like kin selection and reciprocal altruism, can explain sociability in hunter-gatherer societies, up through the level of families, tribes, and other forms of small group sociability. The nonbiological self-organizing mechanisms described in Chapters 11 and 12 can account for the social rules governing somewhat larger groups, where participants number in the hundreds or in some cases thousands. They can also account for the emergence of larger-scale spontaneous order in societies where government and the rule of law exist already. But when spontaneous groups get too large, various public goods problems, like who will negotiate the rules, monitor free riders, and enforce norms, become insuperable. Elinor Ostrom's catalogue of rules regarding common-pool resources constitutes culture with a small "c"—that is, small rules for small communities that we do not generally associate with large and important cultural systems. The spontaneous order literature can give no account of norm formation as it applies to the largest-scale groups—nations, ethnolinguistic groups, or civilizations. Culture with a capital "C," then—whether Islamic, Hindu, Confucian, or Christian—does not have spontaneous roots.

There is a moral problem as well. Ordinary morality is compatible with—indeed, is the precondition for—shocking immorality at higher levels of social organization. A disorganized, individualistic rabble cannot pull off a systematic genocide like the Soviet killing of the kulaks during collectivization in the 1930s. The Southern soldiers of the Confederacy who died to preserve slavery, or the Germans who carried out the Holocaust, often displayed virtues of integrity, courage, and loyalty toward their own communities. The Germans, in particular, are known as sticklers for order, unwilling to cross the street against a red light even as they marched prisoners off to concentration camps. But the kind of ordinary morality that makes an individual not want to disobey a traffic law contributes, at a higher level of community, to the most monstrous crimes. Our desire to be liked and esteemed and to conform leads individuals to carry out the most brutal orders when caught in an evil political system. Morality at the level of humanity as a whole dictates that we violate deeply felt norms of loyalty and reciprocity to our particular group.[1] The great moral conflicts of our time have arisen not over the absence of ordinary morality, but rather over the tendency of human communities to define themselves narrowly on the basis of race, religion, ethnicity, or some other arbitrary characteristic, and to fight it out with other, differently defined communities.

Lawgivers are necessary to the establishment of governments that permit the creation of large-scale communities and the transformation of social order into political order. Human beings go much further than any other animal by creating second- and third-order hierarchies that unite families into tribes and lineages, tribes into coalitions, and finally all subordinate social units into a political community or state.[2] It may be the case that the state, as the political scientist Roger Masters has argued, has biological origins.[3] Aristotle says not that man is a social animal by nature, but a *political* one. He argues this on the grounds that human beings everywhere live in political communities, with the exception of a small number of isolated New Hamelins. Human beings do not simply want to be socially connected to others through family, friends, neighbors, churches, voluntary associations, and the like; they want to *rule,* to lead others and receive recognition for the way in which they shape their communities through hierarchies.

Hierarchy is necessary to correct the defects and limitations of spontaneous order. At a minimum it supplies public goods like defense and the protection of property rights. But beyond that, political order helps to create social order in at least three ways. First, it creates norms directly through legislation. The dictum that "you can't legislate morality" is only partially true; states can't make individuals follow norms that violate important natural instincts or interests. But it can and has shaped informal norms throughout history. The striking down of legal segregation in the United States through the Civil Rights and Voting Rights Acts of the 1960s was critical to changing popular norms on race.

The second way that political order establishes social order is by creating the conditions for peaceful market exchange, and therefore the expansion of the spontaneous order created by markets well beyond the boundaries of face-to-face communities. With secure and enforceable property rights, buyers and sellers can interact over long distances with greater surety that they will have recourse if they are defrauded; investors can invest capital whose prospects for earning a return lie far in the future. Some trade and even less investment will take place in the absence of states and property rights; people truck and barter even in war zones where political order has broken down. But certainly nothing we recognize as the modern economic world will occur in the absence of states.

Finally, politics produces social order through leadership and charisma. I noted earlier that in corporate settings, single individuals can often shape the habits and goals of their organizations. The same is true for politics. The virtues required to create political order are different from those required to produce social order. The virtues practiced by the children of Hamelin are small ones that we have identified with social capital: honesty, promise keeping, reciprocity, and the like. Although they are important to political order as well, the latter requires other, greater and less frequently observed virtues like courage, daring, statesmanship, and political creativity. Statesmen from Solon and Lycurgus to Peter the Great and Abraham Lincoln did not merely codify norms that had bubbled up around them. They were instrumental in the creation of what Machiavelli called "new modes and orders" of political life through the force of their character and personal example. George Washington's modesty in office, his abjuring of elaborate honorific titles, and his willingness to step down after two terms as president, despite the pleading of many of his countrymen to become a quasi-royal president for life, set important precedents for the behavior of subsequent democratically elected U.S. presidents.

In many ways, hierarchical religion has been the handmaiden of politics and virtually indistinguishable from the former as a hierarchical means of building second- and third-order coalitions from lineages to empires. For much of human history, there was no clear dividing line between the hierarchical authority of the state and the hierarchical authority of religion. King and high priest ruled over the same domain and often were united in the same person. Religion legitimated political rule: Confucian doctrine supported the mandarinate in China, Shinto promoted Emperor worship in Japan, and European kings ruled by divine right. Hinduism, Christianity, and Islam all made free use of state power to spread and enforce their doctrines, often at the point of the sword. *Cuius regio, eius religio.*

The largest-scale human communities that transcend the borders of states are religious in nature. Many date back to the so-called axial age, and most sprang from the teachings of either single individuals—Confucius, Christ, Buddha, Muhammad, Luther, Calvin—or relatively small groups of individuals. Although the hierarchical authority of organized religion is not necessary for the production of ordinary moral rules, it was absolutely critical historically for creating civilizations. The great civilizations—Islamic, Jewish, Christian, Hindu, and Confucian—whose boundaries still, according to Samuel Huntington, demarcate the fault lines of world politics—are religious in nature.[4]

Hierarchical religion was important in the shaping of moral norms in another critical way. Neither our biological dispositions favoring social cooperation, nor the kind of spontaneous order we can achieve through decentralized bargaining, will ever result in moral universalism—that is, moral rules that apply to all human beings *qua* human beings, on which current notions of human equality and human rights rest. Natural order and spontaneous order ultimately reinforce the selfishness of small groups and consequently a small radius of trust. They produce the everyday virtues of honesty and reciprocity, and result in hierarchy and order, but only within the relatively small communities in which they are shared. They result in what Mel Brooks would call the morality of Cave 76, where everyone outside the cave can go to hell. Those outsiders are fair targets for communal aggression, just like the victims of the chimps at Gombe.

It might seem strange to credit hierarchical religion with the breaking down of barriers between human communities, since we commonly associate religious passion with communal violence. Sectarian conflicts between Protestants and Catholics in Northern Ireland, Muslims and Orthodox in Bosnia, Hindus and Tamils in Sri Lanka, are regular headlines. But if we look at human history in a longer-term perspective, religion has played a critical role in increasing the radius of trust in human societies. Competition and cooperation are inextricably intertwined in human evolution: we secure domestic order within our community so that we can better compete with other communities. But the scale of those communities has been constantly increasing, beyond the family, beyond the tribe, way beyond Cave 76. The organized religious groups that today are fighting it out among themselves stand at the end of a long process of social evolution that secured order, rules, and peace within ever-larger communities. We owe to religion the fact that it is civilizations rather than families or tribes that are today the basic unit of account.

And it is religion alone that first suggested that the final community within which its moral rules should apply—the ultimate radius of trust— should be mankind itself. This kind of moral universalism is present in many axial religions, including Buddhism, Islam, and Christianity, and it is Christianity that bequeathed the idea of the universal equality of human rights to secular doctrines like liberalism and socialism. The aspiration toward moral universalism may be unrealized by any actual religion, but it is nonetheless an inextricable part of the moral universe created by religion.

It was only in the modern West that the business of building higher-order hierarchies was taken away from religion and given to the state, with its elaborate mechanisms of bureaucracy, formal law, courts, constitutions, elections, and the like. In early modern Europe, sectarian conflict became so destructive that the founders of liberalism like Thomas Hobbes and John Locke established a new basis for community, one that secularized the state and vastly reduced the density and scope of the shared values mandated by state authority. The postindustrial liberal democracies that were the subject of the first part of this book were the ultimate products of this innovation.

Those values that are shared by a modern liberal democracy as a whole increasingly tend to be political rather than religious in character. There was a time when a large majority of Americans would have assented to the characterization of their country as a "Christian nation"; today, this is true only of a small minority, a minority that is looked on with considerable suspicion by others in the society. Most Americans would greatly prefer understanding the nature of their national community in terms of secular values like democracy, equality of rights, and constitutional government. The sheer diversity of the country guarantees that outside of popular culture, there will be fewer and fewer common cultural signposts that can be taken for granted.

It would be even stranger to speak of contemporary Europe as "Christendom," given the secularization of most European societies. Despite the fact that Christianity was critical in shaping their civilization, contemporary Europeans tend to define their cultural identities much more in secular political terms than in religious ones. Those that do, like the various communities of the Balkans, seem like bizarre throwbacks to an earlier period of history. Virtually all contemporary European societies have in effect become multiethnic and multicultural, and although they lag considerably behind the United States in this regard, they, like the United States, must find ways of defining their identities in political and civic rather than ethnic and religious terms. The decisions of the German courts and government in 1998 to include Islam as a religion deserving state recognition and to open citizenship to nonethnic Germans are steps in this direction.

Decentralized Religion

Throughout the developed world, hierarchical religion has been disassociated from state power and has gone into a long-term decline. This does not mean that religion per se has disappeared, however, only that the form has changed. In Chapter 8, I suggested that in many primitive communities, folk religion arises in a decentralized manner, and that in modern societies, communities frequently resort to religious practice for what amount to instrumental reasons. That is, the practice of religion is sustained not by dogmatic belief in revelation but rather because religious teachings constitute a convenient language in which to express the community's existing moral rules. The children of Hamelin, seeking to create social order within their little tribe, may well define the rules they arrive at in religious terms. This does not contradict my earlier point that they will achieve social order without a prophet to bring them the word of God. This kind of decentralized, instrumental religion is a component of spontaneous order, rather than an alternative to it. And while this religious language may seem arational in a way that the language of law and politics is not, it nonetheless serves rational purposes of community building.

No religion sees itself as a mere instrument of social order. Dwight Eisenhower was once ridiculed for saying that Americans should go to church, any church. But in fact, that is precisely how many people approach contemporary religion. They see that their lives are disorderly, that their children need values and rules, or that they are isolated and disoriented; they turn to a particular denomination not because they have become true believers but because that is the most convenient source of rules, order, and community. This type of religious practice does not overcome the problem of moral miniaturization and in fact may well contribute to it. On the other hand, it is a powerful source of social order back inside the cave.

This kind of decentralized religious practice is unlikely ever to disappear, precisely because it is so useful to communities. A generation or two ago, it was commonplace to believe that modernization and secularization went together ineluctably and that belief founded on revelation would eventually be replaced by knowledge founded on reason, science, and empiricism. This seemed plausible given the secularization that was occurring in most European societies, and in the light of the secularization of public life that has taken place in the United States. But there is no well-established social science theory that tells us that a revival of religion is impossible under today's conditions. As Peter Berger, David Martin, and many others have pointed out,[5] the supposed correlation between secularization and modernization that was once a staple of the sociological literature is not true.[6] This supposedly universal law of social development proves to be applicable primarily to Western Europe. Other parts of the developed world, and particularly the United States, have seen little diminution in professed religious belief with higher levels of income and education.[7] Martin has pointed to at least three major religious revivals in the United States since the first Pilgrims settled in Plymouth Bay in 1620: the Great Awakening of the first half of the eighteenth century, the Second Great Awakening of the 1830s and the 1840s, and the Pentecostal upsurge of the mid-twentieth century, a revival that is in some sense still ongoing.[8]

The Cultural Basis for Trust

Despite the decline of hierarchical religion in modern societies, the cultural patterns it established long ago continue to play decisive roles in shaping contemporary trust relationships. One of the weaknesses of any attempt to use human nature to explain phenomena like trust and social capital is that it cannot give an account of the observable differences that exist between human groups. And so too here. The kinds of universal psychological characteristics described earlier as the basis for social capital are sufficient to explain why there should be social cooperation within relatively small groups, but they do not explain why different contemporary human societies have different radii of trust. These kinds of explanations must be entirely cultural in nature, and often need to refer back to a society's religious heritage.

In my earlier book *Trust,* I explored a number of these cultural differences.[9] Chinese societies, for example, often have a radius of trust restricted to family and kinship groups, as a result of Confucianism's emphasis on the family as the primary source of social obligation. A child whose father committed a crime in traditional China was not obligated to report his parent to the police; duties to family trumped duties to the state. This meant that there tended to be strong cooperative bonds within families, but a relative lack of trust between strangers who could not claim a kin relationship. Chinese businesses tend to remain within the family and form alliances based not on any kind of impersonal profit-maximizing criteria, but rather on the basis of family and personal friends.

A similar situation exists in Latin Catholic countries, in both southern Europe and Latin America. The radius of trust tends once again to be limited to family and close personal friends. The economies of countries like Mexico, Peru, Bolivia, and Venezuela are largely controlled by at most a few dozen powerful families, whose businesses span a host of sectors from retailing to manufacturing to insurance. The economic rationale for such networks is not obvious to outsiders until one realizes that they are all based on kinship and personal ties. Outside investors who operate in ignorance of these complex networks of trust do so at their own peril.

A common consequence of a cultural emphasis on kinship as the basis for social capital is that there are two levels of moral obligation—one inside the family and another, lower one for everyone else. In many such familistic societies, there is a high level of public corruption because public service is often regarded as an opportunity to steal on behalf of the family. A popular saying in Brazil is that there is one morality for the family and another for the street. It is hard to make business deals without kinship and personal ties, and strangers are often treated with a kind of flinty opportunism that would never occur within the network of trust.

This is not the place for an extended discussion of the origins of these cultural habits, except insofar as they shed light on the future of the Great Disruption and the prospects for cultural renewal in those countries that have experienced it. Familism in the Latin Catholic world has cultural roots in both the Latin tradition of *familia* and the Catholic emphasis on the family, while in China it is deeply rooted in Confucian ideology. Protestantism, as Max Weber pointed out, laid the basis for a wider radius of trust by deemphasizing what he called the "sib" or family, and enjoining on believers a universal obligation for honesty and moral behavior. The United States was not simply culturally Protestant when it became an independent nation; its version of Protestantism was highly sectarian, decentralized, and congregational in internal organization. Unlike Europe with its state-sanctioned religions, the United States disestablished all of its churches by the early nineteenth century and made religion entirely voluntary. The profusion of voluntary associations in the United States was therefore in large measure fueled by sectarian Protestantism; the latter explains the relatively higher density of civil associations there than in virtually any other developed nation. The World Values Survey provides ample confirmation of this. In 1991, 71 percent of Americans reported that they were members of a voluntary organization, compared to 38 percent in France, 64 percent in Canada, 52 percent in Britain, and 67 percent in the former West Germany.[10] Lester Salamon also finds that the U.S. nonprofit sector represents a significantly larger share of U.S. employment and GDP than for any other developed country.[11] What Weber called "the ghost of dead religious beliefs," in the form of a secular art of association, continues to haunt American society.

The failure to expand the radius of trust beyond the natural circle of family and friends can be the product of bad government. A transparent rule of law creates grounds for trust between strangers. But such a rule of law cannot be taken for granted. Some states have failed to protect property rights adequately or secure public safety; others have been arbitrary and rapacious in the way they tax and regulate society. Under these circumstances, the family becomes a kind of safe haven, a restricted sphere in which one can be relatively confident in the trustworthiness of other people. The Chinese reliance on family is rooted in the arbitrary and exploitative system of taxation in imperial China, reinforced by the horrendous political history of twentieth-century China. Families keeping a separate set of books for the family and for the tax collector made sense in a society where tax farming was common. Diego Gambetta explains that the Sicilian mafia emerged in the late nineteenth century because the government in southern Italy for various reasons never adequately protected property rights.[12] In the absence of an effective court system to which individuals could turn in civil matters, they were forced to go to a mafioso to guarantee that they could get restitution in case they were cheated. Something similar has been unfolding in post-Soviet Russia, where the state has been ineffective in protecting property rights and personal safety, forcing individuals to turn to private sources of protection in the form of the local mafia. A universal, fairly enforced rule of law, by contrast, promotes a much wider radius of trust by giving unrelated strangers a basis for working with one another and resolving disputes.

Back to the Cave

In this and the previous chapter, I have outlined the limitations of natural and spontaneous order, and explained why hierarchical authority in the form of religion and political authority has been necessary to create social order and the totality of norms we label culture. On an organizational level as well, I have shown why hierarchy will never disappear altogether, and why the great advantages of networks and spontaneously organized workplaces will never be sufficient to meet all of the ends that organizations seek. One might be tempted to ask, in the light of all of these limitations, why I have bothered to discuss the natural and spontaneous sources of order in the first place, since they must be supplemented in so many ways by hierarchical order, and what relevance they have to the Great Disruption.

The answer is, to combine metaphors a bit, that the children of Hamelin are already outside the cave. What they have lost is not scale or moral universalism but the ordinary morality that they were initially able to create for themselves. That is, the advanced societies of North America and Europe are already large, politically stable entities, endowed with plenty of hierarchical authority that can enforce universalistic principles of individual rights and citizenship. Although they may not live up to these principles fully and there has been an ongoing process of moral miniaturization, residents of these societies are not yet living in hostile, self-regarding caves or "burbclaves" where the radius of trust extends no farther than the edge of the neighborhood. None of them has become a Bosnia or Rwanda. They can presuppose certain common political principles that allow them to be large, rich societies in which diversity can be an advantage as well as a problem.

The kinds of endemic distrust that exist in southern Italy and contemporary Russia are unlikely to be self-correcting anytime in the near future. The natural capabilities of their inhabitants to create spontaneous order will not be sufficient to permit them to correct cultural habits that lead to a restricted radius of trust. The latter is reinforced by a history of bad government and the absence of mediating social groups—civil society—groups that cannot be called into existence overnight. But that is not the problem faced by the United States or any of the other developed countries experiencing the Great Disruption. The United States, in particular, has a culture that encourages voluntary association; whatever decline in trust may have occurred, it still ranks above Italy and France in this regard. Its society is flexible, dynamic, and relatively unencumbered by ritualization and tradition. We might draw an analogy here to economic development. Development economists are aware that the postulates of modern neoclassical economics do not seem to apply to many Third World countries. These countries lack political and economic institutions that developed societies can take for granted, like banking regulation or a functioning commercial court system, and face cultural obstacles that do not exist in the relatively fluid society of, say, the United States. The idea, for example, that entrepreneurship will flourish when regulatory burdens are lifted does not always apply to countries with cultures hostile to innovation or risk taking. In some cases deregulation leads to criminal behavior and anarchy. This does not mean, however, that these laws won't work in developed societies where the theories were generated in the first place.

The American difficulty is of a different sort. Due to technological change and the very scale and diversity of contemporary society, it has lost much of the ordinary morality the children of Hamelin would have enjoyed while still living in the cave. The reconstitution of social order for the United States and other societies in a similar position, then, is not a matter of rebuilding hierarchical authority. It is a matter of reestablishing habits of honesty, reciprocity, and an enlarged radius of trust under changed technological circumstances.

Hence, knowing that there are important natural and spontaneous sources of social order is not a minor insight. It suggests that culture and moral values will continue to evolve in ways that will allow people to adapt to the changing technological and economic conditions they face and that this spontaneous evolution will interact with hierarchical authority to produce an "extended order of human cooperation." Neither self-organization nor hierarchy is dispensable as a source of rules. Family life cannot be restored in the United States or any other developed country through government fiat, nor can the state dictate how women are going to balance work with responsibilities to children. Crime control is often the responsibility of neighborhoods, which set standards for public behavior. These cultural rules will have to be worked out by individuals and communities interacting with one another on a daily basis. On the other hand, public policy can shape social choices around the margin in ways that are both helpful and unhelpful, by ensuring public safety, on the one hand, or by creating perverse incentives for single-parent families on the other. Although contemporary societies can no longer depend on the authority of religion as they once could, religion has not disappeared and remains a helpful source of common values. But we should presume that people will continue to use their innate capabilities and reason to evolve rules that serve their long-term interests and needs. Human beings have been doing this for tens of thousands of years, so it would be a surprise if they ceased doing so at the end of the twentieth century.

What remains, then, is to turn from this abstract account of the origins of social order to a more concrete discussion of how we might get beyond the Great Disruption as our information age societies continue to mature. In a sense, we have already begun to do this in the discussion of networks and the uses of social capital in high-tech workplaces. Although the development of contemporary capitalism has destabilized industrial era social norms, we need to ask whether it does not contain in it other sources of social order. We can also gain some insight into the future by looking at the past and examining the ways in which societies have historically rebuilt moral values in the face of rapid technological change. These, then, will be the subjects of Part Three.

PART THREE

THE
GREAT
RECONSTRUCTION

15

Does Capitalism Deplete Social Capital?

M any people intuitively believe that capitalism is bad for moral life. Markets put a price on everything and replace human relationships with the bottom line. By this view, a modern capitalist society consumes more social capital than it produces. Phenomena like decreasing confidence in institutions, a smaller radius of trust, higher crime, and fragmenting bonds of kinship in North America and Europe raise the troubling possibility that these advanced societies are spending their social capital without being able to build it back up again. Are capitalist societies destined to become materially wealthier but morally poorer as time goes on? Is the very ruthlessness and impersonality of markets undermining our social connectedness and teaching us that only money, not values, matters? Is modern capitalism destined to undermine its own moral basis, and thereby bring about its own collapse?

The truth of the matter is that contemporary technological societies continue to require social capital, use it up, and then replenish it, much as before. The types of demand and the sources of supply have changed, but there is little evidence that the need for informal ethical norms will disappear, or that human beings will cease to set moral standards for themselves and seek to live up to them. As we have seen from the discussion of natural and spontaneous order in Part Two, human beings will produce moral rules for themselves, partly because they are designed by nature to do so and partly as a result of their pursuit of self-interest. In the past, social capital may have come from sources like hierarchical religion or age-old tradition that in parts of the modern world appear to be relatively weak. But that is not their only source.

The process by which societies regenerate social capital is complex and often difficult. In many cases, it is a multigeneration process that leaves many victims in its wake, as older cooperative norms are destroyed without anything to take their place. The Great Disruption will not correct itself automatically. People have to recognize that their communal lives have deteriorated, that they are engaging in self-destructive behaviors, and that they have to work actively to renorm their society through discussion, argument, cultural argument, and even culture wars. There is evidence that this has happened to some extent already, and earlier periods in human history give us a certain confidence that renorming or remoralization is possible.

Cultural Contradictions of Capitalism?

The question of how the modern economic order relates to moral order is an old one that has been addressed by numerous writers. It may be helpful to review some earlier thinking on this subject before proceeding to see how the supply of social capital may be created in even the most technologically sophisticated parts of the global economy. As the economist Albert Hirschman has pointed out, there have been a number of completely contradictory views as to whether the spread of modern, technologically driven capitalism helps or hurts moral life.[1]

One view is that associated with Edmund Burke, who in effect traced the depletion of social capital to the Enlightenment. Reacting to the excesses of the French Revolution, Burke criticized the effort to establish a new and just political and social order on the basis of abstract principles imposed coercively by a centralized state. The workability of such an order depended not just on the wisdom of the social engineers who designed the society, but on the assumption that human beings could be adequately motivated by rational self-interest. Burke argued that most workable social rules could not be discerned through a priori reasoning, but rather emerged on a trial-and-error basis through the continuous evolution of societies. This was not necessarily a rational process; religion and ancient social custom played an important role in the shaping of rules. There is also a relativistic element to Burkean conservatism. Each society will generate a different set of rules in response to its own environment and history, which reason is incapable of fully comprehending. For Burke, the French Revolution, and the Enlightenment project more broadly, represented a human disaster because they sought to replace these traditional rules with rational ones, to be obeyed by individuals under no threat of divine sanction. But reason is insufficient to create the moral constraints needed to hold societies together, and so the Enlightenment project would fall apart owing to its own internal contradictions.

There have been more recent versions of the Burkean critique of the Enlightenment. The contemporary British writer John Gray, for example, has argued that with the collapse of the Berlin Wall, the internal contradictions of the Enlightenment have been laid bare for all to see and are manifest in the crime rates and social disorder of advanced countries like the United States.[2] Capitalism reinforces this process: by placing self-interest ahead of moral obligation and being endlessly innovative through the replacement of one technology by another, it destroys the bonds built up over the centuries within human communities and leaves them with nothing but naked self-interest as the grounds for social cohesion.

According to this line of thought, to the extent that modern societies haven't literally fallen apart, it is only because they are living on a certain kind of historical social capital that is only spent and never replenished. Critical to this process of decline is the secularization of the world, for if religion is the great source of moral action, then the decline of religion in the face of modernization means the end of social order. This was stated explicitly by Fred Hirsch in his book *Social Limits to Growth:* "Social virtues such as 'truth, trust, acceptance, restraint, obligation,' needed for the functioning of an 'individualistic, contractual economy' are grounded, to a considerable extent, in religious belief, but 'the individualistic, rationalistic basis of the market undermines religious support.'"[3]

Along similar lines is the substantial literature on the "cultural contradictions of capitalism," which argues that capitalist development ultimately undermines itself by producing norms at odds with those necessary for the operation of markets. Perhaps the most famous exponent of this view was Joseph Schumpeter, who argued in *Capitalism, Socialism, and Democracy* that capitalism tended to produce a class of elites over time that was hostile to the very forces that had made their lives possible, and that they would eventually seek to replace market economies with socialist ones.[4] Daniel Bell argued that abundance makes the work ethic appear unnecessary and also creates a cultural elite that is in perpetual revolution against the status quo. The very essence of artistic modernism, he observed, is the desire to violate established norms, question authority, and defy community standards.[5] Each generation finds the task of norm violation harder because there are fewer norms left to be undermined and fewer people who can be shocked out of their complacent conformism. This explanation accounts for the steady escalation in outrageousness from the pointless dadaism of the 1920s to the obscene, sacrilegious, and offensive performance art of the late twentieth century. Ultimately, according to Bell, a cultural elite that stands perpetually in opposition to all middle-class values ends up destroying the productive basis of the market society that makes its own existence possible.

The potential conflict between a market society and social order was noted not only by Bell, but by numerous other writers, like Michael Sandel, Alan Wolfe, and William J. Bennett.[6] Informal community norms are best generated and enforced in small, stable groups, yet capitalism is so dynamic that it is constantly tearing communities apart through downsizing, rightsizing, and moving jobs overseas. Giant, efficient Wal-Marts replace mom-and-pop retailers, thereby destroying the personal connections the latter engendered, all for the sake of lower prices. Market society produces an entertainment industry that will show people whatever they want to see, whether or not the depiction of sex and violence is good for them or their children. Market society tends to elevate as heroes those who are proficient at either making money or attracting notoriety (often, both) at the expense of those who may have far greater but non-monetizable virtues.[7]

In years past, many sectors of the American economy were protected from competition through regulation, professional standards, or segmented markets. With the deregulation and the opening of the U.S. economy to greater domestic and global competition in the 1980s and 1990s, many of these formerly protected sectors have been subject to greater competitive forces which arguably have had negative effects on social capital. Bankers who could hit the golf links at 3:00 P.M. in the 1950s and 1960s also had time and funds to devote to community service; with banking deregulation, both their time and their discretionary funds are in much shorter supply. The sort of arguments Johnnie Cochran used to help acquit O. J. Simpson—jury nullification based on racial solidarity—would have been severely frowned on by an earlier generation of American jurists. The ability of professional associations to enforce such informal norms, however, has been severely eroded by the much more competitive environment faced by lawyers today. Cochran not only helped his client to beat a murder rap, but also got himself a job on *Court TV* as part of the bargain.

The problem with the "contradictions of capitalism" literature, apart from the fact that capitalism has not yet collapsed or otherwise undermined itself, is that it is extremely one-sided. We can accept the fact that capitalism is often a destructive, disruptive force that breaks apart traditional loyalties and obligations. But it also creates order and builds new norms to replace the ones it destroyed. Indeed, it is likely that capitalism is a net creator of norms and thus a net moralizing force in modern societies. The thrust of the spontaneous order literature cited in Part Two illustrates ways that decentralized groups of people will tend to produce order if left to their own devices.

This was certainly the view of a number of Enlightenment thinkers, who argued that capitalism, far from undermining morals, actually improved them. This idea was first articulated by Montesquieu, who argued that "commerce . . . polishes and softens barbaric ways as we can see every day."[8] Perhaps the clearest statement of this point of view was one by Samuel Ricard in 1704 that was widely quoted throughout the eighteenth century:

> Commerce attaches [men] to one another through mutual utility. . . . Through commerce, man learns to deliberate, to be honest, to acquire manners, to be prudent and reserved in both talk and action. Sensing the necessity to be wise and honest in order to succeed, he flees vice, or at least his demeanor exhibits decency and seriousness so as not to arouse any adverse judgment on the part of present and future acquaintances.[9]

Although Ricard knew nothing of game theory, he is describing an iterated game in which a reputation for honesty becomes an asset. Adam Smith as well believed in the moralizing effects of *doux commerce,* arguing that it promoted punctuality, prudence, and honesty, and improved the lives of the working poor by making them less dependent on their social superiors.[10] More broadly, he made a case for capitalism based less on economic than on moral grounds.[11] Aristocratic societies were based on the desire for honor, which could be satisfied only through military struggle and conquest. Bourgeois societies replaced the aristocratic principle with one founded on a narrower form of self-interest—in Hirschman's phrase, they replaced the passions with the interests—and in the process, softened the brutal and violent habits of aristocratic orders.[12] Members of commercial societies developed long-term interests in industriousness, honesty, self-discipline, and a host of other small virtues that may have failed to achieve the greatness of aristocratic societies but nonetheless avoided their vices. Hirsch's assertion that a virtue like honesty necessary for commerce must depend on religion for its survival is, in the end, absurd. The self-interest of businessmen is sufficient to ensure that honesty (or at least the appearance of honesty) will continue to exist.

In the end, it would be best to take an intermediate position—that the progress of capitalism simultaneously improves and injures moral behavior. The shift from passions to interests is not one of pure gain. The aristocratic love of honor is at the core of all great political ambition, making political life dependent in many respects on it. Great and noble enterprises are not begun by people who are merely honest, prudent, punctual, and reliable. Adam Smith in particular was conscious of the limitations of the kinds of small virtues that commerce tended to encourage—for him, prudence commanded only "cold esteem"—and the ends sought by the bourgeois seeking to "better their condition" were based on the illusion that wealth could buy happiness.[13]

Even if we were to restrict our consideration to the bourgeois virtues, it is possible to admit that market society simultaneously injures and strengthens moral relationships. Putting a price on love or firing a long-term employee for better efficiency may indeed make people cynical. But the reverse also happens: people acquire social connectedness in the workplace and learn honesty and prudence by being forced to work with other people on a long-term basis. Not only that, social capital and internalized, informal norms become even more important as we move from an industrial to a postindustrial or information age economy and as the complexity and technological level of an economy grows. Complex activities need to be self-organizing and self-managing. The capabilities for doing so, if not given in the underlying culture, will be supplied by private firms because their productivity depends on it. We can see this in the new forms of organization that have spread in American factories and offices over the past twenty years, and particularly in the concept of the network.

Modern, postindustrial capitalist economies will generate a continuing demand for social capital. *In the long run,* they should also be able to supply sufficient quantities of social capital to keep up with demand as well. We can be reasonably confident about this because we know that private agents seeking their own selfish ends will tend to produce social capital and the virtues associated with it, like honesty, reliability, and reciprocity. God, religion, and age-old tradition are helpful to this process but not necessary. Montesquieu and Adam Smith were right in arguing that commerce tended to improve morals; Burke, Daniel Bell, and John Gray are wrong to assert that capitalism necessarily undercuts its own moral basis or more broadly that the Enlightenment is self-undermining.

There is a great deal of confusion over this point. James Coleman, the sociologist who was responsible for resurrecting the term *social capital* in recent years, argued that it is a public good that therefore tends to be underproduced by free markets.[14] That is, social capital is of benefit to society as a whole; the group of individuals who embody social capital cannot capture the benefits for themselves and therefore will not have sufficient incentive to create it in the first place. This means it needs to be supplied by nonmarket forces—by either governments (as when they provide public education that has a socializing effect) or nongovernmental actors like families, churches, charities, or other types of voluntary associations that are not in it for the money. Many participants in the social capital debate believe, consistent with this view, that there is a sharp distinction between a profit-making corporation like Intel or Gillette and a nongovernmental organization like the Sierra Club or the AARP. Only the latter embody social capital and are legitimately part of civil society.

The view that social capital is a public good is wrong. Social capital will in fact be produced by private markets because it is in the long-term interests of selfish individuals to produce it. The corporation that requires a high degree of honesty and civility in its customer service, or the firm that immediately takes a defective product off store shelves, or the CEO who takes a pay cut to show solidarity with his workers during a recession are not acting altruistically: each has a long-term interest in a reputation for honesty, reliability, quality, and fairness or for simply being a great benefactor. These virtues become economic assets and as such are sought after by individuals and firms interested only in the bottom line. Similarly, the whalers or ranchers or fishermen who devise rules for the fair, long-term exploitation of common-pool resources are not doing this out of a sense of environmental correctness; they have a self-interest that the resource not be depleted so that they can get their fair share over the long run.

Nevertheless, social capital has a different character from physical or human capital. In the economist Partha Dasgupta's phrase, social capital is not a public good, but it is nonetheless pervaded by externalities.[15] That is, private individuals may produce social capital for their own selfish reasons, but once produced, it has a host of beneficial spillover effects on the broader society. Corporations seeking to burnish their reputations for quality and reliability will raise the general level of quality and reliability in the broader society. Individuals who believe that honesty is the best policy (i.e., that honesty has a selfish value) end up acting not that differently from those who believe that honesty should be valued for its own sake. Not only does social capital produce externalities, it is often itself produced as a by-product or externality of some other activity. Max

Weber's famous Puritans did not seek wealth by capital accumulation; they sought to demonstrate their status as elect in the eyes of God. But as an accidental consequence of their frugality, self-discipline, and desire to prove election, they created businesses in the here-and-now that were ultimately the source of enormous wealth.

So if we accept the fact that social capital is not a public good but rather a private good pervaded by externalities, then we can see that a modern market economy will generate social capital all the time. In the case of individual firms, social capital can and is built through direct investment in education and training in cooperative skills. There is, of course, a huge business literature on creating corporate cultures, which are nothing other than attempts to socialize workers in a firm into a series of norms that will improve their willingness to cooperate with one another, and build a sense of group identity.[16] The Japanese are past masters at this, sending their executives on brutal communal training exercises that test endurance and build bonds of mutal dependence.[17] As we saw in Chapter 12, many firms that have moved to flat forms of organization, teams, and similar management structures have found that they have had to invest heavily in teaching their blue-collar workers to exercise what are in effect white-collar managerial skills.

The State as Friend and Enemy of Social Capital

The fact that social capital can be produced by private firms does not mean, of course, that it is not also produced by public agencies. Anyone who thinks that government cannot inculcate values need only observe the U.S. Marine Corps, which over the years has excelled in taking boys from lower-class and poor neighborhoods, many from single-parent families and bad neighborhoods, and turning them into Marines with an extraordinarily well-developed set of internal organizational rules and norms. The Marines do this in an utterly hierarchical and authoritarian manner during their eleven-week basic training, when recruits are deliberately broken of their individualism and forbidden to use the personal pronoun "I."

One of the most important sources of social capital in contemporary societies is the educational system, which in most countries is provided by the state as a public good. Schools have traditionally not simply provided students with knowledge and skills; they have also sought to socialize them into certain cultural habits ultimately designed to make them better citizens. In the first decades of the twentieth century, many public educators in the United States saw as one of their goals assimilating the many immigrant children who poured into the country at the beginning of the century into the broader American culture. Trust, as we have seen, is highly correlated with level of education.

At higher levels of education, schools continue to do a good job of creating social capital. As I noted in the earlier discussion of high-tech R&D, professional education often serves as an important source of norms and social connectedness. Fields of expertise, professional standards, and the experience of higher education itself all create communities in which people share knowledge and experience and in which norms are established and enforced. Levels of postsecondary education have increased in virtually all developed countries in the past two generations and are likely to continue to do so as the returns to education increase. It should not be surprising, then, that social capital is relatively abundant at the top end of a society's educational and income distribution. As the discussion of civil society in Chapter 4 suggested, what has changed is not society's total stock of social capital but its distribution and character.

While governments are capable of building social capital, they are also adept at destroying it. I noted in earlier chapters how states that fail to provide for public safety or stable property rights tend to breed citizens who distrust not only the government but also each other and find it difficult to associate. The growth of modern welfare states, the centralization of their functions, and their intrusion into virtually all walks of life have tended to undermine spontaneous sociability. In European countries like Sweden and France, there is what passes for a vigorous private associational life, but almost all of it depends in some manner on the government for subsidy or regulation; in the absence of the state, many apparently voluntary organizations would collapse. In the United States, localities and states lost power to the federal government during the period of the Great Disruption, and when the government intervened, it was often hostile to the goal of private association. The decriminalization of social disorder described earlier, carried out by the judicial system, is just one example of how the modern liberal state has been able to rob local communities of their ability to set rules and norms for themselves in the name of individual rights.

To take another case, John Miller has pointed out that one of the biggest shortcomings of the contemporary American public education system is the fact that it has given up on the goal of assimilation.[18] Civics and training in American history and values have become less common; many schools have had problems maintaining simple order and preventing violence in classrooms, much less shaping the characters of their students according to common cultural patterns. Schools in many instances are being asked to socialize children whose parents have failed to provide their offspring with adequate social capital and are not managing to keep up. In other instances, the public school system has actually decreased the stock of social capital by promoting innovations like bilingualism and multiculturalism, whose ostensible purpose of building the self-esteem of minority groups has the practical effect of erecting unnecessary cultural barriers between groups.

The question for the future is whether there is some kind of inexorable necessity for modern liberal states to grow in power and to use that power to promote recognition of an ever-widening sphere of individual rights at the expense of community. Although the record of the United States in this regard has not been encouraging over the past generation, I know of no deterministic historical force that makes such outcomes inevitable when they manifestly violate the interests of large majorities of citizens. Perhaps the dismantling of bilingualism in California as a result of the passage of Proposition 227 indicates that modern democracies can still shape their own futures in this regard.

Economic Exchange and Moral Exchange

Many people would not accept the fact that something done by a corporation in its own self-interest can have any moral content. This stems, in my view, from the perfectly reasonable distinction most people make between altruistic or moral intentions and rational self-interest. This is all the more true of economists, who want to keep their science free of any kind of dependence on moral motivation.[19] Commonsense moral reasoning tells us, in effect, that if I am honest and helpful to you only because I want to have your repeat business in the future, then I am not *really* being honest and helpful, just calculating. A virtue is not a virtue unless it is practiced for its own sake.

This Kantian view of moral behavior stressing intentions rather than results is important to keep in mind, particularly when judging people's character. But in practice the line between moral and self-interested behavior is not easy to draw. We often start out obeying a norm for self-interested reasons, but continue obeying it for what amount to moral considerations. You go to work for Company X because you need a job and want to pay your mortgage, but after working there for a couple of years, you find that you have developed a sense of loyalty, if not to the company as an abstract entity, then at least to your fellow workers as people. You begin to make sacrifices of your own self-interest—staying late at the office, using your personal contacts to help the company out—not just because you want that bonus but because you feel you owe it to your coworkers. If Company X betrays you in the end by downsizing your job out of existence, you feel it not just as an impersonal economic decision but as a moral betrayal: "I've given ten years of my life to that firm and this is what I get in return!"

And while it is important to maintain a distinction between moral behavior undertaken for its own sake and rational self-interest, it is difficult and often unreasonable to delink moral behavior entirely from self-interest. Consider the difference between market exchange and reciprocal altruism, which is grounded in biology (as shown in Chapter 9). In a market transaction, buyers and sellers exchange goods and money for mutual benefit. In a situation of reciprocity, two people similarly exchange benefits with one another to each other's long-term benefit. We consider market exchange an amoral transaction, whereas we invest reciprocity with moral meaning. Why?

In the abstract, the only difference between the two situations is a time shifting of when the exchange occurs. In a market transaction, the goods are exchanged simultaneously, whereas in a situation of reciprocal altruism, one person may confer a benefit and not expect any immediate return. But this makes all the difference in the world. If my friend calls and asks me to help her move out of her apartment, and I say "Okay, but only if you help me paint my house tomorrow," we suspect she won't be my friend for long. Supposing a man is robbed, beaten, and left for dead at the side of the road. If a stranger comes up and offers to help, but only if he is paid money on the spot, most people would feel angry at an offer of what amounts to fair economic exchange. Had the stranger been a good Samaritan, however, and helped the man to the hospital, he and most other people would feel obliged to seek the stranger out later to try to return the kindness or at least to thank him. The latter constitutes exchange, but with a very different moral meaning.

There are very few moral relationships outside of kinship that involve acts of true one-way altruism rather than reciprocal exchange. If we confer benefits on a friend who rudely spurns us and starts to repay favors with insults and harm, we quickly come to a point where the loyalty seems less like a virtue and more like stupidity. Wealthy benefactors who donate large sums of money to charities late in life frequently explain that they are seeking to "give back to the community" favors they received when they were young. In the climactic scene of Frank Capra's classic movie *It's a Wonderful Life*, the citizens of Bedford Falls repay George Bailey (played by Jimmy Stewart) for a lifetime of favors he has done them when his savings and loan is about to go bankrupt. What gives the scene its sentimental power is not the fact that George Bailey was altruistic, but rather the reassurance it conveys that in a true human community, altruism is ultimately rewarded—in this case, with large amounts of cold, hard cash. We do not believe—unless we are Kantians of a rather extreme sort—that George Bailey's moral behavior was diminished in any way because it ultimately led to economic benefit. Nor, on the other hand, would we ever equate the time-shifted exchange of benefits within this community with market exchange. That is the province of Old Man Potter, the hard-hearted banker who is the villain of the movie.

Market exchange is therefore not the same as the reciprocal altruism that goes on within moral communities, but the two are not completely unrelated either. Market exchange promotes habits of reciprocity that carry on from economic life into moral life. Moral exchange promotes the self-interest of the people who participate in it. The sharp dichotomy that is often drawn between self-interested and moral behavior is in many instances difficult to maintain.

The problem that modern capitalist societies pose for moral relationships does not therefore lie in the nature of economic exchange itself. The problem, rather, lies in technology and technological change. Capitalism is so dynamic, such a source of creative destruction, that it is constantly altering the terms of exchange that go on within human communities. This is true for both economic exchange and moral exchange, and was the source of the Great Disruption.

16

Reconstructions Past,
Present, and Future

It is now time to return to the Great Disruption and raise the question of what comes next. Are we fated to slide into ever-increasing levels of social and moral disorder, or is there reason to expect that the disruption is merely a temporary condition, and that the United States and other societies that have experienced it will successfully renorm themselves? And if the renorming takes place, what form will it take? Will it happen spontaneously, or will it require the intervention of government through public policies? Or do we have to await some kind of unpredictable and very likely uncontrollable religious revival to restore social values? In Part Two we drew a four-quadrant matrix in which order was said to be natural, self-organized, religious, or political in nature. On which of these sources of order can we draw in the future?

The easiest of these questions to answer is the first: the Great Disruption does not represent the finale of a long-term moral decline that was made necessary by the advent of the Enlightenment, secular humanism, or any other deep historical source. While the cultural emphasis on individualism is deeply rooted in that tradition, the Great Disruption had much more proximate causes like the shift from an industrial to a postindustrial economy and the changes in labor markets this made possible.

Perhaps the easiest way to get a handle on answering the question of the Great Disruption's future is to look at Great Disruptions of the past. Indices of social order have increased and decreased over time, suggesting that although social capital may often seem constantly in the process of depletion, its stock has also increased in certain historical periods. Ted Robert Gurr estimates that in England, homicide rates were three times higher in the thirteenth century than the seventeenth, three times higher in the seventeenth than in the nineteenth, and in London in the early nineteenth century twice as high as in the 1970s.[1] Both conservatives decrying moral decline and liberals celebrating increased individual choice sometimes talk as if there has been a steady movement away from the Puritan values of the early 1600s to the present. But while a secular trend toward greater individualism has been evident over this long time period, there have been many fluctuations in behavior that suggest that societies have been perfectly capable of increasing the degree of constraint on individual choice through moral rules.

This happened during the nineteenth century. I began this book by noting that the great classics of sociology were written to describe the shift in norms that took place as societies in North America and Europe moved from agricultural to industrial ones, the shift captured in the dichotomy between gemeinschaft and gesellschaft. This transition took place first in Britain and then in the United States, the first two countries to industrialize, and somewhat later in the various parts of continental Europe. There is considerable evidence that the late eighteenth and early nineteenth centuries were periods of rising social disorder and moral confusion, in which various indices of social capital declined for both Britain and the United States.

In the United States, the colonial period was not one of great propriety or social engagement, despite the high degree of political participation. In the 1790s, according to historian Richard Hofstadter, perhaps as many as 90 percent of Americans were "unchurched," without any formal affiliation to a church or other religious organization.[2] Given the critical importance of Protestant religiosity to the American art of association that Tocqueville described, this figure suggests that many Americans remained relatively isolated in their farms and villages, without the kinds of civic structures that were to blossom later in the nineteenth century.

Rates of social deviance were high relative to those of the seventeenth century and of later time periods as well. In the early 1800s, per capita consumption of alcohol stood at six gallons of absolute alcohol for every person in America over the age of fifteen, compared to rates of less than three gallons in the late twentieth century.[3] One scholar estimates that by 1829, per capita consumption had risen to an astonishing ten gallons.[4] Taverns were significantly more popular than churches as poles of social interaction, and drunken farmers stumbling home to their farmhouses, or workmen downing a pint of whiskey on their way to work, were not uncommon sights. According to historian William Rorabaugh, in the early nineteenth century, "The male drinking cult pervaded all social and occupational groups. A western husbandman tarried at the tavern until drunk; an eastern harvest laborer received daily a half pint or a pint of rum; a southern planter was considered temperate enough to belong to the Methodist Church if he restricted his daily intake of alcohol to a quart of peach brandy."[5]

It is naturally very difficult to come by quantitative evidence of sexual behavior in this period. Statistics on phenomena like illegitimacy were not kept regularly until the twentieth century. Some social historians have suggested, however, that sexual norms became less restrictive in this period than they were under the seventeenth-century Puritans. Parental control over choice in marriage partners declined, and, according to one study, premarital pregnancy rates increased from 10 percent in the 1600s to perhaps 30 percent by the second half of the 1700s.[6]

The same can be said for crime. Although there does not seem to have been much crime in colonial times, most social historians seem to agree that rates began to go up rapidly in the first decades of the nineteenth century: Boston, Philadelphia, and New York all saw increases. In early nineteenth-century America, there were more and more occasions for young men to be off on their own. Prior to that time, most wage labor was household based. Domestic servants, apprentices, or journeymen would live and work under the same roof as their employers and could be controlled just like members of the employer's family. With the growth of the factory system, however, working men and women were employed outside households for the first time and began establishing their own neighborhoods. The American West was settled primarily by young men, with women and children appearing on the scene only later. All of these conditions promoted higher levels of crime. This phenomenon was not limited to America: Gurr has shown that crime rates increased in London and Stockholm in this period as well.[7] London, like the American frontier, saw an increase in the relative numbers of young males in the period from 1821 to 1841.[8]

In addition to increasing deviance, the shift from country to city meant that country people were bringing their manners with them into new, crowded urban environments. The crudeness of life in this period is often forgotten. Consider James Lincoln Collier's description of early nineteenth-century America:

> Few people had beds to themselves, and sometimes a bed was shared with two or more, especially in the large families that were typical of the day. They bathed infrequently and put on the same clothes morning after morning. They lived surrounded by manure. . . . Chamber pots were emptied into the streets, without much regard for passersby. . . . Broken windows, sagging doors, rotting clapboards went unrepaired for months if not years, and houses were repainted infrequently. Junk—the remains of broken tools, furniture, carts—was allowed to lie in farmyards for years. . . . Men and a great many women chewed tobacco, and gobbets of brown spit were everywhere, not merely on tavern floors but on church floors as well. Many people ate their meals with knives only, and some depended primarily on their fingers.[9]

What applies to farm families in the United States also characterized peasants and the urban poor in Britain and other European countries in this same period.

The Victorian period in Britain and America may seem to many to be the embodiment of traditional values, but when this era began in the mid-nineteenth century, they were anything but traditional. Victorianism was in fact a radical movement that emerged in reaction to the kinds of social disorder that seemed to be spreading everywhere at the beginning of the nineteenth century, a movement that deliberately sought to create new social rules and instill virtues in populations that were seen as wallowing in degeneracy. The shift toward Victorian values began in Britain but was quickly imported into the United States beginning in the 1830s and 1840s. Many of the institutions that were responsible for its spread were overtly religious in nature, and the change they brought about occurred with remarkable speed. In the words of Paul E. Johnson, "In 1825 a northern businessman dominated his wife and children, worked irregular hours, consumed enormous amounts of alcohol, and seldom voted or went to church. Ten years later the same man went to church twice a week, treated his family with gentleness and love, drank nothing but water, worked steady hours and forced his employees to do the same, campaigned for the Whig Party, and spent his spare time convincing others that if they organized their lives in similar ways, the world would be perfect."[10] The nonconformist churches in England and the Protestant sects in the United States, particularly the Wesleyan movement, led the Second Great Awakening in the first decades of the century that followed hard on the rise in disorder and created new norms to keep that order under control. The Sunday school movement grew exponentially in both England and America between 1821 and 1851, as did the YMCA movement, which was transplanted from England to America in the 1850s. According to Richard Hofstadter, U.S. church membership doubled between 1800 and 1850, and there was a gradual increase in the respectability of church membership itself as ecstatic, evangelical denominations became more restrained in their religious observances.[11] At the same time, the temperance movement succeeded in lowering per capita alcohol consumption on the part of Americans back down to a little over two gallons by the middle of the century.[12]

Religion, and in particular sectarian Protestantism, was also intimately connected with the spread of voluntary associations and the growth of civil society in this period. It was in the 1830s that Tocqueville visited the United States and noticed the density of civil associations there. Although he gives religion its due, if anything he understates its importance to the spread of organizations and the habit of associating. By the year 1860, approximately one-fifth of New York's adult Protestant population served on any number of lay boards of civic associations.[13]

The historian Gregory Singleton notes how critical religious institutions were to the civilizing of the West:

> In Quincy, Illinois, for example, the American Home Missionary Society, the American Tract Society, and the American Sunday School Union were influential in rapidly establishing a voluntaristic social basis. . . . By 1843, there were in Quincy seventeen different missionary, reform, and benevolence organizations, fifteen of them affiliated with national associations. By 1860, there were fifty-nine voluntary associations, containing approximately ninety per cent of the adult population.[14]

These attempts to renorm British and American society from the 1830s on in what we now label the Victorian era were a monumental success. The impact on social capital in both societies was extraordinary, as masses of rude, illiterate agricultural workers and urban poor were converted into what we now understand as the working class. Under the discipline of the time clock, these workers understood they had to keep regular hours, stay sober on the job, and maintain minimal standards of decent behavior.

Increasing social capital is also evident from simple indicators like crime rates. Virtually all efforts to estimate crime rates in the nineteenth century agree that from the middle of this period to the end, there was a gradual decrease in rates of deviance. Figure 16.1 shows rates of serious offenses for England and Wales from 1805 until the end of the century. Crime increases steadily from the period of the Napoleonic Wars on, but then decreases just as steadily after peaking in the 1840s.[15] In individual American cities, the peaks may have come a bit later; Gurr suggests that the crest in Boston and other American cities may have come in the 1870s.[16] The decreases in crime in the second half of the nineteenth century are all the more remarkable for having occurred in a period when one would expect rising crime. From the American Civil War on, people were pouring into new urban centers from the countryside and villages, new immigrants with different cultures and habits were arriving, and the new rhythms of industrial life were upsetting old social relationships.[17]

In Britain, illegitimacy followed the same path as crime. The proportion of illegitimate births to all births rose from a little over 5 percent at

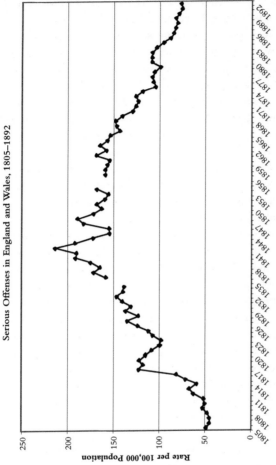

Figure 16.1

Serious Offenses in England and Wales, 1805–1892

Year

Rate per 100,000 Population

Source: E. A. Wrigley, ed. *Nineteenth-Century Society* (Cambridge: Cambridge University Press, 1972), pp. 387–395.

the beginning of the nineteenth century, to a peak of 7 percent in 1845. Thereafter it fell back to 4 percent by the end of the century.[18]

It would be wrong to assert that the greater social order that came to prevail in Britain and America during the Victorian period was simply the result of changing informal moral norms. Both societies in this period established modern police forces, which replaced the hodgepodge of local agencies and poorly trained deputies that existed at the beginning of the nineteenth century. After the Civil War in the United States, police focused attention on minor offenses against public order like public drinking, vagrancy, and loitering, leading to a peaking of arrests for this kind of behavior around 1870.[19] Toward the end of the century, many American states had begun to establish systems of universal education that sought to put all children into free public schools, a process that began somewhat later in Britain.

But the essential change that took place was a matter of values rather than institutions. At the core of Victorian morality was the inculcation of impulse control in young people, the shaping of what economists would today call their preferences so that they would not indulge in casual sex, alcohol, or gambling that would be bad for them in the long run. Victorians sought to create respectable personal habits in societies where the vast majority of inhabitants can be described only as crude. Today the desire for respectability is usually derided as an expression of insufferable middle-class conformism, but it had an important meaning in the first half of the nineteenth century when civility could not be taken for granted. Teaching people habits of cleanliness, punctuality, and politeness was critical in an era when all three of these bourgeois virtues were lacking.

There are examples from other cultures of moral renovation. Tokugawa Japan—that nation's feudal period, when power was held by various *daimyo* or warrior-lords—was one of frequent violence and insecurity. The Meiji Restoration in 1868 brought the country under a single, centralized state and stamped out once and for all the kind of banditry that took place in feudal Japan. The country developed a new moral system as well. We think of customs like lifetime employment, practiced by large Japanese firms, as a deeply cultural and ancient tradition, but in fact it dates only to the late nineteenth century. In that period, there was a high degree of labor mobility; skilled craftsmen in particular were in short supply and constantly on the move between one company and another. Large Japanese firms like Mitsui and Mitsubishi found they could not attract the skilled labor they needed, and so, with the help of the government, they embarked on a campaign to elevate the virtue of loyalty above others. Unlike the crude campaigns waged in the former Soviet Union and other communist countries to encourage people to be altruistic by forcing them to donate their labor to the cause of world socialism, Japanese elites waged a subtle campaign to persuade people to remain loyal to company, nation, and emperor. Loyalty was, of course, a cardinal virtue within the samurai or aristocratic warrior class, but was never widely practiced among merchants or farmers. The Meiji rulers succeeded in persuading these classes as well that loyalty to a firm was tantamount to loyalty to the *daimyo.* Even so, loyalty to company was at first honored more in the breach; it was only after World War II that lifetime employment became more widespread throughout the large company sector.

The Reconstitution of Social Order

The question raised by the Great Disruption is, Could the pattern experienced in the second half of the nineteenth century in Britain and America, or in Japan, repeat itself in the next generation or two?

Evidence is growing that the Great Disruption has run its course and that the process of renorming has already begun. Rates of increase in crime, divorce, illegitimacy, and distrust have slowed substantially and even reversed in the 1990s in many of the countries that earlier experienced an explosion of disorder. This is particularly the case in the United States, where levels of crime have fallen more than 15 percent from the peak levels of the early 1990s. Divorce rates peaked in the early 1980s, and the proportion of births to single mothers has stopped increasing. Welfare rolls have dropped almost as dramatically as crime rates, in response to both the welfare reform measures passed in 1996 and to the opportunities provided by a nearly full-employment economy in the 1990s. Levels of trust in both institutions and individuals have also recovered significantly from the early to the late 1990s.

In the past generation, a sea change has occurred in what Marx would have called the ideological superstructure built around society. When the Moynihan report was issued thirty years ago at the beginning of the Great Disruption, it was almost universally condemned by respectable opinion for "blaming the victim" and being ethnocentric. Today the weight of scholarly opinion has shifted 180 degrees: family structure and values are widely recognized as playing an important role in determining social outcomes. Academic treatises do not directly influence individual behavior, of course, but as Keynes once suggested, abstract ideas have a way of filtering down to the level of popular consciousness in a generation or two.

Any number of other signs suggest that culturally, the period of ever-expanding individualism is coming to an end, and that at least some of the norms swept away during the Great Disruption are being restored. In the 1990s, one of the biggest phenomena in daytime radio in the United States is a call-in show hosted by Dr. Laura Schlessinger, who in a brusque and often censorious tone regularly lectures her listeners to stop indulging themselves and accept responsibility for spouses and children. Her message could not be more different from that of the generation of liberationist therapists who in the 1960s and 1970s advised people to "get in touch with their feelings" and discard social constraints that would stand in the way of "personal growth."

Two of the largest marches in Washington, D.C., during the 1990s were the Million Man March of African Americans organized by Nation of Islam leader Louis Farrakhan, and the march by the Promise Keepers, a conservative Christian group. What is interesting about both of these events was their stress on the decline of male responsibility for their families and the need for men to step up to their duties as fathers, providers, and role models within families. The fact that such large numbers of men could be mobilized around the theme of male responsibility suggests a recognition in the broader society that in the wake of the sexual and feminist revolutions, something was amiss in the expectations that society had of men, and that men had of themselves.

Both the Nation of Islam and the Promise Keepers are highly suspect groups in the eyes of many Americans, the first because of the overtly anti-Semitic views that Farrakhan and other Nation of Islam leaders have expressed over the years, and the latter because of the suspicion of many women that the Promise Keepers seeks to resubordinate women to men. These particular efforts to renorm men have thus run into sharp limits: the Nation of Islam's scapegoating of outsiders as a means of building communal solidarity clashes directly with American liberal principles; the Promise Keepers organization fell apart because of its inability to raise funds to support its own bureaucracy.

Nonetheless, we should expect the conservative trend toward more restrictive norms to continue. The first reason comes out of the theoretical discussion of the sources of order in Part Two: people are social animals by nature and, in addition, rational creators of cultural rules. Both nature and rationality ultimately support the development of the ordinary virtues like honesty, reliability, and reciprocity that constitute the basis for social capital.

Consider the issue of family norms. Norms governing the behavior of both men and women with respect to families changed dramatically after the 1960s in ways that ended up hurting the interests of children: men abandoned families, women conceived children out of wedlock, and couples divorced for what were often superficial and self-indulgent reasons. The interests of parents and the interests of their children frequently conflict: time spent taking a son or daughter to sports or school is time spent away from a job, girlfriend, or leisure activity; living with a less-than-perfect spouse for the sake of the children gets in the way of new opportunities for companionship and sex. But parents will also have a strong natural interest in the well-being of their children. If it can be demonstrated to them that their behavior is seriously injuring the life chances of their offspring, they are likely to behave rationally and to want to alter that behavior in ways that help their children.

The process of reaching a rational set of norms is not an automatic one. During the Great Disruption, the culture produced many cognitive constructs that obscured from people the consequences of their personal behavior on people close to them. They were told by social scientists that growing up in a single-parent family was no worse than growing up in an intact family. They were reassured by family therapists that children were better off if the parents divorced than if they remained in a conflict-strained household. These same therapists told them their children would be happy only if *they* were happy, and thus that it was alright to put their own needs first. And parents were bombarded by images from the popular culture that glamorized sex and portrayed traditional nuclear family life as a hotbed of hypocrisy, repression, and vice. Changing these perceptions requires discussion, argument, even the sort of conflict that James Davison Hunter labeled "culture wars."[20] When Vice President Dan Quayle raised the issue of "family values" during the 1992 presidential campaign and criticized the glamorization of single parenthood on the television series *Murphy Brown,* he was roundly criticized as bigoted and ignorant. But he set off a cultural debate that had important repercussions. President Clinton soon made family values a theme of his own presidency (despite problems in his own family) and helped to legitimize the concept of personal responsibility as a theme in public policy discourse. In the meantime, empirical social science evidence on the deleterious effects of disrupted families continued to accumulate, to the point that it could not be ignored. By the late 1990s, many more people were prepared to accept Barbara Dafoe Whitehead's judgment that "Dan Quayle was right" about the importance of families than even five years earlier.[21]

Social order will not simply be reconstituted through the decentralized interactions of individuals and communities; it will also need to be reconstructed through public policy. This means both action and inaction on the part of government. There is a clear sphere in which governments can act to create social order, through their police powers and through their promotion of education. Crime rates came down in no small measure because jails were built and criminals put away. We have seen how awareness of the social capital dimensions of crime led to innovations like community policing, which arguably had effects in bringing down crime levels in American cities in the 1990s. Beyond crime, however, community policing clearly had an important impact on social capital by creating a greater sense of social order in urban areas and fostering the resettlement of cities by people newly willing to participate in community life and establish stronger community standards. The United States has also embarked on major reforms of its welfare system and of child support collection, both implicated in the problems of the American family during the Great Disruption. The willingness of politicians like New York

City mayor Rudolph Giuliani to reclaim urban areas for middle-class people rather than bending over backward to accommodate the most marginal members of society has laid the basis for a rebuilding of social capital. Other mayors, like Stephen Goldsmith of Indianapolis, have come up with countless creative ways of supporting civic organizations and encouraging citizens to take control of their lives and neighborhoods.[22]

On the other hand, part of the public policy agenda consists not of activism, but of the government getting out of the way of individuals and communities that want to create social order for themselves. In some cases, this means stopping the state from doing counterproductive things like subsidizing illegitimacy or promoting a multiplicity of languages and cultures in the school system. In others, it is a matter of the courts finding a better balance between individual rights and community interests.

How far is this renorming of society likely to go? We are much more likely to see dramatic changes in levels of crime and trust than in norms regarding sex, reproduction, and family life. Indeed, the process of renorming in the first two spheres is already well underway. With regard to sex and reproduction, however, the different technological and economic conditions of our age make it extremely unlikely that anything like a return to Victorian values will take place. Extremely strict rules about sex make sense in a society in which unregulated sex has a high probability of leading to pregnancy, and where having a child out of wedlock is likely to lead to destitution, if not early death, for both mother and child. The first of these conditions largely disappeared with birth control, and the latter was greatly mitigated, though not eliminated, by a combination of female incomes and welfare subsidies. While the United States can and has cut back sharply on welfare, no one is about to propose making birth control illegal or reversing the movement of women into the workplace. The individual pursuit of rational self-interest will also not solve the problems posed by declining fertility. It is precisely the rational interest of parents in their children's long-term life chances that induces them to have fewer. The importance of kinship as a source of social connectedness will probably continue to decline, and the stability of nuclear families is likely never to recover fully. Societies like Japan and Korea that until now have bucked this trend are more likely to shift toward Western practices than the reverse.

What we can hope for in the future, however, are different cultural adaptations that will make information age societies more hospitable to children. The desire of women to work rather than to raise children clearly has a strong cultural component. In many contemporary societies, and particularly in regions like Scandinavia, stay-at-home mothers are looked down on with scorn by their working counterparts because that is the currently fashionable opinion. If it proves, however, that the failure of mothers to stay at home with their children when they are young has a clearly detrimental effect on their children's later life chances, then the cultural norms may change. The ability to take a few years off from work to stay with young children may become the mark of high-status, well-to-do families; it may be only working-class mothers and those on welfare who are forced to give their children up to day care or sitters when they are infants.[23]

Longevity may also have an unanticipated consequence in helping to close the gender gap in incomes. The increase in the length of working lives, coupled with heightened educational requirements for work and greater competitiveness in markets, means that the old model by which a young person got an education that would last an entire working life is becoming less viable. Lifetime employment in the same job or same company has become a thing of the past for many in the United States. European countries like France that are trying to hold on to lifetime employment, or even seeking to lower retirement ages, will find themselves saddled with high permanent unemployment and huge bills for social services. Many of the victims of corporate downsizing in the United States during the 1980s and 1990s were male middle managers in their late forties or fifties. They were forced to start new careers or, if they lacked the flexibility, simply dropped out of the labor force altogether through early retirement. In the future, when people are routinely healthy enough to work well into their seventies, that constant retraining will become necessary and common. But people starting out with new skills and new careers at later points in their lives cannot expect to reenter the workforce at the top of the pay pyramid; falling off the career ladder and downward mobility is likely to become a routine male experience. Much of the existing difference in female and male incomes has to do with women dropping out of the labor force to raise children, which puts them on a lower-paying "mommy track." In a world where work is more fragmented and men are starting out again at advanced ages, the mommy-track disadvantage may appear to be less burdensome. Combined with a greater perception of the importance of mothers to their children, what remains of the gender gap in wages may be seen in time as something less of an injustice requiring urgent remedy.

Technology may help brake the decline in kinship and family life in other ways. Modern networks and communications technology have allowed people to work increasingly out of their homes. The idea that home and work should be located in different places is entirely a creation of the industrial era. Prior to that, the vast majority of people were farmers or peasants who lived on the land they worked; although there was a division of labor within the family, household and production physically took place next to each other. Manufacturing as well often took place within households, where workers were considered part of an extended family. It was only with the advent of the industrial-era factory and office that husbands and wives began to spend their days apart from one another. With women moving into the workforce in large numbers in the second half of the twentieth century, the opportunities for sex outside the home vastly increased, creating the new issue of sexual harassment and adding to the strains already besetting the nuclear family.

Today countless men and women have been downsized out of their Taylorite factory or office and now work out of their homes, connected to the outside world by telephone, fax, e-mail, and the Internet. They may at first feel uncomfortable with this arrangement because they have been brought up to believe that home and work should occur in different places. But this is just a prejudice: it is if anything more natural and more in keeping with the experience of human beings throughout history that home and work should be co-located. It may be that technology, which has infinite capabilities of alienating us from our natural desires and inclinations, may in this instance be able to restore something of the wholeness and integration of life that industrialism took away from us.

Religious Revivals, Then and Now

As the account of the nineteenth-century reconstruction given above indicates, religion played an extremely important role in the Victorian renorming of British and American society. Victorianism was closely allied with Protestantism and the Protestant elites that dominated both societies. In the battles against alcoholism, gambling, slavery, delinquency, and prostitution and in the building of a dense network of voluntary institutions, Methodist, Congregational, Baptist, and other ministers and lay believers were the foot soldiers. They used not just churches but their control over the public school system later in the nineteenth century to achieve these cultural purposes. Religious symbolism was used heavily by Japan's post-Meiji rulers as well in establishing new rules of behavior for an industrial era Japan. The role of religion in past cultural reawakenings raises the question of whether it will play a comparable role in reversing the Great Disruption. If it doesn't play such a role, then we might legitimately question whether a Great Reconstruction will happen at all.

Some religious conservatives hope, and many liberals fear, that the problem of moral decline will be resolved by a large-scale return to religious orthodoxy, a Western version of Ayatollah Khomeini returning to Iran on a jetliner. For a variety of reasons, this seems unlikely. Modern societies are so culturally diverse that it is not clear whose version of orthodoxy would prevail. Any true form of orthodoxy is likely to be seen as a threat to large and important groups in the society, and hence would neither get very far nor serve as a basis for a widening radius of trust. Instead of integrating society, a conservative religious revival may in fact accelerate the movement toward fragmentation and moral miniaturization that has already occurred: the various varieties of Protestant fundamentalists will argue among themselves over doctrine, orthodox Jews will become more orthodox, and newer immigrant groups like Muslims and Hindus may start to organize themselves as political-religious communities.

A return to religiosity is far more likely to take a more benign, decentralized form, in which religious belief is less an expression of dogma than of the community's existing norms and desire for order. In some respects, this has already started to happen in many parts of the United States. Instead of community arising as a by-product of rigid belief, people will come to belief because of their desire for community. In other words, people will return to religious tradition not necessarily because they accept the truth of revelation, but precisely because the absence of community and the transience of social ties in the secular world make them hungry for ritual and cultural tradition. They will help the poor or their neighbors not because doctrine tells them they must, but because they want to serve their communities and find that faith-based organizations are the most effective ways of doing so. They will repeat ancient prayers and reenact age-old rituals not because they believe that they were handed down by God, but rather because they want their children to have the proper values and want to enjoy the comfort of ritual and the sense of shared experience it brings. In this sense they will not be taking religion seriously on its own terms. Religion becomes a source of ritual in a society that has been stripped bare of ceremony, and thus a reasonable extension of the natural desire for social relatedness that all human beings are born with. It is something that modern, rational, skeptical people can take seriously, much as they celebrate their national independence, dress up in traditional ethnic garb, or read the classics of their own cultural tradition. Understood in these terms, religion loses its hierarchical character, and the dividing line between spontaneous rational and arational authority becomes blurred.

The reconstruction of values that has started in the 1990s, and any re-norming of society that may happen in the future, has and will come out of all four quadrants of the norms taxonomy defined in Chapter 8: political, religious, self-organized, and natural. The state is neither the source of all our problems nor the instrument by which we can solve them. But its actions can deplete or restore social capital in ways large and small. We have not become so modern and secularized that we can do without religion. But we are also not so bereft of innate moral resources that we need to wait for a messiah to save us. And nature, which we are constantly trying to evict with a pitchfork, always keeps running back.

Social Capital and History

I said earlier that there were two main sources of an enlarged radius of trust: religion and politics. In the West, Christianity first established the principle of the universality of human dignity, one that was brought down from the heavens and turned into a secular doctrine of universal human equality by the Enlightenment. Today we ask politics to bear nearly the entire weight of this enterprise, and it has done a remarkably

279

good job. Human communities have been based on any number of principles that produce a restricted radius of trust, including family, kinship, dynastic principle, sect, religion, race, ethnicity, and national identity. What the Enlightenment recognized was that all of these traditional sources of community were ultimately irrational. In terms of domestic politics, they implied social conflict, since virtually no society was ever homogeneous with regard to any of these characteristics. And in foreign policy, they paved the way to war, since communities based on different principles were constantly bumping into one another on the world stage. Only a political order based on the universal recognition of human dignity—of the essential equality of all human beings based on their capacity for moral choice—could avoid these irrationalities and lead to a peaceful domestic and international order. Kant's republican form of government, the American Declaration of Independence and Bill of Rights, Hegel's universal and homogeneous state, the Universal Declaration of Rights, and the rights enumerated in the basic laws of virtually all contemporary liberal democracies today enshrine this principle of universal recognition.

Nations built on these universal liberal principles have been surprisingly resilient over the past two hundred years, despite frequent setbacks and shortcomings. A political order based on Serb ethnic identity or Twelver Shi'ism will never grow beyond the boundaries of some miserable corner of the Balkans or Middle East, and could certainly never become the governing principle of large, diverse, dynamic, and complex modern societies like those that make up, for example, the Group of Seven. Not only do they face unresolvable political contradictions concerning religious or ethnic minorities, but their hostility to innovation closes them off from free economic exchange and therefore participation in the modern economic world. The logic of a liberal and democratic political order becomes more pressing as societies develop economically, since reconciliation of all of the diverse interests that make them up requires both participation and equality. The unfolding of modern natural science drives economic development, and economic development drives—with lags, setbacks, and wrong turns—a process of political development in the direction of liberal democracy. We can therefore expect a long-term progressive evolution of human political institutions in the direction of liberal democracy.[24]

The central problem with this essentially optimistic view of historical progress is that social and moral order do not necessarily follow in the wake of political order and economic development. There are two reasons that the cultural preconditions for political order cannot be taken for granted. The first is that liberal societies buy political order at the price of moral consensus. The only moral guidelines a liberal society provides are universal obligations for tolerance and mutual respect. This was not initially a problem because many liberal societies, like the United States, Britain, and France, started out as relatively homogeneous ones in cultural terms, dominated by a single ethnic group and religion. But over time they have become larger and far more culturally diverse. Declining population, pressures for greater immigration, and national borders made permeable by cheap transportation and pervasive communications all suggest that the trend toward greater diversity will continue everywhere. Even countries like Japan that have thus far managed to maintain a fair degree of cultural and ethnic homogeneity will face similar pressures in the future.

In the United States and other English-speaking democracies, as well as in France, these centrifugal cultural forces have been offset traditionally by the creation of a new, civic identity not rooted in either ethnicity or religion. "Americanization," derived equally from democratic political ideals and Anglo-Saxon cultural traditions, was something open to all immigrant children in the United States. French citizenship, based on classical republicanism and French literary culture, was in theory at least equally open to a black from Senegal or an Arab from Tunisia, though immigration there has produced a much more severe backlash in the form of Jean-Marie Le Pen's Front National.

The chief question for the future is whether these universalistic forms of cultural identity will survive the onslaught from a principled belief in multiculturalism that goes beyond the toleration of cultural diversity to its active celebration and promotion. The moral miniaturization that was described in the earlier discussion of American civil society has come about only partly because the underlying society has become more diverse. The more important driver of this process is the spread of a principled belief in moral relativism—the idea that no particular set of values or norms can or ought to be authoritative. When this relativism extends to the political values on which the regime itself is based, then liberalism begins to undermine itself.

The second problem that liberal societies face in safeguarding their own cultural bases is the threat posed by technological change. Social capital is not some rare and precious commodity that was once created in the Age of Faith and handed down like an heirloom from ancient tradition. It is not something with a fixed supply that is now being remorselessly depleted by us modern, secular people. But although the stock of social capital is constantly being replenished, the process is not automatic, easy, or cheap. The same innovation that increases productivity or launches a new industry undermines an existing community or makes an entire way of life obsolete. Societies caught on the escalator of technological progress find themselves constantly having to play catch-up as social rules evolve to meet changed economic conditions. Machine production moves people from country to city and separates husbands from families, while information technology moves them back to the country while pushing women into the workforce. Nuclear families disappear with the invention of agriculture, reappear with industrialization, and start breaking down with the transition to the post industrial era. People can adjust over time to all of these changed conditions, but the rate of technological change can often exceed the rate of social adjustment. When the supply of social capital fails to match the demand, societies must pay a high cost.

There seem to be two processes working in parallel. In the political and economic sphere, history appears to be progressive and directional, and at the end of the twentieth century has culminated in liberal democracy as the only viable alternative for technologically advanced societies. In the social and moral sphere, however, history appears to be cyclical, with social order ebbing and flowing over the space of multiple generations. There is nothing that guarantees that there will be upturns in the cycle. Our only reason for hope is the very powerful innate human capacities for reconstituting social order. On the success of this process of reconstitution depends the upward direction of the arrow of History.

APPENDIX: ADDITIONAL DATA AND SOURCES

Figures A.1 through A.5 present trends on violent crime, theft, fertility, divorce, and illegitimacy for ten OECD countries in addition to the United States, England and Wales, Sweden, and Japan, that were presented in the text of the book. The data underlying these and other figures in this book can been seen at the author's web site, *http://mason.gmu.edu/~ffukuyam/*.

FIGURE A.1
Violent Crime Rates, 1950–1996

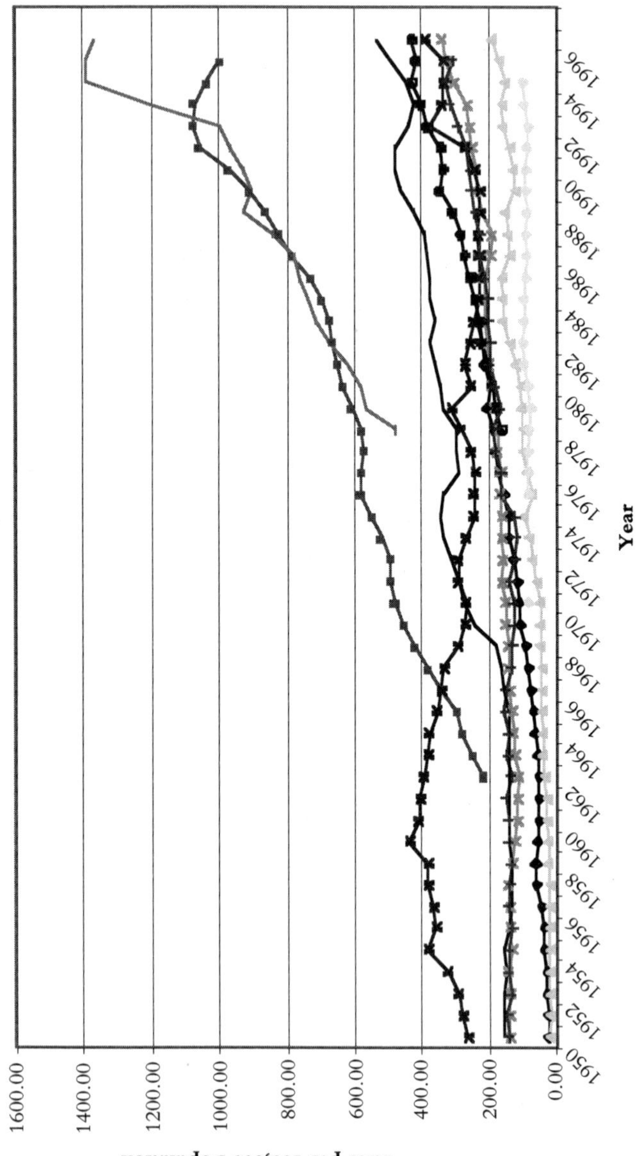

284

FIGURE A.2
Theft Rates, 1950–1996

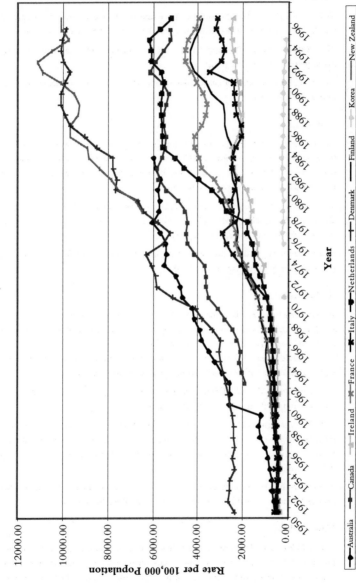

285

Canada

Violent Crime Rates: From the Violent Crime category. Includes homicide, attempted murder, various forms of sexual and nonsexual assault, robbery, and abduction.

Theft Rates: From the Property Crime category. Includes breaking and entering, fraud, possession of stolen goods.

Source: Statistics Canada, *Canadian Crime Statistics 1995* (Ottawa: Canadian Centre for Justice Statistics, 1995).

Denmark

Violent Crime Rates: From the Sexual Offences category, which includes rape and offenses against decency, and from the Crimes of Violence category, which includes assault versus public servant in discharge of his duties, homicide and attempted homicide, and violence against the person.

Theft Rates: From the Offences Versus Property category. Includes forgery, arson, burglary, theft, fraud, robbery, theft of registered vehicles, motorcycles, mopeds, and bicycles, and malicious damage to property.

Source: Danmarks Statistik (Statistics Denmark), *Kriminalstatistik (Criminal Statistics)* (Copenhagen: Statistics Denmark, 1996).

Netherlands

Violent Crime Rates: Available for 1978–1996 only. From the Violent Crime category. Includes completed and attempted offense against life (available for all years as offenses against life pre-1978); help with suicide and abortion (broken down only for 1992–1996); assault; threat (1992–1996 only); culpable of death or grievous bodily harm; rape; sexual assault; other sexual offenses; theft with violence; and extortion.

Theft Rates: From Property Crimes category. Includes simple theft; theft with breaking and entering (burglary); and other aggravated theft.

Note: Violent Crimes and Property Crimes categories do not equate with source-provided major crime types. Also, the problem of coverage of crime types and years makes it difficult to account fully for these major categories and crimes classified within them.

Source: Personal correspondence from Ministry of Justice, Netherlands National Bureau of Statistics, revised by Ministry of Justice, WDOC/SIBa, January 1998.

New Zealand

Violent Crime Rates: From the Violent Crime category, includes homicide, kidnapping and abduction, robbery, grievous assaults, serious assaults, minor assaults, intimidation and threats, and group assemblies. Also from Sexual Offences category, includes sexual attacks, sexual affronts, abnormal sexual relationships, immoral behavior, indecent videos, and films, videos, public classification.

Theft Rates: Taken from the Dishonesty category. Includes burglary, vehicle take/interfere, theft, receiving, and fraud.

Source: Personal correspondence with P. E. C. Doone, Commissioner of Police, New Zealand Police.

Finland

Violent Crime Rates: From the table under offenses against the penal code includes manslaughter, murder, homicide, attempted murder or manslaughter, assault, rape, and robbery.

Theft Rates: From the table under offenses against the penal code. Includes theft/petty theft; aggravated theft; and unauthorized taking or theft of a motor vehicle.

Note: Legislation, penal code, or law amended for robbery in 1972, aggravated assault in 1972, unauthorized taking of a vehicle or theft of a motor vehicle in 1991, and fraud, embezzlement in 1991.

Source: Statistics Finland, *Yearbook of Justice Statistics 1996* (Helinski: Statistics Finland, 1997), and Statistics Finland, *Crime Nomenclature 1996* (Helinski: Statistics Finland, 1997).

France

Violent Crime Rates: From Offenses Against the Person category (no crime types provided).

Theft Rates: From Thefts (including handling stolen goods) category (no crime types provided).

Source: Personal correspondence, Bernard Gravet, the Directeur central de la police judicaire, Ministry of Interior, Republic of France. The source is listed as the French statistical agency, Institut National de la Statistique et des Etudes Economiques (INSEE).

Ireland

Violent Crime Rates: From Group 1 Offenses Against the Person, includes (among many detailed types) murder, various types of manslaughter, various types of assaults, rape, other sexual offenses, kidnapping, abduction, intimidation, cruelty to children, and infanticide. Also from Group 2 Offenses Against Property with Violence, includes aggravated burglary, armed aggravated burglary, robbery and assaults with intent to rob, robbery with arms, assaults on dwelling houses using firearms or explosives, arson, killing and maiming cattle, and causing an explosion likely to endanger life or damage property.

Theft Rates: From Group 2 Offenses Against Property with Violence; includes sacrilege, burglary, possess article with intent, housebreaking, breaking into shops, warehouses, attempts to break into houses, shops, etc., threatening to publish or publishing with intent to extort, malicious damage to schools, other malicious injury to property, attempting to cause an explosion, possession of explosive substances, malicious injuries to property, and other offenses against property with violence. Also from Group 3 Offenses with Property without Violence (also called Larcenies, Etc.); includes (among many detailed types) various forms of larcenies and handling stolen goods. Excludes fraud and related offenses.

Source: Central Statistics Office, *Statistical Abstract* (Cork: Central Statistics Office, annual editions).

Italy

Violent Crime Rates: From source table. Includes premeditated homicide and manslaughter, manslaughter, injury to persons, robbery, extortion, kidnapping, and offenses against the family.

Theft Rates: From source table. Includes theft.

Note: Offenses against the morality and public disturbance are excluded, as they seem to refer to criminal offenses that fall outside my major categories and to be consistent with other countries where they are excluded (e.g., the Netherlands).

Source: Personal correspondence from Claudia Cingolani, head, International Relations Department, Istituto Nazionale Di Statistica (ISTAT). Data from 1950–1985 from a publication and 1986–1996 from an internally generated table.

Japan

Violent Crime Rates: From source table. Includes murder, robbery, robbery resulting in death, robbery resulting in bodily injury, rape on the occasion of robbery, bodily injury, assault, intimidation, extortion, unlawful assembly with dangerous weapons, rape, indecent assault, indecent behavior in public, distribution of obscene material, arson, and kidnapping.

Theft Rates: From source table. Includes larceny.

Source: Koichi Hamai, senior research officer, First Research Department, Research and Training Institute, Ministry of Justice, Government of Japan translated the data taken from the annual White Paper on Crime. The full citation is: Government of Japan, *Summary of the White Paper on Crime* (Tokyo: Research and Training Institute, Ministry of Justice, annual editions).

Sweden

Violent Crime Rates: From source table. Includes murder, manslaughter, and assault resulting in death, assault and aggravated assault, sex crimes, and robbery.

Theft Rates: From source table. Includes property damage, burglary, and property crimes minus robbery and burglary.

Source: Statistics Sweden (Statistika Centralbyran), *Kriminalstatistik 1994* (Stockholm: Statistics Sweden, 1994).

United States

Violent Crime Rates: From Part I offense data. Includes murder and nonnegligent manslaughter, forcible rape, robbery, and aggravated assault.

Theft Rates: From Part I offense data. Includes burglary, larceny-theft, and motor vehicle theft.

Sources: Personal correspondence from the Program Support Section, Criminal Justice Information Services Division, Federal Bureau of Investigation, U.S. Department of Justice. Data are obtained on a voluntary basis through the Uniform Crime Reporting (UCR) program managed by the FBI.

England and Wales

Violent Crime Rates: From Class I Offenses Against Person category, 1950–1972, and Violence Against Person categories, 1973–1997; Sexual Offenses categories; and Robbery Offenses Against Person categories. Includes murder, manslaughter, and infanticide (homicide), attempted murder, threat or conspiracy to murder, child destruction, wounding or other acts of endangering life, endangering railway passengers, endangering life at sea, other wounding, etc., assault (after 1988 these were not included as they became summary offenses), abandoning a child aged under two years, child abduction, procuring illegal abortion, and concealment at birth. Sexual Offenses include buggery, indecent assault on male, indecency between males, rape, indecent assault on a female, unlawful intercourse with a girl under age thirteen, unlawful intercourse with a girl under age sixteen, incest, procuration, abduction, bigamy, and gross indecency with a child.

Theft Rates: From Class II Offenses Against Property with Violence (except for Robbery and Blackmail), 1950–1972, and Burglary categories, and Class III Offenses Against Property without Violence (excluding embezzlement, obtaining by false pretenses, frauds by agents, etc., and falsifying accounts) and Theft categories. Includes various types of burglaries and thefts.

Sources: Home Office, *Criminal Statistics: England and Wales* (London: Her Majesty's Stationery Office, various years).

Australia

Violent Crime Rates: From Crimes Reported to the Police. Includes homicide, murder and manslaughter (not by driving) (1971–1997 only), rape (1964–1987 only), robbery, and serious assault.

Theft Rates: From Crimes Reported to the Police. Includes burglary or break, enter, and steal (total); larceny/stealing; and motor vehicle theft.

Sources: For 1964–1973, statistics from Satyanshu K. Mukherjee, Anita Scandia, Dianne Dagger, and Wendy Matthews, *Sourcebook of Australian Criminal and Social Statistics* (Canberra: Australian Institute of Criminology, 1989), and for 1974–1997 from Satyanshu K. Mukherjee and Dianne Dagger, *The Size of the Crime Problem in Australia,* 2d ed. (Canberra: Australian Institute of Criminology, 1990) and personal correspondence with John Myrtle, Principal Librarian, Australian Institute of Criminology.

Republic of Korea (South Korea)

Violent Crime Rates: For 1970 and 1975–1994, from Violent Offenses in cases. Includes murder, rape, robbery, and aggravated assault.

Theft Rates: For 1970 and 1975–1994, from Property Offenses in cases. Unclear as to what offenses are included.

Sources: National Statistical Office, Republic of Korea, *Social Indicators in Korea 1995* (Seoul, Korea: National Statistical Office, 1995).

FIGURE A.3
Total Fertility Rates, 1950–1996

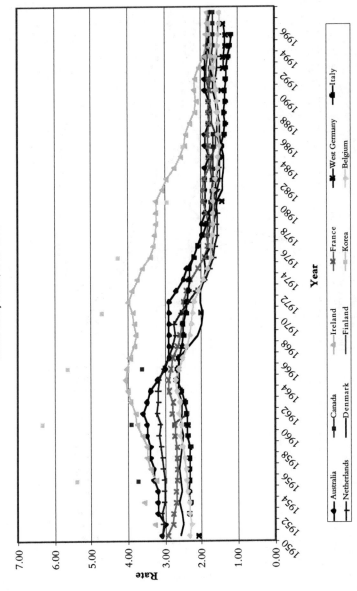

FIGURE A.4
Divorce Rates, 1950–1996

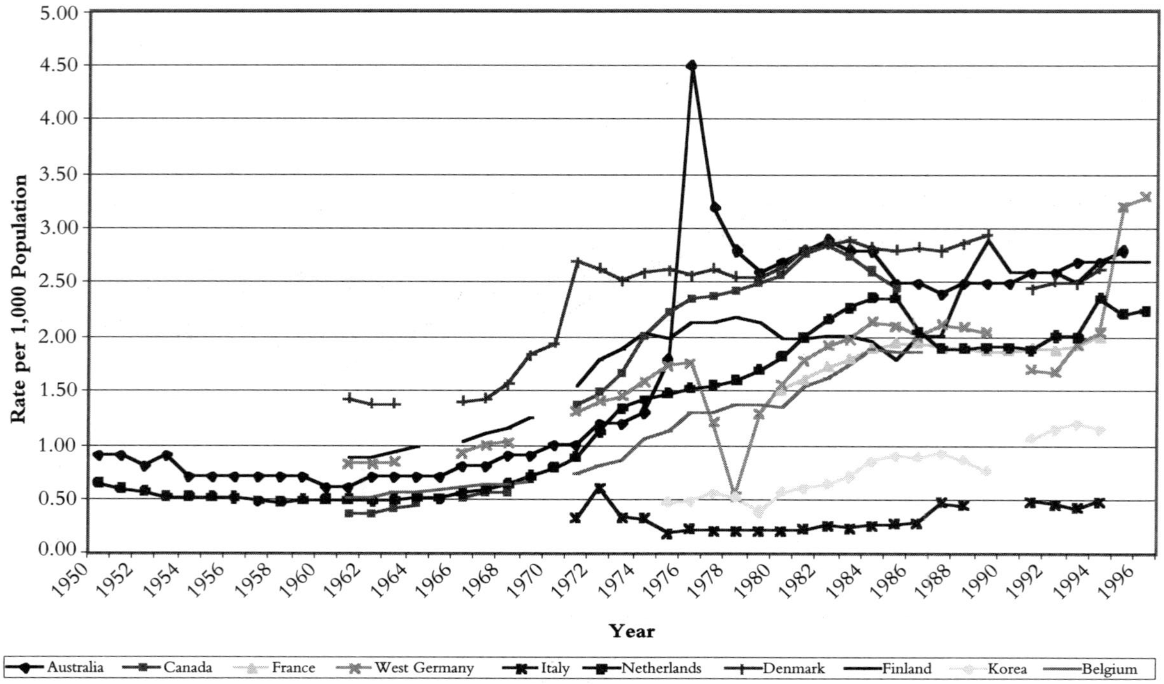

292

FIGURE A.5
Births to Single Mothers, 1950–1996

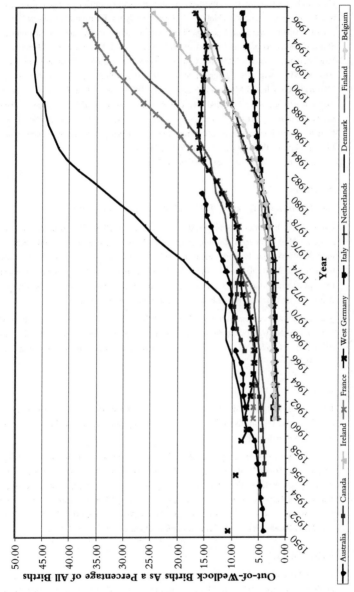

Data on births to unmarried mothers for all European countries are taken from Eurostat, *Demographic Statistics* (New York: Haver Analytics/Eurostat Data Shop, 1997). Data for Japan come from Japanese Ministry of Health and Welfare, Department of Statistics and Information. Sources for U.S. data are S. J. Ventura et al., "Report of Final Natality Statistics," *Monthly Vital Statistics Report* 46, No. 11 supplement (Hyattsville, Md.: National Center for Health Statistics, 1996), and S. J. Ventura et al., "Births to Unmarried Mothers: United States, 1980–1992," *Vital Health Statistics* 21 (53) (Hyattsville, Md.: National Center for Health Statistics, 1995). Source for data on Australia and Canada is United Nations Department for Economic and Social Information and Policy Analysis, Statistical Division, *Demographic Yearbook* (New York: United Nations Publications, 1965, 1975, 1981, 1986).

Sources for other data are given by country.

Australia

Total Fertility Rates: Excludes "full blood Aborigines" prior to 1966.

Divorce Rates: Excludes "full blood Aborigines" prior to 1966. The crude divorce rate is the number of decrees absolute granted per 1,000 of the estimated population at June 30 of that year. For years prior to 1994, the crude marriage rate is based on the mean resident population for the calendar year. In interpreting this rate, it must be kept in mind that a large and varying proportion of the population used in the denominator is unmarried or below the minimum age of marriage.

Sources: Personal correspondence, March 2, 1998, Christine Kilmartin, coordinator, Family Trends Monitoring. Australian Institute of Family Studies, Australian Bureau of Statistics, *Catalog No. 3301.0* (Canberra: Australian Government Publishing Service, 1995).

Canada

Divorce Rate: Data exclude annulments and legal separations unless otherwise specified. Rates are the number of final divorce decrees granted under civil law per 1,000 midyear population.

Sources: United Nations Department for Economic and Social Information and Policy Analysis, *World Population Prospects: The 1996 Revision—Annex 1—Demographic Indicators* (New York: United Nations Publication, 1996); U.S. Bureau of the Census, *International Database,* International Programs Center; United Nations Department for Economic and Social Information and Policy Analysis, Statistical Division, *Demographic Yearbook* (New York: United Nations Publications, 1965–1995).

United States

Divorce Rates: Data refer only to events occurring within the United States. Alaska included beginning 1959 and Hawaii beginning 1960. Rates per 1,000 population enumerated as of April 1 for 1950, 1960, 1970, and 1980, and estimated as of July 1 for all other years.

Sources: S. J. Ventura, J. A. Martin, T. J. Mathews, and S. C. Clarke, *Report of Final Natality Statistics, 1996,* Monthly Vital Statistics Report, Vol. 46, No. 11 supplement (Hyattsville, Md.: National Center for Health Statistics, 1998); S. J. Ventura, *Births to Unmarried Mothers: United States, 1980–1992,* National Center for Health Statistics, Vital Health Statistics 21(53) (Hyattsville, Md.: National Center for Health Statistics, 1995); U.S. Department of Health and Human Services, *Vital Statistics of the United States,* Vol. 1: *Natality,* Publication No. (PHS) 96-1100 (Hyattsville, Md.: National Center for Health Statistics, 1996); S. C. Clark, *Advance Report of Final Divorce Statistics, 1989 and 1990,* Monthly Vital Statistics Report, Vol. 43, No. 8 supplement (Hyattsville, Md.: National Center for Health Statistics, 1995); National Center for Health Statistics, *Births, Marriages, Divorces and Deaths for 1996,* Monthly Vital Statistics Report, Vol. 45, No. 12 (Hyattsville, Md.: National Center for Health Statistics, 1997).

Japan

Sources: Japanese Ministry of Health and Welfare, Department of Statistics and Information.

South Korea

Divorce Rate: Completeness of figures not specified from source or data are deemed incomplete.

Sources: United Nations Department for Economic and Social Information and Policy Analysis, *World Population Prospects: The 1996 Revision—Annex 1—Demographic Indicators* (New York: United Nations Publications, 1996); U.S. Bureau of the Census, *International Database,* International Programs Center; United Nations Department for Economic and Social Information and Policy Analysis—Statistical Division, *Demographic Yearbook* (New York: United Nations Publications, 1980–1995).

Denmark

Divorce Rate: Data exclude Faeroe Islands and Greenland.

Sources: Jean-Paul Sardon, *General Natality* (Paris: National Institute of Demographic Studies, 1994); U.S. Bureau of the Census, *International Database,* International Programs Center; United Nations Department for Economic and Social Information and Policy Analysis—Statistical Division, *Demographic Yearbook* (New York: United Nations Publications, 1965–1995).

Finland

Sources: United Nations Department for Economic and Social Information and Policy Analysis, *World Population Prospects: The 1996 Revision—Annex 1—Demographic Indicators* (New York: United Nations Publications, 1996); U.S. Bureau of the Census, *International Database,* International Programs Center; United Nations Department for Economic and Social Information and Policy Analysis—Statistical Division, *Demographic Yearbook* (New York: United Nations Publications, 1965–1985); personal correspondence, January 23, 1998, Anja Torma, information specialist–library; Statistics Finland, *Vital Statistics 1996* (Helsinki: Statistics Finland, 1996).

France

Sources: Jean-Paul Sardon, *General Natality* (Paris: National Institute of Demographic Studies, 1994); Roselyn Kerjosse and Irene Tamby, *The Demographic Situation in 1994: Movement of the Population* (Paris: National Institute of Statistics—Economic Studies, 1994).

Germany/Former East Germany

Sources: Ministry for Families, Senior Citizens, Women, and Youth, *Die Familie im Spiegel der Amtlichen Statistik: Aktuel und Erweiterte Neuauflage 1998* (Bonn, 1997); United Nations Department for Economic and Social Information and Policy Analysis, *World Population Prospects: The 1996 Revision—Annex 1—Demographic Indicators* (New York: United Nations Publications, 1996); United Nations Department for Economic and Social Information and Policy Analysis—Statistical Division, *Demographic Yearbook* (New York: United Nations Publications, 1965–1995).

Ireland

Sources: Jean-Paul Sardon, *General Natality* (Paris: National Institute of Demographic Studies, 1994); U.S. Bureau of the Census, *International Database,* International Programs Center.

Italy

Divorce Rates: Completeness of figures not specified from source.

Sources: Personal correspondence, April 17, 1998, Viviana Egidi, Direzione Centrale delle Statistiche su Popolazione e Territorio. Istituto Nazionale Di Statistica (ISTAT); United Nations Department for Economic and Social Information and Policy Analysis, Statistical Division, *Demographic Yearbook* (New York: United Nations Publications, 1990–1995).

Netherlands

Divorce Rate: Figures include divorces by death and divorce.

Sources: Personal correspondence, March 4, 1998, Ursula van Leijden, Population Department, Statistics Netherlands.

Sweden

Sources: Jean-Paul Sardon, *General Natality* (Paris: National Institute of Demographic Studies, 1994); personal correspondence, June 11, 1998, Ake Nilsson, Statistics Sweden; *Population Statistics 1996, Part 4, Vital Statistics* (Stockholm: Statistics Sweden, 1997).

United Kingdom

Divorce Rates: Figures for 1964–1970 are for England and Wales only. Rates are computed on population including armed forces outside the country and merchant seamen at sea, but exclude commonwealth and foreign armed forces stationed in the area.

Sources: United Nations Department for Economic and Social Information and Policy Analysis, *World Population Prospects: The 1996 Revision—Annex 1—Demographic Indicators* (New York: United Nations Publications, 1996); United Nations Department for Economic and Social Information and Policy Analysis, Statistical Division, *Demographic Yearbook* (New York: United Nations Publications, 1965–1995); Council of Europe, *Recent Demographic Developments in Europe* (Strasbourg: Council of Europe Publishing, 1997).

NOTES

Chapter One. Playing by the Rules

1. Daniel Bell, *The Coming of Post-Industrial Society: A Venture in Social Forecasting* (New York: Basic Books, 1973).

2. For general treatments of the characteristics of "information societies," see Alvin Toffler, *The Third Wave* (New York: William Morrow, 1980), and Manuel Castells, *The Rise of the Network Society* (Malden, Mass.: Blackwell Publishers, 1996).

3. The first major technological disruption was the invention of agriculture. The transition from hunter-gatherer to agricultural societies occurred much more slowly than economic transitions since the start of the Industrial Revolution, however, and is one about which we have much less information.

4. Ferdinand Tönnies, *Community and Association* (London: Routledge and Kegan Paul, 1955).

5. Sir Henry S. Maine, *Ancient Law: Its Connection with the Early History of Society and Its Relation to Modern Ideas* (Boston: Beacon Press, 1963; originally published 1861), pp. 163–164; see also the parallel discussion in Max Weber, *Economy and Society* (Berkeley: University of California Press, 1978), 1: 40–46; and Robin Fox, *Reproduction and Succession: Studies in Anthropology, Law, and Society* (New Brunswick, N.J.: Transaction Publishers, 1997), pp. 96–100.

6. Samuel P. Huntington, *The Third Wave: Democratization in the Late Twentieth Century* (Oklahoma City: University of Oklahoma Press, 1991).

7. Francis Fukuyama, *The End of History and the Last Man* (New York: Free Press, 1992); see also "Capitalism and Democracy: The Missing Link," *Journal of Democracy* 3 (1992): 100–110.

8. See, for example, the introduction to James M. Buchanan, *The Limits of Liberty: Between Anarchy and Leviathan* (Chicago: University of Chicago Press, 1975).

9. Diego Gambetta, *The Sicilian Mafia: The Business of Private Protection* (Cambridge: Harvard University Press, 1993), p. 35.

10. See, for example, Edward C. Banfield, *The Moral Basis of a Backward Society* (Glencoe,

Ill.: Free Press, 1958), and Robert D. Putnam, *Making Democracy Work: Civic Traditions in Modern Italy* (Princeton, NJ: Princeton University Press, 1993).

11. To my knowledge, the first person to use this term was Lawrence Harrison in *Underdevelopment Is a State of Mind: The Latin American Case* (New York: Madison Books, 1985), pp. 7–8.

12. According to Weber, "The great achievement of ethical religions, above all of the ethical and asceticist sects of Protestantism, was to shatter the fetters of the sib." *The Religion of China* (New York: Free Press, 1951), p. 237.

13. See the discussion of civil society in Larry Diamond, "Toward Democratic Consolidation," *Journal of Democracy* 5 (1994): 4–17.

14. This argument is made by Ernest Gellner in *Conditions of Liberty: Civil Society and Its Rivals* (London: Hamish Hamilton, 1994).

15. Lyda Judson Hanifan, "The Rural School Community Center," *Annals of the American Academy of Political and Social Science* 67 (1916): 130–138.

16. Jane Jacobs, *The Death and Life of Great American Cities* (New York: Vintage Books, 1961), p. 138.

17. Glenn Loury, "A Dynamic Theory of Racial Income Differences," in P. A. Wallace and A. LeMund, eds., *Women, Minorities, and Employment Discrimination* (Lexington, Mass.: Lexington Books, 1977); Ivan H. Light, *Ethnic Enterprise in America* (Berkeley: University of California Press, 1972).

18. James S. Coleman, "Social Capital in the Creation of Human Capital," *American Journal of Sociology* Supplement 94 (1988): S95–S120, and "The Creation and Destruction of Social Capital: Implications for the Law," *Journal of Law, Ethics, and Public Policy* 3 (1988): 375–404.

19. Putnam, *Making Democracy Work,* and "Bowling Alone: America's Declining Social Capital," *Journal of Democracy* 6 (1995): 65–78.

20. Everett C. Ladd, "The Data Just Don't Show Erosion of America's 'Social Capital,'" *Public Perspective* (1996): 4–22; Michael Schudson, "What If Civic Life Didn't Die?" *American Prospect* (1996): 17–20; John Clark, "Shifting Engagements: Lessons from the 'Bowling Alone' Debate," *Hudson Briefing Papers,* no. 196 (October 1996).

21. This study folds a number of different negative social capital measures into a single index. See National Commission on Civic Renewal, *The Index of National Civic Health* (College Park, Md.: National Commission on Civic Renewal, 1998), and *A Nation of Spectators: How Civic Disengagement Weakens America and What We Can Do About It* (College Park, Md.: National Commission on Civic Renewal, 1998).

Chapter Two. Crime, Family, Trust: What Happened

1. Jane Jacobs, *The Death and Life of Great American Cities* (New York: Vintage Books, 1992), pp. 29–54.

2. Ibid., pp. 38–39.

3. For an interesting discussion of the deleterious effects of high-modernist urbanism, see James C. Scott, *Seeing Like a State: How Certain Schemes to Improve the Human Conditions Have Failed* (New Haven, Conn.: Yale University Press, 1998), pp. 132–139.

4. See Robert E. Park, "Community Organization and Juvenile Delinquency," in Ernest W. Burgess, Park, and Roderick D. McKenzie, eds., *The City* (Chicago: University of Chicago Press, 1925), pp. 99–112. Similarly, criminologist John Braithwaite has emphasized the role of what he calls "reintegrative shaming" as a method of crime con-

trol. Communities express disapproval through a process of shaming and stigmatizing those who violate community norms. Reintegrative shaming occurs when communities are willing to accept deviants back into the fold when the latter express guilt or repentance for their acts. According to Braithwaite, reintegration prevents stigmatized deviants from forming their own criminal subcultures. Japan is the premier example: Japan achieves extraordinarily low rates of crime when compared to other developed countries not through the heavy hand of the police, but through informal social pressure to conform to community norms. A great deal of effort is made to rehabilitate criminals morally through active intervention by other members of the community; once this occurs, the individual is welcomed back into normal social life. John Braithwaite, *Crime, Shame, and Reintegration* (Cambridge: Cambridge University Press, 1989).

5. Robert J. Sampson, Stephen W. Raudenbush, and Felton Earls, "Neighborhoods and Violent Crime: A Multilevel Study of Collective Efficacy," *Science* 277 (1997): 918–924.

6. See Erich Buchholz, "Reasons for the Low Rate of Crime in the German Democratic Republic," *Crime and Social Justice* 29 (1986): 26–42.

7. James Q. Wilson, *Thinking About Crime,* rev. ed. (New York: Vintage Books, 1983), p. 15.

8. George Kelling and Catherine Coles, *Fixing Broken Windows: Restoring Order and Reducing Crime in Our Communities* (New York: Free Press, 1996), pp. 14–22.

9. Ibid., p. 47.

10. Wesley G. Skogan, *Disorder and Decline: Crime and the Spiral of Decay in American Neighborhoods* (New York: Free Press, 1990).

11. There have been relatively few compilations of comparative crime data for developed countries since Dane Archer and Rosemary Gartner published *Violence and Crime in Cross-National Perspective* (New Haven, Conn.: Yale University Press, 1984). For other surveys, see Antoinette D. Viccica, "World Crime Trends," *International Journal of Offender Therapy* 24 (1980): 270–277.

12. On the question of methodological problems with regard to international crime comparisons, see James Lynch, "Crime in International Perspective," in James Q. Wilson and Joan Petersilia, eds., *Crime* (San Francisco: ICS Press, 1995), pp. 11–38.

13. W. S. Wilson Huang, "Are International Murder Data Valid and Reliable? Some Evidence to Support the Use of Interpol Data," *International Journal of Comparative and Applied Criminal Justice* 17 (1993): 77–89.

14. See U.S. Department of Justice, Bureau of Justice Statistics, *Criminal Victimization, 1973–95* (Washington, D.C.: U.S. Government Printing Office, 1997).

15. One such recent study for fourteen developed countries is Jan J. M. Van Dijk and Pat Mayhew, *Experiences of Crime Across the World* (Deventer, Netherland: Kluwer, 1991).

16. Pat Mayhew and Philip White, *The 1996 International Crime Victimisation Survey,* Home Office Research and Statistics Directorate Research Findings No. 57 (London: Research and Statistics Directorate, 1997).

17. A second methodological problem has to do with cross-cultural comparisons of crime. Crimes are defined in different ways in different societies. Even in the case of murder, Interpol data include attempted murders in its murder data; the United States does not. "Murder" and "homicide" are sometime considered identical categories, and sometimes not; some national police agencies lump indecent behavior together with other violent crimes, while others do not. Even within the same society, crime definitions can change over time. This is particularly true of sexual crimes like rape

NOTES TO PAGES 35–37

and child abuse, where social norms have changed dramatically. Today in the United States a man can be charged with date rape in a way he could not have been thirty years ago; verbal and emotional abuse are now considered components of child abuse. There can also be cross-national differences within identically defined categories: property crimes in Holland include a far greater proportion of bicycle thefts than auto thefts or burglaries than in the United States, simply because there are more bicycles to steal in the Netherlands.

Because of the frequent arbitrariness of crime definitions, there is a school in criminology that holds that crime is simply whatever the dominant elites in a given society choose to label as crime and that what is deviant for one group is normal for another. This was implicit in Edwin Sutherland's explanation that delinquency arose because of "an excess of definitions" favorable to violation of law, and continued through the so-called labeling theory school of criminology. By this account, law enforcement becomes a kind of coercive cultural prejudice. Since conservatives had made crime a political issue in the 1960s and 1970s, many liberals reacted by echoing Durkheim to the effect that "deviance is normal," that is, there is no society free of crime and deviance. All sorts of sordid crimes were committed in Victorian society and in suburban America of the 1950s, it was argued; to look back on these periods as a kind of golden age was an exercise in nostalgia.

There are two separate answers to the question of cultural bias. One is narrow and technical. Studies have shown that international data sets are reasonably consistent with one another. If crime categories are defined differently between two societies or within the same society over time, then these categories must obviously be disaggregated in any detailed study seeking particular causes or remedies for particular types of crimes. As long as the categories are used consistently over time, however, this should not affect the data on trends. The second, and broader, issue of whether crime is merely a kind of prejudiced way of stigmatizing minorities and other marginalized people surely cannot apply to the broad social phenomena at issue here. There are no societies in the world, and certainly no developed societies, that regard murder or the theft of property as legitimate. The fact that we have been willing to tolerate higher levels of crime and deviant behavior over time doesn't imply that there is less social disorder; it is, rather, another case of "defining deviancy down."

See W. S. Wilson Huang, "Assessing Indicators of Crime Among International Crime Data Series," *Criminal Justice Policy Review* 3 (1989): 28–48; Piers Beirne, "Cultural Relativism and Comparative Criminology," *Contemporary Crises* 7 (1983): 371–391; Gregory C. Leavitt, "Relativism and Cross-Cultural Criminology: A Critical Analysis," *Journal of Research in Crime and Delinquency* 27 (1990): 5–29; Edwin Sutherland and Donald Cressy, *Criminology* (Philadelphia: Lippincott, 1970); Frank Tannenbaum, *Crime and the Community* (New York: Columbia University Press, 1938); Howard S. Becker, *Outsiders: Studies in the Sociology of Deviance* (Glencoe, Ill.: Free Press, 1963).

18. Ted Robert Gurr, "Contemporary Crime in Historical Perspective: A Comparative Study of London, Stockholm, and Sydney," *Annals of the North American Academy of Political and Social Science* 434 (1977): 114–136.

19. W. S. Wilson Huang, "Are International Murder Data Valid?"

20. James S. Coleman, *Foundations of Social Theory* (Cambridge, Mass.: Harvard University Press, 1990), p. 300.

21. Companies with fewer than twenty employees account for 19.5 percent of private

sector employment in the United States in 1995. Small Business Administration, Office of Advocacy, Small Business Answer Card 1998.

22. The total fertility rate is the average number of births a woman would have during her reproductive life if she was exposed to the fertility rates characteristic of various childbearing age groups in that year. See the Appendix for sources of data.

23. I am indebted to Nicholas Eberstadt for much of the analysis in this section. See his article, "World Population Implosion?" *Public Interest,* no. 129 (Fall 1997): 3–22.

24. Nicholas Eberstadt, "Asia Tomorrow, Gray and Male," *National Interest,* no. 53 (Fall 1998): 56–65.

25. On this period, see Michael S. Teitelbaum and Jay M. Winter, *The Fear of Population Decline* (Orlando, Fla.: Academic Press, 1985).

26. David Popenoe, *Disturbing the Nest: Family Change and Decline in Modern Societies* (New York: Aldine de Gruyter, 1988), p. 34.

27. Sara McLanahan and Lynne Casper, "Growing Diversity and Inequality in the American Family," in Reynolds Farley, ed., *State of the Union: America in the 1990s,* vol. 2: *Social Trends* (New York: Russell Sage Foundation, 1995).

28. William J. Goode, *World Change in Divorce Patterns* (New Haven, Conn.: Yale University Press, 1993), p. 54. Some Catholic countries like Chile have not legalized divorce to this day.

29. U.S. Bureau of the Census, *Statistical Abstract of the United States* (Washington, D.C.: U.S. Government Printing Office, 1996), Table 98, p. 79.

30. Ibid.

31. U.S. Department of Health and Human Services, Centers for Disease Control, *National Vital Statistics Report* 47, no. 4 (Washington, D.C.: USHHS, October 7, 1998), p. 15.

32. These changes only bring rates back to where they were in the early 1980s, however. Stephanie J. Ventura, Sally C. Curtin, and T. J. Matthews, "Teenage Births in the United States: National and State Trends, 1990–96," *National Vital Statistics System* (Washington, D.C.: National Center for Health Statistics, U.S. Department of Health and Human Services, 1998).

33. See, for example, McLanahan and Casper, "Growing Diversity," p. 11.

34. Ibid.

35. U.S. Department of Health and Human Services, *Report to Congress on Out-of-Wedlock Childbearing* (Hyattsville, Md.: U.S. Government Printing Office, 1995), p. 70; Larry L. Bumpass and James A. Sweet, "National Estimates of Cohabitation," *Demography* 26 (1989): 615–625.

36. McLanahan and Casper, "Growing Diversity," p. 15. The statistic for Sweden is based on personal correspondence with the Swedish Ministry of Health and Social Affairs, Division for Social Services.

37. Louis Roussel, *La famille incertaine* (Paris: Editions Odile Jacob, 1989).

38. Richard F. Tomasson, "Modern Sweden: The Declining Importance of Marriage," *Scandinavian Review* (1998): 83–89.

39. Elise F. Jones, *Teenage Pregnancy in Industrialized Countries* (New Haven, Conn.: Yale University Press, 1986).

40. These data are for the United States. Larry L. Bumpass and James A. Sweet, "National Estimates of Cohabitation," *Demography* 26 (1989): 615–625.

41. This is true even when controlling for age, education, income, and other factors related to domestic aggression. See Jan E. Stets, "Cohabiting and Marital Aggres-

sion: The Role of Social Isolation," *Journal of Marriage and the Family* 53 (1991): 669–680.

42. Popenoe, *Disturbing the Nest*, p. 174; Ailsa Burns and Cath Scott, *Mother-Headed Families and Why They Have Increased* (Hillsdale, N.J.: Erlbaum, 1994), p. 26.

43. Sara McLanahan and Gary Sandefur, *Growing Up with a Single Parent: What Hurts, What Helps* (Cambridge, Mass.: Harvard University Press, 1994), p. 2.

44. David Popenoe, *Life Without Father: Compelling New Evidence That Fatherhood and Marriage Are Indispensable for the Good of Children and Society* (New York: Free Press, 1996), p. 86. Andrew Cherlin points out that even assuming the validity of this comparison, the rate of family breakup due to divorce still exceeds any historically experienced rate of family dissolution due to other causes. Andrew J. Cherlin, *Marriage, Divorce, Remarriage*, 2d ed. (Cambridge, Mass.: Harvard University Press, 1992), p. 25.

45. Popenoe, *Life Without Father*, pp. 151–152.

46. Goode, *World Change*, p. 35.

47. Ralf Dahrendorf, *Life Chances: Approaches to Social and Political Theory* (Chicago: University of Chicago, 1979).

48. This view is supported by a study by John Brehm and Wendy Rahn that, based on General Social Survey, data, shows that civic engagement is a good predictor of levels of trust. Wendy Rahn and John Brehm, "Individual-Level Evidence for the Causes and Consequences of Social Capital," *American Journal of Political Science* 41 (1997): 999–1023.

49. On this point, see the first chapter of my book *Trust: The Social Virtues and the Creation of Prosperity* (New York: Free Press, 1995). See also Diego Gambetta, *Trust: Making and Breaking Cooperative Relations* (Oxford: Blackwell, 1988).

50. For a general analysis of this problem, see Joseph S. Nye, Jr., ed., *Why People Don't Trust Government* (Cambridge, Mass.: Harvard University Press, 1997).

51. Karlyn Bowman and Everett C. Ladd, *What's Wrong: A Survey of American Satisfaction and Complaint* (Washington: AEI Press and the Roper Center for Public Opinion Research, 1998), Table 5-20.

52. *American Enterprise* (Nov–Dec. 1993), pp. 94–95.

53. Ladd and Bowman, *What's Wrong*, Tables 6-1 to 6-23.

54. Wendy Rahn and John Transue, "Social Trust and Value Change: The Decline of Social Capital in American Youth, 1976–1995," unpublished paper, 1997.

55. Tom W. Smith, "Factors Relating to Misanthropy in Contemporary American Society," *Social Science Research* 26 (1997): 170–196.

56. Ibid., pp. 191–193.

57. Alan Wolfe, *One Nation, After All* (New York: Viking, 1998), p. 231.

58. Rahn and Transue, "Social Trust."

59. Mancur Olson, *The Rise and Decline of Nations* (New Haven, Conn.: Yale University Press, 1982).

60. Everett C. Ladd, *The Ladd Report* (New York: Free Press, 1999). Earlier versions of this were published as Ladd, "The Data Just Don't Show Erosion of America's 'Social Capital,'" *Public Perspective* (1996); and Everett C. Ladd, "The Myth of Moral Decline," *Responsive Community* 4 (1993–94): 52–68.

61. Robert D. Putnam, "Bowling Alone: America's Declining Social Capital," *Journal of Democracy* 6 (1995): 65–78.

62. Calvert J. Judkins, *National Associations of the United States* (Washington, D.C.: U.S. Department of Commerce, 1949). I am grateful to Marcella Rey for this and other ref-

erences concerning measures of group memberships. See her "Pieces to the Association Puzzle" (paper presented at the annual meeting of the Association for Research on Nonprofit Organizations and Voluntary Action, November 1998).

63. Lester M. Salamon, *America's Nonprofit Sector* (New York: Foundation Center, 1992).

64. W. Lloyd Warner, J. O. Low, Paul S. Lunt, and Leo Srole, *Yankee City* (New Haven, Conn.: Yale University Press, 1963).

65. Apart from the difficulty in counting the number of such groups, there are a number of complex issues in assessing the quality of the relationships engendered by them. Ladd contests Putnam's dismissal of many new advocacy groups as mere "membership groups." He shows that not only have memberships in large environmental organizations like the Nature Conservancy or the World Wildlife Fund grown substantially, but the quality of the relationships formed among these groups' members goes well beyond writing a yearly dues check. He points to one study that shows how a single local chapter of a single environmental organization sponsored countless hikes, bike trips, backpacking classes, and the like, all of which presumably fostered personal relationships and had spillover effects on social capital.

66. National Opinion Research Center (NORC), *General Social Survey* (Chicago: NORC, various editions). The General Social Survey was first conducted in 1972. Other years include 1973–1978, 1980, 1982, 1983–1993, 1994, 1996, and 1998.

67. Wolfe, *One Nation,* pp. 250–259.

68. Rahn and Transue, "Social Trust."

69. Pew Research Center for the People and the Press, *Trust and Citizen Engagement in Metropolitan Philadelphia: A Case Study* (Washington, D.C.: Pew Research Center, 1997). This study showed that Philadelphians indeed expressed a marked distrust of others. In Philadelphia itself (as opposed to the suburban counties also included in the survey), only 28 percent of the respondents said that "most people can be trusted," whereas 67 percent agreed that "you can't be too careful," corresponding roughly to the results from broader surveys like the GSS. As in the national surveys, large institutions came in for a great deal of distrust: public schools, the region's newspapers, city and local government, as well as the federal government in Washington, all had less than 20 percent of respondents expressing trust in them. On the other hand, there was evidence of high levels of civic participation: 60 percent had volunteered for some type of organization in the past year, 49 percent in the past month; 49 percent joined with coworkers to solve a common problem, and 30 percent had contacted an elected official. Although these rates were somewhat lower than national averages, there was no evidence of civic disengagement.

70. The WVS asks a question, "Generally speaking, would you say that most people can be trusted or that you can't be too careful in dealing with people?" which is comparable to those posed by Roper, the GSS, and other U.S. polls. Surprisingly, it shows levels of trust rising between 1981 and 1990 for many industrialized countries, including the United States. Trust levels drop only for Britain, France, and Spain among Western industrialized countries. The finding about the United States is not consistent with other data from the GSS and other polls that showed a substantial drop in trust for the United States over this period. According to GSS data, general trust among Americans dropped from 44.3 to 38.4 percent between 1980 and 1990.

71. These countries were the United States, Belgium, Britain, Canada, Denmark, Finland, France, Ireland, Italy, the Netherlands, Norway, Spain, Sweden, and the former West Germany.

72. See also Ronald Inglehart, "Postmaterialist Values and the Erosion of Institutional Authority," in Nye (1997), pp. 217–236.

73. Excluded from the summary are a number of questions on ethical values whose relationship to general social trust is dubious or weak, including whether the respondent has smoked marijuana or hashish and whether one believes that homosexuality or abortion is not justified.

74. Putnam, "Bowling Alone," asserts that there is a correlation between levels of trust and the density of civil society when we look at a cross-section of countries around the world. This correlation is a very weak one if we take into account institutional trust as well as interpersonal trust, and doesn't apply at all to the United States. The WVS confirms the often-asserted fact that Catholic countries, and particularly Latin Catholic ones (e.g., France, Italy, and Spain), have lower levels of generalized social trust than the Protestant countries in northern Europe. These countries as a group also tend to have lower levels of participation in voluntary organizations, a by-product (at least in the case of France and Spain) of their histories of political centralization under a unitary bureaucratic state. On the other hand, the United States has a much higher level of participation in voluntary associations than any other industrialized country, but a level of generalized social trust that is no higher than several other European countries, and levels of institutional distrust that are considerably higher than for Europe.

75. Pew Research Center for the People and the Press, *Deconstructing Distrust: How Americans View Government* (Washington, D.C.: Pew Research Center, 1998), pp. 53–54.

76. Ronald Inglehart and Paul R. Abramson, *Value Change in Global Perspective* (Ann Arbor: University of Michigan Press, 1995); see also Inglehart, *Modernization and Postmodernization: Cultural, Economic, and Political Change in 43 Societies* (Princeton, N.J.: Princeton University Press, 1997).

77. See Lester M. Salamon and Helmut K. Anheier, *The Emerging Sector: An Overview* (Baltimore: Johns Hopkins Institute for Policy Studies, 1994); and Lester M. Salamon, "The Rise of the Nonprofit Sector," *Foreign Affairs* 73 (1994): 109–122.

78. Lester M. Salamon, *Partners in Public Service: Government-Nonprofit Relations in the Modern Welfare State* (Baltimore: John Hopkins University Press, 1995), p. 243.

79. Ibid., p. 246.

80. Ibid., p. 247.

81. As an example, for many years I worked for the RAND Corporation, which was founded in 1948 as a private, nonprofit think tank by the U.S. Air Force to do research on national security issues. RAND would qualify, by Salamon's definition, as part of American civil society, yet it scarcely makes sense to place it there since the great bulk of its work is done under contract for the Department of Defense or the armed services. While having this research conducted by a quasi-autonomous nonprofit organization provides a little extra flexibility in terms of personnel, research agenda, and insulation from political pressure, it could in theory be done as well directly by the federal government. The same is true for all of the nonprofit research laboratories around the United States that are funded by the National Science Foundation, the National Institutes of Health, or the Defense Department.

82. Measurement problems that are severe in the developed world become overwhelming in a Third World country like India or the Philippines, where Salamon (1994) also claims an associational revolution has been taking place. In such societies, foreign researchers are likely to learn a great deal about new, Westernized NGOs because those

are the points of contact to the outside world; but for every new NGO, how many traditional village networks, extended families, or clans have disappeared?

83. See Francis Fukuyama, "Falling Tide: Global Trends and United States Civil Society," *Harvard International Review* 20 (1997): 60–64.

Chapter Three. Causes: The Conventional Wisdom

1. Seymour Martin Lipset, *American Exceptionalism: A Double-Edged Sword* (New York: W. W. Norton, 1995), pp. 46–51.

2. Ruth A. Ross and George C. S. Benson, "Criminal Justice from East to West," *Crime and Delinquency* (January 1979): 76–86.

3. See, for example, Lipset, *American Exceptionalism,* and Robert K. Merton, "Social Structure and 'Anomie,'" *American Sociological Review* 33 (1938): 672–682. This argument has recently been restated in a somewhat different form in Steven F. Messner and Richard Rosenfield, *Crime and the American Dream,* 2d ed. (Belmont, Calif.: Wadsworth, 1997). See also the arguments about the sources of crime related directly to American minorities in Richard Cloward and Lloyd Ohlin, *Delinquency and Opportunity* (New York: Free Press, 1960).

4. Steven Stack, "Social Structure and Swedish Crime Rates: A Time-Series Analysis, 1950–1979," *Criminology* 20 (November 1982): 499–513.

5. On crime rates see James Lynch, "Crime in International Perspective," in James Q. Wilson and Joan Petersilia, eds., *Crime* (San Francisco: ICS Press, 1995), pp. 16, 36–37. On the underclass overseas see Cait Murphy, "Europe's Underclass," *National Interest,* no. 50 (1997): 49–55.

6. This argument has been made recently by Derek Bok, *The State of the Nation: Government and the Quest for a Better Society* (Cambridge, Mass.: Harvard University Press, 1997); see also Peter Flora and Jens Albert, "Modernization, Democratization, and the Development of Welfare States in Western Europe," in Peter Flora and Arnold J. Heidenheimer, eds., *The Development of the Welfare State in Europe and America* (New Brunswick, NJ: Transaction, 1987), pp. 37–80.

7. U.S. Bureau of Census, *Statistical Abstract of the United States, 1996* (Washington, D.C.: U.S. Government Printing Office, 1996), p. 448.

8. David Popenoe, *Disturbing the Nest* (New York: Aldine de Gruyter, 1988), p. 156, surveys the relationship between the Swedish welfare state and family breakdown there.

9. Japan does not maintain large income-transfer programs from the well-off to the poor, though it does in effect protect many low-skill jobs by limiting competition and in effect allocating credit to companies to keep them viable.

10. Sara McLanahan and Lynne Casper, "Growing Diversity and Inequality in the American Family," in Reynolds Farley, ed., *State of the Union: America in the 1990s,* vol. 2, *Social Trends* (New York: Russell Sage Foundation, 1995), pp. 31–32.

11. Lionel Tiger, *The Decline of Males* (New York, Golden Books, 1999).

12. Judith R. Blau and Peter M. Blau, "The Cost of Inequality: Metropolitan Structure and Violent Crime," *American Sociological Review* 47 (1982): 114–129; Harvey Krahn, Timothy Hartnagel, and John W. Gartell, "Income Inequality and Homicide Rates: Cross-National Data and Criminological Theories," *Criminology* 24 (1986): 269–295; Rosemary Gartner, "The Victims of Homicide: A Temporal and Cross-National Comparison," *American Sociological Review* 55 (1990): 92–106; Richard Rosenfeld, "The Social Sources of Homicide in Different Types of Societies," *Sociological Forum* 6 (1991): 51–70.

13. The theory linking economic inequality to crime is also muddled: do people at the bottom of a very large society like that of the United States compare themselves to those at the very top (for example, by watching television), or do they compare themselves to others that they see around them in their neighborhoods or localities? Does absolute poverty lead to crime, or relative poverty, and if the latter, what types of relative deprivation are most significant? For further discussion, see Ineke Haen Marshall and Chris E. Marshall, "Toward a Refinement of Purpose in Comparative Criminological Research: Research Site Selection in Focus," *International Journal of Comparative and Applied Criminal Justice* 7 (1983): 89–97; Harvey Krahn et al., "Income Inequality and Homicide Rates: Cross-National Data and Criminological Theories," *Criminology* 24 (1986): 269–295; W. Lawrence Neuman and Ronald J. Berger, "Competing Perspectives on Cross-National Crime: An Evaluation of Theory and Evidence," *Sociological Quarterly* 29 (1988): 281–313; Steven F. Messner, "Income Inequality and Murder Rates: Some Cross-National Findings," *Comparative Social Research* 3 (1980): 185–198; and Charles R. Tittle, "Social Class and Criminal Behavior: A Critique of the Theoretical Foundation," *Social Forces* 62 (1983): 334–358.

14. Alan Wolfe, *One Nation, After All* (New York: Viking, 1998), pp. 234–250.

15. See Daniel Yankelovich, "How Changes in the Economy are Reshaping American Values," in Henry J. Aaron and Thomas Mann, eds., *Values and Public Policy* (Washington, D.C.: Brookings Institution, 1994).

16. This argument was made originally in Charles Murray, *Losing Ground* (New York: Basic Books, 1984). It had been made earlier by Gary Becker in his *A Treatise on the Family* (Cambridge, Mass.: Harvard University Press, 1981).

17. The disqualification of married women ended in many states during the 1980s, particularly after passage of the Family Support Act of 1988. See Gary Bryner, *Politics and Public Morality: The Great American Welfare Reform Debate* (New York: W. W. Norton, 1998), pp. 73–76.

18. For a description of the welfare reform measure, see Rebecca M. Blank, "Policy Watch: The 1996 Welfare Reform," *Journal of Economic Perspectives* 11 (1997): 169–177.

19. Gary S. Becker, "Crime and Punishment: An Economic Approach," *Journal of Political Economy* 76 (1968): 169–217.

20. "Defeating the Bad Guys," *Economist,* October 3, 1998, pp. 35–38.

21. Based on a personal interview with officials at the Bureau of Justice Statistics, U.S. Department of Justice.

22. James Q. Wilson, "Criminal Justice in England and America," *Public Interest* (1997): 3–14.

23. See the summary of studies on this issue in Robert Moffitt, "Incentive Effects of the United States Welfare System: A Review," *Journal of Economic Literature* 30 (1992): 1–61.

24. In a survey of the existing empirical studies of the relationship between welfare and illegitimacy in the United States, Murray himself notes that the relationship is weak for the period after the mid-1970s when average benefit levels in real terms began to decrease, and weaker for blacks than for whites. See Charles Murray, "Welfare and the Family: The United States Experience," *Journal of Labor Economics* 11 (January 1993): S224–262.

25. This issue is made more complex by how one calculates the total value of welfare

benefits, e.g., whether one includes the implicit value of Medicaid in addition to AFDC payments. See Moffitt, "Incentive Effects"; Robert Moffitt, "The Effect of the United States Welfare System on Marital Status," *Journal of Public Economics* 41 (1990): 101–124; Greg J. Duncan and Saul D. Hoffman, "Welfare Benefits, Economic Opportunities, and Out-of-Wedlock Births Among Black Teenage Girls," *Demography* 27 (1990): 519–535; Robert D. Plotnick, "Welfare and Out-of-Wedlock Childbearing: Evidence from the 1980s," *Journal of Marriage and the Family* 52 (1990): 735–746.

26. See William A. Galston, "Beyond the Murphy Brown Debate: Ideas for Family Policy" (speech to the Institute for American Values, Family Policy Symposium, New York, 1993); and Mark R. Rosenzweig and Kenneth J. Wolpin, "Parental and Public Transfers to Young Women and Their Children," *American Economic Review* 84 (1994): 1195–1212.

27. James L. Nolan, *The Therapeutic State: Justifying Government at Century's End* (New York: NYU Press, 1998).

28. Margaret Mead, *Coming of Age in Samoa: A Psychological Study of Primitive Youth for Western Civilisation* (New York: William Morrow, 1928).

29. James L. Collier, *The Rise of Selfishness in America* (New York: Oxford University Press, 1991), pp. 141–142.

Chapter Four. Causes: Demographic, Economic, and Cultural

1. James Q. Wilson and Richard Herrnstein, *Crime and Human Nature* (New York: Simon & Schuster, 1985), pp. 104–147.

2. James Wilson, *Thinking About Crime,* rev. ed. (New York: Vintage Books, 1983), p. 20.

3. Glenn D. Deane, "Cross-National Comparison of Homicide: Age/Sex-Adjusted Rates Using the 1980s United States Homicide Experience as a Standard," *Journal of Quantitative Criminology* 3 (1987): 215–227.

4. Wilson, *Thinking About Crime,* p. 23.

5. Rosemary Gartner and Robert N. Parker, "Cross-National Evidence on Homicide and the Age Structure of the Population," *Social Forces* 69 (1990): 351–371. See also Robert G. Martin and Rand D. Conger, "A Comparison of Delinquency Trends: Japan and the United States," *Criminology* 18 (1980): 53–61.

6. Henry Shaw and Clifford McKay, *Juvenile Delinquency and Urban Areas* (Chicago: University of Chicago Press, 1942).

7. Rodney Stark, "A Theory of the Ecology of Crime," in Peter Cordella and Larry Siegel, *Readings in Contemporary Criminological Theory* (Boston: Northeastern University Press, 1996), pp. 128–142.

8. See Fox Butterfield, "Why America's Murder Rate Is So High," *New York Times,* July 26, 1998, p. WK1.

9. See, for example, Henry B. Hansmann and John M. Quigley, "Population Heterogeneity and the Sociogenesis of Homicide," *Social Forces* 61 (1982): 206–224.

10. Richard Cloward and Lloyd Ohlin, *Delinquency and Opportunity* (New York: Free Press, 1960).

11. See Matthew G. Yeager, "Immigrants and Criminality: Cross-National Review," *Criminal Justice Abstracts* 29 (1997): 143–171.

12. "Decline of Violent Crime Is Linked to Crack Market," *New York Times,* December 28, 1998, p. A16.

13. Eleanor Glueck and Sheldon Glueck, *Unraveling Juvenile Delinquency* (New York: Commonwealth Fund, 1950).

14. See Travis Hirschi and Michael Gottfredson, *A General Theory of Crime* (Stanford, Calif.: Stanford University Press, 1990), esp. p. 103.

15. Rolf Loeber and Magda Stouthamer-Loeber, "Family Factors as Correlates and Predictors of Juvenile Crime Conduct Problems and Delinquency," in Michael Tonry and Norval Morris, *Crime and Justice,* vol. 7 (Chicago: University of Chicago Press, 1986).

16. Robert J. Sampson and John H. Laub, *Crime in the Making: Pathways and Turning Points Through Life* (Cambridge, Mass.: Harvard University Press, 1993).

17. J. Rankin and J. E. Wells, "The Effect of Parental Attachments and Direct Controls on Delinquency," *Journal of Research in Crime and Delinquency* 27 (1990): 140–165; Ruth Seydlitz, "Complexity in the Relationships Among Direct and Indirect Parental Controls and Delinquency," *Youth and Society* 24 (1993): 243–275; J. E. Wells and J. H. Rankin, "Direct Parental Controls and Delinquency," *Criminology* 26 (1988): 263–285; Rosemary Gartner, "Family Stucture, Welfare Spending, and Child Homicide in Developed Democracies," *Journal of Marriage and the Family* 53 (1991): 231–240; Shlomo G. Shoham and Giora Rahav, "Family Parameters of Violent Prisoners," *Journal of Social Psychology* 127 (1987): 83–91.

18. Robert J. Sampson, "Urban Black Violence: The Effect of Male Joblessness and Family Disruption," *American Journal of Sociology* 93 (1987): 348–382.

19. Wilson and Herrnstein, *Crime,* pp. 213–218.

20. Robin Fox, *The Red Lamp of Incest,* rev. ed. (South Bend, Ind.: University of Notre Dame Press, 1983), p. 76.

21. Thomas E. Ricks, *Making the Corps* (New York: Scribners, 1997).

22. Children's Defense Fund, *The State of America's Children Yearbook 1997* (Washington, D.C.: Children's Defense Fund), p. 52.

23. Andrea J. Sedlak and Diane D. Broadhurst, *Third National Incidence Study of Child Abuse and Neglect* (Washington, D.C.: U.S. Department of Health and Human Services, September 1996), p. 3-3.

24. In addition, standards for what constitutes child abuse have changed over time. The Department of Health and Human Services now tries to keep tabs not just on physical and sexual abuse, but on "emotional abuse" as well—a notoriously imprecise category of offense. Parents tend to resort to corporal punishment less, and there is a significant group of child care and child development professionals who would today regard simple spanking as tantamount to child abuse. Between 1988 and 1997 in the United States, one survey found that the number of parents who had resorted to spanking as a means of disciplining their children had fallen from 62 to 46 percent of those questioned. See National Commission to Prevent Child Abuse, *Public Opinion and Behaviors Regarding Child Abuse Prevention: A Ten Year Review of NCPCA's Public Opinion Poll Research* (Chicago: NCPCA, 1997), p. 5.

25. Martin Daly and Margo Wilson, *Homicide* (New York: Aldine de Gruyter, 1988), p. 83; Martin Daly, "Child Abuse and Other Risks of Not Living with Both Parents," *Ethology and Sociobiology* 6 (1985): 197–210.

26. Robert Whelan, *Broken Homes and Battered Children: A Study of the Relationship Between Child Abuse and Family Type* (Oxford: Family Education Trust, 1994), pp. 22–23.

27. Sedlak and Broadhurst, *Third Study,* pp. 5-18–5-19, 5-28.

28. Martin Daly and Margo Wilson, "Children Fathered by Previous Partners: A Risk

Factor for Violence Against Women," *Canadian Journal of Public Health* 84 (1993): 209–210

29. According to the U.S. Census Bureau, *Statistical Abstract of the United States, 1997* (Washington, D.C.: U.S. Government Printing Office, 1997), the percentage of Americans living in poverty in 1980 was 13.0 versus 14.5 in 1994. The rate climbed as high as 15.2 percent in 1983.

30. For a somewhat pessimistic view of the ability of families to adapt to substitute parents, see Andrew J. Cherlin and Frank F. Furstenberg, Jr., "Stepfamilies in the United States: A Reconsideration," *Annual Review of Sociology* 20 (1994): 359–381.

31. Given both the strong natural and empirical reasons for thinking that child abuse and family breakdown are connected, it is curious that the relationship between these two developments is not stronger in the public eye or among the professionals who deal with such issues. The failure to recognize systematic behavioral differences between biological and substitute parents is reflected in the continuing tendency of government and advocacy agencies involved with child welfare *not* to distinguish between types of perpetrators in child abuse cases, lumping natural, substitute, and other kinds of caregivers into the same category. Much of the social science literature on child abuse tends to be dismissive of biological theories that might provide some understanding of the evolutionary grounding of contemporary behavior. See Owen D. Jones, "Law and Biology: Toward an Integrated Model of Human Behavior," *Journal of Contemporary Legal Issues* 8 (1997): 167–208, and "Evolutionary Analysis in Law: An Introduction and Application to Child Abuse," *North Carolina Law Review* 75 (1997): 1117–1241 esp. pp. 1230–1231; and Marilyn Coleman, "Stepfamilies in the United States: Challenging Biases and Assumptions," in Alan Booth and Judy Dunn, *Stepfamilies: Who Benefits? Who Does Not?* (Hillsdale, N.J.: Erlbaum, 1994).

32. Robert D. Putnam, "Tuning In, Tuning Out: The Strange Disappearance of Social Capital in America," *PS: Political Science and Politics* (1995): 664–682.

33. Eric Uslaner, "The Moral Foundations of Trust," unpublished manuscript, 1999, chap. 7.

34. Tom Smith "Factors Relating to Misanthropy in Contemporary American Society," *Social Science Research* 26 (1997): 170–196; Wendy Rahn and John Transue, "Social Trust and Value Change," unpublished manuscript, 1997.

35. Smith, "Factors," p. 193. Minority status does not appear to explain the rise in distrust, since African Americans, the most distrusting racial or ethnic minority, have remained a stable percentage of the American population. It is true that immigration exploded over the 1965–1995 time period, and the argument is often made that by undermining common cultural norms, immigration breeds distrust. But distrust is only weakly linked to immigrant status, and the United States has been, overall, quite welcoming of immigrants. It is possible that Americans strongly opposed to immigration have become more distrustful over time. However, opposition to immigration correlates to a large extent with socioeconomic status (it is primarily low-skill workers whose jobs are threatened by immigration) so it is difficult to disentangle the two factors.

36. Rahn and Transue, "Social Trust." For many people, evidently, the fact that the chief authority figure has walked out of their family does not necessarily affect their ability to trust and work with other people to whom they are not related. This ability to compartmentalize one's sex and family life from one's relations with strangers may seem at first glance puzzling, but it is in fact common. The French writer Albert

Camus behaved abominably toward the women who loved him and drove one wife to madness and suicide. This fact did not prevent him from being regarded as one of the most important moral voices of his generation. When President Clinton got into trouble for lying about a series of sexual escapades, a large majority of Americans felt that this had no bearing on his trustworthiness as a political leader; they were much less willing to trust Richard Nixon, who as far as anyone knows was never unfaithful to his wife.

37. Seymour Martin Lipset, *American Exceptionalism* (New York: W. W. Norton, 1995), pp. 60–67.

38. On this point, see Adam Seligman, *The Problem of Trust* (Princeton, N.J.: Princeton University Press, 1997).

Chapter Five. The Special Role of Women

1. Gary Becker, *A Treatise on the Family,* enl. ed. (Cambridge, Mass.: Harvard University Press, 1991), pp. 135–178.

2. Naohiro Ogawa and Robert D. Retherford, "The Resumption of Fertility Decline in Japan: 1973–92," *Population and Development Review* 19 (1993): 703–741.

3. In economic terms, there has not just been a change in relative prices for the cost of raising children and the opportunity cost of women's labor, but an autonomous change in the preference for children. They simply aren't wanted as much any more.

4. Quoted in Michael Specter, "Population Implosion Worries a Graying Europe," *New York Times,* July 10, 1998, p. A1.

5. Alice Rossi, "The Biosocial Role of Parenthood," *Human Nature* 72 (1978): 75–79.

6. Alice Rossi, "A Biosocial Perspective on Parenting," *Daedalus* 106 (1977): 2–31.

7. Lionel Tiger and Robin Fox, *The Imperial Animal* (New York: Holt, Rinehart, and Winston, 1971), p. 64.

8. In fact, while birds pair-bond, they are often not monogamous. See "Infidelity Common Among Birds and Mammals, Experts Say," *New York Times,* September 27, 1998, p. A25.

9. See William J. Hamilton III, "Significance of Paternal Investment by Primates to the Evolution of Adult Male-Female Associations," in David M. Taub, *Primate Paternalism* (New York: Van Nostrand Reinhold, 1984).

10. Robert Trivers, *Social Evolution* (Menlo Park, Calif.: Benjamin/Cummings, 1985), p. 214.

11. Ibid., p. 215.

12. For a more extended discussion of this issue, see Matt Ridley, *The Red Queen: Sex and the Evolution of Human Nature* (New York: Macmillan, 1993), pp. 181–183.

13. Tiger and Fox, *Imperial Animal,* p. 67.

14. Ibid., p. 71.

15. For a historical account of how theories of the family have changed over time, see David Popenoe, *Disturbing the Nest* (New York: Aldine de Gruyter, 1988), pp. 11–21.

16. See Stevan Harrell, *Human Families* (Boulder, Colo.: Westview, 1997), pp. 26–50.

17. Adam Kuper, *The Chosen Primate: Human Nature and Cultural Diversity* (Cambridge, Mass.: Harvard University Press, 1993), p. 174.

18. Ibid., p. 170.

19. See Peter Laslett and Richard Wall, *Household and Family in Past Time* (Cambridge:

Cambridge University Press, 1972); and Peter Laslett and Richard Wall, *Family Forms in Historic Europe* (Cambridge: Cambridge University Press, 1983).

20. David Blankenhorn, *Fatherless America: Confronting America's Most Urgent Social Problem* (New York: Basic Books, 1995), p. 3.

21. Margaret Mead, *Male and Female* (New York: Dell, 1949), pp. 188–191. This point has been made by a number of observers, including David Blankenhorn, *Fatherless America.*

22. On this point, see Becker, *Treatise,* pp. 141–144.

23. I am grateful to Lionel Tiger for pointing this out.

24. U. S. Department of Health and Human Services, *Report to Congress on Out-of-Wedlock Childbearing* (1995), p. 72.

25. See George Akerlof, Janet Yellen, and Michael L. Katz, "An Analysis of Out-of-Wedlock Childbearing in the United States," *Quarterly Journal of Economics* 111 (May 1996): 277–317.

26. Becker, "Treatise," pp. 347–361.

27. Gary S. Becker and Elisabeth M. Landes, "An Economic Analysis of Marital Instability," *Journal of Political Economy* 85 (1977): 1141–1187. See also Cynthia Cready and Mark A. Fossett, "Mate Availability and African American Family Structure in the United States Nonmetropolitan South, 1960–1990," *Journal of Marriage and the Family* 59 (1997): 192–203.

28. Shoshana Zuboff, *In the Age of the Smart Machine: The Future of Work and Power* (New York: Basic Books, 1984), p. 37.

29. Lawrence F. Katz and Kevin M. Murphy, "Changes in Relative Wages, 1963–1981: Supply and Demand Factors," *Quarterly Journal of Economics* 107 (February 1992): 35–78.

30. June O'Neill and Solomon Polachek, "Why the Gender Gap in Wages Narrowed in the 1980s," *Journal of Labor Economics* 11 (1993): 205–228.

31. Valerie K. Oppenheimer, "Women's Rising Employment and the Future of the Family in Industrial Societies," *Population and Development Review* 20 (1994): 293–342.

32. Ibid.

33. Annette Bernhardt, Martina Morris, and Mark S. Handcock, "Women's Gains or Men's Losses? A Closer Look at the Shrinking Gender Gap in Earnings," *American Journal of Sociology* 101 (1995): 302–328.

34. O'Neill and Polachek, "Why the Gender Gap?"

35. Elaine Reardon, "Demand-Side Changes and the Relative Economic Progress of Black Men: 1940–90," *Journal of Human Resources* 32 (Winter 1997): 69–97. The author suggests that while white women were replacing white men, black men were being replaced by middle-class white men.

36. Bernhardt, Morris, and Handcock, "Women's Gains or Men's Losses?" p. 314.

37. John Bound and Richard B. Freeman, "What Went Wrong? The Erosion of Relative Earnings Among Young Black Men in the 1980s," *Quarterly Journal of Economics* (1992): 201–232; John M. Jeffries and Richard L. Schaffer, "Changes in the Economy and Labor Market Status of Black Americans," in National Urban League, *The State of Black America, 1996* (Washington, D.C.: National Urban League, 1997).

38. Cordelia W. Reimers, "Cultural Differences in Labor Force Participation Among Married Women," *ABA Papers and Proceedings* 75, no. 2 (1985): 251–255.

39. Herbert G. Gutman, *The Black Family in Slavery and Freedom, 1750–1925* (New York: Vintage Books, 1977).

40. See William Julius Wilson, *The Truly Disadvantaged: The Inner City, the Underclass, and Public Policy* (Chicago: University of Chicago Press, 1988), and *When Work Disappears: The World of the New Urban Poor* (New York: Knopf, 1996).

41. Tamar Lewin, "Wage Difference Between Men and Women Widens," *New York Times,* September 15, 1997, p. A1. One suggestion is that the lower skills of former welfare recipients now in the workforce since the onset of welfare reform in the mid-1990s have dragged down the earnings for women as a whole.

Chapter Six. Consequences of the Great Disruption

1. Already in Italy there are as many people over the age of sixty as there are under twenty. Under the low-growth variant that the United Nations's Population Division started estimating for the first time in 1997, the dependency ratio—the number of dependent people over sixty-five as a percentage of the working population—will shift dramatically. It is currently 20 percent for the West as a whole today (one dependent person for every five working people), but will move to 60 percent in Germany, 65 percent in Japan, and an amazing 80 percent in Italy by the year 2050. In the absence of immigration, median ages will rise as well, to fifty-five in Germany, fifty-three in Japan, and fifty-eight in Italy. These estimates are based on the assumption that fertility rates will continue their downward trend slightly before bottoming out and that there is no large increase in immigration. We cannot, of course, know that there won't be a sudden upturn in fertility in the next fifty years. However, estimates of dramatically falling and aging populations in Europe and Japan do not require heroic assumptions about changes in future behavior; they are the outcomes of fertility patterns that were established during the Great Disruption. See Nick Eberstadt, "World Population Implosion?" *Public Interest* no. 129 (1997): 18.

2. Jean Fourastié, "De la vie traditionelle à la vie tertiaire," *Population* (Paris) 14 (1963): 417–432.

3. Eberstadt, "World Population Implosion?" p. 21.

4. Lionel Tiger, *The Decline of Males* (New York: Golden Books, 1999).

5. James S. Coleman et al., *Equality of Educational Opportunity* (Washington, D.C.: U.S. Department of Health, Education and Welfare, 1966).

6. Daniel P. Moynihan, *The Negro Family: A Case for National Action* (Washington, D.C.: U.S. Department of Labor, 1965).

7. See, for example, Carol Stack, *All Our Kin: Strategies for Survival in a Black Community* (New York: Harper & Row, 1974); see also William J. Bennett, "America at Midnight: Reflections on the Moynihan Report," *American Enterprise* 29 (1995).

8. Among the first to make this argument were Elizabeth Herzog and Cecilia E. Sudia, "Children in Fatherless Families," in B. Caldwell and H. H. Ricciuti, eds., *Review of Child Development Research,* vol. 3 (Chicago: University of Chicago Press, 1973). For a more recent version of this argument, see Michael Katz, *The Undeserving Poor: From the War on Poverty to the War on Welfare* (New York: Pantheon, 1989), pp. 44–52.

9. See the evidence summarized in Sara McLanahan and Gary Sandefur, *Growing Up with a Single Parent* (Cambridge, Mass.: Harvard University Press, 1994), pp. 79–94.

10. Ibid., pp. 24–25; Greg J. Duncan and Saul D. Hoffman, "A Reconsideration of the Economic Consequences of Marital Disruption," *Demography* 22 (1985): 485–498.

11. On the paucity of research into the impact of fathers on children, see Suzanne M.

Bianchi, "Introduction to the Special Issue, 'Men in Families,'" *Demography* 35 (May 1998): 133.

12. One of the best summaries of work on this subject is David Popenoe's *Life Without Father* (New York: Free Press, 1996). See also Patricia Cohen, "Daddy Dearest: Do You Really Matter?" *New York Times,* July 11, 1998, p. A13.

13. See, for example, David Blankenhorn, *Fatherless America* (New York: Basic Books, 1995).

14. Robert Putnam, "Tuning In, Tuning Out," *PS* (1995).

15. James Q. Wilson, *Thinking About Crime,* rev. ed. (New York: Vintage Books, 1983), p. 26.

16. Dorothy Rabinowitz's articles include "Kelly Michaels's Orwellian Ordeal," *Wall Street Journal (WSJ),* April 15, 1993, p. A14; "A Darkness in Massachusetts," *WSJ,* January 30, 1995, p. A20; "A Darkness in Massachusetts II," *WSJ,* March 14, 1995, p. A14; "A Darkness in Massachusetts III," *WSJ,* May 12, 1995; "Wenatchee: A True Story," *WSJ,* September 29, 1995, p. A14; "Wenatchee: A True Story—II," *WSJ,* October 13, 1995, p. A14; "Wenatchee: A True Story—III," *WSJ,* November 8, 1995, p. A20; "Verdict in Wenatchee," *WSJ,* December 15, 1995, p. A14; "The Amiraults: Continued," *WSJ,* December 29, 1995, p. A10; "Justice and the Prosecutor," *WSJ,* March 21, 1997, p. A18; "The Amiraults' Trial Judge Reviews His Peers," *WSJ,* April 10, 1997; "Justice in Massachusetts," *WSJ,* May 13, 1997, p. A22; "The Snowden Case, at the Bar of Justice," *WSJ,* October 14, 1997; "Through the Darkness," *WSJ,* April 8, 1998, p. A22; "From the Mouths of Babes to a Jail Cell," *Harper's* (May 1990): 52–63.

17. June Kronholz, "Chary Schools Tell Teachers, 'Don't Touch, Don't Hug'," *Wall Street Journal,* May 28, 1998, p. B1.

18. James Q. Wilson and George Kelling, "Broken Windows: The Police and Neighborhood Safety," *Atlantic Monthly* 249 (1982): 29–38.

19. For an overview of community policing, see Robert Trojanowicz, Victor E. Kappeler, Larry K. Gaines, and Bonnie Bucqueroux, *Community Policing: A Contemporary Perspective,* 2d ed. (Cincinnati, Ohio: Anderson Publishing, 1996).

20. "The challenge that the police face in getting informaton is that there must [be] some level of trust for citizens to cooperate with the police." Ibid., p. 10.

21. Wesley G. Skogan, *Disorder and Decline: Crime and the Spiral of Decay in American Neighborhoods* (New York: Free Press, 1990), p. 15.

22. George Kelling and Catherine Coles, *Fixing Broken Windows* (New York: Free Press, 1996), pp. 12–13.

23. For an account of this process, see Nicholas Lemann, *The Promised Land: The Great Black Migration and How It Changed America* (New York: Alfred A. Knopf, 1991), pp. 347–348.

Chapter Seven. Was the Great Disruption Inevitable?

1. See James Q. Wilson, "Thinking about Crime," in Wilson, *Thinking About Crime,* rev. ed. (New York: Vintage Books, 1983).

2. Kingsley Davis and Pietronella Van den Oever, "Demographic Foundations of New Sex Roles," *Population and Development Review* 8 (1982): 495–511.

3. See, for example, Fareed Zakaria, "A Conversation with Lee Kuan Yew," *Foreign Affairs* 73 (1994): 109–127.

4. See Francis Fukuyama, "Asian Values and the Asian Crisis," *Commentary* 105 (1998): 23–27.

5. Japan and Korea have experienced changes in social norms that are in some ways similar to those of the West. For example, in the World Values Survey, both countries showed a decrease in confidence in major institutions between 1981 and 1990, beginning with the government—not surprising for Japan, which experienced a series of scandals, and Korea, whose democratic institutions were incompletely formed and less than three years old in 1990. In Japan, confidence decreased for the church, armed forces, the education and legal systems, trade unions, and police and increased for the press, parliament (very slightly), civil service, and major companies. In Korea, confidence in all institutions except for trade unions decreased. As in the West, trends in organizational memberships are inconclusive, tending to fall slightly in Japan and rise in Korea (especially memberships in religious groups). In both countries, and particularly Japan, fertility has declined dramatically during the past generation. Family structure has changed as well, as multigenerational families have given way to nuclear ones (a process that began substantially earlier in Japan than in Korea). Changes in family structure have been similar in Asia and the West in other ways as well, including the separation of workplace from home, education in institutional settings, and greater access of children to economic resources. See Arland Thornton and Thomas E. Fricke, "Social Change and the Family: Comparative Perspectives from the West, China, and South Asia," *Sociological Forum* 2 (1987): 746–779.

6. Organization for Economic Cooperation and Development, *Employment Outlook* (Paris, July 1996), and personal correspondence.

7. Marguerite Kaminski and Judith Paiz, "Japanese Women in Management: Where Are They?" *Human Resource Management* 23 (1984): 277–292.

8. Eiko Shinotsuka, "Women Workers in Japan: Past, Present, Future," in Joyce Gelb and Marian Lief Palley, eds., *Women of Japan and Korea* (Philadelphia: Temple University Press, 1994); Andrew Pollack, "For Japan's Women, More Jobs and Longer and Odder Hours," *New York Times,* July 8, 1997, p. D1.

9. Shinotsuka, "Women Workers," p. 100.

10. Roh Mihye, "Women Workers in a Changing Korean Society," in Gelb and Paley, *Women of Japan.*

11. This was not always the case. In the West, in Japan, and in contemporary Asia, light manufacturing (e.g., textiles) has been a major source of employment for young women. See Claudia Goldin, "The Historical Evolution of Female Earnings Functions and Occupations," *Explorations in Economic History* 21 (1984): 1–27.

12. Miho Ogino, "Abortion and Women's Reproductive Rights: The State of Japanese Women, 1945–1991," in Gelb and Paley, *Women of Japan,* pp. 72–75; see also Naohiro Ogawa and Robert Retherford, "The Resumption of Fertility Decline in Japan," *Population and Development Review* 19 (1993): 703–741.

13. Ronald R. Rindfuss and S. Philip Morgan, "Marriage, Sex, and the First Birth Interval: The Quiet Revolution in Asia," *Population and Development Review* 9 (1983): 259–278.

14. Gavin W. Jones, "Modernization and Divorce: Contrasting Trends in Islamic Southeast Asia and the West," *Population and Development Review* 23 (1997): 95–114.

15. There is some evidence that these problems may already have started. See Mary Jord

and Kevin Sullivan, "In Japanese Schools, Discipline in Recess," *Washington Post* (January 24, 1999): A1, A22.

16. In many countries, and particularly in Catholic ones, it is often the case that while the family remains relatively intact as a formal and legal institution, men have mistresses or girlfriends on the side. Although this situation is more hypocritical, it has the virtue of better protecting the legal rights of dependents than the serial polygamy practiced in countries like the United States with Puritan traditions.

Chapter Eight. Where Do Norms Come From?

1. This account is based on Lee Lawrence, "On the Trail of the Slug: A Journey into the Lair of an Endangered Species," *Washington Post,* August 10, 1997, p. 1 ("Style" section).

2. Although slugging was not created by the state, the state subsequently intervened, when the Metropolitan Police of the District of Columbia sought to curb the "slug lines" on Fourteenth Street. In response, Representative James Moran of Virginia introduced legislation to protect the interests of the slugs. Informal rules are thus being transformed into formal ones, with the intervention of hierarchical authority. See "Slugfest," *Washington Post,* August 2, 1998, p. C8.

3. Friedrich A. Hayek, *The Fatal Conceit: The Errors of Socialism* (Chicago: University of Chicago Press, 1988), p. 5; see also his *Law, Legislation and Liberty* (Chicago: University of Chicago Press, 1976).

4. On this point, see the discussion in Kevin Kelly, *Out of Control: The New Biology of Machines, Social Systems, and the Economic World* (Reading, Mass.: Addison-Wesley, 1994), pp. 5–7. See also John H. Holland, *Hidden Order: How Adaptation Builds Complexity* (Reading, Mass.: Addison-Wesley, 1995).

5. This is the theme of Richard Dawkins, *The Blind Watchmaker* (New York: W. W. Norton, 1986).

6. For a description of the genesis of the Santa Fe Institute, see M. Mitchell Waldrop, *Complexity: The Emerging Science at the Edge of Order and Chaos* (New York: Simon & Schuster, 1992).

7. See Emile Durkheim, *The Rules of Sociological Method* (Glencoe, Ill.: Free Press, 1938), pp. 23–27. See also Dean Neu, "Trust, Contracting and the Prospectus Process," *Accounting, Organizations, and Society* 16 (1991): 243–256.

8. Max Weber, *The Protestant Ethic and the Spirit of Capitalism* (London: Allen and Unwin, 1930).

9. Dennis Wrong, "The Oversocialized Conception of Man in Modern Sociology," *American Sociological Review* 26 (1961): 183–196.

10. Viktor Vanberg, "Rules and Choice in Economics and Sociology," in Geoffrey M. Hodgson, ed., *The Economics of Institutions* (Aldershot: Edward Elgar Publishing Co., 1993).

11. Ronald A. Heiner, "The Origin of Predictable Behavior," *American Economic Review* 73 (1983): 560–595, and "Origin of Predictable Behavior: Further Modeling and Applications," *American Economic Review* 75 (1985): 391–396.

12. For a description of the new institutionalism and how it differs from the older variety, see Geoffrey M. Hodgson, "Institutional Economics: Surveying the 'Old' and the 'New,'" *Metroeconomica* 44 (1993): 1–28.

13. Douglass C. North, *Institutions, Institutional Change, and Economic Performance* (New York: Cambridge University Press, 1990).

14. The classic sociological account of small group behavior was George C. Homans, *The Human Group* (New York: Harcourt, Brace, 1950).

15. On this point, see Adam Kuper, *The Chosen Primate* (Cambridge, Mass.: Harvard University Press, 1993), pp. 98–99.

16. This subdiscipline starts with John von Neumann and Oskar Morgenstern, *Theory of Games and Economic Behavior* (New York: John Wiley, 1944).

17. On the original liberal "isolated rights bearer," see Mary Ann Glendon, *Rights Talk: The Impoverishment of Political Discourse* (New York: Free Press, 1991), pp. 67–68.

18. For a discussion of methodological individualism and a partial critique, see Kenneth J. Arrow, "Methodological Individualism and Social Knowledge," *AEA Papers and Proceedings* 84 (1994): 1–9.

19. Some people might question whether laws promulgated by democratic political processes should be put in the hierarchical category, since democracies by definition are committed to some form of voter equality and reflect, if they are well implemented, the wishes of the broader community. *Hierarchical* as it is used here refers to the way laws are issued and enforced, however, and not to the process by which they are legislated. A democratically decided law is still promulgated from the top down and carries with it the full enforcement powers of the state.

Chapter Nine. Human Nature and Social Order

1. For a history of how the social constructionist view arose out of the abuse of nineteenth-century Darwinism, see Carl N. Degler, *In Search of Human Nature: The Decline and Revival of Darwinism in American Social Thought* (New York: Oxford University Press, 1991), pp. 59–83. See also Francis Fukuyama, "Is It All in the Genes?" *Commentary* 104 (Sept. 1997): 30–35.

2. For a critical description of this model, see J. H. Barkow, Leda Cosmides, and John Tooby, *The Adapted Mind* (New York: Oxford University Press, 1992), p. 23.

3. Clifford Geertz, *The Interpretation of Cultures* (New York: Basic Books, 1973), chap. 1.

4. Robin Fox, *The Red Lamp of Incest* (New York: Dutton, 1983). See also his article "Sibling Incest," *British Journal of Sociology* 13 (1962): 128–150.

5. See in particular Degler, *In Search of Human Nature*, pp. 245–269; Adam Kuper, *Chosen Primate* (Cambridge, Mass.: Harvard University Press, 1993), pp. 156–166; Matt Ridley, *The Red Queen* (New York: Macmillan, 1993), pp. 282–287.

6. Degler, *In Search of Human Nature*, pp. 258–260.

7. Fox, *Red Lamp*, p. 76.

8. Claude Levi-Strauss, *The Elementary Structures of Kinship* (Boston: Beacon Press, 1969).

9. Edward O. Wilson, "Resuming the Enlightenment Quest," *Wilson Quarterly* 22 (1998): 16–27.

10. For examples of economists who have looked to biology for models and evidence, see Jack Hirshleifer, "Economics from a Biological Viewpoint," *Journal of Law and Economics* 20 (1977): 1–52; Gary S. Becker, "Altruism, Egoism, and Genetic Fitness: Economics and Sociobiology," *Journal of Economic Literature* 14 (1976): 817–826; Richard E. Nelson and Sidney G. Winter, *An Evolutionary Theory of Economic Change* (Cambridge: Belknap/Harvard University Press, 1982); and Robert H.

Frank, *Passions Within Reason: The Strategic Role of the Emotions* (New York: Norton, 1988).

11. On the role of methodological individualism in the social sciences, see Kenneth Arrow, "Methodological Individualism and Social Knowledge," *ABA Papers and Proceedings* 84 (1994): 1–90. See also James Coleman, *Foundations of Social Theory* (Cambridge, Mass.: Harvard University Press, 1994), p. 5.

12. Karl Marx's characterization of man as a "species being" presupposes a degree of natural altruism toward the species as a whole.

13. See Vero C. Wynne-Edwards, *Animal Dispersion in Relation to Social Behaviour* (New York: Hafner Publishing, 1967), and *Evolution Through Group Selection* (Oxford: Blackwell Scientific, 1986). For a critique of Wynne-Edwards, see Robert Trivers, *Social Evolution* (Menlo Park, Calif.: Benjamin/Cummings, 1985), pp. 79–82. See also Ridley, *Red Queen,* pp. 32–33.

14. George C. Williams, *Adaptation and Natural Selection: A Critique of Some Current Evolutionary Thought* (Princeton, N.J.: Princeton University Press, 1974).

15. Jack Hirshleifer points to the substantive conclusions concerning human nature suggested by new findings in biology but fails to push them further. Jack Hirshleifer, "Natural Economy Versus Political Economy," *Journal of Social Biology* 1 (1978): 319–337.

16. Frans de Waal, *Chimpanzee Politics: Power and Sex Among Apes* (Baltimore: Johns Hopkins University Press, 1989).

17. Richard Wrangham and Dale Peterson, *Demonic Males: Apes and the Origins of Human Violence* (Boston: Houghton Mifflin, 1996), p. 191.

18. Ibid.

19. Lionel Tiger, *Men in Groups* (New York: Random House, 1969).

20. John Locke suggests that grooming in primates serves purposes similar to small talk for humans. See John L. Locke, *The De-voicing of Society: Why We Don't Talk to Each Other Anymore* (New York: Simon & Schuster, 1998), pp. 73–75.

21. On this issue, see Lawrence H. Keeley, *War Before Civilization* (New York: Oxford University Press, 1996), chap. 2.

22. Mary Ann Glendon, *Rights Talk* (New York: Free Press, 1991), pp. 47–75.

23. *Politics* Book I 1253a.

24. Aristotle bases the judgment that human beings are political animals in part on the fact that they alone have language by which they can express opinions about good and bad, right and wrong, and that the highest forms of virtue can only come about in a city. *Politics* Book I 1253b.

Chapter Ten. The Origins of Cooperation

1. See William D. Hamilton, "The Genetic Evolution of Social Behavior," *Journal of Theoretical Biology* 7 (1964): 17–52. For an overview of the development of kin selection theory, see Leda Cosmides and John Tooby, "Cognitive Adaptations for Social Exchange," in J. H. Barkow, Leda Cosmides, and John Tooby, eds., *The Adapted Mind* (New York: Oxford University Press, 1992), pp. 167–168.

2. Richard Dawkins, *The Selfish Gene* (New York: Oxford University Press, 1989).

3. The extraordinary social altruism shown by haplodiploid species like ants and bees, where individuals forgo reproduction in order to help raise their sisters, is due to the

curious fact that the sisters in such social species actually share three-quarters of their genes.

4. P. W. Sherman, "Nepotism and the Evolution of Alarm Calls," *Science* 197 (1977): 1246–1253.

5. See Robert L. Trivers, "Parental Investment and Sexual Selection," in Bernard Campbell, ed., *Sexual Selection and the Descent of Man* (Chicago: Aldine, 1972), pp. 136–179.

6. Martin Daly and Margot Wilson, *Homicide* (New York: Aldine de Gruyter, 1988), chap. 1.

7. Ibid., Owen D. Jones, "Evolutionary Analysis in Law: An Introduction and Application to Child Abuse," *North Carolina Law Review* 75 (1997): 1117–1241; and Owen D. Jones, "Law and Biology: Toward an Integrated Model of Human Behavior," *Journal of Contemporary Legal Issues* 8 (1997): 167–208.

8. Cosmides and Tooby, "Cognitive Adaptations," p. 169.

9. This is described in Robert Trivers, *Social Evolution* (Menlo Park, Calif.: Benjamin/Cummings, 1985), pp. 47–48.

10. Francis Fukuyama, *Trust: The Social Virtues and the Creation of Prosperity* (New York: Free Press, 1995), pp. 83–95.

11. On this point see Robert Trivers, "The Evolution of Reciprocal Altruism," *Quarterly Review of Biology* 46 (1971): 35–56; also Trivers, *Social Evolution,* pp. 47–48.

12. See Matt Ridley, *The Origins of Virtue: Human Instincts and the Evolution of Cooperation* (New York: Viking, 1997), p. 61.

13. Robert Axelrod, *The Evolution of Cooperation* (New York: Basic Books, 1984).

14. See Daniel B. Klein, ed., *Reputation: Studies in the Voluntary Elicitation of Good Conduct* (Ann Arbor: University of Michigan Press, 1996).

15. Trivers, *Social Evolution,* p. 386.

16. Ridley, *The Origins of Virtue,* pp. 96–98.

17. Adam Kuper, *The Chosen Primate* (Cambridge, Mass.: Harvard University Press, 1993) p. 228.

18. Richard D. Alexander, *How Did Humans Evolve? Reflections on the Uniquely Unique Species* (Ann Arbor: Museum of Zoology, University of Michigan, 1990), p. 6.

19. On defensive modernization, see Francis Fukuyama, *The End of History and the Last Man* (New York: Free Press, 1992), pp. 74–76.

20. Nicholas K. Humphrey, "The Social Function of Intellect," in P. P. G. Bateson and R. A. Hinde, eds., *Growing Points in Ethology* (Cambridge: Cambridge University Press, 1976), pp. 303–317; Alexander, *How Did Humans Evolve?* pp. 4–7; Richard Alexander, "The Evolution of Social Behavior," in Richard F. Johnston, Peter W. Frank, and Charles D. Michener, eds., *Annual Review of Ecology and Systematics,* vol. 5 (Palo Alto, Calif.: Annual Reviews, 1974), pp. 325–385. See also Steven Pinker and Paul Bloom, "Natural Language and Natural Selection," in Barkow et al. (1992); and Robin Fox, *The Search for Society: Quest for a Biosocial Science and Morality* (New Brunswick, N.J.: Rutgers University Press, 1989), pp. 29–30.

21. Matt Ridley, *The Red Queen* (New York, Macmillan, 1993), pp. 329–331.

22. John L. Locke, "The Role of the Face in Vocal Learning and the Development of Spoken Language," in B. de Boysson-Bardies, ed., *Developmental Neurocognition: Speech and Face Processing in the First Year of Life* (Netherlands: Kluwer Academic Publishers, 1993).

23. This was a subject of particular interest to Darwin, who wrote an entire book on the

subject. See his *The Expression of Emotion in Man and Animals* (New York and London: D. Appleton and Co., 1916).

24. Some biologists speculate that language evolved out of grooming. See Robin Dunbar, *Grooming, Gossip, and the Origin of Language* (Cambridge, Mass.: Harvard University Press, 1996).

25. For a general description of the brain and its functions, see George E. Pugh, *The Biological Origin of Human Values* (New York: Basic Books, 1977), pp. 140–143.

26. Locke (1998), pp. 48–57.

27. Ridley, *Red Queen*, p. 338.

28. See the earlier reference to male and female incentives in Part One.

29. See Martin Daly and Margo Wilson, "Male Sexual Jealousy," *Ethology and Sociobiology* 3 (1982): 11–27. See also Ridley (1993), pp. 243–244.

30. Michael S. Gazzaniga, *Nature's Mind: The Biological Roots of Thinking, Emotions, Sexuality, Language, and Intelligence* (New York: Basic Books, 1992), pp. 60–61, 113–114. Other biologists have suggested that there are other forms of innate knowledge: Edward O. Wilson speculates that fear of snakes may be genetically rather than culturally transmitted. This assertion is impossible to prove or disprove based on Wilson's evidence. Edward O. Wilson, *On Human Nature* (Cambridge, Mass.: Harvard University Press, 1978), chap. 1.

31. For an overview of this research, see Michael S. Gazzaniga, *The Social Brain: Discovering the Networks of the Mind* (New York: Basic Books, 1985), and "The Split Brain Revisited," *Scientific American* 279 (1998): 50–55.

32. Tooby and Cosmides, "Cognitive Adaptations," pp. 181–185.

33. Plato, *Republic* 359d.

34. Robert Frank, *Passions Within Reason* (New York: Norton, 1988) pp. 18–19.

35. Pugh, *Biological Origin,* p. 131.

36. Antonio R. Damasio, *Descartes' Error: Emotion, Reason, and the Human Brain* (New York: G. P. Putnam, 1994); and Antonio R. Damasio, H. Damasio, and Y. Christen, eds., *Neurobiology of Decision-Making* (New York: Springer, 1996).

37. Damasio, *Descartes' Error,* pp. 34–51; R. Adophs, D. Tranel, A. Bechara, H. Damasio, and Damasio, "Neuropsychological Approaches to Reasoning and Decision-making," in Damasio, Damasio, and Christen, *Neurobiology,* pp. 157–179.

38. P. S. Churchland, "Feeling Reasons," in Damasio, Damasio, and Christen, *Neurobiology,* p. 199.

39. Robert Axelrod, "An Evolutionary Approach to Norms," *American Political Science Review* 80 (1986): 1096–1111; also see his *The Complexity of Cooperation: Agent-Based Models of Competition and Collaboration* (Princeton, N.J.: Princeton University Press, 1997).

40. Robert Trivers, "The Evolution of Reciprocal Altruism," *Quarterly Review of Biology* 46 (1971): 35–56,

41. Frank, *Passions,* pp. 4–5.

Chapter Eleven. Self-Organization

1. Robert C. Ellickson, *Order Without Law: How Neighbors Settle Disputes* (Cambridge, Mass.: Harvard University Press, 1991), pp. 138–140.

2. For a commentary on Michael Rothschild's Bionomics Institute, see Paul Krugman, "The Power of Biobabble: Pseudo-Economics Meets Pseudo-Evolution," *Slate,* October 23, 1997.

3. Armen A. Alchian, "Uncertainty, Evolution, and Economic Theory," *Journal of Political Economy* 58 (1950): 211–221; Arthur de Vany, "Information, Chance, and Evolution: Alchian and the Economics of Self-Organization," *Economic Inquiry* 34 (1996): 427–443. See also Jack Hirshleifer, "Natural Economy versus Political Economy," *Journal of Social Biology* 1 (1978): 320–321.

4. For an overview, see Karl-Dieter Opp, "Emergence and Effects of Social Norms—Confrontation of Some Hypotheses of Sociology and Economics," *Kyklos 32* (1979): 775–801.

5. Garrett Hardin, "The Tragedy of the Commons," *Science* 162 (1968): 1243–1248.

6. See, for example, Russell Hardin, *Collective Action* (Baltimore: Johns Hopkins University Press, 1982).

7. For a critique of Garrett Hardin, see Carl Dahlman, "The Tragedy of the Commons that Wasn't: On Technical Solutions to the Institutions Game," *Population and Environment* 12 (1991): 285–295.

8. Mancur Olson, *The Logic of Collective Action: Public Goods and the Theory of Groups* (Cambridge, Mass.: Harvard University Press, 1965).

9. H. Demsetz, "Toward a Theory of Property Rights," *American Economic Review* 57 (1967): 347–359.

10. Douglass C. North and Robert P. Thomas, "An Economic Theory of the Growth of the Western World," *Economic History Review*, 2d ser. 28 (1970): 1–17; and Douglass C. North and Robert P. Thomas, *The Growth of the Western World* (London: Cambridge University Press, 1973).

11. Strictly speaking, Coase himself did not postulate a "Coase theorem." Ronald H. Coase, "The Problem of Social Cost," *Journal of Law and Economics* 3 (1960): 1–44. This is the single most commonly cited article in the legal literature today.

12. Andrew Sugden, "Spontaneous Order," *Journal of Economic Perspectives* 3 (1989): 85–97, and *The Economics of Rights, Cooperation and Welfare* (Oxford: Basil Blackwell, 1986).

13. Ellickson, *Order Without Law,* p. 192.

14. Ibid., pp. 143ff.

15. Elinor Ostrom, *Governing the Commons: The Evolution of Institutions for Collective Action* (Cambridge: Cambridge University Press, 1990).

16. Ibid., pp. 103–142.

Chapter Twelve. Technology, Networks, and Social Capital

1. Ludwig von Mises, *Socialism: An Economic and Sociological Analysis* (Indianapolis: Liberty Classics, 1981); Friedrich A. Hayek, "The Use of Knowledge in Society," *American Economic Review* 35 (1945): 519–530.

2. For a longer discussion of the problems of hierarchical management, see Gary J. Miller, *Managerial Dilemmas: The Political Economy of Hierarchy* (New York: Cambridge University Press, 1992).

3. Jeremy R. Azrael, *Managerial Power and Soviet Policy* (Cambridge, Mass.: Harvard University Press, 1966).

4. See Alfred D. Chandler, *The Visible Hand: The Managerial Revolution in American Business* (Cambridge, Mass.: Harvard University Press, 1977), and *Scale and Scope: The Dynamics of Industrial Capitalism* (Cambridge, Mass.: Harvard University Press/Belknap, 1990).

5. Ronald H. Coase, "The Nature of the Firm," *Economica* 6 (1937): 386–405; also see

the works of Oliver Williamson, including *The Nature of the Firm: Origins, Evolution and Development* (Oxford: Oxford University Press, 1993).

6. The Coase theory of the firm has not been universally accepted. Alchian and Demsetz have argued that firms can be adequately understood as market relationships. Armen Alchian and H. Demsetz, "Production, Information Costs, and Economic Organization," *American Economic Review* 62 (1972): 777–795.

7. See, for example, Gernot Grabher, *The Embedded Firm: On the Socioeconomics of Industrial Networks* (London: Routledge, 1993); Nitin Nohria and Robert Eccles, eds., *Networks and Organizations: Structure, Form, and Action* (Boston: Harvard Business School Press, 1992); Walter W. Powell, "Neither Market Nor Hierarchy: Network Forms of Organization," *Research in Organizational Behavior* 12 (1990): 295–336; John L. Casti et al., *Networks in Action: Communications, Economies and Human Knowledge* (Berlin: Springer-Verlag, 1995); Michael Best, *The New Competition: Institutions of Industrial Restructuring* (Cambridge, Mass.: Harvard University Press, 1990).

8. Thomas W. Malone and Joanne Yates, "Electronic Markets and Electronic Hierarchies," *Communications of the ACM* 30 (1987): 484–497.

9. See, for example, Nitin Nohria, "Is a Network Perspective a Useful Way of Studying Organizations?" in Nohria and Robert Eccles, *Networks and Organizations* (Boston: Harvard Business School Press, 1992).

10. Thomas Malone et al., "Electronic Markets"; see also Malone, "The Interdisciplinary Study of Coordination," *ACM Computing Surveys* 26 (1994): 87–199.

11. Mark S. Granovetter, "The Strength of Weak Ties," *American Journal of Sociology* 78 (1973): 1360–1380.

12. Max Weber, *Economy and Society* (Berkeley: University of California Press, 1978).

13. See Kenneth J. Arrow, "Classificatory Notes on the Production and Transmission of Technological Knowledge," *American Economic Review* 59 (1969): 29–33.

14. This point is made in Masahiko Aoki, "Toward an Economic Model of the Japanese Firm," *Journal of Economic Literature* 28 (March 1990): 1–27.

15. See, for example, Kenneth J. Arrow, "Classifactory Notes on the Production and Transmission of Technological Knowledge," *American Economic Review* 59 (1969): 29–33.

16. Harry Katz, *Shifting Gears: Changing Labor Relations in the United States Automobile Industry* (Cambridge, Mass.: MIT Press, 1985).

17. Allan Nevins, with Frank E. Hill, *Ford: The Times, the Man, the Company* (New York: Scribner's, 1954); p. 517.

18. See James P. Womack et al., *The Machine That Changed the World: The Story of Lean Production* (New York: Harper Perennial, 1991).

19. Annalee Saxenian, *Regional Advantage: Culture and Competition in Silicon Valley and Route 128* (Cambridge, Mass.: Harvard University Press, 1994).

20. In this respect, I wrongly overemphasized the importance of firm size in *Trust*. Large firm size can reflect social capital insofar as it involves the willingness of individuals to trust people outside their immediate families; it can also reflect an absence of social capital, since it is possible to organize large firms on low-trust, Taylorite lines. Firm size is much less important than the existence of social norms linking individuals. These norms can exist within the boundaries of a single organization; they can also transcend individual organizations.

21. Don E. Kash and Robert W. Ryecroft, *The Complexity Challenge: Technological Innovation for the 21st Century* (London: Pinter, 1999).

22. Saxenian, *Regional Advantage,* pp. 32–33.

23. Ibid., p. 33.

24. See, for example, Bernardo A. Huberman and Tad Hogg, "Communities of Practice: Performance and Evolution," *Computational and Mathematical Organization Theory* 1 (1995): 73–92; John Seely Brown and Paul Duguid, "Organizational Learning and Communities-of-Practice: Toward a Unified View of Working, Learning, and Innovation," *Organization Science* 2 (February 1991): 40–57.

25. Masahiko Aoki, paper presented to the Samsung Economic Research Institute, June 1996.

26. Michael E. Porter, "Clusters and the New Economics of Competition," *Harvard Business Review* (November–December 1998): 77–90; also Porter, *On Competition* (Boston: Harvard Business Review Books, 1998), pp. 197–287.

Chapter Thirteen. The Limits of Spontaneity and the Inevitability of Hierarchy

1. Elinor Ostrom, *Governing the Commons* (Cambridge: Cambridge University Press, 1990) p. 90.

2. Robert J. Sampson et al., "Neighborhoods and Violent Crime," *Science* 277 (1997).

3. "Spring Breakers Drink in Cancun's Excess," *Washington Post,* April 3, 1998, p. A1.

4. Francis Fukuyama, *Trust: The Social Virtues and the Creation of Prosperity* (New York: Free Press, 1995), p. 28.

5. This was the formulation of "amoral familism" given by Edward Banfield, *The Moral Basis of a Backward Society* (Glencoe, Ill.: Free Press, 1958).

6. Max Weber, *The Religion of China* (New York: Free Press, 1951), p. 237.

7. See, for example, the introduction to James Buchanan, *The Limits of Liberty* (Chicago: University of Chicago Press, 1975).

8. For a sophisticated treatment of this subject, see Leo Strauss, *Natural Right and History* (Chicago: University of Chicago Press, 1953).

9. See Mark J. Roe, "Chaos and Evolution in Law and Economics," *Harvard Law Review* 109 (1996): 641–668.

10. Ibid.

11. W. Brian Arthur, "Increasing Returns and the New World of Business," *Harvard Business Review* 74 (1996): 100–109, "Positive Feedbacks in the Economy," *Scientific American* (1990): 92–99.

12. Friedrich Hayek, *Law, Legislation, and Liberty* (Chicago: University of Chicago Press, 1976), pp. 88–89.

13. Robert L. Simison and Robert L. Rose, "In Backing the UAW, Ford Rankles Many of Its Parts Suppliers," *Wall Street Journal,* February 6, 1997.

14. This experiment is described in Kevin Kelly, *Out of Control* (Reading, Mass,: Addison-Wesley, 1994), pp. 8–11.

15. For a description of the problems at Sears, see Gary Miller, *Managerial Dilemmas* (New York: Cambridge University Press, 1992), pp. 90–94.

16. Ibid., p.99.

17. See Edgar H. Schein, *Organizational Culture and Leadership* (San Francisco: Jossey-Bass, 1988), pp. 228–253.

18. James Q. Wilson, *Bureaucracy: What Government Agencies Do and Why They Do It* (New York: Basic Books, 1989), pp. 96–98.

19. See Robert H. Frank, *Choosing the Right Pond* (Oxford: Oxford University Press, 1985), pp. 21–25.

20. M. Raleigh, M. McGuire, W. Melega, S. Cherry, S.-C. Huang, and M. Phelps, "Neural Mechanisms Supporting Successful Social Decisions in Simians," in Antonio Damasio et al., *Neurobiology of Decision-Making* (New York: Springer, 1996), pp. 68–71.

21. There is a long tradition in Western political philosophy that emphasizes the importance of pride in political life. Plato understood the underlying psychological phenomenon as *thymos,* or spiritedness, which he regarded as a separate part of the soul from the reasoning and desiring parts. For Hegel, the struggle for recognition is the chief motor of human history. For a fuller account, see Francis Fukuyama, *The End of History and the Last Man* (New York: Free Press, 1992), pp. 143–161.

22. Adam Smith, *The Theory of Moral Sentiments* (Indianapolis: Liberty Classics, 1982), pp. 50–51.

23. Frank, *Choosing the Right Pond,* pp. 96–99.

24. Ibid., pp. 26–30.

Chapter Fourteen. Beyond Cave 76

1. This point is made in James Q. Wilson, *The Moral Sense* (New York: Free Press, 1993), pp. 121–122.

2. The only animals that are known to create higher-order hierarchies are dolphins.

3. Roger D. Masters, "The Biological Nature of the State," *World Politics* 35 (1983): 161–193.

4. Samuel P. Huntington, *The Clash of Civilizations and the Remaking of World Order* (New York: Simon & Schuster, 1996).

5. See, for example, Peter L. Berger, "Secularism in Retreat," *National Interest* (1996): 3–12.

6. For a general work on the subject, see David Martin, *A General Theory of Secularization* (New York: Harper & Row, 1978). Martin's views have been revised since then; see his *Tongues of Fire: The Explosion of Protestantism in Latin America* (Oxford: Basil Blackwell, 1990) and "Fundamentalism: An Observational and Definitional Tour d'Horizon," *Political Quarterly* 61 (1990): 129–131.

7. Seymour Martin Lipset, *American Exceptionalism* (New York: Norton, 1995), pp. 60–67.

8. Martin, *Tongues of Fire,* chap. 1.

9. See Francis Fukuyama, *Trust* (New York: Free Press, 1995), especially pp. 61–67.

10. James E. Curtis, Douglas E. Baer, and Edward G. Grabb, "Voluntary Association Membership in Fifteen Countries: A Comparative Analysis," *American Sociological Review* 57 (1992): 139–152.

11. The nonprofit sector represents 6.8 percent of total employment in the United States, compared to 4.2 percent for the next highest country, France; the sector's output as a percentage of GDP is 6.3, compared to the next highest country (the United Kingdom), where the figure is 4.8 percent. Lester Salamon and Helmut Anheier, *The Emerging Sector* (Baltimore: Johns Hopkins Institute for Policy Study, 1994), pp. 32, 35.

   The type of association to which Americans belong is quite different from other countries, however, and shows the continuing impact of religion in American society. The countries with the next highest levels of religious participation, South Korea, the Netherlands, and Canada, are all well below U.S. levels. On the other hand, in the United States, Britain, and Canada, membership rates in unions were much lower in 1981 than in continental Europe or, particularly, Scandinavia, and fell substantially in the following decade; in the Nordic countries, rates actually rose during the same period.

12. Diego Gambetta, *The Sicilian Mafia* (Cambridge, Mass.: Harvard University Press, 1993), pp. 18–22.

Chapter Fifteen. Does Capitalism Deplete Social Capital?

1. Albert O. Hirschman, "Rival Interpretations of Market Society: Civilizing, Destructive, or Feeble," *Journal of Economic Literature* 20 (1982): 1463–1484.

2. John Gray, *Enlightenment's Wake: Politics and Culture at the Close of the Modern Age* (London: Routledge, 1995).

3. Quoted in Hirschman, "Rival Interpretations," p. 1466.

4. Joseph A. Schumpeter, *Capitalism, Socialism and Democracy* (New York: Harper Brothers, 1950).

5. Daniel Bell, *The Cultural Contradictions of Capitalism* (New York: Basic Books, 1976); see also John K. Galbraith, *The Affluent Society* (Boston: Houghton Mifflin, 1958).

6. Michael J. Sandel, *Democracy's Discontent: America in Search of a Public Philosophy* (Cambridge, Mass.: Harvard University Press, 1996), particularly pp. 338–340; Alan Wolfe, *Whose Keeper? Social Science and Moral Obligation* (Berkeley: University of California Press, 1989), pp. 78–104; William J. Bennett, "Getting Used to Decadence," *Vital Speeches* 60, no. 9 (February 15, 1994), p. 264; see also Larry Reibstein, "The Right Takes a Media Giant to Political Task," *Newsweek* 125 (June 12, 1995), p. 30.

7. For a cultural defense of commercial society, see Tyler Cowen, *In Praise of Commercial Culture* (Cambridge, Mass.: Harvard University Press, 1998).

8. Montesquieu, *The Spirit of the Laws,* Book 20, chap. 1.

9. Quoted in Hirschman, "Rival Interpretations," p. 1465.

10. Adam Smith, *The Theory of Moral Sentiments* (Indianapolis: Liberty Classics, 1982), pt. 1, I.4.7; pt. 7, IV.25; *Lectures on Jurisprudence* (Indianapolis: Liberty Press, 1982), pt. B 326; *An Inquiry into the Nature and Causes of the Wealth of Nations* (Indianapolis: Liberty Classics, 1981), Book 1, VIII.41–48. I am grateful to Charles Griswold for these insights.

11. Charles L. Griswold, Jr., *Adam Smith and the Virtues of Enlightenment* (Cambridge: Cambridge University Press, 1999), pp. 17–21.

12. Albert O. Hirschman, *The Passions and the Interests: Political Arguments for Capitalism Before Its Triumph* (Princeton, N.J.: Princeton University Press, 1977).

13. Smith, *Theory,* pt. VI.

14. Coleman (1988).

15. Partha Dasgupta, "Economic Development and the Idea of Social Capital," unpublished paper, March 1997.

16. See, for example, Edgar Schein, *Organizational Culture and Leadership* (San Francisco: Jossey-Bass, 1988).

17. See, for example, Thomas P. Rohlen, "'Spiritual Education' in a Japanese Bank," *American Anthropologist* 75 (1973): 1542–1562.

18. John J. Miller, *The Unmaking of Americans: How Multiculturalism Has Undermined the Assimilation Ethic* (New York: Free Press, 1998).

19. See, for example, Oliver E. Williamson, "Calculativeness, Trust, and Economic Organization," *Journal of Law and Economics* 36 (1993): 453–502, who argues that trust

ends up as an empty category when you subtract out the apparently trustworthy behavior that can be explained on the basis of rational self-interest.

Chapter Sixteen. Reconstruction Past, Present, and Future

1. Ted Robert Gurr, "On the History of Violent Crime in Europe and America," in Egon Bittner and Sheldon L. Messinger, *Criminology Review Yearbook,* vol. 2 (Beverly Hills, Calif.: Sage, 1980).

2. James Collier, *The Rise of Selfishness in America* (New York: Oxford University Press, 1991), p. 5.

3. Ibid., p. 5.

4. James Q. Wilson, *Thinking About Crime* (New York: Basic Books, 1975), p. 232.

5. William J. Rorabaugh, *The Alcoholic Republic* (New York: Oxford University Press, 1979), pp. 14–15.

6. Collier, *Rise of Selfishness,* p. 6.

7. Ted Robert Gurr, "Contemporary Crime in Historical Perspective," *Annals of the American Academy of Political and Social Science* 434 (1977): 114–136.

8. Ted Robert Gurr, Peter N. Grabosky, and Richard C. Hula, *The Politics of Crime and Conflict: A Comparative History of Four Cities* (Beverly Hills, Calif.: Sage, 1977).

9. Collier, *Rise of Selfishness,* pp. 6–7.

10. Paul E. Johnson, *A Shopkeeper's Millennium: Society and Revivals in Rochester, New York, 1815–1837* (New York: Hill and Wang, 1979).

11. Richard Hofstadter, *Anti-Intellectualism in American Life* (New York: Vintage Books, 1963), p. 89.

12. Wilson, *Thinking About Crime,* p. 233.

13. Gregory H. Singleton, "Protestant Voluntary Organizations and the Shaping of Victorian America," in Daniel W. Howe, ed., *Victorian America* (Philadelphia: University of Pennsylvania Press, 1976), p. 50.

14. Ibid., p. 52.

15. See also Gurr, Grabosky, and Hula, *Politics,* pp. 109–129.

16. Gurr in Bittner and Messinger, eds. (1980), p. 417.

17. Wilson, *Thinking About Crime,* p. 225.

18. Gertrude Himmelfarb, *The De-Moralization of Society: From Victorian Virtues to Modern Values* (New York: Knopf, 1995), pp. 222–223.

19. Wesley Skogan, *Disorder and Decline* (New York: Free Press, 1990).

20. James Davison Hunter, *Culture Wars: The Struggle to Define America* (New York: Basic Books, 1991).

21. Barbara Dafoe Whitehead, "Dan Quayle Was Right," *Atlantic Monthly* 271(1993): 47–84.

22. Stephen Goldsmith, *The Twenty-First Century City: Resurrecting Urban America* (Lanham, Md.: Regnery Publishing, 1997).

23. One of the most important criticisms of the 1996 welfare reform act is that it encourages single mothers on welfare to work while their children are small. What is needed, but elusive, is a public policy to bring back the missing fathers of those children so as to increase their base of support.

24. This is a much-shortened version of an argument I made in *The End of History and the Last Man* (New York: Free Press, 1992).

BIBLIOGRAPHY

Aaron, Henry J., et al., eds., *Values and Public Policy.* Washington, D.C.: Brookings Institution, 1994.

Akerlof, George A., et al. "An Analysis of Out-of-Wedlock Childbearing in the United States." *Quarterly Journal of Economics* 111 (1996): 277–317.

Alchian, Armen A. "Uncertainty, Evolution, and Economic Theory." *Journal of Political Economy* 58 (1950): 211–221.

Alchian, Armen A., and H. Demsetz, "Production, Information Costs, and Economic Organization," *American Economic Review* 62 (1972): 777–795.

Alexander, Richard D. *How Did Humans Evolve? Reflections on the Uniquely Unique Species.* Ann Arbor: Museum of Zoology, University of Michigan, 1990.

Aoki, Masahiko. "Toward an Economic Model of the Japanese Firm." *Journal of Economic Literature* 28 (March 1990): 1–27.

Archer, Dane, and Gartner, Rosemary. *Violence and Crime in Cross-National Perspective.* New Haven, Conn.: Yale University Press, 1984.

———. "Violent Acts and Violent Times: A Comparative Approach to Postwar Homicide Rates." *American Sociological Review* 41 (1976): 937–963.

Arrow, Kenneth J. "Classificatory Notes on the Production of Transmission of Technological Knowledge." *American Economic Review* 59 (1969): 29–33.

———. "Methodological Individualism and Social Knowledge," *AEA Papers and Proceedings* 84 (1994): 1–9.

Arthur, W. Brian. "Increasing Returns and the New World of Business." *Harvard Business Review* 74 (1996): 100–109.

———. "Positive Feedbacks in the Economy." *Scientific American* (1990): 92–99.

Australian Bureau of Statistics. *Births. Catalog No. 3301.0.* Canberra: Australian Government Publishing Service, 1995.

———. *Marriages and Divorces. Catalog No. 3301.0.* Canberra: Australian Government Publishing Service, 1995.

Austrian Central Statistical Office. *Republik Osterreich 1945–1995.*

Axelrod, Robert. "An Evolutionary Approach to Norms." *American Political Science Review* 80 (1986): 1096–111.

———. *The Complexity of Cooperation: Agent-Based Models of Competition and Collaboration.* Princeton, N.J.: Princeton University Press, 1997.

———. *The Evolution of Cooperation.* New York: Basic Books, 1984.

Axelrod, Robert, and Hamilton, W. D. "The Evolution of Cooperation." *Science* 211 (1981): 1390–1396.

Azrael, Jeremy R. *Managerial Power and Soviet Policy.* Cambridge: Harvard University Press, 1966.

Banfield, Edward C. *The Moral Basis of a Backward Society.* Glencoe, Ill.: Free Press, 1958.

Barkow, J. H., Cosmides, Leda, and Tooby, John, eds. *The Adapted Mind.* New York: Oxford University Press, 1992.

Bateson, P. P. G., and Hinde, R. A., eds. *Growing Points in Ethology.* Cambridge: Cambridge University Press, 1976.

Becker, Gary S. *A Treatise on the Family.* Enl. ed. Cambridge: Harvard University Press, 1991.

———. "Altruism, Egoism, and Genetic Fitness: Economics and Sociobiology." *Journal of Economic Literature* 14 (1976): 817–826.

———. "Crime and Punishment: An Economic Approach." *Journal of Political Economy* 76 (1968): 169–217.

Becker, Gary S., et al. "An Economic Analysis of Marital Instability." *Journal of Political Economy* 85 (1977): 1141–87.

Becker, Howard S. *Outsiders: Studies in the Sociology of Deviance.* Glencoe, Ill.: Free Press, 1963.

Beirne, Piers. "Cultural Relativism and Comparative Criminology." *Contemporary Crises* 7 (1983): 371–391.

Bell, Daniel. *The Coming of Post-Industrial Society: A Venture in Social Forecasting.* New York: Basic Books, 1973.

———. *The Cultural Contradictions of Capitalism.* New York: Basic Books, 1976.

Bennett, William J. "America at Midnight: Reflections on the Moynihan Report." *American Enterprise* 29.

———. "Getting Used to Decadence." *Vital Speeches* 60, no. 9 (February 15, 1994), p. 264.

Berger, Peter L., "Secularism in Retreat." *National Interest* (1996): 3–12.

Bernhardt, Annette, et al. "Women's Gains or Men's Losses? A Closer Look at the Shrinking Gender Gap in Earnings." *American Journal of Sociology* 101 (1995): 302–328.

Best, Michael. *The New Competition: Institutions of Industrial Restructuring.* Cambridge: Harvard University Press, 1990.

Bianchi, Suzanne M. "Introduction to the Special Issue, 'Men in Families.'" *Demography* 35 (1998): 133.

Bittner, E., and Messinger, S. L. *Criminology Review Yearbook.* Vol. 2. Beverly Hills: Sage, 1980.

Blank, Rebecca M. "Policy Watch: The 1996 Welfare Reform." *Journal of Economic Perspectives* 11 (1997): 169–177.

Blankenhorn, David. *Fatherless America: Confronting America's Most Urgent Social Problem.* New York: Basic Books, 1995.

Blau, Judith R., and Blau, Peter M. "The Cost of Inequality: Metropolitan Structure and Violent Crime." *American Sociological Review* 47 (1982): 114–129.

Bok, Derek. *The State of the Nation: Government and the Quest for a Better Society.* Cambridge: Harvard University Press, 1997.

Booth, Alan, and Dunn, Judy. *Stepfamilies: Who Benefits? Who Does Not?* Hillsdale, N.J.: Erlbaum, 1994.

Bound, John, and Freeman, Richard B. "What Went Wrong? The Erosion of Relative Earnings and Employment Among Young Black Men in the 1980s." *Quarterly Journal of Economics* (1992): 201–232.

Bowman, Karlyn, and Ladd, Everett. *What's Wrong: A Study of American Satisfaction and Complaint.* Washington: AEI Press and the Roper Center for Public Opinion Research, 1998.

Braithwaite, John. *Crime, Shame, and Reintegration.* Cambridge: Cambridge University Press, 1989.

Brown, John Seely, and Daguid, Paul. "Organizational Learning and Communities-of-Practice: Toward a Unified View of Working, Learning, and Innovation." *Organization Science* 2 (1991): 40–57.

Bryner, Gary. *Politics and Public Morality: The Great American Welfare Reform Debate.* New York: W. W. Norton, 1998.

Buchanan, James M. *The Limits of Liberty: Between Anarchy and Leviathan.* Chicago: University of Chicago Press, 1975.

Buchholz, Erich. "Reasons for the Low Rate of Crime in the German Democratic Republic." *Crime and Social Justice* 29 (1986): 26–42.

Bumpass, Larry L., and Sweet, James A. "National Estimates of Cohabitation." *Demography* 26 (1989): 615–625.

Burgess, Ernest W., Park, Robert E., and McKenzie, Roderick D., eds. *The City* (Chicago: University of Chicago Press, 1925).

Burns, Ailsa, and Scott, Cath. *Mother-Headed Families and Why They Have Increased.* Hillsdale, N.J.: Erlbaum, 1994.

Caldwell, B., and Ricciuti, H. H. *Review of Child Development Research.* Vol. 3, Chicago: University of Chicago Press, 1973.

Campbell, Bernard, ed. *Sexual Selection and the Descent of Man.* Chicago: Aldine, 1972.

Castells, Manuel. *The Rise of the Network Society.* Malden, Mass.: Blackwell, 1996.

Casti, John L., et al. *Networks in Action: Communications, Economies and Human Knowledge.* Berlin: Springer-Verlag, 1995.

Central Statistical Office and Ireland. *Statistical Abstract,* various annual editions (Cork).

Chandler, Alfred D. *Scale and Scope: The Dynamics of Industrial Capitalism.* Cambridge: Harvard University Press/Belknap, 1990.

———. *The Visible Hand: The Managerial Revolution in American Business.* Cambridge: Harvard University Press, 1977.

Cherlin, Andrew J. *Marriage, Divorce, Remarriage,* 2nd ed. (Cambridge, Mass.: Harvard University Press, 1992).

Cherlin, Andrew J., and Furstenberg, Frank F., Jr. "Stepfamilies in the United States: A Reconsideration." *Annual Review of Sociology* 20 (1994): 359–381.

Children's Defense Fund. *The State of America's Children Yearbook 1997.* Washington, D.C.: Children's Defense Fund, 1998.

Clark, John. "Shifting Engagements: Lessons from the 'Bowling Alone' Debate." *Hudson Briefing Paper.* No. 196, October 1996.

Cloward, Richard, and Ohlin, Lloyd. *Delinquency and Opportunity.* New York: Free Press, 1960.

Coase, Ronald H. "The Nature of the Firm." *Economica* 6 (1937): 386–405.

———. "The Problem of Social Cost." *Journal of Law and Economics* 3 (1960): 1–44.

Coleman, James S. *Foundations of Social Theory.* Cambridge: Harvard University Press, 1990.
———. "Social Capital in the Creation of Human Capital." *American Journal of Sociology Supplement* 94 (1988): S95–S120.

———. "The Creation and Destruction of Social Capital: Implications for the Law." *Journal of Law, Ethics, and Public Policy* 3 (1988): 375–404.

Coleman, James S., et al. *Equality of Educational Opportunity.* Washington, D.C.: U.S. Department of Health, Education and Welfare, 1966.

Collier, James L. *The Rise of Selfishness in America.* New York: Oxford University Press, 1991.

Cordella, Peter, and Siegel, Larry. *Readings in Contemporary Criminological Theory.* Boston: Northeastern University Press, 1996.

Cowen, Tyler. *In Praise of Commercial Culture.* Cambridge: Harvard University Press, 1998.

Cready, Cynthia, et al. "Mate Availability and African American Family Structure in the US Nonmetropolitan South, 1960–1990." *Journal of Marriage and the Family* 59 (1997): 192–203.

Curtis, James E., et al. "Voluntary Association Membership in Fifteen Countries: A Comparative Analysis." *American Sociological Review* 57 (1992): 139–152.

Dahlman, Carl. "The Tragedy of the Commons That Wasn't: On Technical Solutions to the Institutions Game." *Population and Environment* 12 (1991): 285–295.

Dahrendorf, Ralf. *Life Chances: Approaches to Social and Political Theory.* Chicago: University of Chicago, 1979.

Daly, Martin. "Child Abuse and Other Risks of Not Living with Both Parents." *Ethology and Sociobiology* 6 (1985): 197–210.

Daly, Martin, and Wilson, Margot. "Children Fathered by Previous Partners: A Risk Factor for Violence Against Women." *Canadian Journal of Public Health* 84 (1993): 209–210.

———. *Homicide.* New York: Aldine de Gruyter, 1988.

Daly, Martin, et al. "Male Sexual Jealousy." *Ethology and Sociobiology* 3 (1982): 11–27.

Damasio, Antonio R. *Descartes' Error: Emotion, Reason, and the Human Brain.* New York: G. P. Putnam, 1994.

Damasio, Antonio R., et al. *Neurobiology of Decision-Making.* New York: Springer, 1996.

Darwin, Charles. *The Expression of Emotion in Man and Animals.* New York: Appleton and Co., 1916.

Dasgupta, Partha. "Economic Development and the Idea of Social Capital." Unpublished paper. 1997.

Davis, Kingsley, and Van den Oever, Pietronella. "Demographic Foundations of New Sex Roles." *Population and Development Review* 8 (1982): 495–511.

Dawkins, Richard. *The Blind Watchmaker.* New York: W. W. Norton, 1986.

———. *The Selfish Gene.* New York: Oxford University Press, 1989.

de Boysson-Bardies, B., ed. *Developmental Neurocognition: Speech and Face Processing in the First Year of Life.* Netherlands: Kluwer, 1993.

de Vany, Arthur. "Information, Chance, and Evolution: Alchian and the Economics of Self-Organization." *Economic Inquiry* 34 (1996): 427–443.

de Waal, Frans. *Chimpanzee Politics: Power and Sex Among Apes.* Baltimore: Johns Hopkins University Press, 1989.

Deane, Glenn D. "Cross-National Comparison of Homicide: Age/Sex-Adjusted Rates Using the 1980s US Homicide Experience as a Standard." *Journal of Quantitative Criminology* 3 (1987): 215–227.

Degler, Carl N. *In Search of Human Nature: The Decline and Revival of Darwinism in American Social Thought*. New York: Oxford University Press, 1991.

Demsetz, H. "Toward a Theory of Property Rights." *American Economic Review* 57 (1967): 347–359.

Denzau, Arthur, and North, Douglass C. "Shared Mental Models: Ideologies and Institutions." *Kyklos* 47 (1994): 3–31.

Diamond, Larry. "Toward Democratic Consolidation." *Journal of Democracy* 5 (1994): 4–17.

Dunbar, Robin I. M. *Grooming, Gossip, and the Origin of Language*. Cambridge, Mass.: Harvard University Press, 1996.

Duncan, Greg J., and Hoffman, Saul D. "A Reconsideration of the Economic Consequences of Marital Disruption." *Demography* 22 (1985): 485–498.

———. "Welfare Benefits, Economic Opportunities, and Out-of-Wedlock Births Among Black Teenage Girls." *Demography* 27 (1990): 519–535.

Durkheim, Emile. *The Rules of Sociological Method*. Glencoe, Ill: Free Press, 1938.

Eberstadt, Nicholas. "Asia Tomorrow: Gray and Male." *National Interest*, No. 53 (Fall 1998): 56–65.

———. "World Population Implosion?" *Public Interest*, No. 129 (1997): 3–22.

Ellickson, Robert C. *Order Without Law: How Neighbors Settle Disputes*. Cambridge: Harvard University Press, 1991.

Eurostat. *Demographic Statistics*. New York: Haver Analytics/Eurostat Data Shop, 1997.

Farley, Reynolds. *State of the Union: America in the 1990s*. Vol. 2: *Social Trends*. New York: Russell Sage Foundation, 1995.

Federal Bureau of Investigation and Uniform Crime Reporting Program. *Crime in the United States*. Washington, D.C.

Flora, Peter, and Heidenheimer, Arnold J. *The Development of the Welfare State in Europe and America*. New Brunswick, N.J.: Transaction, 1987.

Fourastié, Jean. "De la vie traditionelle à la vie tertiaire." *Population* 14 (1963): 417–432.

Fox, Robin. *Reproduction and Succession: Studies in Anthropology, Law, and Society*. New Brunswick, N.J.: Transaction, 1997.

———. "Sibling Incest." *British Journal of Sociology* 13 (1962): 128–150.

———. *The Red Lamp of Incest*, rev. ed. South Bend, Ind: University of Notre Dame Press, 1983.

———. *The Search for Society: Quest for a Biosocial Science and Morality*. New Brunswick, N.J.: Rutgers University Press, 1989.

Frank, Robert H. *Choosing the Right Pond: Human Behavior and the Quest for Status*. Oxford: Oxford University Press, 1985.

———. *Passions Within Reason: The Strategic Role of the Emotions*. New York: Norton, 1988.

Fukuyama, Francis. "Asian Values and the Asian Crisis." *Commentary* 105 (1998): 23–27.

———. "Capitalism and Democracy: The Missing Link." *Journal of Democracy* 3 (1992): 100–110.

———. "Falling Tide: Global Trends and US Civil Society." *Harvard International Review* 20 (1997): 60–64.

———. "Is It All in the Genes?" *Commentary* (1997): 30–35.

———. *The End of History and the Last Man*. New York: Free Press, 1992.

———. *Trust: The Social Virtues and the Creation of Prosperity*. New York: Free Press, 1995.

Galbraith, John K. *The Affluent Society*. Boston: Houghton Mifflin, 1958.

Galston, William A. "Beyond the *Murphy Brown* Debate: Ideas for Family Policy." Speech to the Institute for American Values, Family Policy Symposium. New York, 1993.

Gambetta, Diego. *The Sicilian Mafia: The Business of Private Protection.* Cambridge: Harvard University Press, 1993.

———. *Trust: Making and Breaking Cooperative Relations.* Oxford: Blackwell, 1988.

Gartner, Rosemary. "Family Stucture, Welfare Spending, and Child Homicide in Developed Democracies." *Journal of Marriage and the Family* 53 (1991): 231–240.

———. "The Victims of Homicide: A Temporal and Cross-National Comparison." *American Sociological Review* 55 (1990): 92–106.

Gartner, Rosemary, and Parker, Robert N. "Cross-National Evidence on Homicide and the Age Structure of the Population." *Social Forces* 69 (1990): 351–371.

Gazzaniga, Michael S. *Nature's Mind: The Biological Roots of Thinking, Emotions, Sexuality, Language, and Intelligence.* New York: Basic Books, 1992.

———. *The Social Brain: Discovering the Networks of the Mind.* New York: Basic Books, 1985.

———. "The Split Brain Revisited." *Scientific American* 279 (1998): 50–55.

Geertz, Clifford. *The Interpretation of Cultures.* New York: Basic Books, 1973.

Gelb, Joyce, and Palley, Marian Lief. *Women of Japan and Korea.* Philadelphia: Temple University Press, 1994.

Gellner, Ernest. *Conditions of Liberty: Civil Society and Its Rivals.* London: Hamish Hamilton, 1994.

Glendon, Mary Ann. *Rights Talk: The Impoverishment of Political Discourse.* New York: Free Press, 1991.

Glueck, Eleanor, and Glueck, Sheldon. *Unraveling Juvenile Delinquency.* New York: Commonwealth Fund, 1950.

Goldin, Claudia. "The Historical Evolution of Female Earnings Functions and Occupations." *Explorations in Economic History* 21 (1984): 1–27.

———. *Understanding the Gender Gap: An Economic History of American Women.* New York: Oxford University Press, 1990.

Goldsmith, Stephen. *The Twenty-first Century City: Resurrecting Urban America.* Lanham, Md.: Regnery Publishing, 1997.

Goode, William J. *World Changes in Divorce Patterns.* New Haven, Conn.: Yale University Press, 1993.

Government of Japan and Ministry of Justice. *Summary of the White Paper on Crime* (Tokyo, annual).

Grabher, Gernot. *The Embedded Firm: On the Socioeconomics of Industrial Networks.* London: Routledge, 1993.

Granovetter, Mark S. "The Strength of Weak Ties." *American Journal of Sociology* 78 (1973): 1360–1380.

Gray, John. *Enlightenment's Wake: Politics and Culture at the Close of the Modern Age.* London: Routledge, 1995.

Griswold, Charles L., Jr. *Adam Smith and the Virtues of Enlightenment.* Cambridge: Cambridge University Press, 1999.

Gurr, Ted Robert. "Contemporary Crime in Historical Perspective: A Comparative Study of London, Stockholm, and Sydney." *Annals of the American Academy of Political and Social Science* 434 (1977): 114–136.

Gurr, Ted Robert, et al. *The Politics of Crime and Conflict: A Comparative History of Four Cities.* Beverly Hills, Calif.: Sage, 1977.

Gutman, Herbert G. *The Black Family in Slavery and Freedom, 1750–1925*. New York: Vintage Books, 1977.

Hamilton, William D. "The Genetic Evolution of Social Behavior." *Journal of Theoretical Biology* 7 (1964): 7–52.

Hanifan, Lyda Judson. "The Rural School and Community Center." *Annals of the American Academy of Political and Social Science* 67 (1916): 130–138.

Hansmann, Henry B., and Quigley, John M. "Population Heterogeneity and the Sociogenesis of Homicide." *Social Forces* 61 (1982): 206–224.

Hardin, Garrett. "The Tragedy of the Commons." *Science* 162 (1968): 1243–1248.

Hardin, Russell. *Collective Action*. Baltimore: Johns Hopkins University Press, 1982.

Harrell, Stevan. *Human Families*. Boulder, Colo.: Westview, 1997.

Harrison, Lawrence E. *Underdevelopment Is a State of Mind: The Latin American Case*. New York: Madison Books, 1985.

Hayek, Friedrich A. *Fatal Conceit: The Errors of Socialism*. Chicago: University of Chicago Press, 1988.

———. *Law, Legislation and Liberty*. Chicago: University of Chicago Press, 1976.

———. "The Use of Knowledge in Society." *American Economic Review* 35 (1945): 519–530.

Heiner, Ronald A. "Origin of Predictable Behavior: Further Modeling and Applications." *American Economic Review* 75 (1985): 391–396.

———. "The Origin of Predictable Behavior." *American Economic Review* 73 (1983): 560–595.

Himmelfarb, Gertrude. *The De-Moralization of Society: From Victorian Virtues to Modern Values*. New York: Knopf, 1995.

Hirschi, Travis, and Gottfredson, Michael. *A General Theory of Crime*. Stanford, Calif.: Stanford University Press, 1990.

Hirschman, Albert O. "Rival Interpretations of Market Society: Civilizing, Destructive, or Feeble." *Journal of Economic Literature* 20 (1982): 1463–1484.

———. *The Passions and the Interests: Political Arguments for Capitalism Before Its Triumph*. Princeton, N.J.: Princeton University Press, 1977.

Hirshleifer, Jack. "Economics from a Biological Viewpoint." *Journal of Law and Economics* 20 (1977): 1–52.

———. "Natural Economy Versus Political Economy." *Journal of Social Biology* 1 (1978): 319–337.

Hodgson, Geoffrey M. "Institutional Economics: Surveying the 'Old' and the 'New.'" *Metroeconomica* 44 (1993): 1–28.

———, ed. *The Economics of Institutions*. Aldershot: Edward Elgar Publishing Co., 1993.

Hofstadter, Richard. *Anti-Intellectualism in American Life*. New York: Vintage Books, 1963.

Holland, John H. *Hidden Order: How Adaptation Builds Complexity*. Reading, Mass.: Addison-Wesley, 1995.

Homans, George C. *The Human Group*. New York: Harcourt, Brace, 1950.

Home Office. *Criminal Statistics: England and Wales*. London: Her Majesty's Stationery Office, various years.

Howe, D. W., ed. *Victorian America*. Philadelphia: University of Pennsylvania Press, 1976.

Huang, W. S. Wilson. "Are International Murder Data Valid and Reliable? Some Evidence to Support the Use of Interpol Data." *International Journal of Comparative and Applied Criminal Justice* 17 (1993): 77–89.

———. "Assessing Indicators of Crime Among International Crime Data Series." *Criminal Justice Policy Review* 3 (1989): 28–48.

335

Huberman, Bernardo A., and Hogg, T. "Communities of Practice: Performance and Evolution." *Computational and Methodological Organizational Theory* 1 (1995): 73–92.

Hunter, James Davison. *Culture Wars: The Struggle to Define America.* New York: Basic Books, 1991.

Huntington, Samuel P. *The Clash of Civilizations and the Remaking of World Order.* New York: Simon and Schuster, 1996.

———. *The Third Wave: Democratization in the Late Twentieth Century.* Oklahoma City: University of Oklahoma Press, 1991.

Inglehart, Ronald. *Modernization and Postmodernization: Cultural, Economic, and Political Change in 43 Societies.* Princeton, N.J.: Princeton University Press, 1997.

Inglehart, Ronald, and Abramson, Paul R. *Value Change in Global Perspective.* Ann Arbor: University of Michigan Press, 1995.

Jacobs, Jane. *The Death and Life of Great American Cities.* New York: Vintage Books, 1992.

Johnson, Paul E. *A Shopkeeper's Millennium: Society and Revivals in Rochester, New York, 1815–1837.* New York: Hill and Wang, 1979.

Johnston, Richard F., et al. *Annual Review of Ecology and Systematics,* vol. 5. Palo Alto, Calif.: Annual Reviews, 1964.

Jones, Elise F. *Teenage Pregnancy in Industrialized Countries.* New Haven, Conn.: Yale University Press, 1986.

Jones, Gavin W. "Modernization and Divorce: Contrasting Trends in Islamic Southeast Asia and the West." *Population and Development Review* 23 (1997): 95–114.

Jones, Owen D. "Evolutionary Analysis in Law: An Introduction and Application to Child Abuse." *North Carolina Law Review* 75 (1997): 1117–1241.

———. "Law and Biology: Toward an Integrated Model of Human Behavior." *Journal of Contemporary Legal Issues* 8 (1997): 167–208.

Judkins, Calvert J. *National Associations of the United States.* Washington, D.C.: U.S. Department of Commerce, 1949.

Kaminski, Marguerite, and Paiz, Judith. "Japanese Women in Management: Where Are They?" *Human Resource Management* 23 (1984): 277–292.

Kash, Don E., and Ryecroft, Robert W. *The Complexity Challenge: Technological Innovation for the 21st Century.* London: Pinter, 1999.

Katz, Harry. *Shifting Gears: Changing Labor Relations in the U.S. Automobile Industry.* Cambridge: MIT Press, 1985.

Katz, Lawrence F., and Murphy, Kevin. "Changes in Relative Wages, 1963–1987: Supply and Demand Factors." *Quarterly Journal of Economics* 107 (February 1992): 35–78.

Katz, Michael. *The Undeserving Poor: From the War on Poverty to the War on Welfare.* New York: Pantheon, 1989.

Keeley, Lawrence H. *War Before Civilization.* New York: Oxford University Press, 1996.

Kelling, George, and Coles, Catherine. *Fixing Broken Windows: Restoring Order and Reducing Crime in Our Communities.* New York: Free Press, 1996.

Kelly, Kevin. *Out of Control: The New Biology of Machines, Social Systems, and the Economic World.* Reading, Mass.: Addison-Wesley, 1994.

Kerjosse, Roselyn, and Tamby, Irene. *The Demographic Situation in 1994: The Movement of the Population.* Paris: National Institute of Statistics and Economic Studies, 1994.

Klein, Daniel B., ed. *Reputation: Studies in the Voluntary Elicitation of Good Conduct.* Ann Arbor: University of Michigan Press, 1996.

Krahn, Harvey, et al. "Income Inequality and Homicide Rates: Cross-National Data and Criminological Theories." *Criminology* 24 (1986): 269–295.

Krugman, Paul R. "The Power of Biobabble: Pseudo-Economics Meets Pseudo-Evolution." *Slate,* October 23, 1997.

Kuper, Adam. *The Chosen Primate: Human Nature and Cultural Diversity.* Cambridge: Harvard University Press, 1993.

Ladd, Everett C. *Silent Revolution: The Reinvention of Civic America.* New York: Free Press, 1999.

———. "The Data Just Don't Show Erosion of America's 'Social Capital.'" *Public Perspective* (1996): 4–22.

———. "The Myth of Moral Decline." *The Responsive Community* 4 (1993–94): 52–68.

Laslett, Peter, and Wall, Richard. *Family Forms in Historic Europe.* Cambridge: Cambridge University Press, 1983.

———. *Household and Family in Past Time.* Cambridge: Cambridge University Press, 1972.

Leavitt, Gregory C. "Relativism and Cross-Cultural Criminology: A Critical Analysis." *Journal of Research in Crime and Delinquency* 27 (1990): 5–29.

Lemann, Nicholas. *The Promised Land: The Great Black Migration and How It Changed America.* New York: Alfred A. Knopf, 1991.

Levi-Strauss, Claude. *The Elementary Structures of Kinship.* Boston: Beacon Press, 1969.

Light, Ivan H. *Ethnic Enterprise in America.* Berkeley: University of California Press, 1972.

Lipset, Seymour Martin. *American Exceptionalism: A Double-Edged Sword.* New York: W. W. Norton, 1995.

Locke, John L. *The De-voicing of Society: Why We Don't Talk to Each Other Anymore.* New York: Simon & Schuster, 1998.

Maine, Henry. *Ancient Law: Its Connection with the Early History of Society and Its Relation to Modern Ideas.* Boston: Beacon Press, 1963.

Malone, Thomas W. "The Interdisciplinary Study of Coordination." *ACM Computing Surveys* 26 (1994): 87–199.

Malone, Thomas W., et al. "Electronic Markets and Electronic Hierarchies." *Communications of the ACM* 30 (1987): 484–497.

Marshall, Inkeke Haen, and Marshall, Chris E. "Toward Refinement of Purpose in Comparative Criminological Research: Research Site Selection in Focus." *International Journal of Comparative and Applied Criminal Justice* 7 (1983): 89–97.

Martin, David. *A General Theory of Secularization.* New York: Harper & Row, 1978.

———. "Fundamentalism: An Observational and Definitional Tour d'Horizon." *Political Quarterly* 61 (1990): 129–131.

———. *Tongues of Fire: The Explosion of Protestantism in Latin America.* Oxford: Basil Blackwell, 1990.

Martin, Robert T., and Conger, Rand D. "A Comparison of Delinquency Trends: Japan and the United States." *Criminology* 18 (1980): 53–61.

Masters, Roger D. "The Biological Nature of the State." *World Politics* 35 (1983): 161–193.

Mayhew, Pat, and White, Philip. *The 1996 International Crime Victimization Survey.* London: Home Office Research and Statistics Directorate, 1997.

McLanahan, Sara S., and Sandefur, Gary D. *Growing Up with a Single Parent: What Hurts, What Helps.* Cambridge: Harvard University Press, 1994.

Mead, Margaret. *Coming of Age in Samoa; A Psychological Study of Primitive Youth for Western Civilisation.* New York: William Morrow, 1928.

———. *Male and Female.* New York: Dell, 1949.

Merton, Robert K. "Social Structure and 'Anomie.'" *American Sociological Review* 33 (1938): 672–682.

Messner, Steven F. "Income Inequality and Murder Rates: Some Cross-National Findings." *Comparative Social Research* 3 (1980): 185–198.

Messner, Steven F., and Rosenfeld, Richard. *Crime and the American Dream,* 2d ed. Belmont, Calif.: Wadsworth Publishing Co., 1997.

Miller, Gary J. *Managerial Dilemmas: The Political Economy of Hierarchy.* New York: Cambridge University Press, 1992.

Miller, John J. *The Unmaking of Americans: How Multiculturalism Has Undermined the Assimilation Ethic.* New York: Free Press, 1998.

Ministry of Families. Senior Citizens. and Women, and Youth. Federal Republic of Germany. *Die Familie im Spiegel der Amtlichen Statistik: Aktual unf Erweiterte Neuaufalge 1998.* Bonn, 1998.

Mitchell, B. R. *International Historical Statistics: Europe 1750–1988.* New York: Stockton Press, 1992.

Moffitt, Robert. "Incentive Effects of the US Welfare System: A Review." *Journal of Economic Literature* 30 (1992): 1–61.

———. "The Effect of the US Welfare System on Marital Status." *Journal of Public Economics* 41 (1990): 101–124.

Moynihan, Daniel P. *The Negro Family: A Case for National Action.* Washington, D.C.: U.S. Department of Labor, 1965.

Mukherjee, Satyanshu, and Dagger, Dianne. *The Size of the Crime Problem in Australia.* 2d ed. Canberra: Australian Institute of Criminology, 1990.

Mukherjee, Satyanshu, and Scandia, Anita. *Sourcebook of Australian Criminal and Social Statistics.* Canberra: Australian Institute of Criminology, 1989.

Murphy, Cait. "Europe's Underclass." *National Interest,* No. 50 (1997): 49–55.

Murray, Charles. *Losing Ground.* New York: Basic Books, 1984.

———. "Welfare and the Family: The US Experience." *Journal of Labor Economics* 11 (1993): S224–S262.

National Center for Health Statistics. "Births, Marriages, Divorces and Deaths for 1996." Washington, D.C.: Public Health Service, 1997.

———. *Vital Statistics of the United States, 1992.* Vol. 1: *Natility.* Washington, D.C.: Public Health Service, 1995.

National Commission on Civic Renewal. *A Nation of Spectators: How Civic Disengagement Weakens America and What We Can Do About It.* College Park, Md.: National Commission on Civic Renewal, 1998.

———. *The Index of National Civic Health.* College Park, Md.: National Commission on Civic Renewal, 1998.

National Commission to Prevent Child Abuse. *Public Opinion and Behaviors Regarding Child Abuse Prevention: A Ten Year Review of NCPCA's Public Opinion Research.* Chicago: NCPCA, 1997.

National Statistical Office and Republic of Korea. *Social Indicators in Korea 1995.* Seoul: National Statistical Office, 1995.

National Urban League. *The State of Black America 1996.* Washington, D.C.: National Urban League, 1997.

Nelson, Richard E., and Winter, Sidney G. *An Evolutionary Theory of Economic Change.* Cambridge: Belknap/Harvard University Press, 1982.

Neu, Dean. "Trust, Contracting and the Prospectus Process." *Accounting, Organizations and Society* 16 (1991): 243–256.

Neuman, W. Lawrence, and Berger, Ronald J. "Competing Perspectives on Cross-National Crime: An Evaluation of Theory and Evidence." *Sociological Quarterly* 29 (1988): 281–313.

Nevins, Allan, with Frank E. Hill. *Ford: The Times, the Man, the Company.* New York: Scribner's, 1954.

Nohria, Nitin, and Eccles, Robert. *Networks and Organizations: Structure, Form, and Action.* Boston: Harvard Business School Press, 1992.

Nolan, James L. *The Therapeutic State: Justifying Government at Century's End.* New York: NYU Press, 1998.

North, Douglass C. *Institutions, Institutional Change, and Economic Performance.* New York: Cambridge University Press, 1990.

North, Douglass C., and Thomas, Robert P. "An Economic Theory of the Growth of the Western World." *Economic History Review,* 2d ser. 28 (1970): 1–17.

———. *The Growth of the Western World.* London: Cambridge University Press, 1973.

Nye, Joseph S., Jr., ed. *Why People Don't Trust Government.* Cambridge: Harvard University Press, 1997.

O'Neill, June, and Polachek, Solomon. "Why the Gender Gap in Wages Narrowed in the 1980s." *Journal of Labor Economics* 11 (1993): 205–228.

Ogawa, Naohiro, and Retherford, Robert D. "The Resumption of Fertility Decline in Japan: 1973–92." *Population and Development Review* 19 (1993): 703–741.

Olson, Mancur. *The Logic of Collective Action. Public Goods and the Theory of Groups.* Cambridge: Harvard University Press, 1965.

———. *The Rise and Decline of Nations.* New Haven, Conn.: Yale University Press, 1982.

Opp, Karl-Dieter. "Emergence and Effects of Social Norms—Confrontation of Some Hypotheses of Sociology and Economics." *Kyklos* 32 (1979): 775–801.

Oppenheimer, Valerie K. "Women's Rising Employment and the Future of the Family in Industrial Societies." *Population and Development Review* 20 (1994): 293–342.

Organization for Economic Cooperation and Development. *Employment Outlook.* Paris, July 1996.

Ostrom, Elinor. *Governing the Commons: The Evolution of Institutions for Collective Action.* Cambridge: Cambridge University Press, 1990.

Ostrom, Elinor, and Walker, J. *Rules, Games and Common-Pool Resources.* Ann Arbor: University of Michigan Press, 1994.

Pew Research Center For the People and the Press. *Deconstructing Distrust: How Americans View Government.* Washington, D.C.: Pew Research Center, 1998.

———. *Trust and Citizen Engagement in Metropolitan Philadelphia: A Case Study.* Washington, D.C.: Pew Research Center, 1997.

Plotnick, Robert D. "Welfare and Out-of-Wedlock Childbearing: Evidence from the 1980s." *Journal of Marriage and the Family* 52 (1990): 735–746.

Popenoe, David. *Disturbing the Nest: Family Change and Decline in Modern Societies.* New York: Aldine de Gruyter, 1988.

———. *Life Without Father: Compelling New Evidence that Fatherhood and Marriage are Indispensable for the Good of Children and Society.* New York: Free Press, 1996.

Porter, Michael E. "Clusters and the New Economics of Competition." *Harvard Business Review* (November–December 1998): 77–90.

———. *On Competition.* Boston: Harvard Business Review Books, 1998.

Posner, Richard A., and Landes, Elisabeth M. "The Economics of the Baby Shortage." *Journal of Legal Studies* 323

Powell, Walter W. "Neither Market Nor Hierarchy: Network Forms of Organization." *Research in Organizational Behavior.* 12 (1990): 295–336.

Pugh, George E. *The Biological Origin of Human Values.* New York: Basic Books, 1977.

Putnam, Robert D. "Bowling Alone: America's Declining Social Capital." *Journal of Democracy* 6 (1995): 65–78.

———. *Making Democracy Work: Civic Traditions in Modern Italy.* Princeton, N.J.: Princeton University Press, 1993.

———. "Tuning In, Tuning Out: The Strange Disappearance of Social Capital in America." *PS: Political Science and Politics* (1995): 664–682.

Rabinowitz, Dorothy. "From the Mouths of Babes to a Jail Cell." *Harper's* (1990): 52–63.

Rahn, Wendy, and Brehm, John. "Individual-Level Evidence for the Causes and Consequences of Social Capital." *American Journal of Political Science* 41 (1997): 999–1023.

Rahn, Wendy, and Transue, John. "Social Trust and Value Change: The Decline of Social Capital in American Youth, 1976–1995." Unpublished paper, 1997.

Rankin, J., and Wells, J. E. "The Effect of Parental Attachments and Direct Controls on Delinquency." *Journal of Research in Crime and Delinquency* 27 (1990): 140–165.

Reardon, Elaine. "Demand-Side Changes and the Relative Economic Progress of Black Men: 1940–1990." *Journal of Human Resources* 32 (1997): 69–97.

Reimers, Cordelia W. "Cultural Differences in Labor Force Participation Among Married Women." *ABA Papers and Proceedings* 75, no. 2 (1985): 251–255.

Republic of China and Directorate-General of Budgeting, Accounting and Statistics. *Statistical Yearbook of the Republic of China 1992.* Taipei: Directorate General of Budgeting, Accounting and Statistics, 1992.

Rey, Marcella. "Pieces to the Association Puzzle." Paper presented to the annual meeting of the Association for Research on Nonprofit Organizations and Voluntary Action, November 1998.

Ricks, Thomas E., *Making the Corps.* New York: Scribner's, 1997.

Ridley, Matt, *The Origins of Virtue: Human Instincts and the Evolution of Cooperation.* New York: Viking, 1997.

———. *The Red Queen: Sex and the Evolution of Human Nature.* New York: Macmillan, 1993.

Rindfuss, Ronald R., and Morgan, S. Philip. "Marriage, Sex, and the First Birth Interval: The Quiet Revolution in Asia." *Population and Development Review* 9 (1983): 259–278.

Roe, Mark J. "Chaos and Evolution in Law and Economics." *Harvard Law Review* 109 (1996): 641–668.

Rohlen, Thomas P. "'Spiritual Education' in a Japanese Bank." *American Anthropologist* 75 (1973): 1542–1562.

Rorabaugh, William J. *The Alcoholic Republic.* New York: Oxford University Press, 1979.

Rosenfeld, Richard. "The Social Sources of Homicide in Different Types of Societies." *Sociological Forum* 6 (1991): 51–70.

Rosenzweig, Mark R., and Wolpin, Kenneth J. "Parental and Public Transfers to Young Women and Their Children." *American Economic Review* 84 (1994): 1195–1212.

Ross, Ruth A., and Benson, George C. S. "Criminal Justice from East to West." *Crime and Delinquency* (1979): 76–86.

Rossi, Alice. "A Biosocial Perspective on Parenting." *Daedalus* 106 (1977): 2–31.

———. "The Biosocial Role of Parenthood." *Human Nature* 72 (1978): 75–79.

Roussel, Louis. *La famille incertaine*. Paris: Editions Odile Jacob, 1989.

Salamon, Lester M. *America's Nonprofit Sector: A Primer*. New York: Foundation Center, 1992.

———. "Government and the Voluntary Sector in an Era of Retrenchment: The American Experience." *Journal of Public Policy* 6 (1986): 1–19.

———. *Partners in Public Service: Government-Nonprofit Relations in the Modern Welfare State*. Baltimore: Johns Hopkins University Press, 1995.

———. "The Rise of the Nonprofit Sector." *Foreign Affairs* 73 (1994): 109–122.

Salamon, Lester M., and Anheier, Helmut K. *The Emerging Sector: An Overview*. Baltimore: Johns Hopkins Institute for Policy Studies, 1994.

Sampson, Robert J. "Urban Black Violence: The Effect of Male Joblessness and Family Disruption." *American Journal of Sociology* 93 (1987): 348–382.

Sampson, Robert J., and Laub, John H. *Crime in the Making: Pathways and Turning Points Through Life*. Cambridge: Harvard University Press, 1993.

Sampson, Robert J., et al. "Neighborhoods and Violent Crime: A Multilevel Study of Collective Efficacy." *Science* 277 (1997): 918–924.

Sandel, Michael J. *Democracy's Discontent: America in Search of a Public Philosophy*. Cambridge: Harvard University Press, 1996.

Sardon, Jean-Paul. *General Natality*. Paris: National Institute of Demographic Studies, 1994.

Saxenian, Annalee. *Regional Advantage: Culture and Competition in Silicon Valley and Route 128*. Cambridge: Harvard University Press, 1994.

Schein, Edgar H. *Organizational Culture and Leadership*. San Francisco: Jossey-Bass, 1988.

Schudson, Michael. "What If Civic Life Didn't Die?" *American Prospect* (1996): 17–20.

Schumpeter, Joseph A. *Capitalism, Socialism and Democracy*. New York: Harper Brothers, 1950.

Scott, James C. *Seeing Like a State: How Certain Schemes to Improve the Human Conditions Have Failed*. New Haven: Yale University Press, 1998.

Sedlak, Andrea J., and Broadhurst, Diane D. "Third National Incidence Study of Child Abuse and Neglect." Washington, D.C.: U.S. Dept of Health and Human Services, 1996.

Seligman, Adam B. *The Problem of Trust*. Princeton, N.J.: Princeton University Press, 1997.

Seydlitz, Ruth. "Complexity in the Relationships among Direct and Indirect Parental Controls and Delinquency." *Youth and Society* 24 (1993): 243–275.

Shaw, Henry, and McKay, Clifford. *Juvenile Delinquency and Urban Areas*. Chicago: University of Chicago Press, 1942.

Sherman, P. W. "Nepotism and the Evolution of Alarm Calls." *Science* 197 (1977): 1246–1253.

Shoham, Shlomo G., and Rahav, Giora. "Family Parameters of Violent Prisoners." *Journal of Social Psychology* 127 (1987): 83–91.

Skogan, Wesley G. *Disorder and Decline: Crime and the Spiral of Decay in American Neighborhoods*. New York: Free Press, 1990.

Smith, Adam. *An Inquiry into the Nature and Causes of the Wealth of Nations*. Indianapolis: Liberty Classics, 1981.

———. *Lectures on Jurisprudence*. Indianapolis: Liberty Press, 1982.

———. *The Theory of Moral Sentiments*. Indianapolis: Liberty Classics, 1982.

Smith, Tom W. "Factors Relating to Misanthropy in Contemporary American Society." *Social Science Research* 26 (1997): 170–196.

Stack, Carol. *All Our Kin: Strategies for Survival in a Black Community.* New York: Harper and Row, 1974.

Stack, Steven. "Social Structure and Swedish Crime Rates: A Time-Series Analysis, 1950–1979." *Criminology* 20 (1982): 499–513.

Stack, Steven, and Kowalski, Gregory S. "The Effect of Divorce on Homicide." *Journal of Divorce and Remarriage* 18 (1992): 215–218.

Statistics Canada. *Canadian Crime Statistics 1995.* Ottawa, Onatario: Canadian Centre for Justice Statistics, 1995.

Statistics Denmark. *Kriminalstatistik (Criminal Statistics).* Copenhagen, 1996.

Statistics Finland. *Crime Nomenclature.* Helsinki: Statistics Finland, 1996.

Statistics Finland. *Yearbook of Justice Statistics 1996.* Helsinki: Statistics Finland, 1997.

Statistics Norway and Statistik Sentralbyra. *Crime Statistics 1995.* Oslo-Kongsvinger: Statistics Norway, 1997.

Statistics Norway. *Historic Statistics 1994.* Oslo: Statistics Norway, 1995.

Statistics Sweden and Statistika Centralbyran. *Kriminalstatistik 1994.* Stockholm: Statistics Sweden, 1994.

Statistics Sweden. *Population Statistics 1996. Part 4, Vital Statistics.* Stockholm: Statistics Sweden, 1997.

Stets, Jan E. "Cohabiting and Marital Aggression: The Role of Social Isolation." *Journal of Marriage and the Family* 53 (1991): 669–680.

Strauss, Leo. *Natural Right and History.* Chicago: University of Chicago Press, 1953.

Sugden, Andrew. "Spontaneous Order." *Journal of Economic Perspectives* 3 (1989): 85–97.

———. *The Economics of Rights, Cooperation and Welfare.* Oxford: Basil Blackwell, 1986.

Sutherland, Edwin, and Cressy, Donald. *Criminology.* Philadelphia: J. B. Lippincott, 1970.

Tannenbaum, Frank. *Crime and the Community.* New York: Columbia University Press, 1938.

Taub, David M. *Primate Paternalism.* New York: Van Nostrand Reinhold, 1984.

Teitelbaum, Michael S., and Winter, Jay M. *The Fear of Population Decline.* Orlando, Fla.: Academic Press, 1985.

Thornton, Arland, and Fricke, Thomas E. "Social Change and the Family: Comparative Perspectives from the West, China, and South Asia." *Sociological Forum* 2 (1987): 746–779.

Tiger, Lionel. *The Decline of Males.* New York: Golden Books, 1999.

———. *Men in Groups.* New York: Random House, 1969.

Tiger, Lionel, and Fowler, Heather T. *Female Hierarchies.* Chicago: Beresford Book Service, 1978.

Tiger, Lionel, and Fox, Robin. *The Imperial Animal.* New York: Holt, Rinehart, and Winston, 1971.

Tittle, Charles R. "Social Class and Criminal Behavior: A Critique of the Theoretical Foundation." *Social Forces* 62 (1983): 334–358.

Toffler, Alvin. *The Third Wave.* New York: William Morrow, 1980.

Tomasson, Richard F. "Modern Sweden: The Declining Importance of Marriage." *Scandinavian Review* (1998): 83–89.

Tönnies, Ferdinand. *Community and Association.* London: Routledge and Kegan Paul, 1955.

Tonry, Michael, and Morris, Norval. *Crime and Justice.* Vol. 7 Chicago: University of Chicago Press, 1986.

Trivers, Robert. *Social Evolution.* Menlo Park, Calif.: Benjamin/Cummings, 1985.

———. "The Evolution of Reciprocal Altruism." *Quarterly Review of Biology* 46 (1971): 35–56.

Trojanowicz, Robert et al. *Community Policing: A Contemporary Perspective.* Cincinnati, Ohio: Anderson Publishing Company, 1998.

U.S. Bureau of the Census. *International Database, Population.* Washington, D.C.: International Programs Center, 1998.

———. *Statistical Abstract of the United States, 1996.* Washington, D.C.: U.S. Government Printing Office, 1996.

———. *Statistical Abstract of the United States, 1997.* Washington, D.C.: U.S. Government Printing Office, 1997.

U.S. Department of Health and Human Services. *Report to Congress on Out-of-Wedlock Childbearing.* Hyatsville, Md.: U.S. Government Printing Office, 1995.

———. *Vital Statistics of the United States.* Vol. 1: *Natality.* Hyattsville, Md.: National Center for Health Statistics, 1996.

U.S. Department of Justice. *Criminal Victimization, 1973–95.* Washington, D.C.: BJS National Crime Victimization Survey, 1997.

United Nations. *Demographic Yearbook, 1995.* New York: United Nations Publications, 1995.

———. *World Population Prospects: The 1996 Revision-Annex 1—Demographic Indicators.* New York: United Nations Publications, 1996.

United Nations Department for Economic and Social Information and Policy Analysis. *Demographic Yearbook, 1990.* New York: United Nations Publications, 1990.

Van Dijk, Jan J. M., et al. *Experiences of Crime across the World.* Deventer, Netherland: Kluwer Law and Taxation Publishers, 1991.

Ventura, S. J., "Births to Unmarried Mothers: United States, 1980–1992." Hyattsville, Md.: National Center for Health Statistics, 1995.

Ventura, S. J., Martin, J. A., Mathews, T. J., and Clarke, S. C. "Advance Report of Final Natility Statistics, 1994." *National Center for Health Statistics,* 1996.

———. *Report of Final Natility Statistics, 1996.* Hyattsville, Md.: National Center for Health Statistics, 1998.

Viccica, Antoinette D. "World Crime Trends." *International Journal of Offender Therapy* 24 (1980): 270–277.

von Mises, Ludwig. *Socialism. An Economic and Sociological Analysis.* Indianapolis: Liberty Classics, 1981.

von Neumann, John, and Morgenstern, Oskar. *Theory of Games and Economic Behavior.* New York: John Wiley, 1944.

Waldrop, M. Mitchell. *Complexity: The Emerging Science at the Edge of Order and Chaos.* New York: Simon & Schuster, 1992.

Wallace, P. A., and LeMund, A. *Women, Minorities, and Employment Discrimination.* Lexington, Mass.: Lexington Books, 1977.

Warner, W. Lloyd, et al. *Yankee City.* New Haven, Conn.: Yale University Press, 1963.

Weber, Max. *Economy and Society.* Berkeley: University of California Press, 1978.

———. *The Protestant Ethic and the Spirit of Capitalism.* London: Allen and Unwin, 1930.

———. *The Religion of China.* New York: Free Press, 1951.

Wells, J. E., and Rankin, J. H. "Direct Parental Controls and Delinquency." *Criminology* 26 (1988): 263–285.

Whelan, Robert. *Broken Homes and Battered Children: A Study of the Relationship Between Child Abuse and Family Type.* Oxford: Family Education Trust, 1994.

Whitehead, Barbara Dafoe. "Dan Quayle Was Right." *Atlantic Monthly* 271 (1993): 47–84.

Williams, George C. *Adaptation and Natural Selection: A Critique of Some Current Evolutionary Thought*. Princeton, N.J.: Princeton University Press, 1974.

Williamson, Oliver E. "Calculativeness, Trust, and Economic Organization." *Journal of Law and Economics* 36 (1993): 453–502.

———. *The Nature of the Firm: Origins, Evolution and Development*. Oxford: Oxford University Press, 1993.

Wilson, Edward O. *On Human Nature*. Cambridge: Harvard University Press, 1978.

———. "Resuming the Enlightenment Quest." *Wilson Quarterly* 22 (1998): 16–27.

Wilson, James Q. *Bureaucracy: What Government Agencies Do and Why They Do It*. New York: Basic Books, 1989.

———. "Criminal Justice in England and America." *Public Interest* (1997): 3–14.

———. *The Moral Sense*. New York: Free Press, 1993.

———. *Thinking About Crime*. Rev. ed. New York: Vintage Books, 1983.

Wilson, James Q., and Abrahamse, Allan. "Does Crime Pay?" *Justice Quarterly* 9 (1993): 359–378.

Wilson, James Q., and Herrnstein, Richard. *Crime and Human Nature*. New York: Simon & Schuster, 1985.

Wilson, James Q., and Kelling, G. "Broken Windows: The Police and Neighborhood Safety." *Atlantic Monthly* 249 (1982): 29–38.

Wilson, James Q. and Petersilia, Joan, eds. *Crime*. San Francisco: ICS Press, 1995.

Wilson, William Julius. *The Truly Disadvantaged: The Inner City, the Underclass, and Public Policy*. Chicago: University of Chicago Press, 1988.

———. *When Work Disappears: The World of the New Urban Poor*. New York: Knopf, 1996.

Wolfe, Alan. *One Nation, After All: What Middle-Class Americans Really Think About God, Country, Family, Racism, Welfare, Immigration, Homosexuality, Work, The Right, The Left, and Each Other*. New York: Viking, 1998.

———. *Whose Keeper? Social Science and Moral Obligation*. Berkeley: University of California Press, 1989.

Womack, James P., et al. *The Machine That Changed the World: The Story of Lean Production*. New York: Harper Perennial, 1991.

Wrangham, Richard, and Peterson, Dale. *Demonic Males: Apes and the Origins of Human Violence*. Boston: Houghton Mifflin, 1996.

Wrigley, E. A.. *Nineteenth-Century Society: Essays in the Use of Quantitative Methods for the Study of Social Data*. Cambridge: Cambridge University Press, 1972.

Wrong, Dennis. "The Oversocialized Conception of Man in Modern Sociology." *American Sociological Review* 26 (1961): 183–196.

Wynne-Edwards, Vero C. *Animal Dispersion in Relation to Social Behaviour*. New York: Hafner Publishing, 1967.

———. *Evolution Through Group Selection*. Oxford: Blackwell Scientific, 1986.

Yeager, Matthew G. "Immigrants and Criminality: A Cross-National Review." *Criminal Justice Abstracts* 29 (1997): 143–171.

Zakaria, Fareed. "A Conversation with Lee Kuan Yew." *Foreign Affairs* 73 (1994): 109–127.

Zuboff, Shoshana. *In the Age of the Smart Machine: The Future of Work and Power*. New York: Basic Books, 1984.

INDEX